Sandy Tolan has written for the *New York Times Magazine* and more than forty other magazines and newspapers. He has reported from twenty-five different countries, especially in the Middle East and Latin America, and his work has won numerous awards. He served as an oral history consultant for the US Holocaust Memorial Museum, was a 1993 Nieman Fellow at Harvard University and a Fellow at the UC Berkeley Graduate School of Journalism, where he directs the school's project on International Reporting.

D0867656

www.randomhouse.co.uk

Also by Sandy Tolan

Me & Hank: A Boy and His Hero,
Twenty-five Years Later

THE LEMON TREE

The true story of a friendship spanning
four decades of Israeli–Palestinian conflict

SANDY TOLAN

BLACK SWAN

TRANSWORLD PUBLISHERS
61–63 Uxbridge Road, London W5 5SA
A Random House Group Company
www.randomhouse.co.uk

THE LEMON TREE
A BLACK SWAN BOOK: 9780552155144

First published in Great Britain
in 2007 by Bantam Press
a division of Transworld Publishers
Black Swan edition published 2008

This book is a work of non-fiction.

A CIP catalogue record for this book
is available from the British Library.

Addresses for Random House Group Ltd companies outside the UK
can be found at: www.randomhouse.co.uk
The Random House Group Ltd Reg. No. 954009

Typeset in 11/13.5pt Giovanni Book by
Falcon Oast Graphic Art Ltd.

19

Penguin Random House is committed to a sustainable future for
our business, our readers and our planet. This book is made from
Forest Stewardship Council® certified paper.

MIX
Paper from
responsible sources
FSC® C018179

Printed and bound in Great Britain by Clays Ltd, Elcograf S.p.A.

For the children, Arab and Jew, between
the river and the sea.
And for Lamis, who brought me into the story.

CONTENTS

First Words

The house depicted in this book is an actual place, and the lemon tree in its yard is a real one. You could see the place for yourself if you boarded a bus in the West Jerusalem terminal, rode west, climbed and then plunged down the hills toward the Mediterranean, and banked up a two-lane rise until you came to a bustling, industrial town in a place once known as Palestine that is now the state of Israel. When you stepped off the bus, you'd walk down the busy main road known as Herzl Boulevard, past the juice vendors, the kebab stands, and the old storefronts selling trinkets and cheap clothing, and take a left at a street called Klausner. There, at the next corner, you'd spot a run-down gas station, and across the street a modest house with a pillared fence, a towering palm, and stones the color of cream.

This is the place, you could say to yourself. This is the house with two histories. The house with the lemon tree.

AUTHOR'S NOTE

THIS BOOK IS firmly planted in the soil of non-fiction narrative. Many of the events depicted are from fifty, sixty, or seventy years ago; none the less, their retelling relies, like everything else in the book, entirely on the tools of reporting and research: interviews, archival documents, published and unpublished memoirs, personal diaries, newspaper clippings, and primary and secondary historical accounts. For *The Lemon Tree* I conducted hundreds of interviews in Israel, the West Bank, Jordan, Lebanon, and Bulgaria over a period of seven years, mostly since 2002; visited archives in Jerusalem, Ramallah, Beirut, Sofia, London, New York, and Austin, Texas; and consulted hundreds of first- and second-hand sources, many housed in one of the world's great research centers: the Doe Library at the University of California at Berkeley.

I have not taken liberties with the history, no matter how minor. At no point do I imagine what *probably* happened, for example, at a family event in 1936 and state it as fact; nor at any moment do I describe what someone was *thinking* unless those thoughts are based on a specific recounting in a memoir or interview. Rather, the scenes and sections of the narrative are built through a combination of the available sources.

For example: Descriptions of events surrounding the Eshkenazi family are based on family interviews in Jerusalem and Sofia; interviews with other Bulgarian Jews now living in Israel; documents unearthed in the State Archives of Bulgaria, the American Jewish Joint Distribution Committee archives in Queens, New York, and the Central Zionist Archives in Jerusalem; and newspaper clippings and other historical accounts translated from the National Library in Sofia. The portrait of the Khairi family in al-Ramla in 1948 is similarly based on multiple sources: personal interviews of family members; memoirs and other accounts translated from the Arabic; Israeli military intelligence reports; documents from state and kibbutz archives; the memoirs of Yitzhak Rabin and Arab Legion commander John Bagot Glubb; U.S. State Department cables of the day; secondary historical accounts by Middle Eastern scholars; and years of my own interviews with Palestinians in refugee camps in the West Bank, Gaza, and Lebanon. For details and additional historical context, see the source notes section.

An author's refusal to take poetic license does not, of course, ensure that each event depicted speaks an 'objective' truth, especially when the topic at hand represents two highly subjective histories. Where else, after all, would the same event be remembered as the War of Independence by one people and the Nakba, or 'Catastrophe,' by another? In such cases, particularly when the history described is volatile or less familiar to Western readers, I have intensified my basic research approach, endeavoring to gather an even greater multitude of sources from various perspectives, thus ensuring that the emerging narrative is not based primarily on decades-old personal memories.

None of this, of course, means that *The Lemon Tree* represents a definitive history of the conflict between Arabs and Jews since 1948 (or, if you prefer, since 1936, or 1929, or 1921, or 1917, or 1897, or 1858). By juxtaposing and joining the histories of two families, however, and placing them in the larger context of the days' events, I hope to help build an understanding of the reality and the history of two peoples on the same land.

A NOTE ON SPELLING AND PRONUNCIATION

IN THE MIDDLE EAST, the use of a single letter – say, an 'e' instead of an 'a' – can be a political statement, or at the very least a declaration of identity. Take the case of Ramla – or, al-Ramla, or Ramle, or Ramleh, or Ramlah. Present-day Israelis use 'Ramla,' which is how the road signs read in English; in classical Arabic, it's 'al-Ramla'; in spoken Arabic, and throughout its history from the eighth century A.D., including during the British Mandate from 1917 to 1948, it was 'Ramle.' Israeli historians generally use 'Ramle' when referring to the era before 1948, and some Israelis continue to call it 'Ramle' rather than the Hebraized pronunciation of 'Ramla,' because, unlike other cities where Jews lived in antiquity, Ramle was always exclusively an Arab town, founded by Muslims in 715.

How to resolve this dilemma for a writer intent on conveying two histories? I have decided, after much experimentation, to use the classical Arabic 'al-Ramla' when looking at the city through Arab eyes and 'Ramla' when describing the place through the Israeli experience. This way, it is clear that I am referring to the same place –

and, by the way, not to Ramallah, a Palestinian town in the West Bank about twenty miles to the east.

In single references, I tend to use the pronunciation favored by the person through whose eyes the reader is seeing at a particular moment. Thus, Bashir sees the hilltop at Qastal, not Castel, or Kastel, as many Israelis know it; similarly, Dalia looks upon the Judean Hills, known as Jabal Nablus and Jalal al Khalil (Nablus and Hebron Mountains) in Arabic.

For Arabic words, I have chosen not to use accent marks unfamiliar to most readers; rather, I have used spellings in English which will come closest to the actual pronunciation in Arabic. Similarly for the Hebrew. For example, the Hebrew letters kaff and khet, indicated as 'ch' by some writers, are pronounced like an 'h', but in a more guttural way, and I have generally used 'kh', which comes closer. (An exception is where the 'ch' spelling is commonly accepted, as in Chanukah.) This guttural 'kh' is also represented by the Arabic letter kha, and pronounced similarly – as in Khairi, Bashir's family name, and Khanom, Bashir's sister. Bashir's name, by the way, is pronounced bah-SHEER.

Dalia's family name was Eshkenazi, not Ashkenazi; despite how odd that spelling may look to many Jewish readers, it is common for Bulgarians, and Dalia assures me this is how her father always spelled his name in English. Her name at birth was Daizy, and she kept that name until she was eleven years old, when she changed it to Dalia. To avoid confusion, and after consulting Dalia, I have decided to refer to her as Dalia throughout the book.

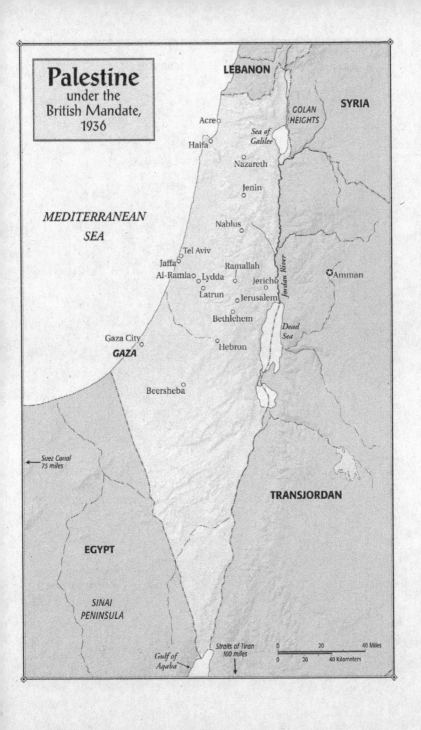

Palestine
under the
British Mandate,
1936

LEBANON

SYRIA

GOLAN
HEIGHTS

Acre

Sea of
Galilee

Haifa

Nazareth

Jenin

MEDITERRANEAN
SEA

Nablus

Tel Aviv

Jaffa

Ramallah

Al-Ramlao

Lydda

Jericho

Amman

Latrun

Jerusalem

Jordan River

Bethlehem

Dead
Sea

Gaza City

Hebron

GAZA

Beersheba

Suez Canal
75 miles

TRANSJORDAN

EGYPT

SINAI
PENINSULA

Gulf of
Aqaba

Straits of Tiran
100 miles

0   20   40 Miles

0   20   40 Kilometers

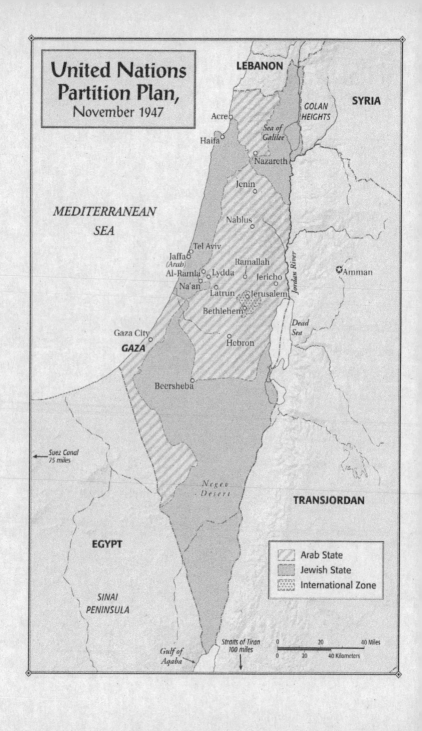

United Nations Partition Plan,
November 1947

LEBANON

SYRIA

Acre

Sea of Galilee

GOLAN HEIGHTS

Haifa

Nazareth

MEDITERRANEAN SEA

Jenin

Nablus

Tel Aviv

Jaffa
(Arab)

Al-Ramla   Lydda

Na'an

Ramallah

Jericho

Latrun   Jerusalem

Bethlehem

Jordan River

Amman

Gaza City

GAZA

Hebron

Dead Sea

Beersheba

Negev Desert

TRANSJORDAN

Suez Canal
75 miles

EGYPT

SINAI PENINSULA

Arab State
Jewish State
International Zone

Straits of Tiran
100 miles

0   20   40 Miles

0   20   40 Kilometers

Gulf of Aqaba

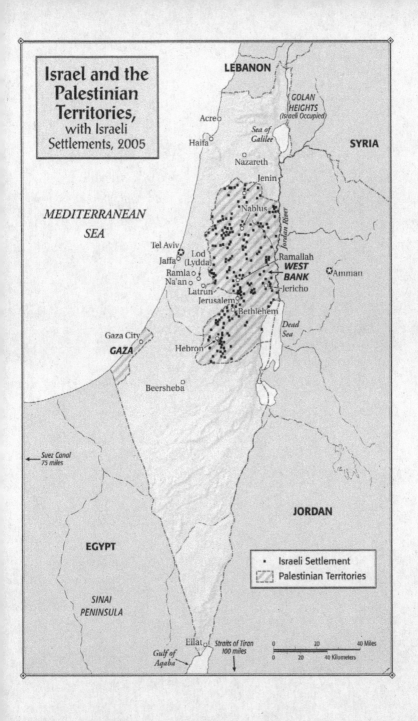

Israel and the Palestinian Territories, with Israeli Settlements, 2005

LEBANON

GOLAN HEIGHTS (Israeli Occupied)

Acre

Sea of Galilee

Haifa

SYRIA

Nazareth

Jenin

MEDITERRANEAN SEA

Nablus

Jordan River

Tel Aviv

Lod (Lydda)

Jaffa

Ramallah

WEST BANK

Ramla

Amman

Na'an

Latrun

Jericho

Jerusalem

Bethlehem

Gaza City

GAZA

Dead Sea

Hebron

Beersheba

Suez Canal 75 miles

JORDAN

EGYPT

- Israeli Settlement

Palestinian Territories

SINAI PENINSULA

Eilat   Straits of Tiran 100 miles

Gulf of Aqaba

0   20   40 Miles

0   20   40 Kilometers

One

BELL

I

THE YOUNG ARAB man approached a mirror in the washroom of Israel's West Jerusalem bus station. Bashir Khairi stood alone before a row of porcelain basins and leaned forward, regarding himself. He turned his head slightly, left to right and back again. He smoothed his hair, nudged his tie, pinched his clean-shaven face. He was making certain all of this was real.

For nearly two decades, since he was six years old, Bashir had been preparing for this journey. It was the breath, the currency, the bread of his family, of nearly every family he knew. It was what everyone talked about, all the time: return. In exile, there was little else worth dreaming of.

Bashir gazed at his reflection. *Are you ready for this journey?* he asked himself. *Are you worthy of it?* It seemed his destiny to return to the place he'd mainly heard about and mostly couldn't remember. It felt as if he were being drawn back by hidden magic; as if he were preparing to meet a secret, long-lost lover. He wanted to look good.

'Bashir!' yelled his cousin Yasser, snapping the younger man back to the moment in the bus station men's room. *'Yallah!* Come on! The bus is leaving!'

The two men walked out into the large waiting hall of the West Jerusalem terminal, where their cousin Ghiath was waiting anxiously.

It was nearly noon on a hot day in July of 1967. All around Bashir, Yasser, and Ghiath, strangers rushed past: Israeli women in white blouses and long dark skirts; men in wide-brimmed black hats and white beards; children in side curls. The cousins hurried toward their bus.

They had come that morning from Ramallah, a Palestinian hill town half an hour to the north, where they lived as refugees. Before they embarked, the cousins had asked their friends and neighbors how to navigate this alien world called Israel: Which bus should we take? How much is a ticket? How do we buy it? Will anyone check our papers once we board the bus? What will they do if they find out we are Palestinians? Bashir and his cousins had left Ramallah in the late morning. They rode south in a group taxi to East Jerusalem and arrived at the walls of the Old City, the end of the first leg of their journey. Only weeks before, these walls had been the site of fierce combat, leading to devastation for the Arabs and the occupation of East Jerusalem by Israel. Emerging from the taxi, the cousins could see soldiers stationed at Damascus Gate, the northern entrance to the Old City. From there the three men turned west and walked away from the ancient walls and across an invisible line.

From the Old City, the cousins had walked west, away from the ancient shrines, across the line of an old boundary between nations. Until a few weeks before, this line had divided West Jerusalem and Israel from Arab East Jerusalem and the West Bank. Now, after defeat of the Arabs in the Six Day War, Israeli forces occupied the West Bank, the Sinai Peninsula, and the Golan Heights and were redeployed to defend the new frontiers. Bashir and his cousins had thus found it easy to cross the old no-man's-land and into a territory simultaneously old and new. They had trudged in the heat for several miles, down crowded lanes and past stone houses that seemed oddly familiar. Finally the narrow streets had given way to busy, modern avenues, where the West Jerusalem bus station had come into view.

Bashir and his cousins hurried across the concrete terminal floor, past the station agents pushing tickets through metal bars, past the kiosk selling candies, gum, and newspapers in a language they could not recognize. On the platforms at the far end of the terminal stood buses bound for lands they had only heard about: the forests in the north; the southern deserts; the coastal plain. The three men held their tickets to al-Ramla and hurried toward platform ten, where their bus, painted in waves of aqua and white, was ready to take them home.

II

The young woman sat alone at the kitchen table. Sunlight streamed in through the south-facing windows of the stone house. The morning was clear, Dalia Eshkenazi remembered, and the quiet would have been broken only by her sips from a steaming mug of tea or the crunch of her teeth on black bread spread thick with Bulgarian cheese.

In recent days, life in Dalia's home and her hometown of Ramla had returned to normal – as normal as could be expected, at least, in the Israel of 1967. The air raid sirens had at last fallen silent, and Dalia's parents were back at work. Dalia, on summer break from Tel Aviv University, now had time to contemplate her emotions of the last few months.

First had come the unbearable tension and the trauma before the six days of war. Alien voices broadcasting from Cairo told her people to go back where they came from or be pushed into the sea. Some Israelis thought the threats were funny, but for Dalia, who had grown up amid the silence of unspeakable atrocities, it was impossible to fully express the depths of fear these threats awakened. For a month before the war, it had felt to her that the end was coming. 'Not just the disintegration of the state, but the end of us as a people,' Dalia remembered. Alongside this fear was a determination, born from the Holocaust, 'to never again be led like sheep to the slaughter.'

Late on the first night of war, Dalia learned that Israel had destroyed the enemy's air force. She knew then that the outcome of the war was essentially decided. Dalia believed God had a hand in Israel's survival and compared her own feeling of awe and wonder with the feeling she imagined her ancestors had when witnessing the parting of the Red Sea.

Dalia's parents had never been religious. They had grown up in Bulgaria, married in 1940, survived a pro-Nazi government, and moved to Israel after the war. Dalia was eleven months old when she arrived.

Dalia's family had been spared the atrocities in Bulgaria by acts of goodwill from Christians she was raised to admire and remember. Now, she believed her people had a destiny on the land of Israel. This was partly why she believed what she had been told: The Arabs who lived in her house, and in hundreds of other stone homes in her city, had simply run away.

III

The 1965 Leyland Royal Tiger let out a low rumble, then a burst of exhaust, as the bus driver downshifted to descend the hills west of Jerusalem. Inside sat the three cousins, riding toward their hometown. They had boarded the bus in prior agreement not to sit together. First, this would eliminate the temptation to speak to one another, thus reducing any suspicion among the other passengers about their identity. By sitting apart, each cousin could also have a window seat, to take in every inch of the journey home. They sat three in a row, absorbing the scenery.

Bashir wasn't sure if he wanted the trip to go quickly or slowly. If it went quickly, he would be in al-Ramla sooner; but if time slowed down, he could more fully take in each bend, each landmark, each piece of his own history.

The bus roared up the curving highway toward the crest of the famous hilltop at Qastal; here, a great Arab commander had fallen in battle nineteen years earlier, breaking the back of his people's army and opening the road to the Holy City for the enemy. Beyond the hilltop, Bashir could see stone minarets of the mosque at Abu Ghosh, one of the few Arab villages that remained standing on the road between Jerusalem and the sea. The village leaders had collaborated with the enemy here, and their village had been spared; Bashir looked upon Abu Ghosh's minarets with mixed feelings.

The Royal Tiger sped down the hillside, easing up as the mountain walls closed in, then opened to a broad valley below. Eight centuries earlier, Bashir's Arab ancestors had battled the Christian invaders in hand-to-hand combat, repelling them for a time. Along the roadside, Bashir looked out the window to see the burned carcasses of vehicles blown up nineteen years earlier, in a more recent war, and the wreaths and fading flowers laid alongside them. The Israelis who placed these wreaths here were honoring what they called their War of Independence; to Bashir this same event was known as the Nakba, or 'Catastrophe.'

The bus entered the valley, slowed, turned right onto a narrow highway bisecting rows of irrigated wheat fields, and angled up a low rise. As they passed near Latrun, Bashir suddenly recalled a journey made in haste and fear two decades earlier. The details were elusive; he was trying to remember the stories from when he was six years old, events he had brooded about nearly every day for the last nineteen years.

Bashir glanced at his seatmate – an Israeli man absorbed in his book. Looking out the window meant nothing to this man, Bashir thought. Perhaps he'd seen it so many times. Decades later, Bashir would recall feeling jealous of the man's inattention to the landscape.

The bus hit a bump – it was the railroad crossing. Simultaneously, the three cousins experienced a familiar sensation, grooved into memory by a repetition two decades distant.

Bashir and his cousins knew they had arrived in al-Ramla.

IV

Dalia finished rinsing the morning dishes, wiped her hands on a towel, and walked to the kitchen doorway, which opened onto the garden. In recent days, since the end of the war, she had been carrying on a silent dialogue with God that she began as a child. *Why*, she thought, *would You allow Israel to be saved during the Six Day War, yet not prevent genocide during the Holocaust? Why would You*

*empower Israel's warriors to vanquish its enemies, yet stand by
while my people were branded and slaughtered a generation
earlier?*

For a child, it was difficult to comprehend the trauma
of the people who surrounded her. Only after probing
could Dalia begin to understand. She had asked her
mother: How were the people branded? Did they stand in
line? Did it hurt? Why would anyone do these things?
Over the years, Dalia's curiosity would fuel her empathy.
It helped her understand the silence of the children she
grew up with – children she would invite home after
school and try to cheer up with her elaborate skits and
solo performances in the garden.

Through the doorway, Dalia looked out at the
jacaranda tree her father had planted amid the flower
beds. As a girl, Dalia had loved to water the deep red
Queen Elizabeth roses, with their overwhelming perfume.
Near the jacaranda stood the lemon tree. Another family
had planted that tree; it was already bearing fruit
when Dalia and her parents arrived nearly nineteen years
earlier. Dalia was aware she had grown up in an Arab
house, and sometimes she wondered about the previous
residents. Had children lived here? How many? How old?
In school Dalia had learned that the Arabs had fled like
cowards, with their hot soup still steaming on the table. As
a younger child, she hadn't questioned this story, but the
older she got, the less sense it made: Why would anyone
voluntarily leave such a beautiful house?

V

Bashir, Yasser, and Ghiath emerged from the bus into a
hot, glaring world at once bizarre and familiar. They could
see the old municipality building, and the town cinema, and

the edge of the neighborhood where they were raised. But none of the streets seemed familiar, at least not at first; they all had new names. Most of the old buildings were covered with brightly colored signs in blocky, indecipherable Hebrew lettering. On some of the building archways, the remnants of the original flowing Arabic cursive remained.

Suddenly Yasser, the eldest, spotted something he knew: the old neighborhood butcher's shop. He quickly walked inside, his cousins following, and threw his arms around the butcher, kissing both his cheeks in the customary way of the Arabs. 'Abu Mohammad!' Yasser shouted in glee. 'Don't you recognize me? *Habibi*, my dear friend, I recognize you! We meet again!'

The Jewish butcher couldn't have been more startled. Abu Mohammad had left many years before. 'You are right, *habibi*,' the man told Yasser, stammering awkwardly in the language of his visitor. 'Once there was Abu Mohammad. Now, no more Abu Mohammad. Now, Mordechai!' The butcher invited his guests to stay for kebab, but the cousins were too stunned by the man's true identity and too distracted by their own mission to accept his offer of food. They walked out, flustered.

'You were pretending you know everything here!' Ghiath teased his older cousin as they left the shop. 'You don't know anything here!'

The three men turned a corner and found themselves in the quieter streets of the neighborhood where they once played. They felt at ease and happy, and they forgot their earlier admonitions about speaking to one another and conversed openly in their mother tongue.

They came upon Yasser's house and approached the door; Yasser stepped forward to knock. A woman in her forties came out, looking at them strangely. 'Please,' said

Yasser, 'all we want is to see the house we lived in before.'

The woman grew agitated. 'If you don't leave the house, I will call the police!' she screamed. The cousins tried to calm her, explaining their purpose. The woman continued shouting, taking a step forward and shoving them back. Neighbors began opening their doors. Eventually the cousins realized they might soon find themselves in trouble with the local authorities, and they retreated in haste.

Yasser drifted along in a silent daze. 'It was as if he had no soul,' Bashir recalled. 'He was a walking body, nothing more.'

'I cannot accept such a feeling,' Yasser said finally. 'It is something that I really cannot bear.'

Soon they came upon the house where Ghiath had grown up. Outside was a large sign they couldn't read and a guard armed with a machine gun. The two-story stone house was now a school. The guard told the men to wait while he went inside, and a moment later the principal came out and invited them in for tea. She introduced herself; her name was Shulamit. She told them they could walk through the rooms when the class period ended, and she left them in her office to wait.

There they sat, silently sipping their tea. Ghiath removed his glasses and wiped his eyes. He put them back on and tried to look cheerful. 'I can't control my feelings,' he whispered.

'I know,' Bashir said quietly. 'I understand.'

When the principal returned, she invited them to tour the house. They did so, Ghiath crying the whole time.

After their visit they left the house and walked in the direction of Bashir's old home. No one could remember exactly where it was. Bashir recalled that it had both a front door and a back door that faced a side street. It had a front gate with a bell, a flowering *fitna*, or plumeria, tree in the front yard, and a lemon tree in the back. After walking in circles in the heat, Bashir realized he'd found the house. He heard a voice from somewhere deep inside himself: *This is your home.*

Bashir and his cousins approached the house. Everything depended on the reception, Bashir told himself. You can't know what the outcome will be, especially after what had happened to Yasser. 'It depends,' he said, 'who is on the other side of the door.'

VI

Dalia sat in a plain wooden chair on the back veranda of the only home she had ever known. She had no special plan for today. She could catch up on her summer reading for the university, where she studied English literature. Or she could peer contentedly into the depths of the jacaranda tree, as she had done countless times before.

VII

Bashir stood at the metal gate, looking for the bell. How many times, he wondered, did his mother, Zakia, walk through this same gate? How many times did his father, Ahmad, pass by, coming home tired from work, rapping his knuckles on the front door in his special knock of arrival?

Bashir Khairi reached for the bell and pressed it.

Two

HOUSE

THE STONE LAY cool and heavy in Ahmad's open hands. Pockmarked and rough, the color of cream, it was cut in foot-thick slabs, with the blunted right angles of the stonemason's chisel. Its dips and rises defined a landscape in miniature, like the hills and wadis of the Palestine it came from.

Ahmad stood in an open field in his coat and tie and Turkish fez. He looked down, crouched low, and laid the first stone upon its foundation. Hundreds of other chiseled slabs, known as white Jerusalem stone, were stacked high beside him. With the first stone in place, Ahmad looked to the cousins, friends, and hired laborers beside him. They began to place stone upon mortar upon stone.

It was 1936, and Ahmad Khairi was building a home for his family. The house was to stand at the eastern edge of al-Ramla, an Arab town of eleven thousand on the coastal plain between Jerusalem and the Mediterranean. To the north lay the Galilee and southern Lebanon; in the Bedouin lands to the south, the sands of Palestine and Sinai.

Al-Ramla was named for sand, some believed, from the Arabic word *raml*. Mostly the soil here was good, bearing

31

citrus, olives, bananas, lentils, and sesame. The year Ahmad Khairi built his house, Arab farmers in Palestine would produce hundreds of thousands of tons of barley, wheat, cabbage, cucumber, tomato, figs, grapes, and melons. The Khairis tended oranges, olives, and almonds in a communal *waaf*, land owned collectively by the extended family and administered under Islamic law.

The Khairis traced their history and landed wealth to the sixteenth century and the religious scholar Khair al-Din al-Ramlawi. Khair al-Din came from Morocco to preside as a judge for the Ottoman Empire. The Ottomans, based in Istanbul, would rule Palestine for four hundred years. At its height, the empire stretched from the outskirts of Vienna through the Balkans, Central Asia, North Africa, and the Middle East. From Istanbul, the Ottoman sultan bequeathed to Khair al-Din the productive *waqf* lands that would sustain the family for centuries.

By 1936, Palestine was under the rule of a new overseer, the British, who had arrived at the end of World War I as the Ottoman Empire collapsed. By this time, the Khairis of al-Ramla had their own family quarter, an expanse of open grounds and houses connected by stone gates and archways that made it possible to travel from home to home without ever leaving the compound. The women rarely ventured out, leaving the shopping to maids and servants.

The Khairis owned the town's cinema, and on Tuesdays it was made available for the exclusive use of the clan. Dozens of family members would come to watch the latest films from Egypt. In the privacy of their own theater, the Khairi women would not be exposed to the looks of strangers, especially men. Khairis rarely married outside the clan, but at his wedding seven years earlier, twenty-two-year-old Ahmad was an exception: His bride, Zakia, nineteen, was from the Riad family of al-Ramla. Quiet, discreet, and loyal, she was considered a good housewife and was much loved by the Khairis.

Ahmad's uncle Sheikh Mustafa Khairi was both the family patriarch and the longtime mayor of al-Ramla. Mustafa was like a father to Ahmad; when Ahmad was seven, his parents died, and Mustafa's family had raised the boy as their own. Mustafa was popular both with the town's citizens and with the British colonial overseers, despite growing tensions.

The British had arrived in 1917, the same year of the historic Balfour Declaration, in which England pledged to help establish a 'national homeland for the Jewish people' in Palestine. This was a triumph for Zionism, a political movement of European Jews founded by Theodor Herzl. The British had authorized 'an appropriate Jewish agency' to help develop public works, utilities, and natural resources – in essence, the beginnings of a Jewish government in Palestine. In recent years, Jewish immigration to Palestine had driven the Arabs and the British further apart, and Sheikh Mustafa, as mayor and town patriarch, had to mediate between the colonial overseers and his restive fellow Arabs.

Ahmad watched his walls go up from the loamy soil on the eastern outskirts of al-Ramla: from foundation to roofline, fourteen layers of Jerusalem stone. His decision to move out of the family compound, and its world unto itself, was unusual. Ahmad wanted to feel independent, however, and he conferred with Sheikh Mustafa. They agreed that from the young man's inheritance, his own share of the Khairi *waqf* income, and the income from his al-Ramla furniture workshop, his family's home would rise. It was time. Zakia, now twenty-six, was pregnant with her fourth child, which Ahmad hoped would finally be a boy.

The young couple had envisioned a house with an open design. Ahmad had gone over the master plan with a British friend and builder, Benson Solli, one of only a few Jews who lived in al-Ramla. For the Khairis, as for many Arabs, Jews like Mr. Solli, as Ahmad's children remembered him, were simply part of the landscape of Palestine. Jews from the *kibbutzim* bartered for wheat, barley, and melons at al-Ramla's Wednesday market. Arab laborers worked in nearby Jewish fields, pushing hand plows made in the *kibbutzim*, and Jewish farmers brought their horses into al-Ramla to be shod. Arabs would recall Jewish engineers and conductors working for the Palestine railroad that passed through town; some remembered bearded, Arabic-speaking Jews riding by donkey to purchase bags of cement at the local factory. For the most part the two communities lived and worked in separate worlds, but their degree of interaction was undeniable. The well-to-do of al-Ramla traveled to Tel Aviv to have suits cut by Jewish tailors, fezzes cleaned by Jewish drycleaners, or portraits taken by Jewish photographers. Khairi women recalled traveling to Tel Aviv to have their dresses made by a Jewish seamstress. One of the Khairi family physicians, Dr. Litvak, was Jewish; and at the Schmidt Girls College in Jerusalem, where Ahmad and Zakia's daughters studied, many of the girls' classmates were Jews. 'They all spoke Arabic and were Palestinians like us,' one Khairi daughter would remember decades later. 'They were there – like us, part of Palestine.' Mr. Solli, an architect and builder, was a quiet man, unassuming, with daughters named Rosalie and Eively. He spoke Arabic and, according to later generations of Khairis, coexisted comfortably among the town's Muslim and Christian Arabs.

Ahmad and Mr. Solli designed large living and sleeping quarters separated by double wooden doors in the center. Workers walled off a small bedroom in a corner. They laid tile, hung wire for electric lights, and ran pipe for indoor plumbing. Zakia would have an inside kitchen with a modern stove. Instead of baking her Arabic bread in the *taboun*, the open-air, wood-fired oven found at most traditional homes, she now had the luxury of sending her dough to the communal ovens in al-Ramla, to be brought back as warm bread ready for the table.

These were new luxuries for the town founded twelve centuries earlier, in 715 A.D., by the Muslim caliph Suleiman Ibn Abdel-Malek. Suleiman, it was said, did not name the place for its *raml*, or sand, but rather for a woman named Ramla who had been generous to him as he had traveled through the area. Suleiman made al-Ramla the political capital of Palestine, and for a time it became more important than Jerusalem. The town lay halfway between Damascus and Cairo, and soon it was a stopover for camel caravans hauling leather, swords, buckets, walnuts, barley, and cloth. Suleiman's workers built the White Mosque, considered one of the most beautiful in the Arab world. They built a six-mile-long aqueduct to carry fresh water to the town's residents and to irrigate its fields. The gently sloping lands surrounding al-Ramla would be considered among the most fertile in Palestine. By the tenth century, a Muslim traveler would write of al-Ramla:

It is a fine city, and well built. Its water is good and plentiful; its fruits are abundant. It combines manifold advantages, situated as it is in the midst of beautiful villages and lordly towns, near to holy places and pleasant hamlets. Commerce here is prosperous, and means of livelihood easy . . . Its bread is of the best and the whitest; its lands are well favoured above all others, and its fruits are of the most luscious. The capital stands among fruitful fields, walled towns, and serviceable hospices. It possesses magnificent hostelries and pleasant baths, dainty food and various condiments, spacious houses, fine mosques and broad roads.

In the next thousand years, al-Ramla would be conquered by the Crusaders, liberated by the Muslim hero Saladin, and ruled by the Ottoman sultans from Istanbul. By the 1930s, the town housed a military garrison used by British forces and a colonial office for a subcommissioner dispatched from London. British officers were fond of hunting fox through the olive groves, over cactus hedges and stone walls, with hounds from the town's kennels. A British subcommissioner filed periodic briefings to His Majesty's government in London. In a cursive scrawl with his blue fountain pen, he noted crops, tonnage, and, by 1936, as Ahmad Khairi's house rose, an increasing disintegration in the public order.

In 1933, Adolf Hitler had taken power in Germany, and the situation for Jews was deteriorating across Europe. Within a few years, demands for Jewish immigration to Palestine increased. Underground Zionist organizations began smuggling boatloads of Jews in ever greater numbers from European ports to Haifa, along the northern Mediterranean coast of Palestine. The British authorities struggled to control the flow. Between 1922 and 1936, the Jewish population of Palestine quadrupled – from 84,000 to 352,000. During the same time, the Arab population had increased by about 36 percent, to 900,000. In those intervening fourteen years, as the Jewish community in Palestine had grown more powerful, a nationalistic fervor began to rise among the Arabs of Palestine. For decades, Arabs had been selling land to Jews arriving from Europe. Gradually, as land sales increased and Jewish leaders pressed their call for a state of their own, many Arabs began to fear Jewish domination. Already more than 30,000 Arab peasant families, or nearly a quarter of the rural population, had been dispossessed through the sale of land to Jews, many by absentee Arab landowners. The families arrived impoverished in the cities of Palestine and in many cases earned wages by building houses for the new Jewish arrivals. By the mid-1930s Arab leaders had declared that selling land to the Jews was an act of treason. They were opposed to a separate Jewish state, and, increasingly, they wanted the British out of Palestine.

Ahmad and his workers hung wooden shutters on the windows. For the exterior fence, they fastened lengths of iron bar to limestone pillars. They laid the tiles for a small garage – for a car that Ahmad didn't yet own but hoped someday he would.

Before long, Ahmad would turn his attention to the garden. In the corner of the yard behind the house, he had chosen a spot for a lemon tree. Once the tree was in the soil, Ahmad knew it would be at least seven years, and probably more, before the strong Palestinian sun and sweet waters of the al-Ramla aquifer would nurture the tree to maturity. The act of planting was thus an act of faith and patience.

The Khairis' stone house was finished by late 1936. To celebrate, the family butchered a lamb and prepared a huge feast: Chicken stuffed with rice and great piles of lamb were common for such occasions, along with handmade couscous, date-filled cookies made with soft buttery dough, and *kanafe*, a hot, pistachio-covered sweet that is shaped like a pizza and looks like shredded wheat. Cousins, sisters and brothers, and Sheikh Mustafa would all have come from the Khairi family compound to admire the new home, with its layers of white Jerusalem stone rising up from the earth. There stood Ahmad, in his coat and tie and fez; a pregnant Zakia; and their three girls – Hiam, six years old; Basima, four; and Fatima, three. Ahmad still waited for a son. He came from a good family with land and wanted to pass on the inheritance in the way of his ancestors. Zakia understood this clearly.

Ahmad and Mr. Solli had designed the house to withstand the weight of three floors. Ahmad and Zakia hoped later to expand the home as the family grew and the income provided.

But the sense of security the Khairis might have hoped for in their new home, on the land their families had inhabited for centuries, was tempered by the reality of daily life in Palestine in late 1936. By then, their homeland was in the midst of a full-scale rebellion.

The Great Arab Rebellion had erupted the previous fall, when an Arab nationalist named Sheikh Izzadin al-Qassam took to the hills near Jenin in northern Palestine with a small band of rebels. Arab nationalists had long suspected the British of favoring the Jews over the Arabs in Palestine. The Balfour Declaration had helped put in motion the machinery for building a Jewish state, including a trade union, a bank, a university, and even a Jewish militia, known as the Haganah. As for the Arabs, Balfour said simply that the Jewish homeland would not adversely affect 'the civil and religious rights of existing non-Jewish communities in Palestine.' In the fall of 1935, when the British authorities uncovered a Zionist arms-smuggling operation but did not find and prosecute the organizers, Arab mistrust of the British deepened, and Sheikh al-Qassam launched his rebellion. He was convinced that only armed insurrection could bring about national liberation for the Arabs.

The British suspected al-Qassam's band of causing two firebomb deaths at a kibbutz and other killings. They called the sheikh an 'outlaw'; Zionist leaders said he was a 'gangster'; both agreed he was a terrorist. In November 1935, al-Qassam, who liked to declare, 'Obey God and the Prophet, but not the British high commissioner,' was hunted down and shot dead near his cave in the hills. 'The band was liquidated by police action,' a British report stated. Arabs of Palestine spent the winter mourning the death of their first Palestinian martyr and organizing for the long fight ahead.

On Wednesday evening, April 15, 1936, as Ahmad Khairi and his friend Benson Solli made plans to break ground in al-Ramla, the trouble began. On a road twenty-five miles north of town, two Jews crossing northern Palestine by car were held up by what the British authorities would later describe as 'Arab highwaymen.' The Arabs robbed the Jews, then shot and killed them. The next night, two Arabs near Tel Aviv were killed by Jewish assailants. In the coming days, Jews stoned Arab delivery trucks and looted Arab-run shops. Rumors, apparently false, spread quickly of the murder of two Arabs at Jaffa, adjacent to Tel Aviv; Arabs responded with violence. The attacks, reprisals, and counterreprisals had begun.

The British brought in military reinforcements to Jaffa and Tel Aviv and imposed a state of emergency. Colonial authorities imposed strict curfews, arrested Jews and Arabs, searched their houses without warrant, and censored letters, telegrams, and newspapers. Arab guerrillas, meanwhile, set up national committees in towns and villages across Palestine to serve as the bases for an insurgency. Leaders of Arab political parties in Palestine had formed the Arab Higher Committee, led by the mufti of Jerusalem, Hajj Amin al-Husseini, who called for a general strike and a boycott of Jewish goods. The mufti, who had been appointed by the British to represent the Muslim community in Palestine, had turned against his former colonial masters. His Arab Higher Committee demanded an end to Jewish immigration, an end of land sales to Jews, and an end to the British Mandate in favor of a single state.

Arab fighters in checkered keffiyehs, or head scarves, struck from the hills, firing on British forces and Jewish kibbutzim. The rebels, known as fedayeen, cut phone and telegraph lines, sabotaged water pipelines, mined bridges, burned forests, derailed trains, and sniped at Jewish settlements and detachments of British forces. 'There have been widespread acts of murder and other outrages by gangs of armed terrorists,' declared a report of His Majesty's government. British troops responded with baton charges, live ammunition, and a new tactic:

demolitions of the stone homes of suspected rebels and their relatives. 'This preliminary work of demolition,' one British communiqué declared, 'will be punctuated by frequent detonations and crashes of falling masonry . . . the neighbourhood should not be surprised, misled, or alarmed when they hear these noises.'

In the summer of 1936, the entire Khairi clan, along with the rest of al-Ramla, prepared for the annual festival of Nabi Saleh. Despite the rebellion and the British crackdown, thousands of Arabs came from across Palestine to honor this early miracle-working prophet who foretold the coming of the Prophet Mohammad. Delegations from each city in Palestine would come to the ancient mosque at Nabi Saleh, planting their city flags. 'Women went to his tomb in al-Ramla to pray for fertility and better health,' Ahmad and Zakia's daughter Khanom remembered. 'There would be singing and dancing and prayer and picnics. This event was the highlight of the year.'

News of the conflict reached the family sporadically. The rebels were exacting a toll. Many Jewish farmers couldn't get their crops or livestock to market, and those who tried were often attacked and their animals killed. Water projects were suspended as survey crews were attacked. Rural guerrillas had mastered hit-and-run tactics, firing upon British patrols, in some cases retreating to nearby villages to disguise themselves as women. A British report underscored the frustration. Colonial troops 'were continually finding themselves shot up on all sides,' only to find 'that the hostile area was apparently populated by unarmed peaceful shepherds and agriculturalists.' On one occasion, 'a small party of British troops were bathing near Beisan on the 12th August [and] were subject to a

41

surprise attack by a large Arab armed band. Unfortunately their Lewis gun 'jammed' and those who were on guard were killed by the band, who succeeded in capturing the Lewis gun and some rifles.' The rebellion was just as alarming to the Zionists. 'On one side, forces of destruction, forces of the desert, have risen,' declared Chaim Weizmann. 'And on the other side stand firm the forces of civilization and building. It is the old war of the desert against civilization, but we will not be stopped.'

At night, fedayeen fighters moved from house to house, sleeping in their muddy boots in the homes of peasants or city dwellers. Family oral history suggests some Khairis were also sheltering rebels. Organizers in the local committees set up networks for smuggling arms and for collecting 'taxes,' sometimes by intimidation, to finance the insurgency. Rebel leaders were pressuring urban Arabs to abandon their fezzes and put on the keffiyeh, so that the rural rebels would not stand out. It isn't clear if Ahmad's furniture workshop was a target of such 'tax collection,' but increasingly, his uncle, Mayor Mustafa Khairi, was facing threats from rebels who saw him as too close to the British. Despite the pressure from all sides, the family tried to continue living normally.

With the birth of baby Khanom, Zakia and Ahmad now had four daughters. Ahmad still waited for his son, and he had begun to wonder if his wife was capable of bearing one. 'We also didn't have any uncles,' Khanom said. 'So it was even more important to have a male baby.' Of her mother, she said, 'Of course we thought she was the most beautiful woman in the world.' At home Zakia always wore a dress: a housedress for family and fancier dresses with dark stockings for visitors. She smelled of Bombay perfume, which she applied from a special flask shaped like an Indian woman. Most people in al-Ramla in those days used the public baths, but the Khairis had their own; sometimes the girls' schoolteachers would come to use the bath, which shocked the children. 'When we were young we thought teachers were like angels and did not need to bathe or eat or sleep,' Khanom recalled.

Usually Zakia would send the servants to buy the food, but sometimes she would do her own shopping. When she left the house to go to Wednesday market, she put on a jacket and dark cape and wore a veil over her face. Occasionally she would take her daughters along.

At the market the girls would gaze up at the stalls of eggplants and peppers; tomatoes, cucumbers, and parsley; spices and herbs; and live chickens and squab. Village men rode to the oil presses perched atop sacks of olives in flatbed trucks. Horse-drawn carts creaked into market overburdened with produce. Village women would barter chicken and eggs – or, in hard times, silver bracelets and old Ottoman coins – for Syrian silk, Egyptian linen, and cotton from Gaza. The women chose dyes for their embroidery: indigo from the Jordan Valley, red from the sumac growing wild in the fields of Palestine, yellow muchra from the soil found near the Egyptian border.

The Khairi girls could see how each villager's dress told a story. Some were embroidered with patterns of sesame branches; others with sunflowers or field tulips. In al-Ramla, a citrus-growing region near the sea, patterns of orange branches were woven into the embroidered bodices. These were surrounded by green triangles to represent the cypress trees used as windbreaks beside the orange groves. Below that, undulating lines of indigo stood for the waves of the nearby Mediterranean.

At home, Zakia and her servants often cooked the girls'

favorite, *makloubeh*, or 'upside down,' a lamb-and-eggplant casserole they would turn over and sprinkle with pine nuts just after it came out of the oven. The girls would gather around their mother in the kitchen as she sprinkled sugar and pistachios atop the *kanafe*. The main meals were served at midday in the dining room. Zakia would call the girls to the table; Ahmad would come home from his carpentry workshop to join them; and the family would dine around a short-legged table called a *tablieh*. When guests came the parents would retire to the salon, where they would sit on couches of engraved wood covered in dark blue velvet, on which the girls were never allowed to sit.

After dinner Ahmad would return to work, where he had built a reputation as an accomplished furniture crafts-man. His vision was bad, and reading therefore difficult, so instead of the university, Ahmad had attended the Schneller's School in Jerusalem, which turned out young men expert in the trades. Now, a decade later, Ahmad had enough work to hire assistants, and his business was prospering despite the Arab Rebellion. His trade, along with the income from the Khairi land, was enough to pro-vide the family a comfortable life.

Ahmad rarely socialized at home; instead, he would join the other Khairis to play cards, drink Arabic coffee, and smoke from the arguileh (water pipe) at the diwan, or social gathering place, in the family compound. There the talk of politics was unending.

By the end of 1936, a relative calm had settled on Palestine. The Arab Higher Committee had suspended its general strike and rebellion in response to a British promise to investigate the underlying causes of the conflict. Lord Peel, the former secretary of state for colonial India, arrived from London dressed in a top hat and tails. The British lord was to direct the parliamentary commission of inquiry, but at times he seemed baffled. 'I did not realise how deep-seated was the Arab fear of Jewish overlordship and domination,' he wrote to a colleague in London. 'As to reconciliation between the two races, nobody makes any attempt to bring it about.' With increasing numbers of European Jews 'pour[ing] into Palestine . . . by means legal and illegal,' Lord Peel decried the 'unpleasant atmosphere of suspicion' and fretted over the futility of making even 'constructive suggestions.'

In July 1937, the Palestine Royal Commission presented its 418-page report to the British Parliament. Declaring 'half a loaf is better than no bread,' Peel and his fellow commissioners recommended Palestine be partitioned into two states – one for the Jews and one for the Arabs. 'Partition offers a prospect,' the Peel Commission concluded, 'of obtaining the inestimable boon of peace.' Hundreds of Arab villages, and at least 225,000 Palestinian Arabs, were inside the proposed boundaries of the new Jewish state; some 1,250 Jews resided on the Arab side of the partition line. An 'arrangement' would have to be made 'for the transfer, voluntary or otherwise, of land and population . . . if then the settlement is to be clean and final, this question of the minorities must be boldly faced and firmly dealt with,' the Peel Commission declared.

The Zionist leadership accepted Lord Peel's recommendations despite internal dissension. Many Jewish leaders did not want to give up the idea of a Jewish homeland across the whole of Palestine, and some leaders even considered Transjordan, the desert kingdom across the

Jordan River, as part of an eventual Jewish state. For them, acceptance of the Peel Commission's report was a major compromise, and their disagreement reflected ideological divisions that would manifest for decades. David Ben-Gurion, the leader of the Mapai Party and the most influential of the Zionists in Palestine, had argued in favor of the plan. At the core of the Peel Commission plan was the idea of transferring the Arabs, a concept that had been advanced for decades by fellow Zionists. In 1895, Theodor Herzl, founder of political Zionism, had written that in purchasing land from the indigenous Arabs for a Jewish homeland, 'we shall try to spirit the penniless population across the border by procuring employment for it in the transit countries, while denying it any employment in our own country . . . Both the process of expropriation and the removal of the poor must be carried out discreetly and circumspectly.'

Forty years later, during Lord Peel's investigation, Ben-Gurion had instructed Jews who met with the commission to recommend the transfer plan. After the release of the commission's report, the Zionist leader wrote: 'We have to uproot from the roots of our hearts the assumption that it is not possible. Indeed it is possible . . . We might be losing a historical chance that won't return. The transfer cause, in my view, is more important than all our demands for additional territory . . . with the evacuation of the Arab population from the valleys, we get for the first time in our history a real Jewish state.' A year later, Ben-Gurion would declare, 'I support compulsory transfer.' Others sympathetic to the Zionist cause had warned against such measures. Albert Einstein and Martin Buber, for example, had long advocated what Einstein called 'sympathetic cooperation' between 'the two great

Semitic peoples,' who 'may have a great future in common.'

The Arabs were as stunned by the Peel Commission's proposal as Ben-Gurion was excited. The Arab Higher Committee, led by the mufti of Jerusalem, promptly rejected it, not only because of the transfer plan, but because of the partition itself. The Arabs would fight for a single, independent, Arab-majority state.

In September 1937, the Arab Rebellion erupted again when Arab assassins gunned down a British commissioner on a winding, narrow road in Nazareth. The British response was swift. The military took control from the civil authorities. Military courts stepped up execution of suspected rebels. Thousands were jailed as British forces occupied cities across Palestine, including al-Ramla. British gunners hunted bands of insurgents from the air, at one point employing 16 airplanes west of al-Ramla to kill more than 150 rebels. 'Terrorism has called for severe counter measures,' wrote the district commissioner for al-Ramla in October, 'and these, inevitably, have exacerbated feelings still further. Moderate opinion has now lost the last shred of influence it possessed, and al-Ramla, where the moderates grouped under Sheikh Mustafa Kheiri [Khairi], the Mayor, exercised some restraining power, has capitulated to the gunmen.'

Ahmad's uncle Sheikh Mustafa was in trouble, caught between the British occupying forces and the fedayeen of the Arab Rebellion. For fifteen years, he had commanded great respect as al-Ramla's mayor and leader of one of its most influential families. Sheikh Mustafa's popularity, according to later generations, was based on his defense of the rural poor and their rights to pay lower taxes. 'When

Sheikh Mustafa came into a room, everyone would stand,' remembered Khanom Khairi. 'When he walked by people on horseback, they would get down from the horse. People who were working would stop working. No one asked them to do so; they did it out of respect.' The sheikh was tall and good-looking, with hazel eyes and a mustache, and he was never without his abaya, or dark cape, and the white turban of the religious scholar. He would wrap the turban himself before placing the dark red *tarbush* (fez) over it.

The charismatic mayor walked a fine line between the imperial power and the rebels. He had opposed the Peel Commission plan and battled with Arab 'notables' who he felt were too close to the British and the Zionists. The mayor, according to later Khairi generations, even secretly used his sons to ferry information on British troop movements to the rebels and to transport weapons in the trunk of a car. If this is true, they did so at the risk of execution.

Still, Mustafa Khairi was a mayor in a land under foreign occupation and by definition needed to cooperate with the British authorities. Despite his self-image as a nationalist, he was known to oppose Hajj Amin al-Husseini, the rebel leader of the Arab Higher Committee. Sheikh Mustafa was for a time a member of the National Defense Party, which was aligned with Husseini's rivals, and considered to be 'collaborators' with the Zionists.

As the rebellion accelerated anew, rumors began to spread that some Arab elites were cooperating with the British and the Zionists, even informing on the rebels by revealing details of operational plans. Equally incendiary were reports that many of these Arab 'notables' had sold land to the new arrivals, prompting evictions of Arabs and the emergence of an angry class of landless peasants. In al-Ramla, townspeople told of a Jewish man from Tel Aviv who was making the rounds, trying to buy more land. It was said that another of Ahmad's uncles, the doctor Rasem Khairi, had angrily sent the man away. Shukri Taji, a cousin of Sheikh Mustafa's and one of the town's most prominent citizens, was said to be going door-to-door in al-Ramla, warning people not to sell their land. But even Taji himself, records would later indicate, had once sold land to Jews. As the reports of informants, collaborators, and land sellers grew, the insurgents killed hundreds of their own people, including, in late 1938, two municipal councillors in nearby Lydda.

According to British accounts, the mayor stood up to the fedayeen by resisting the taxes they demanded to fuel the Arab Rebellion. In October 1938, according to a British subcommissioner's report, Sheikh Mustafa, 'the very able Mayor' of al-Ramla, 'left the country' for Cairo 'because of fear of assassination . . . The loss of the Mayor will be keenly felt.' The British, meanwhile, used the anger over the rebels' tax demands to recruit more informants from among the disgruntled.

Within a month Sheikh Mustafa returned to al-Ramla, pledging to try to stay out of nationalist politics and to focus on municipal affairs in the large stone building along the Jaffa-Jerusalem road.

In May 1939, it appeared to some Arabs that the sacrifices of their rebellion had brought a political victory. With British forces still heavily engaged with the rebels, and with the situation in Europe creating tens of thousands of Jewish refugees, the British government released its White Paper, accepting many of the demands of the Arab Rebellion. The British agreed to strictly limit Jewish immigration and to tighten restrictions on land sales in Palestine. Most important, the White Paper called for a single independent state. Many Arabs in Palestine saw in the White Paper a practical solution to their problem. But Hajj Amin al-Husseini, speaking for the Arab Higher Committee, rejected the White Paper. His word carried the day in Arab Palestine, even though it was made from exile: the ex-mufti had fled Palestine nearly two years earlier, wanted by the British at the height of the Arab rebellion. The ex-mufti's decision was unpopular with many Palestinian Arabs, who believed they had missed an opportunity.

The new British policy marked a sharp change from the Peel Commission plan of only two years earlier. The White Paper was a major concession to the Arabs. For the Jews of Palestine, it was an abandonment of British support for a Jewish national homeland promised in the Balfour Declaration, at a time when the situation for Jews in Europe was growing more perilous. Within weeks, Jewish paramilitary squads were attacking British forces, planting explosives in Jerusalem's central post office, and carrying out attacks on civilians in Arab souks. The White Paper, it was clear, had shaken Jewish-British relations in Palestine. 'Satan himself could not have created a more distressing and horrible nightmare,' David Ben-Gurion wrote in his diary.

By the turn of 1940, the British authorities had finally defeated the Arab Rebellion through what they called 'severe countermeasures': tens of thousands jailed, thousands killed, hundreds executed, countless houses demolished, and key leaders, including the mufti, in exile. In the cities, Arab men had taken off their keffiyehs and replaced them once again with the fez. The Palestinian national movement was deeply divided and utterly un-prepared for any future conflict.

* * *

Two years later, on February 16, 1942, newspaper head-
lines announced British defeats in Burma and Singapore
at the hands of the Japanese. In the sands of Libya and
Egypt, British forces had retreated three hundred miles in
the face of a fresh assault from Nazi brigadier general
Erwin Rommel. Stories of Nazi atrocities had begun to
trickle out of Poland and Germany; Jews in Palestine were
terrified that Rommel, should he reach his prize of the
Suez Canal, would keep marching east toward Tel Aviv.

Compared with a few years earlier, the Holy Land was
quiet. The British high commissioner's monthly telegram
to the secretary of state for the colonies reported 'no genuine political developments' among the Jews and 'on the
surface no political activity on the Arab side.' The commissioner expressed concern over possible Arab recruiting
efforts for a postwar conflict. He mused over the exile of
Hajj Amin al-Husseini. The now ex-mufti had resumed his
nationalist struggle against the British and the Zionists by
taking up with the archenemy of the British Empire: Nazi
Germany. The ex-mufti was now in Berlin.

In his February report on the state of Palestine, the high
commissioner worried about a Jewish 'pseudo-political
terrorist gang known as the Stern group,' which had begun
carrying out assassinations. But mostly the commissioner
advised London, 'Public interest, both Arab and Jewish, has
tended once again to concentrate more on the cost of living
and the supply situation': food rationing, the price of yarn,
the supply of shoes, and the number of meatless days per
week.

In al-Ramla, Mayor Khairi was once again attending to
his municipal duties, confronting black marketeers
illegally hoarding foods to get around wartime rationing,

and dealing with a failed well and subsequent shortage of water in the town. 'The enemies of the Mayor,' wrote the district commissioner, 'are profiting by the shortage of water as well as of food to conduct a campaign against him.'

There was, in other words, a lull in the battle for the future of Palestine. And on February 16, 1942, at least, Sheikh Mustafa Khairi could be distracted by something far more pleasant than water battles, political attacks, and the prospect of fresh violence in Palestine. His nephew Ahmad would become a father for the seventh time. For the first time, Zakia would give birth to a boy. He was born at home, with the help of a midwife. Zakia was happy and relieved.

'I don't believe it – my wife brings only girls into the world,' Ahmad said, according to his daughter Khanom. 'He sent one of the young men from the family to come to the house and unwrap my brother's clothes to see if he was really a boy.'

Many lambs were sacrificed as thanks. Relatives came from Gaza, and the entire Khairi clan celebrated with song and dance.

'It was a great occasion,' Khanom recalled. 'We finally had a brother.'

They called the child Bashir.

Three

RESCUE

THE YOUNG JEWISH salesman walked quickly through the cold down a cobblestone street. Moshe Eshkenazi carried his black leather case full of fine socks, flannel underwear, and other factory samples as he made his rounds from shop to shop in the Bulgarian capital of Sofia. Suddenly he stopped. There in plain view, just at his feet, lay a wallet. It was in good condition, untouched, as if someone had only recently dropped it. Moshe stooped to pick it up. The wallet was filled with money – a small fortune to a struggling Jewish peddler trying to support his family in the Bulgaria of early 1943. During the war, it had become far more difficult for men like Moshe to ensure any security for their families, and for some men, the unexpected find would have been impossible to resist.

Moshe did not hesitate. He made the only decision possible for him. Taking the wallet to the police was the most natural thing in the world to do.

At the police station, the officer on duty was shocked to see the salesman with the yellow star bring in a billfold with its contents intact. He consulted with his fellow policemen, and soon Moshe was sent to another office, where he was introduced to a senior member of the force. The officer looked at his unusual visitor with curiosity:

Moshe stood short and squat, with wavy black hair, a heavy brow, and a clear, steady gaze. Before long, the peddler and the veteran policeman found themselves deep in conversation, and in the coming days, they would develop a friendship. Moshe's daughter, Dalia, who grew up with the story, was not yet born in 1943. She would never hear the specifics of these discussions – whether the two men talked about the war, Bulgaria's alliance with the Nazis, or the country's treatment of its Jews – but at some point the policeman decided to reveal a state secret.

'There is a plan to deport the Jews – soon,' he told Moshe. 'Settle your affairs, take your family away, and clear out of here.' The officer's information, though lacking in some details, had come from senior Bulgarian authorities, and Moshe needed no further warning. His brother, Jacques, had already left the city and joined the Communist resistance in the hills. Moshe had no such intentions, but within days he and his wife, Solia, had gathered their things and were traveling east to her family's home in Sliven, near the Bulgarian Black Sea coast. There, they hoped, it would be safe.

Bulgaria in early 1943 was a monarchy aligned with the Axis powers. Hitler's reach into southeastern Europe had extended to the edge of the Balkans and beyond, where the kingdom of Boris III lay wedged between the Black Sea to the east and Turkey and Greece to the south. In the previous two years under Boris's rule, able-bodied Jewish men like Moshe, Jacques, and Solia's cousin Yitzhak Yitzhaki, along with Communists and other dissidents, had spent the warmer months living in work camps, building roads and railways to fuel the wartime machine of the Axis.

By early 1943, with wind of terrible stories from else-where in Europe drifting over the borders, Bulgarian Jews had become increasingly unsettled. Already the rights of the country's forty-seven thousand Jews had been stripped by sweeping measures built on Germany's Nuremberg laws.

Moshe, Solia, and their families could not have known it then, but even as the young couple rode east through Bulgaria's Valley of the Roses and into the mountains of Sliven, a drama was unfolding that would determine the destiny of the nation's Jews. In the early days of March 1943, the actions of ordinary citizens and a handful of political and religious leaders would change the course of Bulgaria's history. At the center of the drama would be families like the Eshkenazis, clustered in small Jewish communities throughout the country. The central players would come from Kyustendil, a rail town near the western border with Macedonia, and Plovdiv, Bulgaria's second-largest city, where the roundup of the town's Jews would begin early on a frigid morning in March.

A little after midnight on March 9, 1943, the daughter of the rabbi of Plovdiv was sitting in the family den, reading Jack London. Her parents were asleep, and the house was quiet.

The doorbell rang. Susannah Shemuel Behar looked up from her reading.

In high school, Susannah had planned to go to the university and study astronomy. That was before life had changed for Bulgaria's Jews; it was before her father, racing to beat a curfew one night after presiding at a funeral, was jailed briefly for coming home ten minutes late.

Now Susannah was part of Bulgaria's underground

anti-Fascist movement. She had joined the illegal Union of Young Workers and had friends in the Partizan resistance: Communists, roaming the bitter cold Rhodope Mountains with their five-shot Austrian rifles. Susannah and her girlfriends were inclined toward missions of subterfuge and mischief. When comrades set about torching a leather factory or sabotaging an assembly line of canned vegetables bound for Germany, Susannah would stand lookout. At night around town, she posted anti-Fascist flyers – 'Stop the War!'; 'Germans Out!'; 'We Want Jobs!' This work was usually undertaken in mixed pairs so that if a policeman passed by, the co-conspirators could embrace and begin kissing to disguise their mission. At home, Susannah stashed the literature in a perfect hiding place: her father's Bible.

On the doorstep Susannah found Totka, the stout neighborhood bread seller. Susannah was alarmed: Totka was also the wife of a Plovdiv policeman. 'Go wake up your father,' the woman said.

A moment later, the bearded, soft-faced rabbi appeared in his nightclothes. 'They're going to arrest your family soon,' said the policeman's wife. 'Give me your gold. I will keep it and return it to you.'

Her father replied, 'If we had gold, it would burn with us.' Susannah knew what this meant. Her father had been telling her stories about Nazi Germany.

Totka left. An hour later, just after 2:00 A.M., the bell rang again and Susannah opened the door to find a policeman in black boots and a blue cloth coat with shiny silver buttons. He gave the Behars thirty minutes to collect a few belongings and walk to the yard of the Jewish school. From there, they would await further instructions.

Susannah's mother went into shock. She was unable

to pack anything but a few coats and a little bread.

Susannah, her brother, and her parents shuffled along a narrow road in the heart of Jewish Plovdiv, past Susannah's friend Estrella's house, past the Benvenisti home. They were flanked by the uniformed policeman and a plainclothes officer. It was quiet but for their footsteps on the gravel. Susannah looked up to see Big Bear and Little Bear – Ursa Major and Ursa Minor – suspended in the clear early-morning sky. Her mother worried aloud about Susannah's two sisters in the capital; she wouldn't be able to tell them what was happening. Susannah barely heard her mother. She was thinking of something her father had said before they left the house. 'If you have a chance,' the rabbi told his daughter, 'escape.'

The Behars came to a cobblestone road known as Russian Boulevard. There, by chance, they encountered the servant to the Orthodox bishop of Plovdiv, hurrying to the church to light the stove. It was just before 3:00 A.M. 'Where are you taking the family at this hour?' the servant asked the rabbi.

'Please go wake up Bishop Kiril,' Benyamin Behar responded urgently. 'Tell him Plovdiv's rabbi has been arrested along with his whole family and is being held at the Jewish school. I expect more Jewish families will soon be arriving.'

The servant took off at a sprint, the flaps of his coat rising in his wake. It looked to Susannah as if he were flying.

The same day, several hours to the east in the hill country of Sliven, Moshe and Solia Eshkenazi were waiting in silence and fear. Moshe had hoped that the warning of the policeman he had befriended in Sofia would help him find safe haven with Solia's family. These hopes had died when the family received a letter from the Bulgarian authorities: Solia's family was to pack twenty kilograms of food and clothing and be prepared for a journey. To where, it wasn't clear; but Solia, who had heard of atrocities elsewhere in Europe, had no illusions. Years later, recounting the events to her daughter, Dalia, she would vividly recall the feeling: *This is the end.*

Hundreds of other Jewish families across Sliven, Plovdiv, and other Bulgarian cities had received similar orders. On March 9, 1943, it appeared that the fate of the Eshkenazis, of the Behars – of all of Bulgaria's Jews – was to be identical to that of the rest of European Jewry. Indeed, the path had seemed clear for at least two years, since the imposition of the anti-Jewish laws and Bulgaria's alliance with Hitler.

In 1941, King Boris, after struggling to remain neutral in World War II, had finally joined the Axis powers. This averted a German occupation but led to a pro-Fascist government. The Bulgarians who despised Jews the most were put directly in charge of their fate. The key figure was Aleksander Belev, former member of the Fascist Guardians of the Advancement of the Bulgarian National Spirit, or Ratnitsi. Belev was to be the principal authority on the 'Jewish question' in Bulgaria. It was Belev who had traveled to Berlin to study the 1935 Law for the Protection of German Blood and German Honor, and the other Nuremberg racial laws, which would result in Bulgaria's 1941 Law for the Defense of the Nation.

With this law and others like it, the persecution of Bulgaria's Jews would formally begin, as their legal rights would be reduced to those of the Jews of Germany. 'Jewish Residence' signs were required on every Jewish home. Jews were subject to strict curfews and were no longer permitted to be members of political parties or professional associations. Jews could not marry Gentiles, enter air raid shelters, or own cars, telephones, or radios. They were required to wear the yellow star.

Solia Eshkenazi's cousin Yitzhak Yitzhaki, a strong, good-looking twenty-year-old, was sent to a work camp on the Serbian border. He ate daily rations of bean soup, with occasional supplements of sausages, bread, and *kashkavel* (Bulgarian yellow cheese) smuggled in by visiting family members, or brought by local villagers in exchange for medical treatment by Jewish doctor prisoners. The prisoners and the villagers, Yitzhaki recalled, shared the food with the guards. The prisoners spent their days crushing rocks and at night wrote letters home by the light of gas lanterns. In colder months, they had little warm clothing; under the primitive conditions, with limited access to medicines, sickness often spread quickly. Once, during a malaria outbreak, the prisoners tried a home cure: drinking the blood of turtles caught near the camp, after which the animals were roasted over a fire. 'Under those circumstances, the roasted turtles were a delicacy!' Yitzhaki remarked. In the spring the prisoners put on a show: Offenbach's operetta *The Beautiful Helena*. 'The veteran Bulgarian commander, proud of the talent in his camp, invited many other officers for the show,' Yitzhaki remembered. 'In comparison with what was happening in Europe, we were very lucky indeed.'

Treatment in the camps was sometimes harsh – Yitzhaki once was threatened with a firing squad after his comrades inadvertently set a tent on fire – but Bulgaria was in fact different from the rest of Europe. With all the momentum pushing Bulgarian Jews toward annihilation, there was something pushing back. To many patriots across the fatherland, the pro-Fascist laws required a strong response; the laws were at odds with Bulgaria's history and identity.

In 1492, when the Jews were expelled from Spain, the Ottoman sultan in Istanbul sent ships to the Spanish port of Cadiz to welcome thousands of Jews into his empire. 'They say that Ferdinand of Spain is a wise man, but he is a fool,' declared Bayezid II. 'For he takes his treasure and sends it all to me.' Jews would soon spread across the Ottoman Empire, including in Bulgaria. There, in modest communities of horse-drawn carriages and quiet village squares, they would encounter less anti-Semitism, and in a milder form, than did Jews elsewhere in Europe. When Bulgaria struggled for its independence in the 1870s, Jews fought alongside their countrymen to shed the Ottoman 'yoke'; Jews of Plovdiv gave shelter to the hero of the Bulgarian revolution, Vasil Levski. Levski, a kind of Bulgarian George Washington, outlined his own vision for a democratic Bulgaria: 'brotherhood and absolute equality among all nationalities. Bulgarians, Turks, Jews, etc. will be equal in every respect . . .' These words were later enshrined in the country's 1879 constitution, considered at the time to be one of the most progressive in Europe.

Six decades later, when Aleksander Belev helped draft the anti-Jewish laws for King Boris's pro-Fascist government, statements of protest and alarm came flooding in from nearly every sector of Bulgarian society. Letters and telegrams were sent to the king, the national parliament, and the prime minister's office from doctors, politicians, intellectuals, tailors, technicians, cobblers, tobacco workers, street vendors, and the Bulgarian Orthodox Church.

We, the food workers from Plovdiv, are shocked by the existence of such reactionary laws, which will only divide the nation . . .

We the textile workers, who work side by side with the Jewish workers, making goods for the Bulgarian people, and going through the injustices of life, we raise our voices in protest against the Law for the Defense of the Nation, which stands against the interests and ideals of the Bulgarian workers' society . . .

We cannot understand who is going to win from the implementation of the Law for the Defense of the Nation. Not the Bulgarian craftsmen, to be sure. We protest this smashing of tradition . . .

We the pastry workers from Plovdiv express our deep indignation . . . this bill sharply opposes all democratic understanding, which has always been part of the soul of the Bulgarian people.

The Bulgarian Communist Party, through its clandestine newspapers and underground radio station, issued repeated denunciations. 'The fate of 50,000 Jews,' declared an illegal Communist flyer, 'is indissolubly connected with that of our people.'

Former government ministers wrote to the parliament as well:

Poor Bulgaria! We are seven million people, yet we so fear the treachery of 45,000 Jews who hold no positions of responsibility at the national level that we need to pass exceptional laws to protect ourselves from them. And then what? . . . Gentlemen. Decide now! Will you stand behind the Constitution and the Bulgarian people in defense of freedom, or will you march in step with the political

mercenaries and bring shame on yourselves as you under-
mine our country's life and future along the way? In the
cities and in the countryside, they are all saying the same
thing: 'If only Levski ... were here today ... [he] would
chase us down and flog us to make us understand [his]
ideas and just what is this liberty in the name of which [he]
died for Bulgaria ...'

The protests over the law would serve as a warning to
the Bulgarian authorities, from the king to the pro-Fascist
functionaries in charge of the 'Jewish question': ill treatment of the nation's Jews would not go unnoticed.
Consequently, Belev, the most ardent servant of the Nazi
ideals in Bulgaria, worked as swiftly and as quietly as
possible.

In October 1942, Nazi authorities in Berlin sent a
message to their office in Sofia: 'Please approach the
Bulgarian government and discuss with them the
question of evacuation of Jews stipulated by the new
Bulgarian regulations ... We are ready to receive
these Jews.'

As commissar for Jewish questions, Belev now had the
power to oversee the 'expulsion of Jews into the provinces
or outside the kingdom.' Funds for the office were to come
largely from frozen Jewish assets.

In January 1943, the Reich's man for Jewish issues in
Paris, Theodor Dannecker, arrived in Sofia. He was there
to work with Belev on the 'evacuation' of twenty thousand
Jews from the Bulgarian lands. This was to be the first of
several mass expulsions. The next month, the two men
signed the Dannecker-Belev Agreement, identifying railway stations ('in Skopje: 5,000 with 5 trains ... in
Dupnitsa: 3,000 with 3 trains ...'), target dates ('the Jews

concentrated in the cities Skopje and Bitola will be deported after 15 April 1943 . . .'), exceptions ('Jews with contagious diseases are not to be included . . .'), security, payment, schedules, and a pledge of no regrets: 'In no case will the Bulgarian government ask for the return of the deported Jews.'

The agreement stipulated that all 20,000 Jews were to come from the 'newly liberated lands' of Macedonia and Thrace, which Germany had turned over to Bulgaria to occupy. Yet Belev and Dannecker realized that in all of those occupied territories there weren't that many Jews; at least 7,500 would have to come from 'old Bulgaria,' like the Eshkenazis, the Behars, and other Jews who would soon be waiting on instructions from the authorities.

On February 22, the same day Belev signed the agreement with Germany, his office sent a memorandum to twenty-one regional representatives of the Jewish commissariat. 'Private. Extremely confidential,' the memo began.

> Within 24 hours of receipt of this message, please present to the Commissariat a list of all Jews from your town who are wealthy, well-known or are considered public figures. Please include in this list those Jews who have acted as leaders in their own community and are supporters of the Jewish spirit among the local Jewish community, or have expressed any anti-state ideas or feelings . . .

The next day, Belev traveled to the 'new lands,' apparently confident that the deportation of Jews from 'old Bulgaria' was on track. The key, Belev believed, was secrecy. 'The deportation,' he had already stressed in a memo to Petur Gabrovski, the interior minister, 'should be kept in strict confidence.'

But even as Belev rode south to oversee the expulsion of the Jews of Macedonia and Thrace, his airtight plan had sprung leaks back home.

In late February, around the time the Sofia policeman revealed the deportation rumors to Moshe Eshkenazi, a young Bulgarian functionary decided that she, too, could no longer keep a disturbing secret. Liliana Panitsa contacted a Jewish friend and in a clandestine meeting told him of the plan to deport the Jews of Macedonia. Her information was reliable, and she disclosed it at considerable risk: Miss Panitsa was the secretary, and some believed the lover, of Aleksander Belev.

About the same time, at a chance meeting on the street with a Jewish acquaintance, a Sofia optician offered to disclose, for a price, another piece of vital information. The optician received his bribe and quickly revealed the government's plans to deport the Jews of Bulgaria. The optician also had reason to know: He was the brother-in-law of Petur Gabrovski, the interior minister and former member of the Ratnitsi, the Bulgarian Fascist organization.

The optician had grown up in Kyustendil, a tranquil hill town surrounded by orchards and wheat fields close to the mountainous border with Macedonia. For the next several days, this 'fruit basket' of Bulgaria, with its lovely shaded streets, its street vendors with their sugared apples and cherries on a stick, its family cafés serving lamb soup and Bulgarian wine, would become the battleground upon which the future of Bulgaria's Jews would be decided.

* * *

Fears of a coming catastrophe gripped Kyustendil. The owner of a local glass factory passed along the deportation rumors; he often worked with Germans, so his information seemed good. A Macedonian leader had also learned the secret, apparently during a party at Aleksander Belev's house, and quickly warned his Jewish friends. Kyustendil's district governor, despite his official position and reputation for corruption, did not keep quiet, either: When he learned of the plans directly from Belev's office, he alerted a prominent Jewish pharmacist, Samuel Barouh.

Soon virtually every Jew in Kyustendil knew of Belev's secret plans. Terrifying rumors began to circulate: The Fernandes tobacco warehouse was being swept out to store Jews near the train station. A list of Jews had been drawn up by Belev's office, and families began to speculate about whose names were on it. Long chains of boxcars, it was said, had already been assembled in neighboring towns.

In early March, residents caught sight of the trains from Thrace passing near Kyustendil. They were packed with Jews, crying out and begging for food. Shocked local residents and Jews interned in nearby work camps raced alongside the tracks, throwing bread into the cars as the trains rolled by. Similar scenes were recorded by Metropolitan Stefan, the Orthodox bishop and top religious official in the nation. 'What I saw exceeded my notions of horror and my conception of inhumanity,' the bishop wrote. 'In the freight wagons, there were old and young, sick and well, mothers with their nursing babies, pregnant women, packed like sardines and weak from standing; they cried out desperately for help, for pity, for water, for air, for a scrap of humanity.' Stefan had sent a telegram to the prime minister, pleading with him not to send those Jews to Poland, 'a name that had a sinister ring, even to the ears of babies.'

In Kyustendil, as word of the fate of Macedonian and Thracian Jews spread and rumors of new deportations surfaced, Jews began to panic. A young woman named Mati brought her family photo album to the home of a close Gentile friend, Vela. Vela was a fellow resister in the anti-Fascist movement; like Susannah Behar, the rabbi's daughter in Plovdiv, the two friends worked underground in support of the Partizans fighting in the southern mountains near Greece. Mati wore a small black pouch made of silk around her neck. Inside it she had placed lockets of hair from her mother, father, and sister, tokens in case the family became separated.

Mati was crying. 'Vela,' she said, 'if I have the luck to come back, I'll take my album back. But if not, please keep it as a memory for me.' She looked strangely at her friend: 'When you get bars of soap from Poland, please wash your face. Probably this will be soap made from me. And I will touch your face again.'

By March 6, the Jews of Kyustendil had mobilized. That day Samuel Barouh, the pharmacist, sent word of the deportations to his brother, Yako, in Sofia. Yako, politically well connected in the capital, began working his contacts in the ministries and the parliament. After a series of alarming and ultimately fruitless meetings, he called on an old high school classmate, Dimitur Peshev, vice president of the parliament. Peshev had grown up in Kyustendil, and though he had voted for the Law for the Defense of the Nation, his personal relations with Jews were good. He was friends with Yako's brother Samuel, the pharmacist, and had spent many hours with him in

Kyustendil, drinking ouzo and eating baklava at local cafés, or relaxing in the mineral waters of the town's public baths. Peshev's sister was a 'milk sister' to Yako's sister: They nursed each other's babies. Yako now felt he had to approach Peshev; he had run out of options. Yako also had a strategic reason to work with Peshev. He had learned that the law specified that only Jews from the 'newly liberated territories' were targeted for this first round of deportations. Terrible as this was, there appeared to be a loophole in the law that might help save the Jews of 'old Bulgaria.'

That same day, Vladimir Kurtev, the Macedonian leader, arrived in Kyustendil with chilling details culled from conversations in Sofia. He told his Jewish friends that the trains were coming and that all the Jews of Kyustendil were to be deported to Poland.

The Jews of the town began pooling their money. Perhaps Liuben Miltenov, the district governor, would authorize a delegation to Sofia. Jews were not permitted to travel without special papers, and the delegation needed to reach the capital in order to meet with Peshev and others in the parliament. It would be tricky: Even though Miltenov had warned Samuel Barouh, the Jewish pharmacist, of the deportation plans, he also had a reputation as a corrupt politician. The district governor would have to be 'persuaded' to grant the travel permits.

Across town, Jews emptied their pockets. The contributions were brought to a Jewish home in the city center, where an ad hoc group had assembled. The group chose Violeta Conforty, a young woman recently arrived with her three-year-old daughter from Sofia, to take the money to Miltenov. They saved some money for other bribes and for transport for the delegation.

The bills, unfolded, smoothed, and stacked, were placed in a large cloth bag. Violeta had never seen so much cash before, much less carried it in a shopping bag. She walked on that cold, clear morning the short distance to Miltenov's office and thought of her husband in a far-off labor camp. When she arrived at Miltenov's office, 'I gave him the bag,' Violeta recalled. 'And I was told that he was supposed to give me the documents. I said, "Where are the documents?" '

'I cannot give you the documents,' Miltenov said.

'Then give me my money back,' Violeta told the governor.

'No, I'm not giving you the money back,' he replied. 'Please leave the room.'

The young woman with the yellow star stood up and left the office. She returned to the house shaken, with no money and no documents. There would be no Jewish delegation traveling to the capital. It was then, she recalls, that many Jews in Kyustendil began to lose hope; it was then that other citizens of Kyustendil crafted their own plan.

Asen Suichmezov had grown up around Jews. A large man, perhaps six feet five, with a big appetite, he liked to eat kebab and lamb soup at a Jewish café across the street from his Kyustendil leather and coat shop. He even spoke Ladino, the Judeo-Spanish legacy of the Sephardic Jews from Spain and, 450 years later, still the mother tongue for many Balkan Jews.

Early in the war, Suichmezov had traveled to Macedonia on business. There, in Skopje, he had seen Jewish property being sold off. The owners had been deported to Poland; Suichmezov was aghast. In early

March, Suichmezov heard the story of the tobacco warehouse that was to store the Jews of Kyustendil. Fifteen or twenty times a day, anxious Jewish friends would ask him about rumors of huge soup pots arriving in the town to feed the corraled Jews before they boarded the trains. Suichmezov could provide no reassurance.

Jewish friends would pass by Suichmezov's shop, calling out, 'Good-bye, Asen! We're never going to see you again!' Other Jews, resisting this fate, pressed the sympathetic businessman to travel to Sofia and meet with Dimitur Peshev in the parliament on their behalf. Suichmezov agreed. 'I had given my word to the Jews that I would defend them,' the shop owner wrote years later. 'And I would not back out.'

On the early evening of March 8, Suichmezov and three other men began their journey toward Sofia. What had started out as a delegation of forty had now shrunk to four; this would be the entire ad hoc Kyustendil delegation to the parliament and its vice president, Dimitur Peshev.

When the four men arrived at the Kyustendil railway station, a yellow brick building with a broad cobblestone platform, they could see the long lines of freight cars ready to deport the Jews. The final destination, they would learn later, was to be the Treblinka death camp.

As they approached the platform, the men noticed police milling about; it occurred to them that someone had alerted the authorities of their trip to the parliament and that they could be blocked from boarding the train to Sofia. Quickly, they climbed onto a horse-drawn carriage and traveled to Kopelovsky, the next station down the line. From there, the four men got on the train and rode north, toward the capital and their meeting with Dimitur Peshev.

* * *

At about the same time, perhaps on that very same March evening in 1943, Moshe and Solia sat waiting with her parents at their home in the hills of Sliven. No one knew what to pack, what to talk about, how to wait, how even to wonder where they were going. Moshe and Solia had been married three years earlier, in a simple ceremony in the Balkan synagogue in Sofia. Solia had stood with her raven black hair flowing over her shoulders; Moshe, nervous, serious, standing stiffly in his suit, held the weight of responsibility on his shoulders. The young couple had faced the rabbi and the holy ark. Their wedding had taken place just weeks before the anti-Jewish measures went into effect and Moshe was sent away to the labor camps. Now, on that March 1943 evening in Sliven, just beyond the Valley of the Roses, the family sat in silence.

Sixty miles to the southwest, just before 3:00 A.M., Rabbi Behar led his family across Russian Boulevard and toward the Jewish school in Plovdiv. The streets were empty. Presently the school, and its black iron fence surrounding an empty courtyard, came into view. Rabbi Behar and his wife walked through the gate, followed by Susannah, her brother, and the two policemen. The family passed the first cold hour alone in the courtyard. Then, just as the rabbi had predicted, other Jewish families shuffled in, their arms filled with clothing, blankets, yellow cheese, and round loaves of black Bulgarian bread.

Just after sunrise, Bishop Kiril's servant came back to tell the rabbi that the bishop was taking action. Kiril had sent a telegram to King Boris, 'begging him in God's name to have pity on these unfortunate people.' The bishop had also sent a message to the chief of police 'that I, who until now had always been loyal towards the government, now reserved the right to act with a free hand on this matter and heed only the dictates of my conscience.'

By now, Kiril estimated, 'between 1,500 and 1,600 Jews' had assembled in the Jewish school yard in Plovdiv. Other citizens of Plovdiv had learned of this and begun to gather outside the school in protest; now there were crowds on both sides of the fence. 'There was widespread indignation among the public,' Kiril reported.

One eyewitness would recall Kiril himself showing up at the Jewish school that morning, saying, 'My children, I will not let this happen to you. I will lie on the railroad tracks and will not let you go.'

Susannah does not recall this, but she does remember sneaking through a loose board in the back of the school yard outhouse to hatch a contingency plan with a friend: When the time came, she would be spirited away and taken to the Rhodope Mountains with the Partizans. She slipped back into the school yard to update her father on the plan. If the deportations seemed imminent, the rabbi and his daughter agreed, Susannah would escape to join the armed struggle against the pro-Fascist monarchy. Moshe's brother, Jacques, was already there.

In Kyustendil, meanwhile, the town's Jews anxiously waited for news from the delegation that had left for the capital to meet with Dimitur Peshev, vice president of the parliament.

Dimitur Peshev had a fondness for fine suits cut close to his sturdy frame; invariably, a clean white handkerchief poked out in a triangle from his breast pocket. He wore cuff links, and his hair was carefully combed back with oil.

71

Peshev lived alone in a third-floor room above his sister's Sofia apartment. He was partial to backgammon and Voltaire. Often he would come downstairs in his fedora and buttoned-up suit coat to call on his two young nieces. Standing at the door in their lace-bordered dresses and party shoes, they would take their uncle's hand and walk with him to the neighborhood sweet shop.

Dimitur Peshev had spent much time dreaming of 'national ideals and universal human aspirations for something pure and sacred.' He believed in parliamentary democracy. He considered the Bulgarian Nazi imitators, 'spouting borrowed slogans' and marching about in their brown uniforms, as actors in 'a grotesque and pathetic vaudeville.'

Yet Peshev was vice president of the parliament in a pro-Fascist government put in place by King Boris III. The young lawyer had grown disillusioned with the Socialists after witnessing the harsh rule of a peasant regime. He saw his accommodation to the Fascists as part of the reality of European geopolitics. In tying his future to the king's, and to Bulgaria's alliance with the Nazis, Peshev sought to ensure a measure of national sovereignty for Bulgaria. The country's relations with Germany were precarious; somehow, the nation had managed to remain unoccupied and had even recovered old pieces of the fatherland.

Like the king, Peshev seemed to believe that in this dangerous balance, the nation's foreign policy required a nod to Hitler. Years later, he would recall his vote in favor of the Law for the Defense of the Nation, writing, 'This sacrifice was made more palatable by the knowledge that the restrictions on the Jews, however painful, were nonetheless temporary and would not be taken to extremes.' It was in this man's hands, more than anyone's, that the fate of the nation's Jews now rested.

On the morning of March 9, Asen Suichmezov stood at a hat shop on a Sofia street and rang up Dimitur Peshev at home. Suichmezov and his three companions had arrived from Kyustendil the night before. Peshev invited the men to his house, where Suichmezov made Kyustendil's case, speaking through tears about the long lines of train cars at the railway station.

In several previous meetings over recent weeks, the vice president of Bulgaria's national assembly had spent considerable time and energy explaining that there was no plan to deport the Jews. If there were, Dimitur Peshev had assured his worried visitors, surely he would know about it. By the morning of March 9, however, when Suichmezov and the others appeared before him, Peshev had begun to investigate. He had heard the deportation rumors from a close Jewish friend from Kyustendil. He had listened to a fellow parliamentarian describe the wrenching stories from Macedonia: 'old people, men, women, and children, carrying their belongings, defeated, desperate, powerless people begging for help, dragging themselves towards some unknown destination . . . that could only be surmised, to a fate that conjured up everyone's darkest fears.'

In the days just before Suichmezov and the others arrived, Peshev had realized that the rumors he'd been hearing were true. At that point Dimitur Peshev – proroyalist member of the assembly, leader of a parliament that endorsed the alliance with the Nazis, a man who had voted in favor of harsh restrictions against the nation's Jews – faced a choice. It was, perhaps, the most important moment in the complex and fragile narrative that would mark Bulgaria's history as forever distinct from the rest of Europe's.

'I could not remain passive,' Dimitur Peshev decided. 'My conscience and understanding of the grave consequences both for the people involved and for my country did not allow it. It was then I made the decision to do everything in my power to prevent the execution of a plan that was going to compromise Bulgaria in the eyes of the world and brand it with a mark of shame that it did not deserve.'

Peshev told the men to meet him at his office in the parliament that afternoon at 3:00 P.M. It was imperative to try to meet with the prime minister.

The men met again that afternoon in the parliament building. The prime minister, however, refused to see Peshev and the Kyustendil delegation. The deportation order remained in place. It was now late on the afternoon of March 9; the hour for the deportations was growing closer. With few options left, Peshev played his strongest remaining card. He demanded a meeting with the interior minister, Petur Gabrovski.

Within minutes, Peshev, Suichmezov, and eight other men – including fellow members of Parliament and, according to some accounts, several Jewish leaders in Sofia – strode into Gabrovski's office. The men confronted the minister with the scenes from Kyustendil. Gabrovski denied knowledge of what they knew to be true. Peshev, however, would recall that the interior minister seemed tense and nervous. The men pressed him, and again Gabrovski denied any knowledge of the deportations. At that point, someone in the delegation asked about the Dannecker-Belev Agreement – the German-Bulgarian document that laid out the secret plans in detail, down to the train wagons and deportation centers. How, the men wanted to know, could the interior minister not know about that?

Gabrovski lay trapped by his own denials. Either he didn't know what was happening in his own ministry or, far more likely, he was lying. Or, Peshev would charitably recount, 'he was speaking in the kinds of platitudes one might use to extricate oneself from an awkward situation . . .'

It was late afternoon. In just over an hour, the parliament would convene an evening session. Peshev and his fellow MPs in the meeting had made it clear they were prepared to use the session to denounce the secret deportations; if that happened, a national scandal would erupt. This was a crucial difference between Nazi-occupied countries elsewhere in Europe and the quasi-sovereign Axis nation of Bulgaria: There was still some room to maneuver. Dissenters in Bulgaria would not be shot on sight.

Peshev and the others waited for a response from the interior minister. Finally, Gabrovski stood up and left the room – perhaps to speak to the prime minister. When he returned he announced that the deportation order could not be revoked but that its execution could be suspended – temporarily. Peshev called Miltenov, the Kyustendil governor, and told him of the suspension. Other representatives began calling their home districts to repeat the news, while pressing Gabrovski to make his own official calls. The interior minister ordered his secretary to telegram each Bulgarian city where the deportation orders were active.

Evidence would later suggest that King Boris approved the

suspensions. A document from the Gestapo official in Sofia to German authorities in Berlin attributed the decision to suspend the deportations to 'the highest level.' Yet Gabrovski – and therefore, perhaps, Boris – insisted the suspension would be only temporary. Boris was adamant that the orders for the 11,300 Jews of the 'new lands' of Macedonia and Thrace would not be affected. Their deportation would continue. While the king apparently agreed, at least temporarily, to give Bulgaria's 47,000 Jews a chance to live, the Jews from Macedonia and Thrace perished under his watch.

Moments after the meeting with Gabrovski, in the hallway outside the interior ministry, Peshev turned to the leather shop owner and coat maker from Kyustendil. 'Suichmezov, shake my hand,' Peshev said. 'The deportation of the Jews has been stopped. You can phone Kyustendil immediately and tell them the news.'

Suichmezov left the assembly building with the rest of the Kyustendil delegation. At the back door they encountered a group of Jews crowded around the entrance. 'God bless you, Asen!' exclaimed a young man from Kyustendil. Moments later, as they walked toward a liquor store to phone Kyustendil, another man approached. His name was Colonel Avram Tadger, a Jewish veteran of two Bulgarian wars who was forced out of the Union of Reserve Officers by the Law for the Defense of the Nation. 'Which one of you is Asen Suichmezov?' the colonel asked. Suichmezov spoke up; Colonel Tadger seized the coat maker's hand and began to cry. 'I have come to shake your hand,' the veteran exclaimed. 'Bravo for your courage!'

* * *

The Jewish school yard in Plovdiv and the adjacent high-walled gymnasium were packed with hundreds of Jews, surrounded by their flimsy suitcases and cloth sacks jammed with clothes. It was the late morning of March 10; the order to suspend the deportation had still not been delivered to the authorities. Throngs of people were standing outside the fence, shouting, pledging not to let the Jews go.

Susannah Behar would recall the terror she experienced when the police demanded quiet to make an announcement. They ordered all the Jews to line up. Susannah believed it was almost time to escape to join the Partizans; the deportations would now begin.

Instead, the police told everyone to go home.

The physical sensation of relief at that moment – for the Behars in the school yard and the Barouhs and the Confortys in Kyustendil and the Eshkenazis waiting for news in Sliven – would be recalled, sixty years later, as something beyond description.

By afternoon, the Jews of Plovdiv were home. Many found that their houses, left unlocked in the rush to leave, were untouched – watched over by worried neighbors.

In the late afternoon, Bishop Kiril paid a visit to the rabbi's house. Susannah would remember him in his bishop's cap and silver-topped cane, embracing each one in the family before joining the rabbi for a private meeting in her father's study. As he walked toward the study, the bishop stopped and gazed at the rabbi's children. 'The whole Bulgarian Orthodox Church,' he promised, 'will stand up for the Jews.'

And so it did in the months to come. Metropolitan Stefan, the nation's top religious official, applied moral pressure on Boris, imploring the king 'to demonstrate the compassion and lucidity incumbent' on his position 'by defending the right to the freedom and human dignity that the Bulgarian people have always upheld by tradition and by temperament . . . The wails and tears of these Bulgarian citizens of Jewish origin whose rights are being denied them,' Bishop Stefan insisted, 'are a legitimate protest against the injustice being done to them.'

Dimitur Peshev, for his part, realized the authorities still intended to carry out the deportations. Perhaps, he reasoned, public exposure could shame the government. By March 17, Peshev had gathered forty-three signatures for a letter to the prime minister protesting the plan. 'We cannot believe that the deportation of these people outside Bulgaria, as suggested by some evil-intentioned rumor, was planned by the Bulgarian government,' the letter declared. 'Such measure is unacceptable not only because these people of Bulgarian citizenship cannot be expelled outside Bulgaria, but because it would be disastrous and bring ominous consequences upon the country. It would inflict an undeserved stain on Bulgaria's honor . . .'

Peshev's public rebuke of his own government's plan was unprecedented. He was a member of the pro-Fascist majority and supporter of the king and prime minister; yet in the midst of war, he defended a minority against the government's plan to deport them. Peshev would pay for his actions: Within days, the prime minister had him removed from his post as vice president of the parliament. Dimitur Peshev would never again hold public office.

Throughout the late spring of 1943, as the Nazis applied their own pressure on the king, Belev drew up new deportation plans – this time, Jews were to be shipped in barges along the Danube, on the country's northern border. Yet in the end the king, seeing a Germany weakened by its defeat in the battle of Stalingrad and speculating on the possible arrival of Russia or the Western allies in Bulgaria, wavered on the deportations. Instead, in late May he expelled all Jews from Sofia, dispersing them throughout the country, and stepped up the work of the labor camps. If this strategy was an attempt to placate the Nazis, it worked; soon, the Third Reich would be too distracted to worry about forty-seven thousand Bulgarian Jews.

On June 7, 1943, months after the Bulgarian drama played out in the school yard, the railway station, the parliament, and the streets, Germany's ambassador in Sofia sent a report to the Foreign Ministry in Berlin. 'I am firmly convinced that the Prime Minister and the government wish and strive for a final and radical solution to the Jewish problem,' Adolf Beckerle wrote. 'However, they are hindered by the mentality of the Bulgarian people, who lack the ideological enlightenment that we have.'

In fact, King Boris's capitulation to such 'ideological enlightenment' had cost the lives of more than 11,300 Jews from Bulgaria's annexed 'new lands' of Macedonia and Thrace. Almost without exception, they were exterminated.

Yet it is also true that at the critical time, ordinary people – in Kyustendil, in Plovdiv, in Sofia, across the country – stood by the Jews of Bulgaria. As a result, the Jewish population of an entire nation did not perish in the gas chambers at Treblinka.

And so it was that Moshe and Solia Eshkenazi, when the war finally ended, began to piece their lives back together. After seven years of marriage, Solia became pregnant, and a girl named Daizy was born in the Bulgarian capital on December 2, 1947. (She would later change her name to Dalia.)

None of this would have happened without what the Bulgarian-French intellectual Tzvetan Todorov calls 'the fragility of goodness': the intricate, delicate, unforeseeable weave of human action and historical events. If Liliana Panitsa and the others had not leaked the news of the deportations to their Jewish friends; if Asen Suichmezov and the Kyustendil delegation had not boarded the train for Sofia on the night of March 8; if Metropolitan Stefan and Bishop Kiril had followed Europe's Catholic Church and declined to speak out; if one hundred things had not happened, or had happened differently, it is possible that the deportation plan would have picked up momentum, that forty-seven thousand Bulgarian Jews, including Moshe and Solia Eshkenazi, would have perished at Treblinka, and that Dalia would have never been born.

But Dalia was born, on a cold December evening in Sofia. And like the tens of thousands of other Bulgarian Jews who later boarded ships to Palestine, and then Israel, she carried with her an extraordinary legacy.

Four

EXPULSION

ONE DAY IN late February 1942, as the drama surrounding Moshe and Solia Eshkenazi and the Bulgarian Jews began to play out a thousand miles to the north, a large contingent of the Khairi clan rode through the mountains of Palestine toward Hebron. It was ten days since the birth of the firstborn male child of Ahmad and Zakia and time for the aqiqa ceremony at the Tomb of the Patriarchs, named after the Prophet Abraham and known to the family as the Ibrahimi Mosque.

The baby, his parents, his six sisters, his great-uncle Sheikh Mustafa, and several dozen cousins, aunts, and uncles were packed into buses moving southeast on the narrow roads of Palestine. They rolled past the watermelon groves of Na'ani, just south of al-Ramla; past the village of Abu Shusha, with its tightly packed houses on the hill of Tall Jazar; past the cool, sweet springs of Imwas; past the stone minaret of Deir Aban, home of the finest wheat in all of Palestine; past the olive groves and sloping, rain-fed fields of Surif; and into al-Khalil, or Hebron, where the imam would be waiting at the mosque.

'A name should be prescribed for the child,' the Prophet Mohammad had observed. 'Its hair and all filth should be removed, and sacrifice should be performed on his behalf.' At the ceremony inside the Mosque of Abraham, the patriarch of three great faiths, the imam spoke the baby's name: Bashir, Arabic for 'good news' or 'the bearer of good tidings.'

His hair was cut and weighed; the family would give to the poor the value of that weight in gold. Sheep were slaughtered, and two-thirds of the meat would again be given to the poor. The clan had a feast with the rest.

'It was a big event,' Bashir's sister Khanom remembered. She would turn six that year. 'It was a great occasion.'

Back in al-Ramla, the schoolteachers congratulated the Khairi girls on the arrival of their baby brother. At home, they doted on Bashir. As a toddler he would stand on a table, dressed in white trousers and white shoes, making impromptu speeches to his adoring older sisters. 'He was handsome,' his sister Nuha would recall. 'Like King Farouk,' the ruler of Egypt. *'Hali snanek ya Bashir, khalik la'imak ya Bashir,'* the girls would sing when Zakia had prepared a dessert. 'Sweeten your teeth, Bashir; oh, Bashir, may God keep you for your mother.'

Bashir's great-uncle Sheikh Mustafa Khairi had been mayor for more than twenty years, and for him the tension of nationalist politics had given way to the headaches of rations and rising prices under the British wartime rule. The war economy had actually helped Palestine. The British used the territory as a massive staging area for the conflict in North Africa. Smooth asphalt roads began to replace the rutted dirt tracks of old Palestine. Work was plentiful, and Ahmad's furniture business was faring well.

In Africa and Europe, World War II had turned toward the Allies. Soviet troops had held out in the cold and defeated the Nazis in the battle of Stalingrad. Closer to

Palestine, British troops, aided by many Jewish recruits, had driven Rommel out of North Africa and eliminated the prospect of a Nazi march toward Tel Aviv and Jerusalem.

By the end of the war in 1945, Bashir had turned three and the battle for the future of Palestine had reawakened. A quarter million Jewish refugees flooded the Allied displaced persons camps in Europe, and tens of thousands of Jews were smuggled out of the DP camps to Palestine by the Mossad, predecessor of the present-day Israeli spy agency. Most of this immigration was illegal under the British rule in Palestine. The authorities began to intercept boatloads of European Jews and intern them at Cyprus, off the coast of Lebanon. With its White Paper six years earlier, the British had imposed strict immigration limits in the face of the fears, demands, and rebellion of the Palestinian Arabs.

As the details of the atrocities in Europe began to emerge, however, the image of stateless, bedraggled Holocaust survivors in the Cyprus internment camps was seared into the mind of the Western public, and Britain was pressured to loosen its policy. U.S. president Harry Truman pressed Britain to allow one hundred thousand DPs into Palestine as soon as possible, and to abandon restrictions on land sales to Jews – measures sure to increase tensions with the Arabs of Palestine. Arabs argued that the Holocaust survivors could be settled elsewhere, including in the United States, which had imposed its own limits on settlement of European Jews. The Zionists, too, were intent on settling the refugees in Palestine, not anywhere else. In February 1947, when the ship *Exodus* arrived in Palestine's Haifa port, British authorities refused to bend their immigration limits, denying entry to the

4,500 Jewish refugees and forcing them to board other ships and return to Germany. A French newspaper called the ships a 'floating Auschwitz.' The incident shocked the Western world and deepened support for the Zionist movement.

The earlier cooperation between the British Empire and the Zionists had all but vanished, and like the leaders of the Arab Rebellion of the 1930s, Jewish leaders in Palestine wanted the British out. The Jewish Agency had been authorized by the British to create a 'national home for the Jewish people.' Now, nearly three decades later, the Jewish community in Palestine had grown into a potent economic and political force in the midst of its Arab neighbors and British overseer. It had even developed its own militia, the Haganah, which, in addition to the extremist militia groups Irgun and the Stern Gang, fought to expel the former benefactors. In July 1946, operatives of Irgun planted bombs in Jerusalem's King David Hotel, where the British housed their military and intelligence headquarters. The explosion killed more than eighty people. Tensions between the Haganah, controlled by David Ben-Gurion and the Mapai Party, and Irgun and the Stern Gang, led by future prime ministers Menachem Begin and Yitzhak Shamir, sharpened ideological and tactical differences; these would continue for decades. Meanwhile, thousands of Jewish immigrants continued to pour into Palestine, oblivious to such tensions.

Yitzhak Yitzhaki, Solia's cousin, had arrived in Jerusalem from Bulgaria on New Year's Day 1945. He had come overland via the *Orient Express* from Istanbul, traveling through Damascus, where he encountered exotic oranges and bananas in abundance and was fitted for a new suit and shoes, paid for by his sponsor, the Jewish

Agency of Palestine. He wrote home of a troubling encounter in the Damascus market with an Arab who pointed a knife at his own chest and said, 'This is what they will do to you in Palestine.' Yitzhaki arrived in Jerusalem to the sound of church bells and the sight of drunken British soldiers roaming the streets of the Holy City. He found work in a leather tanning factory, on construction sites, and in plowing Jewish fields with a pair of mules, before joining the Haganah for basic military training.

By 1947, the British had eighty-four thousand troops in Palestine who, according to a report by the British Colonial Office, 'received no co-operation from the Jewish community.' Despite their numbers, the troops 'had proved insufficient to maintain law and order in the face of a campaign of terrorism waged by highly organised Jewish forces equipped with all the weapons of the modern infantryman. Communications were attacked throughout the country; Government buildings, military trains and places of entertainment frequented by Britons were blown up; and numbers of Britons, Arabs and moderate Jews were kidnapped or murdered. This wholesale terrorism has continued ever since.'

British officials were under pressure at home to convert factories and revive the postwar domestic economy. The nation was at the end of a colonial era. It was on the verge of quitting India, and in February, British officials announced they would hand over the problem of Palestine to the newly formed United Nations. A UN fact-finding team arrived to investigate the roots of the struggle for Palestine. It was the eleventh such fact-finding body to come to the area since 1919.

* * *

That same month, Bashir turned five. He was known as a shy boy, frightened of dogs and strangers, unlike the most recent addition to the Khairi family, his mischievous younger brother, Bhajat, who always seemed to be getting into trouble. Bashir was more quiet and reserved. He liked to sit inside with his sister Nuha, one year older, gazing out the window at the railroad tracks for hours at a time as they waited for the Jaffa-to-Jerusalem train. Nuha would recall many days in the flower garden at an al-Ramla park, where the family would bring sandwiches for picnics.

On their way to school, looking crisp in their matching uniforms, the children would notice the British soldiers in their khaki shorts and soft brown hats. The older girls, like Khanom, now eleven, began to understand the political context of the soldiers' presence in Palestine. 'I remember one of my teachers,' Khanom recalled. 'She used to read us nationalist poetry, and she told us – perhaps she was not supposed to – about what was going on in the country.'

By the fall of 1947, nearly everyone in Palestine was anxious about the UN investigation and how its recommendations could determine their future. There was talk about a division of Palestine into separate states for Arabs and Jews. Most Palestinian Arabs saw that as a potential catastrophe. No one could predict what would happen to the Arabs on the Jewish side of the partition; more important, they wanted one Palestine. Increasingly, Ahmad would discuss politics over coffee and *arguileh* (water pipe) at the *diwan* in the Khairi family compound, where the conversation would turn inevitably to the sorry state of the Palestinian Arab leadership.

The Arabs of Palestine were weaker and more fractured than ever. Thousands of men had been killed or wounded during the Arab Rebellion and tens of thousands imprisoned; the leader of the revolt, Hajj Amin al-Husseini, the ex-mufti of Jerusalem, was in exile and his image permanently tainted in the West. The ex-mufti had taken up with the Nazis in Berlin, where he tried to mobilize Arab support for the Axis. To many Arabs in Palestine, the ex-mufti was still a nationalist hero fighting against the British and the Zionists, and they looked to him to deliver an independent state across the whole of Palestine and to defend them in the event of war. These would be extremely difficult tasks to perform, especially from exile.

Arabs inside Palestine competed for power in the ex-mufti's absence, but philosophical differences, personal rivalries, and profound mistrust prevented a unified leadership from emerging. Much of the friction had its roots in the Arab Rebellion. Nationalists, aligned with the ex-mufti, saw the elite or 'notable' class as too willing to sell out Palestine to the Jews; for the notables, it was better to get something than nothing: Arabs had to accept the reality of the Zionists.

The surrounding Arab states, just emerging from colonial rule into fledgling independence, had their own agendas. Publicly, Arab governments proclaimed their support for the ex-mufti's goal of a single independent state in Palestine and pledged to send armies to defend the Palestinian Arabs if necessary. Privately, however, some Arab leaders harbored deep reservations about joining any future conflict and were wary of one another's territorial ambitions for Palestine. In November, Transjordan's King Abdullah met secretly with Zionist leaders along the Jordan River, and the two sides forged an agreement to essentially divide Palestine between them: The Jews would have their state, as outlined in the plan being discussed in the United Nations, and Abdullah would expand his desert kingdom to include land on the west bank of the Jordan River, on territory the UN was considering as an independent Arab state.

This gap between public pan-Arab unity and the hidden interests of individual leaders would prove significant in the months and years to come.

The news from the United Nations in New York arrived in the early hours of November 30, 1947. It was after midnight in Palestine, still early in the evening in the United States. Ahmad may have been sitting over his water pipe and backgammon game at the *diwan* in the family compound. The family may have been at home, huddled around its large wooden radio, straining to listen through the static to the honey-voiced commentator Raji Sahyoun on Arab-run Radio Jerusalem. Bashir and the other young children were probably asleep.

Whatever the circumstances, the news itself would not be forgotten: On the recommendation of the United Nations Special Committee on Palestine, the UN General Assembly had voted, thirty-three states in favor, thirteen opposed, with ten abstaining, to partition Palestine into two separate states – one for the Arabs and one for the Jews. A UN minority report, which recommended a single state for Arabs and Jews, with a constitution respecting 'human rights and fundamental freedoms without distinction as to race, sex, language or religions,' was rejected.

Palestine was to be divided. After three decades of colonial rule, the British would leave on May 15, 1948. If all went according to plan, the Arab and Jewish states would be born on the same day.

The Khairis were in shock. Under the UN partition

plan, their hometown of al-Ramla, along with neighboring Lydda and the coastal city of Jaffa, was to become part of an Arab Palestinian state. The plan stipulated that 54.5 percent of Palestine and more than 80 percent of its cultivated citrus and grain plantations would go to a Jewish state. Jews represented about one-third of the population and owned 7 percent of the land. Most Arabs would not accept the partition.

If the partition plan went forward, al-Ramla would lie only a few kilometers from the new Jewish state. At least, Bashir's parents thought, it could have been worse; under the UN plan, the family would not be strangers on its own land. Still, what would happen to the Arabs in what was now to be Jewish territory? The partition would place more than four hundred thousand Arabs in the new Jewish state, making them a 45 percent minority amid half a million Jews.

Reaction to the UN vote was swift: Palestinians, backed by other Arab leaders, immediately rejected the partition and pledged to fight it. Why, they asked, should their homeland become the solution to the Jewish problem in Europe? Jews in Palestine and around the world celebrated. In Jerusalem, Yitzhak Yitzhaki, Solia's cousin, joined a crowd at the Jewish Agency on King George Street 'and danced and danced throughout the night.' In Bulgaria, a thousand miles to the north, Moshe and Solia Eshkenazi were elated. At last, after the Holocaust, the world had seen the justice in the Zionist cause.

Zionist leaders had accepted the partition concept the previous year, abandoning an earlier position that favored a 'Jewish commonwealth' across the whole of Palestine. Still, in the wake of the UN vote for partition, David Ben-Gurion worried about the large Arab minority on the land set aside for the Jews. 'Such a composition does not provide a stable basis for a Jewish state,' Ben-Gurion told Zionist labor leaders shortly after the United Nations vote. 'With such a composition, there cannot be absolute certainty that control will remain in the hands of the Jewish majority. This fact must be viewed in all its clarity and acuteness . . . There can be no stable and strong Jewish state so long as it has a Jewish majority of only sixty [actually 55] percent.'

As soon as the UN vote was announced, Yitzhaki received word 'that the Arabs were not accepting the partition and that intensified attacks on Jerusalem were expected. I was notified to show up the next day to go up to Mt. Scopus as protection for the hospital and the university.' On November 30, Yitzhaki traveled to Mt. Scopus in a convoy of armored Jewish buses. As the convoy approached the Jewish neighborhood of Shimon Ha-Zadik, 'there was an explosion.' Yitzhaki dived onto the wooden floor of the bus and found himself next to a beautiful young woman with thick black braids. 'Don't worry, it will be all right,' he told the woman hopefully as they heard more explosions. Their bus had passed over a mine laid in the road, but it exploded behind the bus just after it passed, saving the passengers, including Yitzhaki and the young woman on the floor beside him. Eventually the bus resumed its journey up Mt. Scopus, and Yitzhaki learned the name of the woman who would become his wife: Varda Carmon.

The same day, Arabs attacked a Jewish bus near al-Ramla, on the Jaffa-Jerusalem road. A three-day Arab strike in protest of the vote led to violent clashes in Jerusalem, with fourteen people dead, Arabs and Jews. It was only the beginning.

Arab states, and the ex-mufti, were making plans to mobilize troops in Palestine. Throngs of people filled the public squares in the Arab capitals, shouting their approval. Egypt's minister of war boasted that 'the Egyptian military is capable on its own of occupying Tel Aviv, the capital of Jews, in fifteen days . . .' It appeared that Arab armies could eliminate the Jewish state before it was even established. On the other side, Zionist forces had been preparing themselves for months, mobilizing to secure arms and to recruit young Jewish men, many of whom were Holocaust survivors fresh from the DP camps in Europe. These battered refugees-turned-soldiers were highly motivated to defend their new homeland and joined an organized infrastructure that had been decades in the making. The Haganah would soon develop detailed battle plans, including the control of Jewish areas beyond the UN partition line, in an area designated as part of an Arab state. The future shape of Palestine, it was increasingly clear, would be determined by the facts on the ground, not by what the United Nations had put on paper. 'The boundaries of the state,' Ben-Gurion wrote, 'will not be determined by a U.N. resolution, but by the force of arms.'

In early 1948, a series of bombs planted by Arab and Jewish militias killed scores of people in Jerusalem – at the Semiramis Hotel, at the Palestine Post, and on Ben Yehuda Street in West Jerusalem. During the same period, the Haganah attacked Arab towns and villages, driving out thousands; the refugees began fleeing for safe haven in the cities. Arab fighters attacked Jewish settlements, blocked roads in the Negev, and continued their attacks on Jewish traffic at two key transit points between Jerusalem and the Mediterranean coast. One was the mountain pass at Bab al-Wad, or the Gate of the Valley; the other was along the Jaffa-Jerusalem road in al-Ramla, where Ahmad and his family had been growing increasingly nervous.

One night in early April 1948, the Khairi home was jolted by a series of blasts coming from the edge of town. Soon the news arrived: The headquarters of Hassan Salameh, the ex-mufti's commander whose base was just outside al-Ramla, had been devastated. Recruits from the Haganah had blown a rocket through the fence surrounding the headquarters, then thrown explosives into the building, bringing it down in a series of spectacular explosions. At least seventeen of the mufti's men were killed. Volunteers rushed to the scene from al-Ramla and Lydda. Eyewitnesses saw body parts hanging from the trees.

The Khairis and the people of al-Ramla grew increasingly worried. If the mufti's commander could not guard even his own headquarters, how could he protect the city's residents?

A few days later, the family learned of another devastating blow: The Arabs of Palestine had lost their most revered commander when Abd al-Qader al-Husseini, nephew of the ex-mufti, was killed in the battle for Qastal. Control of the hill at Qastal meant control of the road, and therefore the supply lines, between Jerusalem and the Mediterranean ports forty miles to the west. The loss of the hill was crippling to the Arab cause. Even this defeat, however, was not as terrifying as the news that reached Ahmad at about the same time: At Deir Yassin, an Arab village just west of Jerusalem, Jewish militia had massacred hundreds of women, children, and unarmed men. Details were scarce, but the family heard stories of innocents being lined up and shot in their homes by the militia of the Irgun and Stern Gang. There were rumors of rape. Ahmad and Zakia were terrified. They had nine children, seven of them girls.

In one day, the Arabs of Palestine had lost their greatest commander, their most important battle, and dozens of innocents at Deir Yassin. Just as disturbing for the Khairis, in the aftermath of the attack on Hassan Salameh's head-quarters, al-Ramla seemed more vulnerable. Already the strategically located town had become a flashpoint in the ongoing struggle to control the supply routes between Jerusalem and the coast. Ahmad and Zakia saw that their children's lives might be in danger.

Yitzhak Yitzhaki had similar concerns. He had written home to Bulgaria of his assignment on Mt. Scopus with the Haganah to protect the university and the hospital. In Sofia, Moshe and Solia were following Yitzhaki's move-ments and had learned through his letters that Arab forces had cut off Jewish supply lines at the mountain pass of Bab al-Wad and that hunger was growing among the Jewish population of Jerusalem. 'But at Mt. Scopus, we had food,' Yitzhaki would recall. 'We received parachuted supplies by night.' At Passover, in early April 1948, Yitzhaki and his fellow Haganah recruits succeeded in securing the road between Jerusalem and Mt. Scopus. 'Then we could take a little twenty-four-hour vacation in Jerusalem.' There he mailed a letter home to Bulgaria, telling his family he was on his way back to Mt. Scopus the next day.

'The next afternoon, I show up at the appointed place ready to go up with the caravan of the three Jewish buses back to Mt. Scopus,' Yitzhaki said. Varda wanted him to stay in Jerusalem for one more night. 'But I have to go back,' Yitzhaki protested. Varda had connections in the Haganah and succeeded in winning her boyfriend another day off, though the commander warned Yitzhaki: 'Tomorrow's caravan will not be as safe as this one.'

That evening, April 13, Yitzhaki and Varda went to see a movie at Cinema Edison in West Jerusalem. Yitzhaki couldn't concentrate. 'I had a bad feeling and I felt very restless. Suddenly, we heard shooting and explosions. "This is our caravan. I know it," I said to Varda. I ran out to the headquarters. There I was told that armed Arabs stopped the caravan.' Arab fighters had attacked the convoy on its way to Hadassah Hospital. The attackers burned the buses and killed everyone inside. Seventy-eight people died. Most were doctors and nurses.

'Up on Mt. Scopus, I was counted as one of the dead,' Yitzhaki said. 'And indeed, I felt that I myself was there in those buses. It was terrible, terrible to live with this. When my family heard of what happened, they were sure that I was killed. What added to the anguish was that most of the bodies could not be identified, except through someone's personal objects, like rings.' In Bulgaria, Moshe's, Solia's, and Yitzhaki's immediate families in Sliven and Burgas went into mourning.

Even in the midst of the fighting, some Arab leaders in al-Ramla and neighboring Lydda were trying to maintain contact with their Jewish neighbors. Two months earlier, the mayor of Lydda received his Jewish counterpart, Ziegfried Lehman, a medical doctor born in Berlin and now a leader from the nearby Jewish settlement of Ben Shemen. The mayor agreed to Dr. Lehman's request to keep the road open between the communities. In a few places, hope remained for a peaceful settlement.

In early May, Bedouin fighters began arriving in al-Ramla from the east on the orders of King Abdullah of Transjordan. 'We slaughtered many lambs in their honor and received them as a liberation army,' Khanom remembered. 'They gave us assurances and the word of King Abdullah himself that we would be safe and be able to stay in al-Ramla.' Many of the Bedouins were barefoot and in the coming days would use their rifles to shoot pigeons for food. They would be remembered as moody, mercenary, and courageous. With their small numbers and meager weapons, they did not appear equipped to defend the town against an invading force and were belittled by some locals as the 'barefoot brigade.' King Abdullah, however, had promised 'enough force to defend Arab lives,' and people in al-Ramla were hopeful that the Bedouins were simply the advance guard of a much larger force. There was reason to worry, however. Elsewhere internal Arab frictions were causing logistical problems: In Haifa, a mixed Arab-Jewish city along the northern coast of Palestine, arms intended for one Arab militia were being intercepted by another. In Jaffa, an Arab town ten miles west of al-Ramla, two military coordinators were each giving separate and sometimes conflicting sets of orders. Divisions among the Arabs, both within and outside of Palestine, were weakening them. On May 13, Jaffa fell, and refugees began filling al-Ramla's streets.

A short time later, scores of other families began drifting into al-Ramla from the south. They had fled Na'ani, a village of orange groves and watermelon fields a few miles away, after a Jewish farmer had galloped into the village on horseback, shouting, 'The Jewish army is coming! You must leave, or you will all be killed!' The people of Na'ani knew this man as Khawaja Shlomo – Shlomo the Stranger. He was a neighbor from Na'an, the kibbutz next door. They had never seen him in such a state of agitation, and at first they didn't take his warnings seriously. But they were on good terms with this Jewish neighbor, and he was insistent, yelling from his horse, 'No, no, no! If you stay, they will kill you!' The villagers were well aware of the horrors of Deir Yassin, which had already caused panic and flight from villages across Palestine. They felt they had no choice but to believe Shlomo. They arrived in al-Ramla carrying virtually nothing, assuming they would return to Na'ani as soon as the danger had passed.

By now Ahmad Khairi found himself living in a town he scarcely recognized. Refugees slept under trees in Khairi orchards, crowded the coffee shops and markets, and choked the streets near Ahmad's furniture workshop.

Ahmad was growing increasingly nervous about allowing Zakia and the children to remain in al-Ramla. He began to consider a temporary safe haven for them. Within forty-eight hours, the British would be leaving Palestine for good, and whatever little order their presence provided in al-Ramla would be gone. Local Arab merchants were hurriedly buying surplus pants, uniforms, and shoes from the British army as the colonial forces packed up their garrison and prepared to sail north toward England.

On May 14, in the nearby coastal city of Tel Aviv, David Ben-Gurion declared Israel's independence in an address to the Jewish Provisional Council. 'It is,' he proclaimed, 'the self-evident right of the Jewish people to be a nation, as all other nations, in its own Sovereign State.' The next day, Ben-Gurion broadcast word of the new state of Israel by live radio to the United States; in the background, listeners could hear the rumble and explosion of Egyptian planes bombing Tel Aviv. The Jewish leader would describe the conflict as 'seven hundred thousand Jews pitted against twenty-seven million Arabs – one against forty.' More relevant were the fighting forces on the ground, and there, in fact, all Jewish and Arab forces were relatively even as the war officially began. Only days before, American diplomats had expressed skepticism that the Arabs would put up more than a 'token' fight. President Harry Truman wrote to Zionist leader Chaim Weizmann, who would become the first president of Israel: 'I sincerely hope that the Palestine situation will work out on an equitable and peaceful basis.'

Truman had barely signed his letter when Egyptian ground forces were attacking Israeli settlements in the Negev and advancing toward Tel Aviv and Jerusalem; Syrian and Iraqi forces were entering Palestine from the east; and soldiers of King Abdullah's Arab Legion were crossing the Jordan River and marching west. Legion forces took up positions in Ramallah and Nablus north of Jerusalem, on lands Abdullah wanted for the 'West Bank' of his desert kingdom.

The same day, May 15, as the Arab troops converged on the new Jewish state, Irgun forces were approaching al-Ramla.

Al-Ramla men lay behind sandbags in shallow trenches they had dug with oxen and hand tools. Their crude defense posts were at the western and southern edges of town. Zafer Khairi, Sheikh Mustafa's son, was in charge of part of the western defenses. Now, with the mufti's soldiers and the Bedouin 'barefoot brigades' alongside, the volunteer fighters would undergo their most serious test.

Bursts of machine-gun fire echoed near the train tracks close to the Khairi home. Then came earsplitting explosions as shells landed nearby. Outside, two hundred Jewish fighters were trying to penetrate al-Ramla from the west. The Irgun was fighting for control of the Jaffa-Jerusalem road, to ensure the flow of goods and to stop Arab attacks on Jewish convoys. The fighting was fierce. In some quarters of the city, Arabs and Jews were struggling desperately with bayonets in hand-to-hand combat. 'The whole city,' one Israeli account declared, became 'one big battlefield. The Arabs have vast amounts of weapons and are fighting tenaciously. Hundreds of shells are falling on houses throughout the city, and the Arabs have suffered heavy casualties . . . Wave after wave, the Jews charged into the street battles.' It wasn't clear who was winning or how long al-Ramla's defenders could hold out.

After the massacre by Irgun forces in Deir Yassin, the specter of that militia penetrating al-Ramla had city leaders in a state of near panic. They sent urgent cables to King Abdullah and to the commander of his Arab Legion, John Bagot Glubb, pleading for immediate help and invoking fears of another slaughter. One voice cried, 'Our wounded are breathing their last breaths, and we cannot help them.'

Abdullah, however, had received similar pleas from Arabs in Jerusalem, begging him to 'save us!' and warning that Jewish forces were scaling the walls of the Old City. The king wrote Glubb that 'any disaster suffered by the people of the city at the hands of the Jews, whether they are killed or driven from their homes, would have the most far reaching results for us.' He ordered his commander to Jerusalem. On May 19, Glubb rolled into the Holy City to confront Israeli forces with a force of three hundred men, four antitank weapons, and a squadron of armored cars. On Arab-run Radio Jerusalem, commentator Raji Sahyoun had promised 'our forth-coming redemption by the hand of Transjordan' and the 'scurrying' and 'collapse' of the 'Haganah kids.'

Abdullah's secret agreement with the Jews did not envision this fighting: It was designed to accept a Jewish state within the UN partition boundaries while the king took over the West Bank and most of the state designated for the Arabs, including al-Ramla and Lydda. Now fight-ing on the ground made all of this uncertain. Yet Arab Legion forces did not cross into territory allotted by the UN partition resolution to the Jewish state.

For some Israeli leaders, however, the king's move on Jerusalem showed his true intentions. It represented a declaration of war and a joining with other Arab forces intent on destroying the Jewish state. Abdullah's move had only deepened the Jewish leaders' sense that they were under siege from all sides. Several days earlier, according to accounts from Kfar Etzion, a Jewish settle-ment bloc south of Jerusalem, Jewish civilians had been massacred by Arab villagers as they tried to surrender to Arab Legion troops. With the king's forces converging on the Jewish quarter in East Jerusalem, Abdullah, they believed, was not to be trusted.

Civilians on each side were under attack. Desperate Arabs within the walls of the Old City, whose urgent pleas compelled the king to act, were relieved when his Arab Legion forces arrived; residents of the Jewish quarter, who would soon surrender, were terrified. In the western part of the city, Arab residents felt mortars shake their homes, growing closer by the hour, and many fled eastward toward Transjordan; Jewish residents would recall enduring thirst, hunger, and dwindling arms and ammunition during the siege by Arab forces.

Glubb had been reluctant to enter Jerusalem. He was more concerned about controlling the supply lines between Jerusalem and the coast, especially at Latrun, a key junction between Jerusalem and al-Ramla. With forces now committed to Latrun and Jerusalem, he told Abdullah, he could not be expected to send additional troops to reinforce the Arab towns of Lydda and al-Ramla. Those towns would have to defend themselves with what they had.

On May 19, as Glubb's Arab Legion entered the Old City and Radio Jerusalem played patriotic Arab songs, Irgun forces attacked al-Ramla for the fourth time in as many days, pounding the city from the west. Dressed in English and American battle fatigues, they moved forward with armored trucks, machine guns, and mortars.

Around this time, a bomb went off at the Wednesday market while Ahmad was there. His sister rushed there to find that he wasn't hurt, but the incident rattled the family. Ahmad moved Zakia and the children out of the house and in with relatives near Sheikh Mustafa, in the family compound. Bashir, six years old, would remember taking refuge near Sheikh Mustafa's house, in the home his uncle, Dr. Rasem Khairi, had converted into an emergency medical clinic. Rasem was tending to the wounded fighters. 'I used to call it the shelter,' Bashir remembered. 'There were a lot of explosions and shooting. I couldn't tell where they were coming from. I was afraid. I was trying to understand. You're not in your house, your room, your bed. There was no freedom of movement. I remember so many bodies, too many to collect.' Sheikh Mustafa had begun convening meetings with town leaders at his house nearby, urging the people of al-Ramla not to abandon the city.

By the morning of May 19, al-Ramla's fighters had pushed back the Irgun. The Jewish militia would count thirty men dead and twenty missing. 'The people are in very low spirits,' read an Israeli intelligence report issued a few days later, 'due to the heavy losses and lack of success.'

The city's defenders had prevailed. It appeared to be an unambiguous victory for the ex-mufti's forces, the barefoot brigade, and the civilian volunteer fighters of al-Ramla. Ahmad, however, had had enough. It was too dangerous to let Zakia and the children stay in the city. Despite Sheikh Mustafa's pleas that no one should abandon al-Ramla, Ahmad would take no more chances. He hired two cars to take the family east, through the hills of Palestine to Ramallah. That trip in itself would be dangerous, Ahmad knew; though Ramallah was only twenty miles away, the roads were bad and pockets of fighting were erupting in unpredictable places. But staying would be more risky than leaving. In Ramallah it was relatively calm. The family could remain there until the fighting subsided.

Bashir, Nuha, Khanom, and their siblings rode northeast in the two large sedans. 'When we first heard we were going to Ramallah, we were happy,' Khanom said. 'For me, Ramallah was something beautiful. Quiet, small, green, nice weather, nice food, nice people. We thought we would go there for a nice time. Only later did we realize.'

A week after the victory over the Irgun, Hassan Salameh, commander of the only regular force defending al-Ramla, was critically wounded by mortar fire during a battle north of the city. A few days later, he died at a local hospital. His death cast a pall over the city and neighboring Lydda. To Firdaws Taji, the second cousin of the Khairis, Salameh's death was an ominous prelude. 'He was a hero,' she recalled. 'Of course it was a bad sign.'

As Jewish and Arab forces battled on several fronts across Palestine, the United Nations increased diplomatic pressure for a truce. Count Folke Bernadotte, a UN mediator, had arrived in Amman, capital of Transjordan, to meet with King Abdullah and press the issue of a cease-fire. He still hoped the warring parties could implement something close to the partition plan the UN member states had approved the previous November. As the diplomatic efforts continued and a truce appeared more imminent, Israeli and Arab forces worked feverishly to gain the advantage before their supplies and positions were frozen in place during the truce.

Glubb, meanwhile, sent a small detachment of troops to al-Ramla. These would not be sufficient to hold the town, he again stressed to Abdullah, but perhaps they would deter any further attacks before the truce began. However, he proposed another measure that could help ensure al-Ramla's safety. In the final hours before the truce, Arab Legion forces could easily take Ben Shemen, the nearby Jewish outpost that could be used by the Haganah to launch a strike. 'But the mayor of Lydda had begged us not to do so,' Glubb later wrote. Lydda and Ben Shemen were only a mile apart and a few miles from al-Ramla. Lydda's mayor 'alleged that he was on good terms with the Jews and proposed to defend the town by diplomacy.' Glubb's British deputy, Captain T. N. Bromage, also pushed for a takeover of Ben Shemen: 'If there had been any hope of defending Lydda from the Israelis,' Bromage wrote, 'that colony would have needed to have been captured as a first step. I had enough force to have taken it by storm . . .' Bromage's request was refused. The attack on Ben Shemen never took place.

The truce went into effect on June 11. All matériel and supplies were to remain frozen in place, with a strict UN arms embargo ostensibly imposed on all parties. In the intervening few weeks, the Israelis managed to break the embargo with shipments of rifles, machine guns, armored cars, artillery, tanks, Messerschmitt planes, and millions of rounds of ammunition from Czechoslovakia. The British, however, exerted pressure on Transjordan to comply with the embargo; the Arab Legion would therefore face any resumption of the war with severe shortages of weapons and ammunition. 'Allies who let one become involved in a war and then cut off our essential supplies,' King Abdullah complained to the British representative in Amman, 'are not very desirable friends.' In early July, Glubb began to urge an extension of the truce.

King Abdullah was now in possession of much of the West Bank. He appeared content with the status quo and was quietly lobbying for an armistice with Israel. UN mediator Bernadotte agreed, proposing the partition of Palestine between Israel and Transjordan. Under this plan, the people of al-Ramla and Lydda would become not citizens of an independent Arab state, but subjects of Abdullah in his kingdom of Transjordan.

Israel rejected Count Bernadotte's proposal. Israelis had narrowly avoided their own civil war in late June when Ben-Gurion ordered Haganah forces to blow up an Irgun ship, the *Altalena*, under the command of Menachem Begin. The ship was carrying arms for Irgun militia members, but Ben-Gurion insisted all military direction come under the command of the Haganah and its successor, the Israel Defense Forces (IDF). With the military consolidation in progress and the new shipments of arms in hand, Israel had grown stronger during the truce.

Member states of the Arab League, having no wish to see Palestine divided between Israel and King Abdullah, voted on July 6 to resume the fight for a single independent Arab-majority state. The king, ironically, had been chosen by his fellow Arab heads of state as the supreme commander of all the Arab forces in Palestine, which were ostensibly to fight for the independent Palestinian state. Given the king's own territorial ambitions, this was a figurehead position at best, and an ironic one at that. Nevertheless, when the other Arab states voted to continue the fight, Abdullah had little choice but to agree and stand in solidarity with the other Arabs. The war would resume.

'But how are we to fight without ammunition?' Glubb asked Abdullah's prime minister, Tawfiq Abul Huda.

'Don't shoot,' Glubb recalled the response, 'unless the Jews shoot first.'

A few days later, in the early afternoon of July 11, 1948, Lieutenant Israel Gefen crept forward in his jeep, the last vehicle in a long convoy belonging to Commando Battalion Eighty-nine, Eighth Brigade, Israel Defense Forces. As the line of the Eighty-ninth edged slowly along an asphalt track between cactus hedges, Gefen could see his battalion's armored trucks, American-made troop carriers known as half-tracks, an armored car captured a day earlier from the Arab Legion, and twenty-odd more jeeps. The jeeps were mounted with stretchers and Czech- and German-made machine guns, each with the capacity of firing at least eight hundred rounds per minute. In all, the force was made up of about 150 men. They were at the edge of Lydda, a few miles from al-Ramla and the Khairi family.

At twenty-six, Lieutenant Gefen was already a ten-year veteran of Middle Eastern conflicts. In 1941, he had fought against Rommel with the British army during the siege of the Libyan port city of Tobruk. Earlier, he had fought in Palestine for the Haganah during the Arab Rebellion. His career began in a kibbutz. Under the nose of the British, Gefen and other young Zionists, sworn to secrecy, helped test weapons invented by an agricultural instructor in his metal workshop. Lieutenant Gefen could see one such invention, the armored 'sandwich truck' – two layers of steel fortified by an inch of hardwood in the middle – in the long column before him.

The battalion was coming from Ben Shemen, the Jewish settlement just to the north. For weeks the open community with access to its Arab neighbors in Lydda had been transformed into a fortress surrounded by barbed wire and concrete pillboxes. Earlier, Dr. Ziegfried Lehman, the Ben Shemen leader, had objected to the militarization of his community. The people of Ben Shemen had purchased cows and even bullets from their Arab neighbors as recently as May. But Lehman's opposition was in vain, and he had left Ben Shemen in frustration.

Lieutenant Gefen's commander, Lieutenant Colonel Moshe Dayan, sat in the third jeep from the front. Dayan's battalion formed part of the northern flank of Operation Dani, a plan to secure the Tel Aviv–Jerusalem road and prevent an attack on Israeli forces from the Arab Legion to the east. The single-file convoy of Battalion Eighty-nine neared the main road to Lydda. Their primary task would be to stun the enemy with overwhelming firepower. Dayan's plan emphasized shock tactics in military assaults, relying on a strategy of 'mobility and fire.' To Lieutenant Gefen, Dayan's plan in action would feel like 'a rocket going through space.' To eyewitnesses, it would look as though they were shooting anything that moved.

In the late afternoon, the main line of the convoy turned left and roared toward Lydda and al-Ramla.

At the edge of Lydda, the streets remained quiet. Then, Gefen recalls, heavy fire came from the direction of a police building. Some of Gefen's fellow soldiers were hit; he would later recount nineteen or twenty dead. The Eighty-ninth Battalion, with machine guns mounted on every jeep, opened fire. In a few minutes at most, tens of thousands of bullets had been fired.

'Practically everything in their way died,' wrote the *Chicago Sun Times* correspondent in a report headlined BLITZ TACTICS WON LYDDA. The reporter from the *New York Times*, writing from Tel Aviv, recounted that 'armored cars swept through the town, spraying it with machine-gun fire. They were met with heavy resistance, but the [Arab] soldiers were taken by surprise and could not reach shelter fast enough.' The *New York Herald Tribune*'s reporter observed 'the corpses of Arab men, women, and even children strewn about in the wake of the ruthlessly brilliant charge.' Many of the dead were refugees who had flooded Lydda and al-Ramla from nearby Arab villages and from the recently fallen city of Jaffa. The *Herald Tribune* reporter described 'a Jewish column which raced through [Lydda's] main districts with machine guns blazing at dusk . . . Apparently stunned by the audacity of the Jewish thrust from the village of Ben Shemen, Lydda's populace did not resist when infantry units swept in after dark behind an armored spearhead.'

The shock battalion was followed quickly into Lydda by the infantry of Israel's regular army, then known as the Palmach, which rumbled down the narrow streets, firing from jeeps. Lieutenant Gefen and the Eighty-ninth moved on toward al-Ramla. There at the edge of town he saw families moving east on foot, carrying bundles in their arms, their donkeys loaded with belongings. Most reports suggest the convoy turned around without firing heavily on al-Ramla. Within hours the Eighty-ninth left the area, moving south into the Negev desert to face the Egyptians.

That morning in al-Ramla, Dr. Rasem Khairi walked under a stone archway and moved quickly toward the wounded. Jewish forces had been attacking the town from the air, strafing neighborhoods and dropping both bombs and leaflets over al-Ramla and Lydda, demanding that the Arabs 'Surrender' and 'Go to Abdullah.' One leaflet showed Arab heads of state in a sinking ship; another demanded that the residents give up. For days the city had been without electricity or running water; rubbish filled the streets and alleys, and food and medical supplies were running out. Bashir's uncle Rasem was forced to work quickly, under increasingly crude conditions.

Sheikh Mustafa had recently returned from an emergency trip to Transjordan. He'd been sent by the townspeople, who had pooled their gold to buy bullets. He brought the ammunition stacked carefully in boxes, but in the face of the current assault it appeared the gold might have been wasted.

At sixteen years old, Firdaws Taji, second cousin of the

Khairis, was a 'Girl Guide,' which in a more normal time would have been an Arab equivalent to the Girl Scouts. In war, Firdaws became more like a nurse, part of the support network for the town's defenders. She had learned to discern the kinds of weapon fire coming from the Arab fighters or their Jewish enemies. 'This is a Tommy gun,' she would say quietly to herself. 'This is a Sten gun.' She had watched the town's defenders set up crude rocket launchers on tree branches, adjusting the trajectory with a string before lighting the fuse.

For days, Firdaws stood near the front lines with the Arab volunteer fighters. She would bring them food. She would knit them crude sweaters. As the fighting escalated, however, she spent most of her time tearing bedsheets into long strips and rolling them into bandages for Dr. Rasem Khairi to take to his clinic.

By early June, after Hassan Salameh had died in battle, his troops had drifted away, leaderless. Six weeks later, with al-Ramla and Lydda vulnerable to collapse, there was talk of a full withdrawal by Glubb's Arab Legion troops to defend other positions. If that happened, Firdaws had no idea who could defend the town. The only fighters left would be townsfolk and the Bedouin 'barefoot soldiers' against a full-scale army.

Sheikh Mustafa still wanted the residents of al-Ramla to stay put. Firdaws would recall his poise during these hours. He wore a maroon fez with a white imami cloth wrapped around it – the sign of a religious scholar. Sheikh Mustafa had been mayor of this town for twenty-nine years. He had recently ended his long reign, and now the town was governed by the head of another prominent family, but Sheikh Mustafa's influence was still felt throughout al-Ramla. All week, the sheikh had been meeting with concerned townspeople on the large out-door veranda of his villa. He sat in a cane rocker beside his garden. Some meetings were small; in others, twenty of the town's notables would sit to discuss strategy. Sheikh Mustafa's message was consistent: *Stay in your houses. No one will leave. Our family will stay.* Some townspeople, how-ever, including Mustafa's nephew Ahmad, had already sent their families away.

At his clinic, Rasem Khairi continued to dress the wounded. All morning people kept coming through the shelter's doorway. Some had just come from Lydda and were seeking protection in al-Ramla. Others were leaving al-Ramla, searching for safety in Lydda. Bodies lay on the road between the towns. Leaders in Lydda were sending urgent telegrams to Arab Legion commanders in Beit Nabala six miles to the northeast, requesting help and reinforcements. 'Keep your morale up,' the response came. 'A flood of gold will be reaching you soon.'

Reinforcements never materialized. The two towns were falling to the Israelis. Word had come that King Abdullah's Arab Legion would be pulling out its sparse troops, leaving a few civilian defenders, a meager supply of weapons, and the bullets Sheikh Mustafa had brought back from Transjordan. This would be no match for the army of Israel.

Soon more people arrived in the shelters with news from Lydda. Jewish soldiers were pulling people out of their homes, marching them to the mosques or St. George's Church. Others were leaving town to the east, to undetermined destinations. A few resisters were holding out from the police fort, but no one expected them to last much longer. After all their preparations – digging trenches, opening a medical clinic, buying an ambulance, stockpiling months of food, even robbing a train with provisions earmarked for the Haganah – it had come down to a word no one had dared speak: surrender.

On the evening of July 11, shortly after Beethoven's First Symphony played on Radio Jerusalem, the Bedouin soldiers slipped out of town to the south, disappearing into the plain.

At the Khairi compound, the remaining family shuttered the windows and closed all the doors. For as long as they could, they would close themselves in, delaying the inevitable. Their world was coming apart, but perhaps they could hold out a bit longer. There was flour in the storehouse, and they could live on bread for a few more days.

In time it became clear, even to Sheikh Mustafa, that defeat was at hand. On the same evening of July 11, he sent his son Husam, along with the new mayor of al-Ramla, to carry the white flag to the Jews. They went by car to Na'an, the kibbutz near the now abandoned Arab village of Na'ani. Na'an was the home of Khawaja Shlomo, the man who two months earlier had galloped into Na'ani on horseback, frantically warning the villagers.

When the Arab delegation arrived, Israeli soldiers woke up the region's civilian security chief, a man named Yisrael Galili B. (The B was to distinguish him from the other Yisrael Galili, the longtime chief of the national staff of the Haganah.) Galili B greeted the men and proceeded with Palmach troops to a small meetinghouse on the kibbutz. There they ironed out the terms of surrender: The Arabs would hand over all their weapons and accept Israeli sovereignty. 'Foreigners' – Arab fighters from outside Palestine – would be turned over to the Israelis. All residents not of army age and unable to bear arms would be allowed to leave the city, 'if they want to.' Implicit in the agreement was that the residents could also choose to stay.

Galili B would soon learn that other plans were in the works for the residents of al-Ramla: 'The Military Governor told me,' Galili B wrote, 'that he had different orders from Ben-Gurion: to evacuate Ramla.' Orders to expel the residents of al-Ramla and Lydda were given in the early afternoon of July 12. The Lydda order, stating, 'The inhabitants of Lydda must be expelled quickly without attention to age,' was given at 1:30 P.M. by Lieutenant Colonel Yitzhak Rabin.

Firdaws heard Israeli soldiers shouting through bullhorns outside: *'Yallah Abdullah! Go to King Abdullah, go to Ramallah!'* Soldiers were going house to house, in some cases pounding on doors with the butts of their guns, yelling at people to leave. Firdaws could hear them announcing the arrival of buses to take residents of al-Ramla to the front lines of the Arab Legion. No matter what the terms of surrender or what Sheikh Mustafa said, it looked as if they wouldn't have any choice. The Arab residents of al-Ramla were being forced to leave their homes.

On the afternoon of July 12, Bechor Shalom Shitrit, the Israeli minister of minority affairs, arrived at a junction of roads between al-Ramla and Lydda, where he was greeted by the sight of throngs of people walking east. He was outraged. As the man responsible for Arabs in the new Israeli state, he protested the expulsions in a conversation with the foreign minister, Moshe Sharett. Like Yisrael Galili B, like the men of al-Ramla who signed the surrender, Bechor Shalom Shitrit had thought the Arabs in the newly conquered towns would be allowed to stay.

Shitrit tried to put a stop to the expulsions. But he was unaware of an earlier meeting between Ben-Gurion, Lieutenant Colonel Yitzhak Rabin, and Yigal Allon, the commander of the Palmach. Rabin, the future prime minister, would recall later that Ben-Gurion, when asked by Allon what they should do with the civilian population of al-Ramla and Lydda, 'waved his hand in a gesture which said, "Drive them out!"'

Not only was Shitrit apparently unaware of these meetings and orders; he also did not know that Allon had already considered the military advantages of expulsion. Driving out the citizens of al-Ramla and Lydda, Allon believed, would alleviate the pressure from an armed and hostile population. It would clog the roads toward the Arab Legion front, seriously hampering any effort to retake the towns. And the sudden arrival of thousands of destitute refugees in the West Bank and Transjordan would place a great financial burden on King Abdullah – who by now, the Israeli military was convinced, was an avowed enemy of the Jewish state.

'Regrettably, our forces have committed criminal acts that may stain the Zionist movement's good name,' Shitrit would say later. 'The finest of us have given a bad example to the masses.'

The victorious Israeli troops had been accompanied to al-Ramla by a few American reporters. Bilby, from the *Herald Tribune*, noted that 'outdoor prison cages were jammed with young Arabs, whose listless demeanor showed that they had no stomach for a fight.' According to Gene Currivan, the reporter from the *New York Times*, 'It seemed as if most were of military age, but apparently they had no interest in fighting for Ramle [al-Ramla], or for that matter, for Palestine.'

A short time later, Currivan noted, 'There was much excitement as Arab troops [civilian defenders] marched in, their hands high, to give themselves up, and others by the hundred, already prisoners, squatted behind barbed-wire fences in front of the fortress-like police station.' Some men of fighting age had managed to escape scrutiny: wearing dark glasses and long cloth coats, they leaned on their walking sticks and limped about in the heat. Family members stared at one another through the barbed wire, and when the women or elderly tried to approach the fence, Jewish soldiers would fire over their heads. Later that day, nine or ten buses pulled up and soldiers ordered the prisoners to board them. One by one the buses drove off; men who rode on them would recall whispering to one another, 'Where are they taking us?' The men were destined for a POW camp, and the Israeli soldiers directed other townspeople onto separate buses leaving town to the east.

The morning of July 14 was cloudless and extremely hot. It was the middle of July, the seventh day of Ramadan. Thousands of people had already been expelled from al-Ramla by bus and truck. Some, like Bashir and his siblings, had left well before the Jewish soldiers arrived, taking temporary refuge in Ramallah. Others in the Khairi clan had remained in al-Ramla.

Firdaws and her cousins, aunts, and uncles sat waiting at al-Ramla's bus terminal. There were perhaps thirty-five in all, the Khairis and their relatives, the Tajis. Sheikh Mustafa was among them.

With them they carried a few suitcases, bundles of clothes, and gold strapped to their bodies. Firdaws, the Girl Guide, had also packed her uniform and brought along her knife and her whistle. They had planned for a short trip, in miles and in days; they were certain they would be coming back soon, when the Arab armies recaptured al-Ramla.

At home the Khairis, the Tajis, and the rest of the people of al-Ramla had left behind their couches and tables, rugs, libraries, framed family pictures, and their blankets, dishes, and cups. They left their fezzes and gallabiyas, balloon pants, spare keffiyehs, sashes, and belts. They left their spices for *makloubeh*, grape leaves in brine, and the flour for the dough of their date pastries. They left their fields of wild peas and jasmine, passiflora and dried scarlet anemone, mountain lilies that grew between the barley and the wheat. They left their olives and oranges, lemons and apricots, spinach and okra and peppers. They left their silk and linen, silver bracelets and chokers, amber, coral, and necklaces with Austrian coins. They left their pottery and soaps, leather and oils, Swedish ovens and copper pots, and drinking goblets from Bohemia. They left their silver trays filled with sugared almonds and sweet dried chickpeas; their dolls, made with glued-together wood chips; their sumac; their indigo.

The bus came; the Khairis and the Tajis boarded it. So did the village idiot. He was carrying two watermelons. Firdaws saw her aunt give two sacks to her mother: one with vitamins for the baby, another with a glass water pipe and tobacco. With all the things left behind, Firdaws wondered, why would it occur to anyone to bring a water pipe?

The bus rolled out of al-Ramla toward the front lines of the Arab Legion at Latrun. There, they were ordered off the bus and told to march north, toward Salbit. It was only four kilometers, but by now it was one hundred degrees.

There was no shade and no road, just a steep rise across cactus and Christ's thorn. This is what the people would later call 'the donkey road' – if the donkey can make it, perhaps people can, too.

The earth was baked hard. Firdaws looked ahead: A line of humanity moved slowly up the hills in the waves of heat. For many of the people of al-Ramla, it was their first glimpse of Khairi women, who had almost never left the family compound. Some of the women were pregnant, and there, in the heat, a woman's water broke. She had her baby on the ground.

The families climbed out of Latrun and back toward Salbit, where there was word the Arab Legion would drive people in trucks to Ramallah. The refugees bent forward under the sun, stumbling over rocks, thorns, and sharp wheat stalks cut short from the recent harvest.

Firdaws caught sight of the village idiot carrying his two watermelons. Wordlessly she took one from him and with her Girl Guide knife sliced into the red flesh. The Khairi families and their neighbors gathered impatiently. The melon was gone quickly, save for the small piece Firdaws held back for herself; but then a young mother came to her, begging the last piece for her son.

White crusts formed around everyone's mouths. How far was Salbit? Were they still going in the right direction? They were always looking for shade and water. They crossed fields of corn, where they plucked ripe ears and sucked the moisture out of the kernels. Firdaws saw a boy peeing into a can and then watched his grandmother drink from it. A man had slung his father over his shoulder like a sack of potatoes, and Firdaws, for a time, carried someone's baby in her arms.

It was late afternoon, and they had been walking for

hours over rocky terrain with no clear idea anymore how to find the village of Salbit. Their rambling journey would turn out to be much longer than four kilometers. Some would say twelve; others would swear it was twenty.

The Khairis and the Tajis began to shed their belongings. Some had actually begun the walk with suitcases; these had been discarded long ago. After a time someone found a well, but the rope was broken. Women removed their dresses, lowered them into the stagnant water, and lifted them back up, placing the fabric to their children's lips so they could suck on the wet cloth.

Perhaps thirty thousand people from al-Ramla and Lydda staggered through the hills that day.

John Bagot Glubb heard the reports. The British commander of the Arab Legion knew it was 'a blazing day in the coastal plains, the temperature about a hundred degrees in the shade.' He knew that the refugees were crossing 'stony fallow covered with thorn bushes' and that, in the end, 'nobody will ever know how many children died.' Still, Glubb would insist until his death that he didn't have sufficient forces to defend al-Ramla and Lydda; that to do so would have required pulling his troops from the front lines at Latrun and possibly losing everything: Ramallah, Nablus, Tulkarm, East Jerusalem, Abdullah's entire prize of the West Bank – an act that 'would have been madness.'

On July 15, before the march from al-Ramla and Lydda was over, David Ben-Gurion wrote in his diary: 'The Arab Legion has wired that there are 30,000 refugees moving along the road between Lydda and Ramla, who are infuriated with the Legion. They're demanding bread. They should be taken across the Jordan River' – into Abdullah's kingdom and away from the new state of Israel.

* * *

In the evening, the Tajis and Khairis came to a grove of fig trees in the village of Salbit. The village was nearly abandoned, except for the hundreds of refugee families resting in the orchards.

Firdaws and her family took shelter under the trees. Someone brought water. She noticed that her mother had one of the two cloth sacks – the vitamins, Firdaws assumed. But it was the water pipe.

That night, the family sat under the fig trees, smoking quietly, the bubbles gurgling in the glass canister.

The next morning, trucks from the Arab Legion took the Khairis and the Tajis to Ramallah. They reached the crest of a hill just west of the city. Below them lay a vast bowl: the valley of Ramallah. The city had long been a Christian hill town and cool summer haven for Arabs from the Levant to the Gulf.

Now tens of thousands of refugees milled about, stunned and humiliated, looking for food and determined to return home.

Five

EMIGRATION

SUNLIGHT FILTERED THROUGH the narrow windowpanes of Sofia's central rail station, casting a hazy glow on the hundreds of Jewish passengers packed inside the waiting hall. It was October 1948, three months after Israeli forces entered al-Ramla. As the Khairis waited in Ramallah a thousand miles to the south, listening for news in the ongoing war for Palestine, Moshe and Solia Eshkenazi inched forward in the long line of Bulgarian Jews in the train station. Solia wore a long skirt and a tailored jacket to match, and her dark hair spilled over her shoulders from beneath a wide-brimmed hat. Many passengers wore dark coats and heavy shoes and stood surrounded by boxes and suitcases. Moshe held the family's identity papers. He was short and square, with the dark olive skin, high cheekbones, and black, deep-set eyes of many Sephardic Jews. Beside them lay their infant, Dalia, asleep in her straw basket.

Moshe and Solia had met eight years earlier, just before Bulgaria entered its alliance with the Nazis. Moshe liked to tell Solia, and later Dalia, that when he'd first seen his future bride at a party, she was ravishing and vibrant, in a ballroom dress, ready to dance. He'd thought, *Now here is someone for my friend Melamed*, the doctor. Moshe had approached the young beauty, but after a few minutes of conversation, he'd thought, *What about me?* Within days they were on their first date, and Moshe wasted no time: He informed Solia of his intention to marry her. She dismissed the remark with a laugh, but Moshe was undaunted. 'It will take as long as it takes,' he vowed, 'but I will marry you.'

At long tables at the front of the lines sat uniformed Bulgarian immigration police. One by one, 3,694 Jews prepared to show their papers and open their suitcases for inspection for hidden cash or gold. They were allowed to take nothing of value, but some travelers had sewn jewels inside their underwear, or strapped French gold coins, known as napoleons, to their bodies. They were not planning to return: When they reached the immigration tables, they would sign documents saying that from this day forward, they would no longer be citizens of the People's Republic of Bulgaria. Later that day, they would board two long trains and ride to the coast of Yugoslavia, where a ship, the *Pan York*, would be waiting to take them to the new state of Israel.

Moshe and Solia were part of a history unlike any other in Europe. They knew that, like nearly everyone else in the railway station, they were lucky just to be alive. Solia believed that were it not for the decency of so many Gentiles in Bulgaria – and particularly of a handful of people who chose to act in early 1943 – she and Moshe could have been on a train to Treblinka, not waiting to board a ship with their infant daughter for a new life in the Jewish state.

The *Pan York* would sail on October 28, 1948 – three days hence, and after years of deliberation that had brought them to this moment of departure.

* * *

More than five years had passed since the night in March 1943 when Moshe and Solia waited in Sliven for the deportation that never came. King Boris died later that year, and in the summer of 1944, with the arrival of the Soviet Red Army, Bulgaria's alliance with the Nazis crumbled. Bulgaria's Partizan fighters, including Moshe's brother, Jacques, and many of Susannah Behar's friends, came down from the Rhodope and Balkan Mountains, and soon Bulgaria's anti-Fascist parties forged a left-Democratic governing coalition, the Fatherland Front. Moshe and Solia returned to Sofia and began to organize their lives. Some Jews dreamed of the new Bulgarian state they would help build after Fascism, but others were already thinking about Palestine.

Zionism, the political movement devoted to the emigration of European Jews to the Holy Land, had taken hold in Bulgaria in the early 1880s, just as the nation freed itself from the Ottoman 'yoke.' In 1895, an early Zionist paper published in Plovdiv broached the idea that Jews could 'arrange their life in Syria and Palestine by settling in the field for agricultural work.' The next year, Bulgarian Jews established Har Tuv, one of the earliest Zionist settlements in Palestine. That same June, Theodor Herzl, the Zionist leader, stopped in Sofia en route to Istanbul on the *Orient Express*, to a triumphant reception at the train station. Herzl, whose book *The Jewish State* laid out the vision of a 'Promised Land' where 'we can live as free men on our own soil,' was already a hero to Jews in Bulgaria. 'I was hailed as Leader, as the Heart of Israel, etc. in extravagant terms,' Herzl wrote in his diary. 'I stood there, I believe, altogether dumbfounded, and the passengers of the *Orient Express* stared at the unusual spectacle with astonishment.'

Herzl believed Europe did not want the Jews, and he argued for a Jewish state 'where we can have hooked noses, black or red beards, and bandy legs, without being despised for it . . . where we can die tranquilly in our homeland . . . where we shall live at peace with all the world . . . So that the derisive cry of "Jew!" may become an honorable appellation, like German, Englishman, Frenchman – in short, like that of all civilized peoples.' In much of Europe, including among Jewish intellectuals and even some rabbis, Herzl's ideas were dismissed as utopian or dangerous; he was called 'the Jewish Jules Verne' and a 'crazy careerist.' In Bulgaria, however, Herzl was praised as 'the new apostle of the new Jewish nationalism.'

On his way back from Istanbul, where he had sought support from the Ottoman Empire to establish a Jewish state, Herzl stopped in Sofia again. 'Sensation throughout the town,' he wrote. 'Hats and caps thrown in the air. I had to request that a parade be dispensed with . . . Later I had to go to the synagogue, where hundreds were awaiting me . . . I stood in the pulpit before the Holy Ark. When I hesitated for a moment as to how to face the congregation without turning my back to the Ark, someone exclaimed: "You may turn your back even to the Ark. You are holier than the Torah." Several wanted to kiss my hand.' An amazed Herzl warned against demonstrations 'and advised a calm demeanor lest popular passions be aroused against the Jews.'

Talk of a return to Zion went on for several decades in the pages of prewar Zionist newspapers in Bulgaria. Arabs already living on the land did not figure in these discussions, and some Bulgarian Jews would recall reading about the 'land without people for a people without land.'

Debates in these pages centered on whether Jews should learn Hebrew in preparation for emigration to Palestine or stay with Ladino, the Judeo-Spanish mother tongue of the Sephardic Jews. Moshe became fluent in Hebrew through a Socialist-Zionist organization called Hashomer Hatza'ir (the Young Guard). Solia was content with her Ladino and its proverbs learned at the hearth and in the kitchen.

The Zionist papers were shut down after the 1941 anti-Jewish Law for the Defense of the Nation. By October 1944, however, less than a month after the liberation from the pro-Fascist regime, Bulgarian Zionists had already begun to regroup. Organizers of local committees sent official greetings to the Fatherland Front; then they established the Palestinski Komitet, which advocated aliyah, or Jewish emigration to Palestine. Their goal was to make aliyah a mass movement among Bulgarian Jews.

For Moshe and Solia and many of their neighbors, the prospect of emigration had at first seemed remote. Their families lived here; their work was here; even after what happened in 1943, they were still Bulgarian. For many Bulgarians, Jews included, the defeat of the Nazis meant that the sacrifice of the Partizans in the Rhodope and Balkan Mountains had not been for naught. Moshe's brother, Jacques, believed that with the Communists in power for the first time in Bulgaria, an egalitarian society could finally be built. Moshe wasn't so sure; for one thing, the country was still suffering from the recent war.

Bulgaria was a devastated landscape. American bombings in late 1943 and early 1944 had flattened much of Sofia, including the parliament building. The relentless blitzes killed many and drove residents into the countryside. Villages were overrun with refugees. Crop failures brought food shortages and hunger, and runaway inflation deepened the crisis. By the late fall of 1944, the new, impoverished government had begun to look beyond its borders for help.

On December 2, less than three months after the country's liberation, David Ben-Gurion arrived in the Bulgarian capital. The leader of the Zionists in Palestine was received by the Bulgarian prime minister, the foreign, interior, and propaganda ministers, and Metropolitan Stefan, the Bulgarian Orthodox bishop, who at substantial personal risk had stood up for the nation's Jews during the war. The central goal of his meeting was to win their agreement to allow Jews to emigrate to Palestine. Rehabilitating the Jews of Bulgaria would be impossible, he told the officials; they had to be allowed to leave. Establishing a Jewish state, Ben-Gurion told the Jews and state dignitaries packed into the Balkan Theatre in Sofia, was 'the task of the moment.' 'Aliyah!' came cries from the audience. By the end of the year, more than 1,300 Jews had left Bulgaria en route to Palestine. One of them, Solia's cousin Yitzhak Yitzhaki, was the first in the family to leave.

Yitzhaki had returned from the work camp after the liberation by the Soviet Red Army. Ten days later, he was drafted and sent to the Turkish border. He was based in his hometown of Sliven. 'Every week one hundred wagons of food arrived, and I, riding on horseback, would be responsible for the safe arrival of this procession to the Turkish border,' he recalled. While awaiting the next caravan of wagons, he would visit his cousin's house, which was filled with boisterous Soviet officers and the entourage of musicians, choirs, and performers that had followed them into Bulgaria. As winter came, and the wagons became stuck in the snow, life became more difficult. By December 1944, when the new Bulgarian army joined the Red Army in the fighting in Austria and Hungary, Yitzhaki's father was worried his son would be placed on the front lines to die in the cold. 'My father arrived in Sliven with a plan,' Yitzhaki said. 'He had dreamed of the land of Israel as far back as the 1930s. Now my father pushed me to the ultimate step: "You will become our avant garde. We will follow you."' Yitzhaki's father had connections with the officer in charge of the Sliven headquarters. Soon Yitzhaki was discharged, and near the end of 1944 he quietly left Bulgaria, traveling overland on the *Orient Express*, the same train Theodor Herzl had ridden half a century earlier, through Istanbul and Syria to Palestine.

For Ben-Gurion, young men like Yitzhaki were the pioneers for a huge migration to follow. The Zionist leader still had no state, but he had a plan. He knew that Bulgaria was in desperate need of cash and basic goods. He was shocked by the devastation in the capital and the poverty in nearby villages and arranged for temporary aid for the nation's Jews, with a long-term goal of bringing them to a new Jewish state. Upon his return to Palestine, Ben-Gurion ordered that five thousand pairs of shoes be shipped to Bulgaria for its Jewish children, though he added, 'Maybe it is a better idea if we try to bring the feet to the shoes.'

A short time later, the Jewish Agency in Palestine opened trade relations with the new Bulgarian government. 'Your Excellency,' wrote the head of the trade department for the Jewish Agency in Tel Aviv to the Bulgarian minister of commerce, 'I take this opportunity to assure you that it is our great desire to commence business relations with Bulgaria, and that every effort will be made on our part to begin transactions as soon as possible.' The Jewish Agency, still under British rule in Palestine, had become in many ways a de facto sovereign government.

At first the Bulgarians and the Jews of Palestine discussed barter deals: Bulgarian pine, beech, and rose oil in exchange for Jewish pharmaceuticals and shoes. 'The shoes must have in all exchanges DOUBLE SOLES,' one Bulgarian response declared. One kilogram of rose oil, it was proposed, would be worth 160 pairs of shoes. A Jewish Agency minister promised that soon, 'ways and means for cash payments' would be found. Pounds sterling was the currency of choice. Before long, the two parties would be discussing Bulgarian dried fruits, strawberry pulp, beehives, blankets, knapsacks, rugs, iron safes, and coal. They signed a trade agreement well before the Jewish state was formally declared.

Postwar funds for Bulgarian Jews also came from the American Jewish Joint Distribution Committee, better known as the JDC, or simply the Joint. In their early work in Bulgaria, JDC officials shipped clothes, blankets, food staples, and medical supplies and helped fund Jewish artists, writers, and artisanal cooperatives. More significant, the JDC had strong ties with the Jewish Agency and with the Mossad, which was organizing the illegal transport of Jews to Palestine in defiance of the British blockades. The JDC's ultimate goal was to help finance the aliyah to the Holy Land.

Talk of another life in another land tantalized some Bulgarian Jews like Moshe – young men and women who had grown up learning Hebrew and hearing about the dream of Palestine. Jewish support for emigration to Palestine, however, was by no means universal. Many Bulgarian Jews, especially supporters of the Fatherland Front, preferred to rebuild the Jewish community at home. Jewish Communists therefore saw the Zionists as a threat. The political differences often became personal, creating fissures within families: If Ben-Gurion's words stirred something in Moshe, a budding Zionist, they were less appealing to his brother, Jacques, a committed Communist and member of the Fatherland Front.

On many occasions, Moshe would visit Jacques in his Sofia law office, and the two would discuss politics. The brothers would keep their disagreements private, but given their opposing political views, it is likely Jacques repeated the admonitions of other Jewish Communists to their Zionist brethren: Jews had to join other Bulgarians to rebuild the country from the ruins of war. This was the challenge facing Bulgarian Jews; to leave the fatherland would be to evade the hard, necessary work facing all of Bulgaria. Palestine was a 'false Zionist fantasy'; home was here. The new Bulgarian regime, Jacques believed, identified with the struggle against anti-Semitism. The Red Army had fought to save the Jews in Bulgaria. Indeed, the Bulgarian people themselves had fought to save the Jews from annihilation; this alone would be reason for a Jew to take to the streets as a patriotic Bulgarian in a new Communist republic. Jacques, his niece Dalia would recall later, was deeply committed to the dream he had harbored as a Partizan in the mountains.

By now, Jewish Communists were denouncing the Zionists as 'reactionaries' who 'don't believe in the Fatherland Front.' For Moshe, these attacks could not have been welcome. Moshe was not alone, and soon

Bulgarian Jews who opposed Zionism had to concede that they were outnumbered.

In April 1945, Jewish leaders from the Fatherland Front met in Sofia. They were worried about the Zionist move toward mass emigration to Palestine – in particular, Ben-Gurion's call for aliyah. Todor Zhivkov, the Party activist who would later become head of the Bulgarian state, warned his colleagues that the Zionist organizations had significant financial and political clout because of the support they received from abroad. That summer, Bulgarian Zionists traveled to London for the World Zionist Organization meeting. There, Ben-Gurion repeated his call for the creation of a Jewish state. Three million Jews would be needed to make aliyah in the next five years, he told the assembly. Jacques Eshkenazi wondered how long his brother and Solia would stay in Bulgaria.

For Moshe and Solia, the decision to stay or to leave remained a difficult one. The promise of Palestine had to be weighed against the prospect of rebuilding their lives with friends and family in Bulgaria. They knew the new government was taking steps to return Jewish property and to punish those responsible for the pro-Fascist policies. Moshe and Solia watched closely.

Already, People's Court Number Seven had tried Aleksander Belev, the former head of the Commissariat for Jewish Affairs and the country's most infamous anti-Semite, and sentenced him to death in absentia. He had escaped Bulgaria near the end of the war. The court had tried and executed Filov, the prime minister under King Boris, and Gabrovski, his interior minister.

Dimitur Peshev had been spared. The former vice president of the wartime parliament had done more than perhaps anyone to spare Bulgaria's forty-seven thousand

Jews; he had pressured Gabrovski to rescind the deportation orders, later denouncing the plan in a public letter in the parliament. During the war, however, Peshev had also pressed Boris's government for the liquidation of the Partizans in the hills. The quiet bachelor was given fifteen years at hard labor; he would be released after three.

Hundreds of others would not be so lucky. As Moshe worked to reestablish himself as a salesman of fine garments, and he and Solia began planning for a family, they were well aware that a few blocks away, at the people's court, the prosecutions were intensifying. The court began to execute pro-Fascist cabinet members, parliamentarians, collaborators, and alleged collaborators by the hundreds; by the spring of 1945, more than 2,100 people had been put to death. Many more were tortured or sentenced to hard labor for their association with the pro-Fascist government.

In November 1945, Georgi Dimitrov came home to Bulgaria. The Communist and anti-Fascist hero had spent the past two decades in the Kremlin. After parliamentary elections, he became president of Bulgaria. Soon he began a series of property seizures. Already the leadership of the Fatherland Front, with its espousal of collective ownership, had been reluctant to return all Jewish property to its owners. The Communist leadership was interested in eliminating bourgeois communities, not reinstating them. With the return of Dimitrov, collectives and cooperatives began replacing grocers, craftsmen, and merchants. Moshe, Solia, and other Jewish families whose modest commerce relied on private enterprise now had another factor weighing in favor of emigration to Israel. But a central question remained: Would they be allowed to go? A few months later, an answer came.

* * *

In May 1947, Andrei Gromyko, the Soviet ambassador to the United Nations, stunned Zionists, the United States, and Great Britain by suggesting in a speech to the General Assembly that the Soviet Union would support a Jewish state in Palestine. A week later, delighted Sofia Jews expressed their gratitude for Gromyko's speech in a telegram to Stalin. On November 30, 1947, when word arrived that the Soviets had joined the United States in supporting the UN plan to partition Palestine into Arab and Jewish states, celebrations broke out in cities across Bulgaria. This was the same news that the Khairis had greeted with shock and disbelief in al-Ramla. In Sofia, joyous Jews took to the streets to wave flags, sing songs of Israel, and brandish placards bearing the names of the heroes of the day: Theodor Herzl, Georgi Dimitrov, David Ben-Gurion, and Joseph Stalin.

Three days after the UN vote on December 2, 1947, Solia Eshkenazi gave birth to Dalia (then called Daizy) in a Sofia hospital. Jacques and his wife, Virginia, visited Moshe and Solia shortly after the couple brought the baby home from the hospital. Virginia would remember an unusually beautiful child, quiet and peaceful – unlike her father, who could not contain his joy. Nor did he want to. 'There is a girl, and her name is Daizy!' Moshe would exclaim as he darted excitedly between an exhausted mother and their child in her straw basket. 'There is a girl, and her name is Daizy!' The couple had wanted a child for seven years; they had even hoped for a girl. Now they had to decide where she would grow up.

The new Soviet support for a Jewish state meant the Bulgarian government would back emigration for those

Jews wishing to leave. Georgi Dimitrov had just returned from a meeting in the Kremlin, where Stalin had reminded him, 'To help the Jews emigrate to Palestine is the decision of the United Nations.' Dimitrov immediately conveyed this message to Jewish Communists who saw the UN partition vote as a defeat. 'The Jewish people, for the first time in their history, are fighting like men for their rights,' Dimitrov told his Jewish comrades in a Politburo meeting in March 1948. 'We must admire this fight . . . We used to be against emigration. We were actually an obstacle to it. Which made us isolated from the masses.'

A few weeks later, on May 3, Jewish Communists publicly declared 'with a great feeling of boundless appreciation the great contribution of the Great Soviet Union for the solution of the Jewish problem and the achievement of an independent, free, democratic Jewish Republic – Eretz Yisrael . . . Long live the People's Republic of Bulgaria and the leader of the Bulgarian people, the relentless fighter against Fascism and anti-Semitism, comrade Gheorghi Dimitroff. Long live the protector of the enslaved and oppressed nations, Generalissimuss Iossif Vissarionovitch Stalin.'

As for the impending departure of so many of the nation's Jews, the Jewish Communists resolved 'with satisfaction that the Government of the People's Republic of Bulgaria gives full opportunities to those Jews who desire to settle in Palestine to immigrate freely.' This was the position Jacques Eshkenazi would also adopt; how he felt about it, and what he told Moshe, died with the two brothers.

The Fatherland Front now controlled all efforts to move Jews wanting to leave the country. Bulgarian Zionist groups would no longer be allowed to work independently. There would be only one Jewish newspaper, run by the government. Zionists and Communists would share the same goal – to facilitate the departure of those Jews who wished to emigrate to the new state of Israel.

Some recall it as a chain reaction, others as a deliberate, joyous step toward an ancient homeland, others as a fever. For years, the decision to emigrate seemed theoretical. Even after it became possible, many said they planned to stay. That changed quickly. A neighbor, Israel the barber, decided to take his family on an early ship. Then Rahel, the housewife across the street, announced her family was leaving. A cousin, Sami the electrician, made aliyah. Then Matilda the tailor was gone. Leon the shoemaker. Haim the police officer. Isak the driver. Buko the cinematographer. Now the rabbi. The grocer. The fruit peddler. The bread maker. The Bulgarian Jewish choir – all one hundred of them – away, together, on a boat to Israel. Suddenly half of the family was gone, half the neighborhood empty. 'It was like a psychosis,' remembered a former Communist, a Jew who chose to stay in Bulgaria. 'In the evening they believed in something. The next morning they believed in something else.'

For Moshe and Solia, by the spring of 1948 there was little left to debate. Hard times showed few signs of lifting. Factories had been nationalized and property seized for the state; Moshe's future livelihood was unclear. The new government, although it seemed to treat Jews and other Bulgarians equally, had in its tortures and executions demonstrated what Moshe saw as an excessive brutality; the near escape in 1943, moreover, was no guarantee of safety in some unknown future Bulgaria.

For Moshe, though, it was not simply that prospects of a harsh life in Bulgaria were a disincentive to stay; it was that he wanted to arrive in someplace new. Moshe had spent most of his years hearing about a new life in a distant place. He thrived on challenges and trusted his instincts, which in this case told him to go.

Solia was less sure. Leaving behind a beloved country weighed heavily on her. As Moshe's wife, however, she would follow his lead: As soon as they could, Moshe, Solia, and Dalia Eshkenazi would move to Israel.

By May 14, as Ben-Gurion declared Israel's independence and the war between the Arabs and the Jews officially began, the Jewish Agency and the Bulgarian government had already drawn up detailed plans for an orderly emigration. First there would be five small ships carrying 150 people each – people whose children, like Yitzhak Yitzhaki, had gone to Palestine during the mandate and whose presence there was the first pull on the chain of migration. These trips would be paid for by the JDC, at about $40 per person, on ships owned and piloted by the Bulgarian merchant marine. The participation of the JDC and other international Zionist organizations would be tolerated, provided they continued to come up with the hard currency still desperately needed to rebuild a devastated and impoverished Bulgaria.

The first big operation, the Bulgarian government decided, would be arranged through the port of Bakar in Yugoslavia. A total of 3,694 Bulgarian Jews would have about three weeks to get their affairs in order. Before leaving, they would be required to submit to medical examinations to certify they were free of tuberculosis, heart disease, typhoid, cholera, and syphilis. Then they would close their homes, say good-bye, and assemble on October 25 at the central railway station in Sofia, where two long trains would be waiting.

* * *

Moshe and Solia moved forward in the crush of passengers on the platform at the Sofia station. Jacques and his wife, Virginia, had come to say good-bye. They helped Moshe and Solia with the boxes and suitcases; someone was carrying Dalia, placid in her straw basket. The atmosphere was heavy with sorrow and buoyant with expectation; brothers and fathers and grandmothers and uncles knew they would be embracing for perhaps the last time.

The air was sharp and bright. South of the platform, the crest of Vitosha mountain rose up, its jagged crown off center like the peak of a rumpled hat. There Solia had often taken fellowship with groups of young friends, singing their way up steep, stony trails through pines and maples filtering afternoon sun. Well to the east lay her home country of Sliven, just beyond the Valley of the Roses, where she would recall her old yard with its apricot tree. It was a country of coal nestled deep in the hills. The soil there was good for fruit trees and for red wine grapes. Solia would remember the winds that whistled down the gorges, raising clouds of dust in her native town.

The train left Sofia in the afternoon, moving slowly, tentatively at first, then picking up speed as it puffed and clacked west, whistling out of the capital, toward the border of Yugoslavia and a boat bound for Israel.

For many of the 1,800 Bulgarian Jews on the train from Sofia – or the tens of thousands of Hungarian, Romanian, or Polish Jews emigrating in the fall of 1948 – the journey to Israel represented a return after two thousand years of exile, a chance to fulfill the Talmudic promise 'He who makes four steps in Israel, all his sins will be forgiven.'

But the train crossing the Yugoslav border at dusk on October 25, 1948, also represented a triumph for a movement critics once dismissed as folly. Theodor Herzl, the father of political Zionism, knew that establishing a Jewish national home meant forging alliances with the imperial powers. They would need to be convinced that a Jewish state, in Palestine or perhaps elsewhere, would be in their interests. 'Moses needed forty years,' Herzl declared. 'We require perhaps twenty or thirty.'

Herzl courted the Ottoman sultan, whose faltering empire was still in control of Palestine. The Zionist leader promised financial backing from 'my friends on all the stock exchanges of Europe' to help alleviate the empire's debt and build a new bridge 'high enough for the largest warships to pass beneath and enter the Golden Horn.' The sultan responded favorably, declaring himself 'a friend of the Jews.' On his way back from Istanbul, Herzl stopped in Sofia and told a Bulgarian acquaintance: 'The Sultan needs money and we need a homeland. I am leaving for Vienna, London and Paris in order to collect the necessary sum of money.'

Herzl also looked to Britain for support. He urged the British colonial secretary, Joseph Chamberlain, to support 'a Jewish colony in a British possession.' Britain would thus 'gain an increase of her power and the gratitude of ten million Jews.' According to Herzl, Chamberlain 'liked the Zionist idea. If I could show him a spot among the British possessions which was not yet inhabited by white settlers, then we could talk.' Britain was not yet in control of Palestine, so the two men discussed a possible Jewish homeland in Cyprus, Sinai, or even Uganda. 'It is hot on the coast,' Chamberlain told the Zionist leader, 'but the climate of the interior is excellent for Europeans. Sugar and cotton can be raised there.'

The Uganda idea was met with hostility from Herzl's fellow Zionists, and after Herzl died in 1904, the Zionist movement focused on Palestine as the goal and intensified their discussions with the Ottoman sultan. 'There is a country [Palestine] without a people, and, on the other hand, there exists the Jewish people, and it has no country,' Chaim Weizmann told a meeting of French Zionists in 1914. The man who would become Israel's first president asked, 'What else is necessary, then, than to fit the gem into the ring, to unite this people with this country? The owners of the country [the Ottomans] must, therefore, be persuaded and convinced that this marriage is advantageous, not only for the [Jewish] people and for the country, but also for themselves.'

In the end, however, World War I would bring about the collapse of the Ottoman Empire, Britain's entry into Palestine, and the 1917 Balfour Declaration, with its promise to help establish a 'Jewish national home.'

Three decades later, in May 1948, as David Ben-Gurion declared independence for the new state of Israel, the dreams of the 'Jewish Jules Verne' had become reality.

The train reached the bluffs of the Dalmatian coast at dusk on October 27, 1948. To the west, at the horizon of the Adriatic, the sky was ablaze with color. Behind Solia and Moshe in the darkened east lay Zagreb, Lubljana, Belgrade, and Sofia. Somewhere in Bulgaria the family's precious belongings – about 440 pounds of them, or 100 kilograms for each adult – lay in crates. Solia had packed a hope chest made of straw; wool blankets and a Bulgarian kilim; special wedding china from Czechoslovakia, the color of cream, with tiny red flowers along the rims; a soup tureen and bowls; etched purple crystal, for sipping Bulgarian brandy; pillow covers, doilies, and other knitted handwork; and a pink bedroom set: two wardrobes, bedboard, and frame. Solia and Moshe weren't the only Jews separated from their belongings. Four thousand tons of crates would soon be stacked up in the Sofia synagogue, where Moshe and Solia had been married, as workers scrambled to find foreign freighters to haul the crates to Israel.

The train hissed to a stop near the port of Bakar. Inside, Solia and Moshe prepared their bags and got Dalia ready in her basket as they waited to disembark. Through the windows, perhaps three hundred yards away, they could see a great masted ship floating at the pier, its lights shining against the night sky.

The *Pan York* was as long as a football field, its three masts towering over the deck; below, its cargo holds, with a capacity of eleven million pounds to haul bananas and phosphates, had been converted to carry 3,694 Bulgarian Jews: 42 Alcalays, 68 Aledjems, 68 Barouhs, 124 Cohens, 20 Daniels, 7 Danons, 4 Djivris, an Elias, an Elder, an Ephraim, and 54 Eshkenazis.

Solia, Moshe, and Dalia followed the line of emigrants up the gangplank. As they stepped into the ship, they were hit by the strong odor of disinfectant. Before them loomed a huge metal cargo hold painted sea green. Wooden bunk beds were stacked three high for as far as the eye could see. This would be their home for the next eight days.

In the ship's storehouses, the crew had stacked thousands of cans of supplies, paid for by the JDC. For the next week, Moshe, Solia, and the rest of the *Pan York*'s passengers would survive on tinned meat and fish, canned milk, juice, bread, margarine, grapefruit marmalade, and small pieces of dark chocolate. The JDC also supplied soap and emergency medical supplies. Passengers would later recall no serious ailments, though many Bulgarians would spend the balance of their journey bent over the rails, vomiting into the high seas. Dalia, her parents would claim in the coming years, was the only one on the ship who didn't get sick. She slept through nearly the entire journey.

Slowly, the Yugoslav coast disappeared from view. The *Pan York*, at maximum speed of fourteen knots, cut south through the Adriatic. From the bow there was only the sky, the horizon, and the late-October seas.

Moshe could only look ahead. He had no idea where his family would live or exactly what awaited them upon their arrival in Haifa. He knew the war was still going on, though Israel had the advantage and new truce talks suggested a settlement soon. It was obvious to Moshe that some kind of Jewish state would survive.

Despite the conflict, many Jewish intellectuals in Palestine had argued that Israel's long-term survival depended on finding a way to coexist with the Arabs. Moshe was part of a Zionist organization that had advocated a binational democratic state for all the people of Palestine. The binational idea had taken root in the 1920s with the formation of Brit Shalom, or Covenant for Peace, which advocated 'understanding between Jews and Arabs . . . on the basis of the absolute political equality of two culturally autonomous peoples . . .' Part of this philosophy was based on a desire to preserve 'the ethical integrity of the Zionist endeavor'; part of it was practical. Arthur Ruppin, a founder of Brit Shalom, declared, 'I have no doubt that Zionism will be heading toward a catastrophe if it will not find common ground with the Arabs.' The spiritual father of coexistence was Martin Buber, the great religious philosopher from Vienna, who had long advocated a binational state based in part on 'the love for their homeland that the two peoples share.'

Jewish advocates for a binational state came together in the 1940s in the leftist political party Mapam. In 1947, Mapam leaders had tried unsuccessfully to persuade Andrei Gromyko, the Soviet representative to the UN, to support their single-state effort. Two separate states, they argued, could lead to greater tensions in the future. This was a nice idea, Gromyko told them, but unrealistic. After the Soviets voted for partition, one Mapam leader, Victor Shemtov, a Bulgarian who had emigrated to Palestine fifteen years before Moshe, thought to himself: *This is the beginning of a long war*. Still, Shemtov celebrated the birth of Israel with the rest of Mapam, dancing in the streets of Haifa. For his part, Moshe would soon come to embrace Mapam's rival, Mapai, the mainstream, centrist party of Ben-Gurion.

Before dawn on the eighth day, lights appeared in the distance. The passengers began to stir and climb up on deck. As land grew closer, they could see that some of the lights appeared to be sitting on top of others. The scattered jewels hanging in the air were actually lights from houses on different elevations of the hillside. This was Carmel, the bluff overlooking Haifa. They were almost there. As light broke on November 4, passengers were crowded toward the bow as the boat powered into Haifa port. Some were crying. They began to sing 'Hatikva,' for sixty years the anthem of the Zionists and now of the new state of Israel. 'A Jewish soul yearns,' they sang.

And towards the east
An eye looks to Zion
Our hope is not yet lost,
The hope of two thousand years,
To be a free people in our land
The land of Zion and Jerusalem.

It felt to many that after all their struggles, they had finally come home.

Onshore, officials of the Jewish Agency sat at tables behind a roped line, processing the passengers family by family. They took names and years of birth; Dalia's birth year was recorded, incorrectly, as 1948. The Eshkenazis received an identity card and were told to proceed to the large metal building just ahead. There, workers with pump sprayers were dousing the Bulgarians with a substance that turned everyone's hair stiff and white. Children were running around, laughing and pointing to one another's DDT hairstyles.

Next they were given sandwiches. Some families were put on buses, others on a yellow narrow-gauge train chugging south along the coast. The Eshkenazis rode toward Pardes Hannah, an old British military barracks about thirty miles away. Just beyond a row of barracks stood lines of tents erected to shelter the waves of new arrivals.

Thus the Eshkenazis began life in Israel. For about ten days, Moshe and Solia lived in a tent alongside a thousand others in the ingathering of nations – dark, curly-haired, Arabic-speaking immigrants from Morocco; pale, dazed Yiddish speakers from Romania, Hungary, and Poland. It was a crowded, smelly place, hot for early November and muddy from the rains.

Soon Moshe and Solia grew restless. Like many others, they were anxious to settle somewhere. Tel Aviv had little space, and Jerusalem was still too dangerous. After ten days, Moshe noticed people sitting at a table, signing up immigrants to move to a town somewhere between this immigrant camp and Jerusalem.

Moshe had never heard of the town. But why not? he thought. *Let us try this place called Ramla.*

Six

REFUGE

THE FLATBED TRUCK rolled to a halt near the center of Ramallah. Idling in the mid-July heat, the lorry of King Abdullah's Arab Legion discharged its load of refugees. They had come from al-Ramla by way of the Arab village of Salbit.

Sheikh Mustafa Khairi, in his black abaya cape and fez wrapped in the white imami cloth, emerged from the bed of the truck to stand in the glare of a scorching day. Firdaws Taji, the teenage Girl Guide with her whistle and her knife, stood nearby with other members of the Khairi and Taji families. They could scarcely believe the scene laid out in front of them. Entire families camped on the ground, huddling around large metal dinner plates to spoon a few fava beans and lentils into their mouths with scraps of bread. Refugees were sitting and lying beneath trees, in doorways, and beside the road. Families had been split up; many family members had left al-Ramla at different times, and now they didn't know where to find one another.

Sheikh Mustafa walked through the city center and toward the Grand Hotel, where he managed to find a small room. Then he set out to find his nephew and family. Ahmad and Zakia had arrived earlier with Bashir and the other children and had rented a room near the Quaker School. Over the last two months, Ahmad had been going back and forth to al-Ramla, bringing food, a few clothes, and other household items from the house back to the family in Ramallah.

In the middle of July 1948, Ramallah, meaning 'Hill of God' in Arabic, had been transformed from a quiet Christian hill town in northern Palestine to a depository of misery and trauma. One hundred thousand refugees crowded into school yards, gymnasiums, convents, army barracks, and any other space they could find in the town and surrounding villages. The more fortunate shared quarters with relatives; family homes now packed ten or fifteen people into each room. Most of the newly homeless families slept in the open air, in olive groves, caves, corrals, barnyards, and on bare ground along the roadside.

'Conditions appalling,' warned a telegram from the American consulate in Jerusalem on August 12, a month after the Israeli army had conquered Lydda and al-Ramla and ordered the expulsions. 'Majority destitute possessing only what they could wear . . . entirely dependent on meager relief assistance . . . Refugees entirely dependent [on] springs for water, standing in line hours for turn fill cans . . . Definitely possible that water supply may give out completely before end of Aug . . . Diet [of] six hundred calories per day in effect approximately three weeks and insufficient sustain life for long . . . malnutrition is everywhere evident . . . families bury own dead within their camps without report to health officer . . . Local authorities overwhelmed by problem and admit own inability cope with situation.'

The scant water supply, according to United Nations investigators, stood 'unprotected and unorganized, infected and a menace to health ... an epidemic of typhoid is almost inevitable.' Red Cross nurses struggled to immunize refugees against such an epidemic, but 'only ten thousand doses vaccine available at present,' according to the American consulate. Officials warned of possible outbreaks of cholera, diphtheria, and meningitis. The refugees hadn't bathed in weeks, and some began to complain of eye and skin ailments.

Sheikh Mustafa arrived at the house near the Quaker School to find Ahmad, Zakia, and their ten children sharing a single room. At home in al-Ramla, Bashir had his own room and bed; now he slept together with his parents and siblings on a pair of mattresses. In other rooms, other Khairis slept. Now, instead of the walled compound in al-Ramla where members of the clan could walk from house to house across orchards and open grounds, dozens of Khairis were jammed into a single house. Under the circumstances, this represented relative comfort, made possible by family connections and resources.

Bashir watched his mother stave off the family's hunger by selling her jewelry in exchange for bread, olives, cooking oil, and vegetables. Gold had long been the resource of emergency for the Arab women of Palestine, and many women, hearing stories of searches and confiscation by the occupying Israeli soldiers, had left al-Ramla and Lydda with their jewelry strapped to their bodies. Zakia's gold held off the worst of the hunger, and Bashir understood that his mother had become the family bank and, for now, its main source of sustenance. She was not alone. In desperation, many women took to Ramallah's chaotic streets. Bashir would watch as women returned from the springs with jugs of water balanced on their heads or hawked handmade sweets at a makeshift street market.

A few people found work from local villagers in the olive harvest: The men would bang the branches with sticks; the women would crouch on the ground and gather the fruit. Others went begging from house to house when there was no other alternative. 'We have lost our homes,' they would say. 'Can you help us with some oil, lentils, flour, fava?' Their families had been reduced to drinking tea from old tobacco tins and fashioning trousers from blankets and burlap sacks. Occasionally the beggars suffered the abuse of an increasingly angry local population, who themselves were overwhelmed by the unfolding calamity. 'You sold your land to the Jews and came here!' they would taunt. 'Why couldn't you defend yourselves?' The crisis brought out the worst in some people. One refugee would recall a wealthy woman and prominent citizen of Ramallah standing on her balcony, tossing out handfuls of sugar-coated nuts, watching with evident pleasure as the new arrivals fought over the sweets.

Among the dispossessed, the men in particular had been shocked literally into silence, their defeat and humiliation at the hands of the Jews compounded by the disdain of many locals. Bashir would remember the peasant men with glazed eyes, sitting on burlap sacks in the shade of olive trees. At home, it was harvest time for the sesame, melons, grapes, cactus fruit, and summer vegetables. This was the men's life work and what they knew how to do; in sudden exile in Ramallah, they were idle and their families hungry. Their spouses endured endless waits at food distribution centers as trucks rumbled up the narrow road from Amman, fifty miles to the east, to deliver large flat biscuits, unleavened loaves, and the occasional sack of tomatoes or eggplants, courtesy of the Red Cross and King Abdullah of Transjordan. The minuscule rations were intended to prevent starvation. Refugees were mostly left to live off their wits. They begged and stole food from the locals, stripped the fruit trees bare, and, in some cases, scoured the army trash bins for scraps of food left by Abdullah's Arab Legion troops.

The Khairis were not enduring hunger on this scale, in part because Zakia was selling her gold, but Bashir began to understand the humiliation of the refugee. For a six-year-old boy, a seemingly simple deprivation would take on enormous meaning: One day Bashir's father told Zakia in frustration that he didn't even have enough to buy his friends a cup of Arabic coffee. For an Arab man, Bashir knew, inviting friends for coffee was an elementary gesture of hospitality – a fundamental expression of the meaning of being at home – and the inability to do so represented a profound humiliation. Bashir would remember this shame for the rest of his life.

On August 16, Count Folke Bernadotte, the UN mediator, dispatched telegrams to fifty-three countries, appealing to them 'to divert to me at Beirut . . . any such stocks' of meat, fruit, grains, or butter already on the high seas.' The UN considered the situation in Palestine a 'large scale human disaster.' By this time, the UN estimated, more than 250,000 Arabs had 'fled or have been forcibly expelled from the territories occupied by the Jews in Palestine.' (Later figures would be three times the early UN estimate.) 'Never have I seen a more ghastly sight than that which met my eye here, at Ramallah,' Bernadotte wrote in September. 'The car was literally stormed by excited masses shouting with Oriental fervour that they

145

wanted food and wanted to return to their homes. There were plenty of frightening faces in the sea of suffering humanity. I remember not least a group of scabby and helpless old men with tangled beards who thrust their emaciated faces into the car and held out scraps of bread that would certainly have been considered uneatable by ordinary people, but was their only food.'

Anger built as the refugees recovered from their shock. A few days after the Khairis arrived, John Bagot Glubb, the British commander of the Arab Legion, had rolled into Ramallah, only to be stoned by furious refugees. His troops had been called 'traitors' and 'worse than Jews!'; on Glubb's journey from Amman through Arab Palestine, his car had been spat on repeatedly. Demonstrations against Glubb, the Arab Legion, and the British had erupted in Nablus, north of Ramallah, and in Amman and Salt, east of the Jordan River. Many of Glubb's Arab soldiers, sickened by the sight of refugees dragging their way through Legion positions, had angrily demanded retaliation against Jewish forces.

Glubb was shocked by the refugees' rage toward him. He continued to believe his troops had done more than any other Arab force: They had fought for East Jerusalem, saving it for the Arabs; and they had held the line at Latrun 'against five times their numbers . . . I knew that they would go on to the last man – to save that country whose people were now calling them traitors.'

Glubb, however, would also recall a sleepless night on the front lines, tossing and turning in bed after news reached him of the thousands of refugees flooding toward Ramallah. 'Admittedly I had never foreseen that the operations in Lydda and Ramle [al-Ramla] would have led to a human catastrophe on this scale,' he recalled. 'But even if I had known, what else could I have done? To have rushed troops impulsively forward to Lydda would have allowed the enemy to break through to Ramallah.' Glubb knew that a redeployment toward al-Ramla and Lydda would have thinned Arab Legion positions in Latrun, which were holding the line against an Israeli advance. 'And then these scenes would have been enacted – not only in Lydda and Ramle, but twenty times magnified over the whole of Palestine. I could not see that I could have taken any other course.'

Many of the Khairis, however, along with other refugees from the two towns, recalled promises of protection sent by King Abdullah through the Bedouin brigade and other soldiers. They felt betrayed by Glubb and by Abdullah. Even Sheikh Mustafa, who had been on good terms with Abdullah, apparently grew angry with the king. 'King Abdullah had told my grandfather before he left al-Ramla that we would be allowed back,' said Samira Khairi, Bashir's cousin and a granddaughter to Sheikh Mustafa. 'So we were under the impression that there had been a behind-the-scenes agreement that we would be able to return.'

Even without such an agreement, Khairi family connections could have delivered them from the disaster in Ramallah – if not back home, at least into Abdullah's kingdom. Abdullah, according to Khairi family oral history, contacted Sheikh Mustafa with a personal offer. 'Cousin,' the king told Sheikh Mustafa, evoking their distant relations going back centuries, 'I cannot allow you to be miserable refugees. Bring your whole family and I will give you a palace in Amman to stay in.'

Mustafa, the longtime mayor of al-Ramla, was not inclined to ignore the thousands of other refugees. 'I am not alone with my family,' Sheikh Mustafa reminded the king. 'I have all the people of al-Ramla to take care of. Shall I bring them, too?'

'Stay where you are,' came the king's reply.

In Amman, King Abdullah was under siege. The desert oasis of Transjordan, which Glubb had only recently considered 'one of the happiest little countries in the world,' was now besieged by tens of thousands of refugees from al-Ramla and Lydda, driven out of their homes and demanding accountability. Enraged wives and parents of Arab Legion soldiers had even tried breaking into Abdullah's palace in Amman.

On July 18, several days after Sheikh Mustafa arrived in Ramallah, the king had angrily faced down demonstrators in Transjordan. Sir Alec Kirkbride, the British minister in Amman, had watched with apparent disdain as 'the tide of miserable humanity' reached the capital of Transjordan. Kirkbride wondered if the refugees could have stayed home 'had they had a little more courage.' The Englishman recounted the same 'ugly mass protest' directed at the king, with about two thousand men 'screaming abuse and demanding that the lost towns should be reconquered at once.' The king appeared on the steps, protected by royal bodyguards quickly thrusting cartridges into their rifles. 'It seemed to me a bloodbath was imminent,' Kirkbride recalled. Instead Abdullah waded into the crowd, smacked one screaming refugee on his head, and demanded that the demonstrators either enlist to 'fight the Jews' or 'get the hell down the hillside!' Most of the protesters, Kirkbride wrote admiringly, 'got to hell down the hillside.'

Despite his bravado, King Abdullah was rattled, just as the Israeli military had hoped and predicted. Abdullah had already summoned Glubb to a meeting at the palace, glowering at the Arab Legion commander as aides accused him of refusing to fight hard enough to defend Palestine. In fact, Glubb's superiors in London were more to blame. British efforts to enforce the UN arms embargo – in particular, the refusal to resupply the Arab Legion with weapons and ammunition – would contribute, more than Glubb, to the fall of al-Ramla and Lydda and the inability of Arab forces to recapture the towns. Most important of all, from Glubb's perspective, was that the Arab Legion was made up of only 4,500 troops – insufficient to wage battle in Jerusalem and at Latrun while simultaneously protecting Lydda and al-Ramla.

In Ramallah, fifty miles to the west, the Khairis and thousands of other refugees still assumed they would be returning home soon – if not on the backs of Arab armies, then as the result of a political agreement.

'Return,' Bashir said, 'was the issue, from day one.'

Strong signs, however, already pointed to Israel's determination not to surrender the two towns and dozens of other villages in Arab Palestine. 'There may be little prospect for the several hundred thousand Arab refugees from Palestine to return to their former homes in Israel,' stated a confidential air gram sent from the American embassy in Cairo to Secretary of State George Marshall in Washington. The dispatch cited 'reported Jewish measures designed to prevent their return and to take over Arab property . . . those who had left as refugees had lost their property and would have nothing to return to. In addition, much of their property [is] under the control of the Israeli Government, which . . . would not relinquish it willingly to the Arabs.'

Israeli officials indeed refused to discuss the return of refugees. The reason, they stated, was that their new state was still at war with several Arab armies. Yet it appeared that Israeli officials had already made up their minds not to allow refugees to return. On June 16, 1948, during the four-week truce with the Arab states, David Ben-Gurion had announced at an Israeli cabinet meeting, 'I do not want those who flee to return . . . I will be in favor of them not returning even after the war.' At the same meeting, Ben-Gurion's foreign minister Moshe Sharett added: 'This is our policy: They are not coming back.'

Two months later, in the wake of the conquest of al-Ramla and Lydda, Israeli officials would not acknowledge that forced expulsions had taken place. In an August 1948 report submitted to the International Red Cross conference in Stockholm, the Israeli delegate declared 'that approximately 300,000 Arabs left their places of residence in the territory occupied by Israeli forces, *but not one of them has been deported or requested to leave his place of residence* [emphasis in original]. On the contrary, in most of the places the Arab inhabitants were given to understand that there is no reason whatsoever for their flight . . .'

It was increasingly clear, however, that the people of al-Ramla had been forcibly expelled. 'According to the Red Cross representative who had been in Tel Aviv,' declared a confidential U.S. State Department air gram, 'the Jews on capturing [al-Ramla] forced all the Arab inhabitants to evacuate the town, except Christian Arabs, whom they permitted to remain. This information was partially confirmed in a recent report from a Controlled American Source.'

* * *

At summer's end in al-Ramla, several hundred Arabs were still locked behind a barbed-wire fence. Most of the families were Christian; they were considered less of a threat to the new Israeli state than the Muslims of al-Ramla. The families that remained were held inside a few square blocks of the Old City, in what was now called the *sakne*, or Arab ghetto. It was near the Khairis' old street, down which Ahmad had walked to his furniture workshop.

Ahmad's house stood in silence, part of an empty neighborhood. Doors were agape and belongings scattered about after looters had their pick. Shop merchandise lay rotting on the street. Military trucks rolled back and forth, laden with beds, mattresses, cupboards, couches, and drapes.

Soldiers from Moshe Dayan's Commando Battalion Eighty-nine, having little to patrol, had been among those looting. 'The men of Battalion 89 residing in our neighborhood in Ben-Shemen have wreaked havoc on roadblock sentries, pointing weapons toward them at Ben-Shemen roadblocks and breaking through them with trucks laden with different goods they collected in the cities of Ramla and Lod [Lydda],' declared an Israeli military field officer in a written report. 'Battalion 89's outrageous behavior peaked when they threatened our inspector with a bullet unless he left the area while they were collecting their loot . . .'

In the late summer and early fall of 1948, Arab men tried to return to their villages from exile in Ramallah and elsewhere. Many crossed porous front lines – Bashir believes his father was among them – entering their villages and fields at night to gather belongings or harvest what they could. The Israeli government considered them 'infiltrators,' and some were shot on sight. Others returned to find their crops burned. To Israeli leaders, the prospect of Arabs working the conquered fields was alarming. If hungry villagers were allowed to return for the harvest, an Israeli intelligence report warned, the next step could be 'resettlement in the villages, something which could seriously endanger many of our achievements during the first six months of the war.' Consequently, eight days later the chief of staff for the Israel Defense Forces had called upon Jews to work the Arab fields, declaring: 'Every enemy field in the area of our complete control we must harvest. Every field we are unable to reap – must be destroyed. In any event, the Arabs must be prevented from reaping these fields.' Control was turned over to local kibbutzim.

A few Israelis raised their voices in alarm. 'We still do not properly appreciate what kind of enemy we are now nurturing outside the borders of our state,' the agriculture minister, Aharon Cizling, warned in a cabinet meeting. 'Our enemies, the Arab states, are a mere nothing compared with those hundreds of thousands of Arabs [that is, Palestinian refugees] who will be moved by hatred and hopelessness and infinite hostility to wage war on us, regardless of any agreement that might be reached . . .'

In mid-September, Bashir and his family remained in the single room near the Quaker School. The prospect of immediate return was fading, and Bashir began to hear his parents talk about moving out of Ramallah to some other place where they could live more comfortably until they were able to move back to al-Ramla. In the two months since the expulsions, the refugee crisis in Ramallah had improved only slightly, if at all. Every day, Transjordan sent twenty-two thousand half-pound loaves of bread to the refugees, but this still wasn't enough. Red Cross officials determined the refugees could survive indefinitely with adequate supplies of flour and sugar and with milk for the children.

On September 16, as relief officials expressed growing alarm over malnourished children, UN mediator Count Bernadotte reported progress on his request for emergency supplies to be diverted for the Arabs of Palestine. Australia had sent 1,000 tons of wheat; France, 150 tons of fruit; Ireland, 200 tons of potatoes; Italy, 20 tons of olive oil; the Netherlands, 50 tons each of peas and beans; Indonesia, 600 tons of rice and sugar; Norway, 50 tons of fish; South Africa, 50 tons of meat. The United States was finalizing plans to ship large quantities of wheat, meat, cheese, butter, and 20 tons of DDT. The American Red Cross had dispatched two ambulances and $250,000 in medical supplies; Christian charities contributed 500 bales of clothing, 175 pounds of vitamins, and $25,000 toward the purchase of flour in Egypt. The Arab American Oil Company (Aramco) donated $200,000 toward the purchase of baby food; the Bechtel Corporation sent $100,000. Other agencies shipped first-aid boxes, syringes, typhoid and cholera vaccines, two trainloads of wheat, and a boxcar full of milk. His Majesty's government in London, only four months after departing Palestine, released $100,000 for the purchase of tents.

Count Bernadotte continued to advocate a division of historic Palestine between Israel and Transjordan, 'in view of the historical connection and common interests of Transjordan and Palestine.' Under this plan, the Khairis and other refugees would go home to al-Ramla and Lydda – not to an independent state, as many Palestinian Arabs had fought for, but to an Arab state that would fall under the rule of Abdullah and his kingdom of Jordan. (After the war, the 'Trans' was dropped and Abdullah's kingdom was known simply as Jordan.) Large parts of the Negev would be returned to the Arabs; the Jews would keep the Galilee and Haifa. The Lydda airport would be 'a free airport' for all; Jerusalem, as the November 1947 UN resolution had outlined, 'should be treated separately and placed under effective United Nations control.' As for al-Ramla and Lydda, Bernadotte's blueprint declared that the towns 'should be in Arab territory.'

The mediator's proposals were based on what he saw as the political realities of the day. 'A Jewish State called Israel exists in Palestine,' he wrote, 'and there are no sound reasons for assuming that it will not continue to do so.' Bernadotte also stressed another point that would have been of great interest to Ahmad, Zakia, and the tens of thousands of refugees sleeping on the ground in Ramallah: 'The right of innocent people, uprooted by the present terror and ravage of war, to return to their homes, should be affirmed and made effective, with assurance of adequate compensation for the property of those who may choose not to return.'

The next day, Count Folke Bernadotte was killed in the Katamon quarter of Jerusalem. An assassin walked up to Bernadotte's UN vehicle, thrust an automatic pistol through the window, and shot him at close range. Six bullets penetrated, one to his heart. A statement from the extremist Jewish militia group the Stern Gang claimed responsibility, calling UN observers 'members of foreign occupation forces.' David Ben-Gurion, Israel's prime minister, detained two hundred members of the Stern Gang, including one of its leaders, future prime minister Yitzhak Shamir, and ordered the other extremist Jewish militia, Irgun, led by another future premier, Menachem

Begin, to disband and turn over its weapons to the Israeli army. The Irgun ceased to function as a separate military unit, and Ben-Gurion's fight to consolidate the militias was now virtually complete. Begin, no longer in charge of his own militia, began to convert the Irgun into a political party, the Herut, which two decades later would form the basis of the Likud Party.

In the wake of Bernadotte's assassination, international pressure mounted on Israel to accept what amounted to the mediator's final wish. This would have required Israel to give back conquered territory in the Negev and in al-Ramla and Lydda. Soon, however, battles resumed in the Negev, with Israel and the Egyptians accusing each other of violating the terms of a truce. As the fighting in the desert continued, Count Bernadotte's proposal, like countless other 'peace plans' that would follow, dissolved into history.

In late 1948, Sheikh Mustafa traveled to Jericho, away from the cold and chaos of Ramallah. He was not in good health, and the family thought the warm air of the Jordan Valley might make him feel better. At about the same time, relief officials called for ten thousand tents and one hundred thousand blankets and the establishment of a massive tent camp in Jericho, so that many of the refugees would not have to pass the winter in Ramallah. Families there searched for firewood, denuding the Ramallah hills to warm themselves with the heat of olive, almond, and pear trees. Some refugees, unaccustomed to campfires and tents, decided to heat their temporary homes from the inside; before long they could not see the front of the tent from the back, and their neighbors could hear them coughing and shouting for help.

Near the end of 1948, Ahmad and Zakia, unable to find

decent work and overwhelmed by the misery around them, decided to move the family to Gaza. It would be much warmer on the Mediterranean coast. Ahmad had better job prospects there, and the family had relatives with property who could help them find a modest home to live in rent-free.

The Khairi family arrived in Gaza in December 1948 and moved into a one-room house with bare walls, cement floors, and a roof of corrugated tin. Ahmad and Zakia gathered a few mattresses, borrowed pots and pans and a camping stove, found an old icebox from some distant cousins, and started looking for work.

In the span of a few months in 1948, two hundred thousand refugees had poured into this narrow band of sand dunes and orange groves along the Mediterranean, more than tripling its population. Two thousand people per square mile were crowded onto a strip of land surrounded by Israel, Egypt, and the sea. All supplies had to travel three hundred miles through the Egyptian desert and cross Gaza's only border with the Arab world – the Sinai Peninsula, to the southwest. 'It is therefore hardly surprising that conditions very rapidly deteriorated,' a UN report stated. Wages plummeted by nearly two-thirds. Refugees scoured the landscape, collecting 'every movable object that could be burnt' for fuel. Thousands of refugees camped in long rows of tents on the Gaza sands.

The Khairis had come to Gaza in the midst of war and political turmoil. Bashir and his family could hear constant shelling as Israel and Egypt clashed near Gaza City and east toward the Negev. Though the Egyptians controlled the Gaza Strip, there were frequent incursions by both sides across battle lines. Egypt, led by King Farouk, was fighting for territory not just with Israel; the king was also worried about his counterpart, Abdullah of Jordan, and his own quest for territory. Palestinian nationalists, meanwhile, still aspired to establish an independent, Arab-majority state across the whole of Palestine, and in the fall of 1948, Egypt allowed a small Palestinian independence group to establish a government-in-exile in Gaza. This was less an Egyptian support of Palestinian sovereignty than King Farouk's attempt to thwart Abdullah's ambitions. Abdullah's response, in December 1948, was to crown himself 'King of United Palestine,' which included not all of Palestine, but what he now called the 'West Bank' of his kingdom.

As Arab governments jockeyed and maneuvered, the refugees never stopped longing for home. The right of return originally advocated by Count Bernadotte was enshrined by the United Nations in December 1948. UN Resolution 194 declared that 'refugees wishing to return to their homes and live at peace with their neighbors should be permitted to do so at the earliest practicable date, and that compensation should be paid for the property of those choosing not to return.' The resolution – known simply as 'one-nine-four' – generated tremendous hope for the Khairis and refugees across Arab Palestine. It was already clear, however, that Israel had no intention of implementing Resolution 194 and that the United Nations had no power to enforce it.

The next year, 1949, a weakened UN acknowledged the reality on the ground and created UNRWA, the United Nations Relief and Works Agency, to generate jobs and housing for the hundreds of thousands of Palestinian refugees in Jordan, Lebanon, Syria, the West Bank, and Gaza. Soon crude cinder-block buildings were rising from the sands of Gaza amid the tents and dug-out latrines.

Alongside stood mud-brick houses with roofs made out of reeds, empty asphalt barrels, and milk cartons. The 'streets' of the refugee camps – narrow dirt lanes separating long rows of low block housing – took on the names of the refugees' onetime homes, like Yaffa, Acca, Haifa, Majdal, Lydda, and al-Ramla.

The poorest of the Gaza refugees survived on a UNRWA diet of 1,600 calories a day, including a standard monthly ration of twenty-two pounds of flour; about a pound each of sugar, rice, and lentils; and milk for children and pregnant women. Without meat or vegetables, the diet contained just enough nutrients and calories to stave off starvation.

Ahmad had found a job in Gaza using his carpentry skills to make wicker furniture for other refugees. UNRWA paid him not in cash, but in extra rations of flour, rice, sugar, and fat. For the Khairis, every cent (or 'mill') of every Palestinian pound was spoken for. Zakia continued sparingly and strategically to sell off her gold, but the proceeds went only for essentials. Though Ahmad remained protective of his daughters, the extreme situation led to what would have previously been unthinkable: The family sought and received permission from Sheikh Mustafa for the women to work. Bashir couldn't recall a single day when his mother and sisters weren't working. Zakia and her elder daughters now made extra money embroidering Palestinian table covers and pillows or knitting sweaters and scarves. Nuha, who was seven when the family moved to Gaza, remembers wearing crudely knit sweaters with pockets so low that her arms could not reach them. Zakia, only months removed from a life of servants, perfumes, and private baths, had become crucial to the family's survival. She removed her veil.

For the refugees – the destitute in the camps or the more well-off like the Khairis – the central trauma was not in selling off gold or finding enough to eat. Rather, it lay in the longing for home and, conversely, in the indignity of dispossession. At all economic levels, the disruption of normal family life was having profound effects on the children.

Bashir and his siblings breathed in the atmosphere of humiliation and defeat, and for Ahmad's firstborn son, avenging the loss of Palestine became a singular goal, even in play. His siblings and neighborhood children would find pieces of wood to fashion as guns and play 'Arabs and Jews,' like cowboys and Indians, in the dirt streets. 'He insisted that he always play the Arab,' Khanom remembered. 'He would be very angry if anyone would try to get him to play the Jew.'

In the spring of 1949, news arrived from Jericho: Sheikh Mustafa had died. He had been visiting relatives in the Jordan Valley. Standing on the front steps of the house of the Dajani family, he had grown dizzy. He went inside to sit while Mrs. Dajani prepared him lemonade. Before she could bring it, he was dead.

Had the Khairis been in al-Ramla, Sheikh Mustafa's body would have been washed, dressed in white cloth, carried to the mosque for prayers, then immediately taken to the cemetery and placed in the earth, all according to Muslim custom. Under their current circumstances, the family arranged for the body to be transported in a closed wooden coffin to the family cemetery in al-Ramla, where the Israelis would allow him his final place of rest.

'He died of a heart attack,' Bashir said. 'But really, it was from a broken heart.'

By the summer of 1949, Jordan, Egypt, Syria, and Iraq had

signed armistice agreements with Israel; the war was officially over. With its capture of territory beyond the UN partition line, Israel was now in control of 78 percent of Palestine. The next April, King Abdullah completed his annexation of the West Bank, infuriating Palestinian nationalists. A year later, he would pay for this prize with his life when a nationalist linked to Hajj Amin al-Husseini, the ex-mufti of Jerusalem, shot the king in the Old City as his teenaged grandson, Hussein, watched in horror. In the aftermath of the Arab loss of Palestine, leaders in Egypt and Syria also fell to assassins' bullets. In Gaza, the Egyptians responded by repressing all forms of political expression, and Palestinian nationalism was forced underground.

Two governments were essentially in place now in Gaza: the Egyptians, who imposed the equivalent of martial law on the stateless Palestinians; and the United Nations, through UNRWA, which was now responsible for feeding, training, and educating the hundreds of thousands of refugees.

'Their clothing after three years has become shabby and ragged,' declared a UN report in 1951. 'The majority of the men employed on Agency road-building projects had no shoes. Both blankets and the tent flies issued as additional protection are often diverted from their proper use and cut up for clothing. The most fortunate are the children in schools (less than half the total number of children on the rolls), who have generally been given both clothing and footwear.' For some formerly well-off, past and present coexisted: One Khairi cousin recalled running around Gaza barefoot, wearing his glasses.

In Gaza City, Bashir, Nuha, and their younger brother, Bhajat, shared the same one-room class in a UNRWA

REFUGE

school. At first they sat on the dirt floors of cramped
UNRWA tents, and later at UNRWA desks in an old brick
house, where the schooling took place in shifts: locals in
the morning, refugees at 1:00 P.M. UNRWA schoolteachers,
who were mostly refugees themselves, doled out UNRWA
pencils, clothes, fish oil, vitamins, and milk. School began
with a salute to the Egyptian flag. Bashir would remember
learning the history of the Nakba, or Catastrophe, which
he, his classmates, and his Palestinian teachers could
speak of from personal experience and with deep conviction: *The Jews expelled us; we have a right to return.*

'Palestine is our country,' the refugee children would
recite at the beginning of each school day:

> Our aim is to return
> Death does not frighten us,
> Palestine is ours,
> We shall never forget her.
> Another homeland we shall never accept!
> Our Palestine, witness, O God and History
> We promise to shed our blood for you!

Bashir was a good student, and his teachers considered
him especially attentive.

Bashir turned ten in 1952. By now the dream of immediate return had transformed into the reality of long-term
struggle. The Palestinians had begun to understand that
their return would not come about through diplomatic
pressure. Though the Palestinian 'right of return'
dominated most conversations in the streets, souks,
and coffeehouses, it was clear that no government
in the world was prepared to force Israel to accept the

terms of the resolution guaranteeing the right of return.

'This sense of injustice, frustration and disappointment has made the refugee irritable and unstable,' a UN report acknowledged. 'The desire to go back to their homes is general among all classes; it is proclaimed orally at all meetings and organized demonstrations, and, in writing, in all letters addressed to the Agency and all complaints handed in to the area officers. Many refugees are ceasing to believe in a possible return, yet this does not prevent them from insisting on it, since they feel that to agree to consider any other solution would be to show their weakness and to relinquish their fundamental right.'

For the Israelis, the idea of return was moot. In a letter to the UN's Palestine Conciliation Commission, the director of Israel's Foreign Ministry wrote that 'it would be doing the refugees a disservice to let them persist in the belief that if they returned, they would find their homes or shops or fields intact . . . Generally, it can be said that any Arab house that survived the impact of the war . . . now shelters a Jewish family.'

Palestinians were frustrated not only by Israel's refusal to accept the UN resolution advocating their return; they also chafed under Egypt's refusal to allow them to organize politically. Banned political groups, including the Communist Party and the Egypt-based Muslim Brotherhood, had begun to hold secret meetings in the camps, advocating armed struggle to make al-Awda (Return) possible. 'There are occasional strikes, demonstrations and small riots,' the UN report noted. 'There have been demonstrations over the census operation, strikes against the medical and welfare services, strikes for cash payment instead of relief, strikes against making any improvements, such as school buildings, in camps . . . in case this might mean permanent resettlement. This then is rich and tempting soil for exploitation by those with other motives than the welfare of the refugee.'

Refugees whose peasant lives had been replaced by squalor and malnutrition proved a receptive audience to the talk of return to a liberated Palestine. Some volunteered to launch attacks across the armistice lines in Israel, as the endless cycle of strike and retaliation took root in the sands of Gaza. In the summer of 1953, Palestinian guerrillas crossed the armistice lines and attacked a family in the new Israeli city of Ashkelon, which was built on the ruins of a Palestinian village. The attack killed a restaurant owner and his daughter. Two weeks later, an IDF soldier named Ariel Sharon led his unit on a nighttime reprisal. Nineteen people died in the el-Bureij refugee camp.

Bashir remembers a daytime attack in 1954 near his school. He and a friend ran from the school in terror; moments later, as the two boys veered in separate directions, Bashir's friend was hit and killed. At school the next day, Bashir stared at his classmate's empty chair.

Bashir later lost his favorite teacher, Salah al-Ababidi, who was slain with his wife. A refugee from Jaffa, al-Ababidi taught gymnastics and led the children each day in patriotic songs. The teacher often spoke of his love for Jaffa, of one day going home, and of freedom fighters for Palestine.

By 1955, Bashir, now thirteen years old, had grown more serious and mature beyond his years. His older sisters looked up to him. 'We never felt Bashir was our brother,' Khanom said. 'Even though we were older, we always felt that he was like our father. He was the dominant figure, he was the one to take care of us.' More than ever, Bashir was focused on return. It would avenge the Palestinian defeat; it would restore his family's dignity; it would repair the loss his father, mother, and siblings had suffered. It would wash away the shame of dispossession. Over the years, for Bashir and hundreds of thousands of other refugees, hope for return had turned to despair and then rage. By the mid-1950s, however, the prospect for return suddenly seemed real again. It was personified around a single figure who would fire the Arab imagination.

His name was Gamal Abdel Nasser, the son of a postal worker, who had come to power in Egypt in 1952 after the expulsion of the British and the exile of King Farouk. As Farouk sailed away on his royal yacht, Nasser began to implement a plan for Arab unity that would include the 'liberation of Palestine' and the return of the refugees. His 'philosophy of revolution' would be unlike any ever expressed by Arab leaders. Bashir saw the Egyptian president as a man who could unify the entire Arab world, or what Nasser sometimes called the Great Arab Nation, and restore its dignity after the humiliating defeat in 1948. For some he was even a hero in the mold of the Saladin, the great warrior who defeated the Crusaders in Jerusalem eight centuries earlier.

Nasser's emergence would rattle officials from Washington to London to Paris to Tel Aviv. Soon he would begin to harness the power of Palestinian nationalism, transforming a group of fedayeen, or guerrillas, into an Egyptian military unit. Tensions between Egypt and Israel would increase in the coming years, resulting in the Suez conflict, a military victory for Israel that would, ironically, fortify Nasser's position as the undisputed leader of a growing pan-Arab movement.

* * *

After nearly nine years in Gaza, Ahmad and Zakia Khairi decided to move the family back to Ramallah. They had come into a family inheritance and would be able to buy a modest property in the West Bank and think about higher education for the children. It was 1957.

Ahmad took the first group – Khanom, Bashir, and their sister Reema, the youngest of the ten children, to Egypt, where they would fly directly to the West Bank airport at Qalandia, just south of Ramallah.

'On the plane my father fainted,' Khanom remembered. The children were alarmed, but the stewardess was flirting with a co-worker and paid them little attention. 'When we landed he was still in what now seemed like a coma. Everyone got out of the plane and we tried to wake him, we tried to push him out of his chair. We hit his face to wake him. He did not wake up. The captain came and said, "It seems he is dead."'

Bashir, fifteen years old, brought his face close to his father's and took his hand. '*Yabba*, wake up!'

Ahmad opened his eyes. 'Yes, my son,' he said. 'What is it?' The family would tell this story for years: Ahmad would respond only to the voice of his firstborn son. 'This was the miracle touch of Bashir,' Khanom recalled.

Father and son emerged from the plane into the cool air of Qalandia, just south of Ramallah, in the West Bank of the Kingdom of Jordan.

Seven

ARRIVAL

O N NOVEMBER 14, 1948, a busload of immigrants approached the town of Ramla from roads to the north and west. The bus slowed as it reached a military blockade at the edge of town. Inside were the first Israeli civilians to come to the conquered city, part of a larger group of three hundred immigrants, mostly Bulgarians, Romanians, Hungarians, and Poles, arriving that day from the transit camps near the Mediterranean coast at Haifa.

As the bus rolled past the checkpoint, Moshe and Solia Eshkenazi looked out at a ghost town. Sheep, dogs, chickens, and cats roamed the streets. Soldiers watched over rows of empty dwellings. Stone houses stood open, their contents spilling out onto the yards. One arriving immigrant would remember a donkey tied to a post in a house with no doors. Smoldering mattresses littered the streets.

The bus passed cactus hedges and lines of olive and orange trees, then it stopped and everyone got out. They were greeted by a representative of the Jewish Agency. Behind him, Moshe and Solia could see a street lined with Arab houses. It was a simple procedure, immigrants would recall; they were free to enter a house, inspect it, and claim it. The paperwork would come later.

Moshe and Solia came upon a house to their liking. It was in good shape and virtually empty, though not brand new. Clearly, someone had lived there before. It was a stone house with an open layout and plenty of space. There was a carport the family might use someday, and in the yard in back there was a lemon tree.

Lying in bed in their new home, the couple knew they had not arrived to the safe haven they had sought. Israeli and Egyptian forces were fighting just south of Ramla, and the line of defense was perilously close to their new home. After two weeks in Ramla, Moshe and Solia celebrated Dalia's first birthday. It was December 2, 1948, a year and three days after the United Nations partition vote and the beginning of the battles over the shape of historic Palestine.

The family had been given a steel-framed bed, blankets, a kerosene lamp, a camping stove, four large candles, and a ration card for sugar, oil, powdered eggs, and milk. Another family of three had moved into an adjacent room. Solia's mother, brother, two sisters, and a brother-in-law were making final plans to leave Bulgaria, and the house would soon shelter eleven. Eventually the families would sign agreements with the state, which had declared itself the 'custodian' of the houses it considered 'abandoned property.' The Eshkenazis lived on 'K.B. Street.' This was a temporary name; a municipal committee would soon prepare lists of Jewish historical figures and recently fallen war heroes to replace the Arabic names on the street signs.

The Eshkenazis landed in a town under military rule in an emerging nation still at war. The spoils of conquest, and of sudden flight, were still being hauled away. Soldiers piled couches, dressers, lamps, and other heavy items into the backs of army trucks. Much of the 'goods, equipment and belongings of absentee owners,' state records would later indicate, were to be 'collected in store-houses' and 'liquidated through sale.' Some of the men found temporary work sweeping out the Arab houses to prepare for more busloads of new immigrants; their children sold cigarettes brought on the boats to the soldiers standing guard. To the children, it was all an adventure. In the afternoons, they would roam the foreign streets, feeling like discoverers, taking over an empty house to set up a secret club, searching the rooms for marbles or other treasures left behind. Often when they returned, they would find the place occupied by immigrants. These new arrivals, many of whom were survivors of the concentration camps in Europe, asked few questions. Most found empty houses to live in, then went looking for work.

In the early months, jobs were scarce and seasonal. A few people were employed building and paving roads. Others walked, hitchhiked, and rode bicycles to the Jewish citrus groves near Rehovoth; decades later, immigrant children of the time would remember fathers and uncles with one hand on the handlebar and the other balancing a ladder, pedaling toward the orchards. Some immigrants were accustomed to reaching their hands between the branches or into the soil, but others, working a strange land in dark European shoes and fraying suit coats, were overwhelmed. As a result, in 1948, Jewish farmers, who had depended on cheap Arab labor, struggled to make their harvest.

Moshe Eshkenazi first worked for the Jewish Agency, delivering the iron bed frames to immigrant families. As he went from house to house, he would inquire about the families' welfare, speaking Hebrew when possible, using his high school German to converse in Yiddish to Eastern and Central European Jews, in Ladino with Jews from Turkey and the Balkans, or in Bulgarian with his countrymen. Later he would communicate in French with the Moroccan Jews.

Job prospects for the immigrants of Ramla began to improve slightly, especially for the first to arrive, as they found ways to use the skills they brought with them from Europe as mechanics, electricians, plumbers, and shopkeepers. By July 1949, seven months after the first Israeli migrants arrived, 697 of the 2,093 families registered with the city had found work in town. There were 25 Jewish shoemakers, 15 carpenters, 10 seamstresses, 7 window framers, 7 bakers, 7 butchers, 4 watchmakers, 4 sausage makers, a sign maker, and an upholsterer. Seventeen cafés had opened along with 37 small groceries; there was a small factory for ice cream and 2 for making seltzer. Henry Pardo opened the first Jewish pharmacy in Ramla; David Abutbul hung a sign for his law office; Shlomo Scheffler sold newspapers.

Solia Eshkenazi opened a shop for baby clothes in the old Arab *sakne*, or ghetto, before taking a job with the new national tax authority. Dalia's aunt Stella went to work as an orderly, mopping floors at the hospital, then opened a makeshift beauty salon in her bedroom in the house in Ramla. Dalia would sit and watch as Bulgarian ladies came to the house for haircuts and conversation. After work Solia would join the discussion, pressing for the smallest bits of news from Bulgaria: Is it getting worse under Georgi Dimitrov? What do you know of the neighbors? Soon Stella's sister Dora opened her own beauty shop in an old Arab storefront, and Stella joined her there.

Their customers would often sit for hours, and if someone had just come from Bulgaria, the news would be accompanied by many bitter jokes about the Communist regime.

One day shortly after the salon opened, Stella and Dora had a surprise visitor: their cousin, Yitzhak Yitzhaki. The sisters were astonished. Yitzhaki had not, after all, been killed in the massacre at Mt. Scopus in 1948. After the attack, he told them, he had continued his army service, but a few months later, he was released and went to work settling Bulgarian immigrants in old Arab neighborhoods of Jerusalem. There was still sporadic fighting nearby, however, and some Bulgarian arrivals told Yitzhaki that they hadn't escaped the Holocaust in Europe to be killed in Jerusalem. Many moved out, to Jaffa and Tel Aviv, and Yitzhaki, much like his brother-in-law Moshe, worked to settle immigrants from Turkey, Hungary, Poland, and Romania. Soon he was doing this 'absorption' work across Israel for the Jewish Agency. It was on a trip for the agency from Jerusalem to Jaffa that he ran into his Aunt Lili, who told him that the Arroyo girls, as he knew them from their youth, were in Ramla. 'I went looking for the famous salon of Dora and Stella in the Ramla souk,' he remembered, 'and sure enough, I found it, to my great joy!'

Stella and Dora took Yitzhaki to the house on K.B. Street. 'I was astonished to see the home in Ramla,' he remembered. To Yitzhaki, the modest stone home was known as 'The Castle'; he considered it 'the most beautiful house in Ramla.' The cousins went inside and there Yitzhaki saw Solia with her daughter, Dalia. She was, as Aunt Virginia had observed in late 1947, an extraordinarily beautiful child. Before leaving, Yitzhaki's cousins presented him with a gift – a big bag of lemons from the tree in the backyard. He carried them home to his family in Jerusalem.

In the meantime, Moshe had turned his job delivering beds into full-time work for the Custodian of Abandoned Properties. He helped respond to the needs of new arrivals who, like his own family, had moved into the houses of the Arabs. Moshe helped repair the houses where necessary, arranging to fix leaks, shore up walls, and the like. As for the former residents, the Israeli government designated them as 'absentees.' They had simply run away, Moshe and Solia were told, with their soup bowls steaming on the table. The Eshkenazis and others living in the Arab homes did not give the past owners much thought. Instead they focused on building a new society.

In the first session of the Israeli parliament (known by its Hebrew name, Knesset) beginning in 1949, legislators authorized dozens of ministries, including Agriculture, Defense, Immigration, Justice, Religions, Social Welfare, and War Victims. The first Knesset passed laws authorizing an army and mandatory service; systems for taxation, customs, compulsory education, and the courts; an independence day; an official day of rest; the 'transfer of Herzl's remains'; and, perhaps most famously, the Law of Return, whereby citizenship 'shall be granted to every Jew who expressed his desire to settle in Israel.' This law would become an endless source of bitterness between Israel and the Arab world for the next half century and beyond. For the Palestinian Arabs in exile, the law, and each wave of Jews admitted to the new state, denied their own dreams of return; for the Israelis, the law went to the core of their identity: to provide a safe haven for every Jew who wished to make aliyah, the Jewish migration to Israel.

In July 1949, David Ben-Gurion announced a four-year plan to build 500 settlements for 150,000 new immigrants. 'Today the Jewish people are again at a period of genesis,' the prime minister declared. 'A waste land must be made fertile and the exiles gathered in.' By this time, 42,000 Bulgarian Jews lived in Israel, the vast majority having come in the previous nine months. Of the entire community of Bulgarian Jews who had collectively escaped the Holocaust, at most 5,000 would remain in the fatherland.

The flood of migrants increased the pressure on Ramla to create jobs. In early 1949, hundreds of immigrants of Ramla marched in Tel Aviv, demanding work and bread. As unemployment grew, so did petty crime, and by July, a year after the surrender of Arab Ramla, Israeli Ramla had established its first criminal court. The *Palestine Post* reported the historic occasion: The first case involved an Arab, a man named Haddad accused of beating his wife; then came a Mr. Aharon, a Jew charged with brandishing a knife at a local bank manager. The increase in crime was linked directly to the sustained hardship of the immigrants. 'The Force was confronted with grave problems,' declared the Ministry of Police. Assaults were up by 150 percent, and 'offences against morality' had tripled, 'a consequence of the rapid growth of the population . . .' By the end of 1949, as Dalia turned two years old and her 'pioneer' parents marked their first year in Ramla, the city surpassed ten thousand residents.

By now, the municipal naming committee had finished its work and Ramla's streets had new signs. The old Jaffa-Jerusalem highway was called Herzl Street; Birket El Jamusi was named Haganah Street; Omar Ibn Khattab was Jabotinsky, named after the founder of Revisionist

Zionism, the ardent right wing of the new Jewish state. The Eshkenazis' street, known before as Sheikh Radwan, was now called Klausner, named after the Revisionist Zionist, literary critic, and scholar of early Christianity.

July 1949 also marked the first City Council meeting of Israeli Ramla. 'Our work is not easy,' declared the mayor, a Bulgarian named Meir Melamed, 'but by joining forces we will overcome all of the difficulties.' Those difficulties included not only water scarcity, unemployment, and an impatient Jewish population, but also what to do with the Arabs of Ramla. Most had been expelled a year earlier, but 1,300 Arabs still lived in the town. With the Israeli military governor scheduled to leave Ramla within weeks, city councillors worried about 'opening the closed off area where the Arabs are . . . and with that comes the question of safety in the city.'

The Arab men who had not been expelled were held as prisoners of war after the capture of Ramla on July 12, 1948. During their incarceration, they were not allowed to work their fields. Across Israel, the Arab olive and orange groves had gone largely untended and in some cases had been plowed under to prevent 'infiltrators' from returning. In Ramla and Lod (as Lydda was known in the Hebrew vernacular), the military governor had trucked in workers from Nazareth, a Christian Arab community in what was now Israel, to work the olive groves near the two towns. The imprisoned men of Ramla and Lod were put to work weaving thatch baskets for the harvest; their POW labor helped others harvest the lands they had recently cultivated themselves.

Local Israeli officials began to worry about the consequences of their policy toward the Arabs of Israel. 'They still have not gotten used to reality and have become apathetic about the future,' wrote an official named S. Zamir in a status report on the Arab community of Ramla. 'The government's declaration of equality and freedom is like a voice calling out in the desert unless we prove it by actions. Their economic situation is very bad. They have enough provisions for the time being, but soon the question will arise: "What will we eat?"'

After their release from the POW camp, the Arab men of Ramla, like Arabs across Israel at the time, were nevertheless still confined with their families to a few fenced-in blocks. These included Bashir's uncle Rasem, the doctor who had stayed after the expulsions. For several years, the Arabs of Israel would live under martial law. Arab residents wishing to leave their neighborhood or village were required to apply to the military authorities for special permits. Movement was restricted on security grounds. Some leaders in the new state continued to argue for the 'transfer' of the remaining Arabs across the Jordan River to Abdullah's kingdom.

The Arabs of the Ramla and Lod 'ghettos' found their former homes occupied by Jewish families and their agricultural lands controlled by kibbutzim. Not at home, but not in exile, they were defined by the Israeli government as 'present absentees.' Many sought legal recourse to move back into their houses or resume farming their lands.

'Though on several occasions since his interview with the Military Governor, Mr. Shomski promised me to return the door and shutters and to re-condition my house,' wrote an Arab resident of Lydda in December 1949, 'up to this date nothing has been done. On the contrary, owing to the absence of doors and windows unknown persons have carried out extensive damage to my house . . . I shall be very much obliged if you will give your instructions . . . to return my doors and window shutters as soon as possible.'

'I beg to submit the following for your kind consideration,' wrote an al-Ramla landowner, an Arab whose plea had begun in March 1949. 'I am the registered owner of the following pieces of land: Parcel No. 69; Block No. 4374; Locality Ramle [Ramla]; Area 5,032 Sq. Metres . . . All these parcels, including my own share, were treated by the Apetropos [Custodian of Abandoned Properties] as Absentee Properties in spite of the fact that I am not an absentee . . .'

'I am the registered owner of Half of Parcel 13,' wrote an Arab appellant to the local council of Kibbutz Gezer, five miles southeast of Ramla. 'I am prepared to pay the Local Council's taxes on my share in the Parcel . . . I shall be obliged also to know who has ploughed my land and with whose authority he did so.'

In a black-and-white photograph taken in the backyard of the stone house in Ramla, Dalia stands beside a lemon tree, looking into the camera with tears in her eyes. The image was taken in the summer, perhaps of 1950; Dalia would have been two and a half. She'd been crying briefly, offended by the sparrows who had chosen to fly away rather than stay and eat bread crumbs out of her hand. 'Why should they fly?' she cried to her aunt. 'Why? I love them.' It is her earliest memory.

In another image Dalia's father stands beside her, his dark wavy hair combed back, his cuffed pants hoisted above his waist, his smile frozen in time by Solia's snap. In the background, behind the lemon tree, Moshe had planted bananas and *guayabas*. To the right, at the edge of the frame, stood a henhouse where the Eshkenazis raised their own chickens. It was the time of the *tsena*, or scarcity (literally 'austerity'), and everyone was expected to pitch in.

During the *tsena*, the Ministry of Supply and Rationing moved to the center of Israeli public life. The ministry's job was to regulate the limited supply of food so that no one went hungry. Israel's rapid growth required it to import 85 percent of its food. Although before 1948 the Jewish Agency had direct (if unofficial) trade relations with other states, Israel's sudden entry into the world economy proved jarring. The state had reduced its trade with the markets of the British Empire, and the Arab countries had imposed economic and political boycotts. Egypt was blockading cargo to and from Israel through the Suez Canal, despite a UN resolution calling for free passage through the vital waterway. Israel had to depend on wheat and processed flour, and imported meats, seasonally discounted fish, and even olive oil, from the United States, Canada, and Australia. With the demise of many of the Arab groves, Israel could supply only 8 percent of its own olive oil demands.

In 1950, officials distributed seven hundred thousand live chickens to new immigrants. Milk was stored in dozens of collection stations around the country. The ministry established a Flour Committee and a Bread Committee and directly oversaw the daily production of tens of thousands of round loaves, rolls, and raisin milk cakes. Ration cards linked the address of each family to the serial number of an assigned retailer. Coupon books provided subsidies for wheat, yeast, and matzo and allowed for extra rations of meat for pregnant women. To do their part, citizens were urged to be creative.

The Eshkenazis, like many Israelis during the early 1950s, innovated their way through the scarcity. A neighbor's cow roamed the street unmolested, revered as if the neighborhood were in India, not Israel. Solia bartered for milk and butter from the cow's owner, using eggs from the family's chicken coop as currency. This cow nourished Dalia and all of her neighbors.

In the Ramla market, held on Wednesdays as it had been before July 1948, Dalia would walk with her father, passing by the stalls of cucumbers, olives, and watermelons; past the mounds of oranges and bananas and the hawkers yelling, 'Sabra! Sabra!' before the fresh cactus fruit atop buckets of ice; and into the dry goods stores for fabric and shoes. With each purchase, Dalia would watch as her father found top quality without paying too much. 'Here,' he would say, fingering a pair of trousers for the feel of its fabric. 'Compare this' – and he would pick another pair – 'to *this*.' Always he seemed to find a slight imperfection and negotiate a lower price.

In the evenings, Moshe and Solia would invite Bulgarian friends for gatherings in the backyard. They laid out plates of black olives, watermelon, and Bulgarian cheese, pouring cold glasses of boza, a sweet Balkan drink made from wheat. They'd talk of news from Bulgaria, and Dalia would hear them telling off-color jokes in Ladino, the fading language of earlier generations that she could understand only slightly.

Often during these gatherings Dalia would walk to the side of the house, half listening, and inhale from the 'candles of the night,' the flowers that opened only after sunset. She compared them with Aunt Stella's *margaritkis* – the white and yellow flowers that would close in the evenings as the night candles opened. Often Solia would put a record on the phonograph, and sultry Spanish music, a legacy of the Eshkenazis' Sephardic roots, would drift out from the house. Dalia would watch her mother and the guests sashay across the veranda that Ahmad Khairi had built, evoking the ballroom days in Sofia when she'd met Moshe. At the end of the evening, Moshe would pick roses from the bushes in the garden and present one to each of the departing women. It was a Bulgarian tradition, and one especially familiar for Solia, who grew up alongside the Valley of the Roses.

By 1955, the year Dalia turned eight, Moshe was rising into the leadership of the local office of the Custodian of Abandoned Properties. Dalia would visit during school vacations, intent on helping her father, answering the phones or showing clients to his office. Usually they were women, often beside themselves with frustration: They had leaks that had needed fixing for months, or after years they still lived in a tent at the edge of town, though they'd been promised better housing. Moshe was genuinely pained by their troubles. He would say, 'I am entering your situation,' and then explain how his budget was so distressingly limited. He would promise to write appeals to the appropriate ministries, insisting, 'I give you my word, I promise to deal with this even if the world turns upside down . . .' Dalia was amazed to see clients leave the office calmed by the sincere, overwhelmed bureaucrat and hoping for the best. On the street people were constantly approaching Moshe, shaking his hand and thanking him for his help; at other times they would come to his house with gifts. 'I understand your gratitude,' he would tell them. 'I appreciate your gift, but as a public servant I cannot accept it.'

On other afternoons, Dalia would stop at the hair salon

her aunts Stella and Dora had opened in a narrow storefront of an old Arab shop. All too often, Stella would put her niece in a chair and work on her until Dalia felt she had hardly any hair at all. 'Just a little trim . . . there, just a little bit more; you like that, don't you?' Once, when Stella was taking a nap at home, Dalia took her revenge, cutting her aunt's hair as she slept, cooing, 'There, just a little bit more; you like that, don't you?' When Stella woke up and looked in the mirror, it seemed she'd been attacked. Stella's brother Daniel was to be married in a few days. She wore a hat to the wedding.

The salon catered mostly to Bulgarians, but the two sisters were gaining a reputation, and soon Polish, Romanian, and Moroccan women would come and the language would switch from Bulgarian to broken French or broken Hebrew. Dalia would recall one regular customer from Poland – unforgettable for her creamy skin and huge blue-green eyes that struck Dalia as especially sad. To Dalia, the woman was every bit as beautiful as Elizabeth Taylor. She would sit in her chair, never smiling, gazing out at nothing. Dalia would watch, riveted, as Stella and Dora combed and snipped, doting on the woman, trying to draw her out.

Dalia had begun to notice how some of her neighbors were different. They were silent about the past, where her own family spoke openly about the rescue in Bulgaria. At school, she had a teacher who, it was whispered, had lost his wife and children in the death camps in Poland. Teacher Haim, as everyone called him, had come to Israel after the war. He was Dalia's favorite: a short man with dark, heavy eyebrows and a forehead that took up most of his face. His eyes were hazel, vibrant, and intense, and he walked quickly with a wide gait, rarely slowing, always looking forward. In class he would call to her, to all the children, 'Come here, *tachsheet sheli*, come here, my jewel, come to the blackboard and show us what you know.'

'He gave us a feeling that he believed in our future,' Dalia remembered. 'He was a strict disciplinarian, but very affirmative. He gave us tools for life.'

Many of Dalia's classmates, however, seemed almost beyond reach. The children of Poles, Romanians, and Hungarians, they had come to the country, like Dalia, in the first days of the Israeli state. In the eyes of these children, Dalia saw a vacancy.

A Polish classmate lived next door. His father's eyes were literally bulging out of their sockets in an expression of 'permanent incredulity,' Dalia would remember, 'a fixed stare of terror and horror.' For hours at night, over the wall from the inside of another Arab house, Dalia could hear this same man scream at his son, ceaselessly, and she wanted to scream back, 'Stop it! Stop it! What do you *want* from him?' Sometimes she actually put her voice to these protests, but she was always drowned out in the din. At school, the silence of this young Polish friend was punctuated occasionally by sudden outbursts of screaming, crying, and kicking. None of the teachers seemed to know what to do with him.

Dalia found this trauma a direct challenge to her faith. Though Moshe and Solia had never been religious – they rarely went to the synagogue and were the essence of 'secular Zionists' – Dalia's own belief in God had, she felt, always been a part of her. Few people in Ramla seemed to want to talk about what had happened in Europe during the war, but Dalia had seen the people with numbers on their arms. As she grew older, she learned about the atrocities in Germany, Poland, Romania, and Hungary.

She found this truth indigestible. *For God to allow this to happen*, she would recall thinking, *is utterly unconscionable*. She was furious. 'You have created human beings!' she would shout to her Creator. 'You have to take responsibility for Your creation! You have to be more active in preventing such things!'

Dalia began to understand these horrors as her people's historical legacy. In school she learned of other atrocities. Burned into her mind was a pogrom in the Ukraine, where Jews were slaughtered by sword-wielding Christians after Good Friday mass. She was taught of the silence of European Christians during the Holocaust, especially that of Pope Pius XII, who did not show the courage of the Bulgarian Orthodox Church.

By the time she went to piano lessons at St. Joseph's Catholic monastery in Ramla, Dalia felt a deep ambivalence about Christianity. It was perhaps 1956; Dalia was soon to turn nine. The heavy cross on the monastery gates reminded her of a sword and invoked an instantaneous fear. Entering the monastery, however, she was drawn in by the silence; by the painted statue of St. Joseph on a pedestal; by the dimly lit corridors with their black and white tiles; and by the portrait of another pope, John XXIII, whose face contained something humane. She began to understand something fundamental. Decades later, she would remember this moment as the beginning of a life of *discernment*: of being able to see the whole and not judge someone or something based simply on a single observation or teaching.

Growing up, Dalia would frequently ask her parents and teachers: 'What are these houses we are living in?'

'These are Arab houses,' she was told.

'What *are* these Arab houses that everyone talks about?' she would reply.

Dalia's school was in an Arab house, and there she would learn Israel's history. She learned about the creation of the state of Israel as a safe haven for the Jews. She studied the War of Independence as the story of the few against the many. The Arabs had invaded, Dalia would read, in order to destroy the new state and throw the Jews into the sea. Most nations confronted with such hostilities would have been paralyzed, but tiny Israel had withstood five Arab armies. Little David had defeated Goliath. As for the Arabs, Dalia's textbooks would report that they ran away, deserting their lands and abandoning their homes, fleeing before the conquering Israeli army. The Arabs, one textbook of the day declared, 'preferred to leave' once the Jews had taken their towns. Dalia accepted the history she was taught. Still, she was confused. Why, she wondered, would anyone leave so willingly?

One afternoon when she was about seven or eight years old, Dalia climbed up the black metal gate that Ahmad Khairi had placed at the end of the stone path in the front yard. Atop the gate perched a delicate piece of wrought iron in the shape of a star and crescent: the symbol of Islam. It bothered Dalia. 'This is not an Arab house,' she said to herself, and she grasped the delicate crescent and began wrenching it back and forth, back and forth, until it came loose in her hands. She clambered down and threw the crescent away.

In the spring of 1956, when Dalia was in the third grade, she began to make a connection between the Arabs she had learned about in school and those her parents talked about at home. Israeli newspapers were full of stories about raids of infiltrators from Gaza backed by the new Egyptian president, Gamal Abdel Nasser. Moshe read in his evening paper, *Ma'ariv*, about the incursions onto Israeli soil by Egyptian and Palestinian fedayeen guerrillas bent on wiping out the Jewish state, and about the swift Israeli responses.

As the Suez Canal crisis made the news, Moshe and Solia understood there would be cause for their nation to go to war. Nasser was defending Egypt's exclusive rights to control the Suez Canal, long overseen by the British, and threatening to close the Straits of Tiran, Israel's only sea link to central and southern Africa. The Egyptian president had also begun to speak of the 'Arab Nation' and in defense of the Palestinian 'right of return.' None of this boded well for Israel.

In late October 1956, war came suddenly when Israeli paratroopers and infantry battalions crossed their south-western border and attacked Egyptian forces in the Sinai Peninsula, then moved across the Sinai and toward the Suez Canal. British and French forces joined the fight on the Israeli side. The European powers were alarmed at the growing threat posed by this third world Arab nationalist leader, and, like the Israelis, they wanted him stopped. The United States and the Soviet Union, however, had not been consulted. The superpowers had their own separate interests in the region and, in rare agreement, demanded that Britain, France, and Israel withdraw. Israel could still claim a military victory, because it had broken the blockade of the Straits of Tiran, but after the British and French withdrew, Nasser was in control of his prize, the Suez Canal. Because of U.S. and Soviet intervention, Nasser had in effect repelled the European attackers and established Egyptian sovereignty over the canal. The popularity of the Egyptian president surged across the Arab world. He began talking about the importance of Palestine to all Arabs.

One day in the spring of 1957, Dalia was playing with her girlfriends after school. They were at a concrete shelter in Ramla, the same claustrophobic bunker where Dalia and her schoolmates had practiced air raid drills during the recent Suez crisis. Most of Dalia's friends had been lighter-skinned girls from Europe. But recently a new wave of olive- and brown-skinned Jewish children had come to Israel from the Arab countries, including many from Iraq, Egypt, and Yemen. No longer welcome to live in the Arab world, the newspapers reported, these 'Oriental Jews' (also known as Sephardim, or *mizrahi*) were immigrating to Israel, which would grant them the safe haven it offered to every Jew. Among many of Dalia's classmates, however, there was a sense that the dark-skinned school-mates were 'bringing the class down.' They were considered dirty and carriers of lice. Dalia had caught lice herself, much to the shame of her entire family: Aunt Stella had washed her hair with gasoline, scrubbing her scalp to a bright red. Dalia stank of petrol for days and walked around in shame.

Still, Dalia was stunned, she would recall later, when her Polish friend stood atop the concrete shelter and, hands on hips, declared her intent to expel the darker, Oriental Jews from their play group. There would now be two competing groups among the girls: a 'black group' – the *cherniti*, the *schwarzes* – and a 'white group.' The other European girls murmured their assent. The 'white group' would be made up of only the lighter-skinned Ashkenazi, plus Dalia and the other Bulgarians. (It was confusing even to Dalia: Her skin was light, lighter than her father's, and her name was Eshkenazi, but in fact, like most Bulgarians she was Sephardic, with roots in Spain.)

The Polish girl picked up a stone and threw it at a dark-skinned classmate. Other lighter-skinned girls followed. Dalia stepped forward. 'Where did you say you came from?' she asked the Ashkenazi girls. 'And remind me, what happened to the Jews there?' She paused. 'Of all people who should know better,' she said. 'Of all people who should know how not to treat someone badly just because they are different. If you are going to have a black group and a white group,' Dalia announced, 'then I am going with the black group.' The issue never rose again among her classmates.

Tens of thousands of Jews had come to Israel from the Arab countries since 1950. In 1958, Avraham Shmil, the director of Ramla's office of the Israeli national labor federation, organized a mass demonstration against the Labor Department of his own ruling party. Many of the *mizrahi*, or Oriental Jews, of Ramla still lived in crude tent camps and shacks on the outskirts of town and were desperate for work and better living conditions. With his protest, Shmil hoped to pressure the Israeli labor secretary into bringing decent-paying factory jobs to the struggling town. When the *mizrahi* arrived, Shmil would recall, most of the 'good jobs' had already been taken by the Ashkenazi elite from Eastern Europe, who clearly already had insider status in the new state. Sometimes the new, darker-skinned immigrants would fume as they stood waiting in line at the employment office while two Europeans spoke endlessly in Yiddish; they didn't under-stand that in some cases these Ashkenazi were only trying to ascertain if certain relatives or friends were still alive.

The Jews from Arab lands, on the other hand, were discouraged from speaking Arabic or from listening to their beloved classical Arabic music, especially with the rise of Nasser. Their Hebrew often was bad, and the only work many of them could find was twelve days per month sweeping streets, maintaining roads, and 'building' forests for the Jewish National Fund.

The forests, part of what the JNF called 'total redemption of the land of Israel for the entire Jewish people,' were part of a legacy of 'BOULDER-STREWN mountains, stagnant swamps, hard, arid soil, and sterile sand dunes [that] must be redeemed from the neglect of twenty centuries.' The forests in many cases were planted on land that had only recently held Arab villages. From 1948 until the mid-1960s, hundreds of villages were demolished – by bulldozers, by army units training demolition crews, and by aerial bombing – to be replaced by new cities, expanded kibbutzim, or JNF forests. The work of the *mizrahi* and other immigrants for the JNF thus served several purposes: It eliminated the former residences of villagers who might attempt to 'infiltrate' across the armistice lines; it cemented Israel's position against the UN resolution that authorized the return of Palestinian refugees; and it ensured low-paying work for thousands of poor Jewish immigrants from the Arab countries and elsewhere.

Yet the problem for the *mizrahi* was not just work. Like many of the early immigrants, they needed to feel they belonged in the Jewish state. In Ramla, Avraham Shmil worked to help the immigrants forge an Israeli identity out of their patchwork of nationalities and more than a dozen languages. Shmil organized field trips to the

Galilee and the Negev for immigrants to take in the breadth of the new state and to begin to get to know one another. In Ramla he organized classes, plays, and concerts in Hebrew; evenings of folklore from Bulgaria, Morocco, and Yemen; and neighborhood culture and hiking clubs.

The model held up for all of the immigrants, especially the men, was the Sabra, the native-born Israeli whose optimism, strength, and mythical heroism was something for all to aspire toward. Sabra came from the Hebrew word *tzabar*: a cactus fruit, thorn-covered but sweet inside. In 1950s Israel, the Sabra was the New Israeli Man: handsome, tough, physically strong, an ardent Zionist, upbeat, without fear, and unencumbered by the weakness of his ancestors. The Sabra, by definition Ashkenazi, from a generation that had come to Palestine before the Holocaust, had shed the shameful baggage of the old country. He had become, in essence, the Israeli embodiment of Ari Ben Canaan, Leon Uris's hero in *Exodus*. The Sabra was, in the words of one Israeli writer, 'the elect son of the chosen people.'

Social engineers consciously cultivated this image as an alternative to the diaspora Jew. In 1949, a Bulgarian-language paper of the leftist Mapam Party serialized a novel by writer Moshe Shamir in which the 'New Jewish Man' is actually a giant, emerging from the sea in a fantastic aliyah to build up the land. The idea, recalled the editor, former Knesset member Victor Shemtov, was to 'wash off that old Jew,' to erase the image of the 'squirming ghetto Jew,' and to focus on the 'new Jew' who was 'standing tall for the first time,' plunging his hands into the soil to create a new country.

For many new Israelis, this potent icon was something

to strive for. They wore the Sabra 'uniform' – khaki shorts and a khaki or faded blue work shirt and 'biblical sandals.' Ramla's first Israeli mayor wore the uniform, as did many immigrants. Some even had Sabra-style khaki weddings. For many children, the Sabra ideal inspired them to adopt 'Israeli' names.

For the older generation of immigrants, the Sabra image was often impossible to attain. For Holocaust survivors, it was absurd. For the Sabra, the Holocaust survivors often represented the shame of Jews going like sheep to the slaughter. Thus, Dalia would recall years later, the phrase *Never again* was not only a promise by Jews not to repeat the past; it indicated a desire, rooted in shame, to distance themselves from the image of the victim.

One observer of an early transit camp in Israel referred to Holocaust survivors as 'difficult human matter' and said 'these people have known such hell that nothing more can move them now. Their senses have been blunted.' David Ben-Gurion famously called Holocaust survivors 'human dust' and said that 'turning these people of dust into a cultured, independent nation with a vision will be no easy task.' An agricultural worker charged with turning Holocaust survivors into productive farmers advised colleagues: 'We must understand who we are working with . . . a community of rejects, of *pathetic and helpless people*. [Emphasis in original.] We must approach their most basic feelings, which are very volatile and unpredictable and full of fear . . . fear of the ground falling away from under their feet . . . Fear of work – The mere thought of taking any personal initiative and having to face unfamiliar conditions terrifies him . . . he has an uncontrollable fear for the future of his children . . .'

For the immigrants from the Arab countries, the pursuit of the Sabra ideal was equally unrealistic. They often struggled mightily with Hebrew, and their experiences in Morocco, Yemen, Egypt, or Iraq had little to do with the swashbuckling warrior image of the native-born Ashkenazi Sabra. Moreover, many Ashkenazis, including some Israeli leaders who established early immigration policy, considered the *mizrahi*, in Ben-Gurion's description of North African Jews, 'savage' and 'primitive'; others referred to them, in actual policy discussions, as 'mentally regressed,' 'hot-tempered,' or 'chronically lazy.'

In Ramla, as in the rest of Israel, each immigrant group quickly attracted its own labels, which ranged from derogatory to affectionate and sometimes were both. A Moroccan was a *sakin*, or knife, because of his reputation as violent; Iraqis were pajamas, because of their dress; Germans were *yeke*, after the jackets they wore in the fields, or *putzes*, a kind of upscale schmuck; Romanians were thieves; Bulgarians were cheap; and a Pole was *dripke*: Yiddish for dustcloth.

Bulgarians, however they were labeled, were widely respected in Israel. They had none of what would come to be known as the 'Holocaust complex.' As Israel grew up, the Bulgarians would gain a reputation as fair-minded and hardworking, with a passion for European high culture. Solia Eshkenazi embodied this. She appreciated that the entire Bulgarian Jewish choir had come on a boat together and that Bulgarians were playing in the new Israeli philharmonic. She loved to read Tolstoy and Chekhov, Victor Hugo, Thomas Mann, and Jack London. Most of all, she adored Austrian writer Stefan Zweig, her beloved, kindred soul whose work she considered profoundly sensitive and who, during the war, had lost faith in humanity and cut open his veins.

Culture could be imported, but much of what Solia loved had been left behind in the Bulgarian landscape. As Dalia grew older, she noticed how often her mother would speak of the winds that would tumble through the narrow corridors of Sliven or the hikes she and her friends used to take up Vitosha mountain.

As a teenager, Dalia began to see her mother as an uprooted tree that couldn't take to new soil. Moshe had brought his skills with him to build a new state. He was a doer who grew exasperated with weak-mindedness and would exclaim, 'What's this indecisiveness? I cannot understand! If it doesn't work for you, just cut it off like a pickled cucumber!' After coming to Ramla, Solia aged quickly. Her job in the tax office did not suit her personality and the radiance and mischief she arrived with; she wasn't good at cooking and sewing; and though she and Moshe would travel occasionally with friends to walk along the beach in Tel Aviv, Solia's world had narrowed. Her sisters thought of her as an extraordinary woman who would 'take the food from her own mouth if she sees anyone in need,' as the Bulgarian saying went. But a light had dimmed, and gradually, as she went to work year after year in the national tax office, Solia grew quieter.

In 1963, as Dalia entered high school, city leaders marked fifteen years since the 'liberation of Ramla' from Arab hands in 1948. A promotional film showed men in narrow ties paddling rowboats through the town's ancient underground cisterns, as a deep voice intoned, 'Near to this ancient monument there are new buildings and factories emerging. The municipality is proud that Ramla was transferred from a pure Arabic city to a place where now live twenty-five thousand citizens most of which are new immigrants.'

Three years later, in 1966, Dalia Eshkenazi graduated from high school and began making plans to enroll at Tel Aviv University to study English literature. She had taken a special English-language curriculum at an international high school in Yafo, now a mixed Arab-Jewish town just south of Tel Aviv. (Arabs still called the town Yaffa.) The Israeli army had recently recruited Dalia into its officers' training corps, a special program for gifted students that allowed them to attend college before their military service.

By the mid-1960s, Ramla, with its cement smokestacks on the outskirts of town, its high percentage of un-employed *mizrahi*, and its Arab 'ghetto,' had gained a reputation across Israel as, above all, rough and gritty. Some people knew Ramla as the 'Liverpool of Israel,' in part because of the growing rock-and-roll scene playing out in the old Arab houses of the ghetto, where bands from Tel Aviv and Jerusalem would come on the week-ends. Life had finally achieved some normality for Dalia and her fellow countrymen. For most of her high school years, conflict with the Arabs had been relatively silent, and she could afford not to think about it much. As she spent her first summer out of high school, however, Dalia noticed a change.

To the outside world, Israel had made it clear, once and for all, that it would never grant the Palestinian refugees the right of return. The year before, the Israel Lands Administration had destroyed some of the last remaining Arab villages in a campaign known as 'Leveling Villages,' and Prime Minister Levi Eshkol, in response to criticism from an Arab Knesset member, replied, 'Not destroying the abandoned villages would be contrary to the policy of development and revitalization of wasteland, which every state is obliged to implement.' For Israel it was clear, eighteen years after its War of Independence, that these lands could never be returned. Outside the state, it was increasingly clear that the land would be restored to the Arabs only through 'armed struggle.' As Nasser's strength grew with the rise of pan-Arab nationalism, and threats emerged from the Arab Nationalist Movement and a new group called the Palestine Liberation Organization (PLO), the relative quiet between Israel and the Arab world seemed doomed.

By the spring of 1967, as Dalia began to hear chilling threats on the radio from Arab broadcasters speaking bad Hebrew, the world around her darkened. She could sense it. War, it seemed, would be impossible to avoid.

Eight

WAR

ON MONDAY MORNING, June 5, 1967, Bashir Khairi stood before a judge in civil court, arguing a case on behalf of his client, a Mr. al-Abed. Bashir was now twenty-five and a recent graduate of Cairo University Law School, specializing in labor matters. The court had convened in Ramallah in the Jordanian-controlled West Bank, the territory King Abdullah had annexed to his kingdom seventeen years earlier. His grandson Hussein was now Jordan's king and head of state.

Ramallah had changed completely since the day in late 1948 when Ahmad and Zakia had taken Bashir and the other children to Gaza. Gone was the desperation of a refugee population sleeping under the trees. Gone, too, were thousands of well-to-do Ramallans, mostly Christians, who had fled the West Bank into the United States in the years following the Nakba. At the edges of town stood the concrete dwellings and narrow, refuse-strewn lanes of the UNRWA refugee camps. Each year, the UN refugee agency was required to submit a budget for renewed funding. Receiving long-term funds or building more permanent-looking housing would imply a UN admission that the refugees were not going home. This position was still unacceptable for the 'host' governments, the grassroots political factions that were based in the camps, and most of all the refugees themselves. For Palestinians, resistance meant no compromise on the right of return, no matter how firm Israel's position. Bashir, like most Palestinians, believed there was only one way the land would come back to his people. Force expelled us from our land, he reasoned, and only force will get it back.

Bashir faced the judge and made the case for Mr. al-Abed. In his opening argument he stated that Abed, a mechanic at a Ramallah garage, had been fired from his job unjustly and that at the very least he should be given his back pay. Bashir sat down, and the attorney for the repair shop began to speak. As he did, a young man darted through the courtroom door, strode swiftly over to Bashir, and began whispering in his ear. It was a little before noon.

For nineteen years, Palestinian refugees had been waiting for the moment when they would return to their homes. At first they had thought this would happen in a matter of weeks. When Israel barred them from coming back, hopes shifted to the UN resolution advocating the right of return. Years later, still in exile, the refugees began to put their faith in 'armed struggle.' Increasingly they turned to Egypt's Nasser. For more than a decade, the Egyptian president had electrified the Arab world with his anticolonial speeches and his aspirations for a great Arab nation.

Bashir, studying law in Cairo, was inspired by Nasser's dream of unifying the Arabs. His focus on return now had a vehicle, and he set aside all other personal ambitions. 'He never bought anything expensive, shirt, shoes, nothing for himself,' Khanom recalled. 'Our father would ask him, "Do you want money?" and Bashir would say,

"No, I have enough."' Bhajat, Bashir's younger brother by a year, was completely different. 'He was spending three or four times what Bashir spent,' Khanom said. 'Bashir never spent money on shoes, never bought himself a suit. We used to call Bashir the son of the beggar and Bhajat the son of the lord. People couldn't even believe they were brothers.' Bashir believed his discipline would be rewarded, and his people delivered, by the heroic Nasser.

Nasser's nationalization of the Suez Canal, to the anger of the United States, Great Britain, France, and Israel, was a source of deep pride for Bashir and millions of others on the Arab streets. Nasser had become a leader, with Nehru of India and Tito of Yugoslavia, of the 'non-aligned movement' that sought an independent, third path between the superpowers. Most important for Palestinians, Nasser's recent championing of their cause had stirred hopes in the diaspora for a great Arab rebirth to avenge the defeat of 1948. Unlike the UN and its resolutions on paper, Bashir believed, Nasser could end the long exile of the Palestinians by force of arms.

In the early 1960s, Bashir had grown deeply involved in student activist politics in Cairo, particularly with the Arab Nationalist Movement. The ANM was led by George Habash, a refugee from Lydda whose sister had been killed by Israeli soldiers in July 1948 and who walked in the heat through the hills to Ramallah. Palestinian political leaders like Habash, and the leaders of the newly formed Palestine Liberation Organization, were rallying around Nasser, urging him to prepare for war. The PLO and its small Palestine Liberation Army would march under Nasser's command. The Egyptian president, however, would say repeatedly that he had no intention of liberating Palestine: The time was not right, especially for attacks on

Israel launched from Arab states. For many Palestinians, though, by the mid-1960s the urgency had deepened; the Negev was filling up with new Jewish immigrants, and rumors were everywhere that Israel was developing a nuclear weapons program.

Bashir and his fellow student activists in Cairo believed Arab unity was the key to return, and they watched this maneuvering closely. Some students began guerrilla training in secret 'special forces' camps in Egypt and elsewhere. They learned how to plant mines and fire antitank weapons. They jumped from airplanes, waded through swamps, slept on hard ground, ate snakes, and went without food for days.

Two young men emerged from the growing guerrilla movement: Yasser Arafat and Khalil al-Wazir, known as Abu Jihad. Arafat and Abu Jihad believed return would come only if it was led by an autonomous Palestinian political and military organization devoted to armed struggle. Neither Abu Jihad, who had been expelled from al-Ramla in 1948, nor Arafat trusted in deliverance from the Arab states, which they believed had sold out the Palestinians in 1948. Together the two men had founded the guerrilla group Fatah in the wake of the Suez conflict.

On New Year's Day 1965, after nine years of relative quiet between Israel and the Arab world following the Suez crisis, Fatah planned its first attack on Israeli soil. Guerrillas were to cross the Lebanese border and lay explosives alongside water pipes near the Sea of Galilee, Israel's main source of water. The control of water was a key source of tension between Israel and the Arab states. Israel had diverted much of the headwaters of the Jordan River away from downstream Arab lands. Israeli jets had bombed Syrian waterworks in the Golan Heights, across from the Galilee, so that Syria could not divert those same waters. When Israeli tractors moved into the demilitarized zones of the Golan to plow disputed land, they drew Syrian fire, which, in turn, brought swift Israeli response. Israel wanted nothing to interfere with its plan to support more immigrants with a pipeline to the Negev desert. Fatah, the small band of guerrillas, sought to foil Israel's pipeline plan; after all, the Negev was part of old Palestine, to which the rebels and their followers intended to return. Their attack on the pipeline was a failure, thwarted by Lebanese security before it began, but Fatah issued a 'military communiqué' proclaiming success by 'detachments of our strike forces' and warning Israel of future actions.

Throughout 1965 and 1966, Fatah, along with a new group called Abtal al-Awda (Heroes of Return), launched dozens more attacks from the West Bank and Lebanon on mostly isolated targets inside Israel. The attacks sharply raised anxieties in the Jewish state, and, as designed, sparked tensions between Israel and its Arab neighbors. By late 1966 these attacks, and the Israeli reprisals, had drawn a reluctant King Hussein deeper into the conflict, and closer to the point of no return.

Before dawn on November 13, 1966, Israeli planes, tanks, and troops attacked the West Bank village of Samu, blowing up dozens of houses and killing twenty-one Jordanian soldiers. The invasion, especially in its massive scale, shocked even some supporters of Israel. U.S. officials immediately condemned the attack. In Washington, the head of the National Security Council, Walt Rostow, in a memo to President Johnson, declared that the '3000-man raid with tanks and planes was all out of proportion to the provocation' – in this case, a Fatah land mine that had killed three Israeli soldiers on November 11. Rostow said of the Israelis, 'They've undercut Hussein. We're spending $500 million to shore him up as a stabilizing factor . . . It makes even the moderate Arabs feel fatalistically that there is nothing they can do to get along with the Israelis no matter how hard they try. It will place heavy domestic and external political strain on King Hussein's regime . . .'

Rostow believed the Israelis, in attacking Jordan rather than Soviet-backed Syria, which was supporting the Palestinian guerrilla factions, had struck at the wrong target. When Eshkol, in a conciliatory note, wrote to President Johnson asking for his support in this 'difficult hour for us,' the president didn't respond. Instead, a week after the attack, Johnson wrote to King Hussein of his 'sense of sorrow and concern . . . words of sympathy are small comfort when lives have been needlessly destroyed.' The president assured the king that 'my disapproval of this action has been made known to the government of Israel in the strongest terms.' He also addressed a fear King Hussein had expressed since the raid. Regarding 'Your Majesty's concern that Israel's policies have changed and that Israel now intends to occupy territory on the West Bank of the Jordan River,' the president assured the king, 'we have good reason to believe it highly unlikely that the events you fear will in fact occur. Should Israel adopt the policies you fear it would have the gravest consequences. There is no doubt in my mind that our position is fully understood and appreciated by the Israelis.'

The king's fears of an Israeli occupation of the West Bank, however, were secondary to his worries at home. American officials in Amman had already warned

Washington that 'the monarchy itself is in jeopardy.' The CIA, in a special memorandum to the president, wrote that the Samu attack 'badly damaged Hussein's position at home. It made him vulnerable to attack by disaffected elements of his population, who argue that his policy of peaceful coexistence with Israel has been dictated by the U.S. and has proved a failure.' The king, according to the American assessment, would now be under great pressure to appear more militant toward Israel, especially as his kingdom grew more restive.

In Amman, the Samu raid had already provoked waves of violent protests against the king's regime. Palestinians accused the army of being weak and unprepared and demanded arms to fight Israel. A PLO broadcast from Cairo called upon the Jordanian army to overthrow the king. Riots broke out in Jordan and the West Bank, Jordanian troops fired at Palestinian demonstrators in Jerusalem, hundreds were arrested, and the king dissolved the parliament, imposed martial law, and secured additional military aid from the United States.

Now the split in the Arab world became more obvious than ever: Egypt and its ally Syria stood in favor of 'pan-Arab unity,' while King Hussein was labeled a pro-Western 'imperialist agent' and 'ally of Zionism.' In the spring of 1967, Syria called for Hussein's overthrow, and Nasser declared that the king was 'ready to sell the Arab nation in the same manner as Abdullah [the king's late grandfather] sold it in 1948.' Bashir, now twenty-five years old, stood firmly on the side of Nasser and the pan-Arab movement.

As Arab leaders sniped at one another, tensions were rising in the demilitarized zone of Syria's Golan Heights. The DZs were narrow bands of land between the Sea of

Galilee and the westernmost edge of the Golan. Syrian and Israeli forces had been exchanging sporadic fire over farming operations and the Syrian waterworks diversions, and Syrian mortar fire had fallen on Israeli kibbutzim. On April 7, 1967, Israeli air force pilots shot down six Syrian fighter jets in a dogfight above the Golan; one of the Israeli planes roared over Damascus in a public display of humiliation for the Syrians and their ally, Nasser. Yitzhak Rabin, the Israeli army's chief of staff, soon threatened to destroy the Syrian regime. Syria, with its backing of Palestinian guerrillas and its confrontation with Israel in the Golan, was antagonizing Nasser.

The Israeli actions were an embarrassment for Nasser, champion of the pan-Arab cause, and King Hussein seized the moment to shed his image as a lackey for the West. If the Egyptian president really wanted to stand up for the Arabs, Jordan Radio challenged, he should send an unmistakable message to Israel: Close the Straits of Tiran to Israeli vessels. After all, the broadcast intoned, some of those vessels would inevitably be transporting weapons to be used against Arabs in any coming conflict. The challenge from Jordan may have been meant simply to divert criticism from the beleaguered king to Nasser, but like the Fatah raids and the Israeli reprisal attack on Samu, it helped drive the region closer to war. Closing the Straits of Tiran would cut off Israel's access to the Red Sea and Africa beyond. Israel would still be able to ship freely from its Mediterranean ports, which accounted for more than 90 percent of its maritime trade, but nevertheless, closing the straits would be a grave step. Indeed, the last time Nasser closed the straits, during the Suez crisis of 1956, he provoked an Israeli attack.

Privately, Nasser had sent signals to supporters and

diplomats that he didn't want war with Israel. By May, however, he was under growing pressure from the millions of people across the Arab world who looked to him for action. On May 15, the Egyptian president sent thousands of troops into Sinai toward the Israeli border. On May 18, he ordered UN peacekeeping troops out of Sinai. The next day, Israel began to mass thousands of its own troops along the border with Sinai.

Three days later, on May 22, 1967, Gamal Abdel Nasser announced the closure of the Straits of Tiran, declaring, 'The Jews threaten us with war and we say to them, *ahlan wa sahlan* [you are welcome]. We are ready!'

As far as Israeli leaders were concerned, this was a declaration of war. That day, May 22, the Israeli government sent a request to the U.S. military for twenty thousand gas masks, and the cabinet went into crisis deliberations. For Israelis, the paralyzing time known as the 'period of waiting' had begun.

Dalia Eshkenazi unfurled the last square of black construction paper and taped it onto the window next to the other black squares. Now no light would escape. Outside, in the carport near the front gate, the family's two-cylinder 'Deux Chevaux' Citroën was similarly darkened. A day or two earlier, the police had stood on Herzl Street with brushes and cans of blue-black paint, stopping cars passing between Tel Aviv and Jerusalem and swabbing their headlights. Blackened headlights would still cast a dim path but not emit light that could be detected by enemy aircraft. Whether those jets would ever come, whether a single shot would ever be fired, no one knew. Across the country, Israelis were mobilizing: Schools were turned into shelters as citizens and soldiers dug trenches, stepped up blood drives, prepared hospital beds, made plans to send their children to Europe, and dug ten thousand graves.

Dalia was nineteen years old, but during this 'period of waiting' she often felt like crawling under a blanket. She had never felt like this, yet she understood that for others something terrible and familiar was reawakening. Later she would recall it as a 'collective fear of annihilation.' Her mother's face wore an expression of perpetual worry. As the waiting period stretched out, the family sat in excruciating silence, listening for a siren. In the Ramla shops people would engage in conversation readily, looking to one another for reassurance; other times, on the streets, they would glance at one another quickly, furtively, one nervous face flashing into the mirror of another.

The radio picked up broadcasts of a serene Egyptian voice, saying, 'Why don't you go back to where you came from? You don't stand a chance.' Dalia would lie on the blue silken cover of her parents' bed, listening to the threats of the Arabs in their accented Hebrew. In the newspapers, Dalia had read about the Arabs promising to push the Jews into the sea. At times she thought she should listen to her Western friends who insisted that the taunting voice from Cairo represented bravado and 'Oriental exaggeration.' She knew that the Israeli army, in whose officers' training corps program she now served, was strong. But in a community where people were still walking around with numbers on their arms, Dalia believed, 'one had to take sick fantasies seriously.' She was petrified; so were her parents; so were Aunt Stella and Aunt Dora. *Ma-ihey-yiheh*? everyone was desperate to know. What will happen?

* * *

On May 23, the day after Nasser closed the Straits of Tiran and taunted the Israeli public, Israel's cabinet sent Foreign Minister Abba Eban on a diplomatic mission to Paris, London, and Washington.

Officials in the Johnson administration were trying to keep Israel from attacking Egypt, while assessing whether Nasser truly wanted war, and, if he did, what the outcome would be. A CIA assessment on May 26 – part political review and part psychological analysis – surmised that Nasser's threats against Israel were made partly in response to Israel's threats to Syria, Egypt's ally: 'He probably felt he had to identify himself with Arab nationalist interests and that some action on his part would refurbish his image in the Arab world.' The CIA memorandum also suggested the Soviets had encouraged Nasser, in part because of the 'bad blood' with the U.S. over Vietnam, and that perhaps Nasser believed his forces were now strong enough to withstand an attack from Israel. In addition, the CIA report concluded, 'There may have been some element of desperation in Nasser's attitude, arising from . . . perhaps a fatalisitic conclusion that a showdown with Israel must come sooner or later, and might best be provoked before Israel acquired nuclear weapons.'

The previous day, Lucius Battle, the U.S. undersecretary of state and recent ambassador to Egypt, had suggested to the president another possible reason for Egypt's actions: that Nasser 'had gone slightly insane.' For it was clear to U.S. officials that the Egyptian forces in the Sinai were 'defensive in character' and were not preparing to invade Israel. Repeated U.S. and British intelligence estimates cited fifty thousand Egyptian troops in the Sinai. Israel's estimates, cited often by latter-day historians, are of one hundred thousand Egyptian troops – estimates Walt

Rostow of the NSC called 'highly disturbing.' The CIA had concluded that these estimates were a political 'gambit intended to influence the U.S.' to '(a) provide military supplies, (b) make more public commitments to Israel, (c) approve Israeli military initiatives, and (d) put more pressure on Nasser . . .' The U.S. had determined, in its own military analysis and in meetings with high-level British officials, that Israel would win any conflict against its Arab enemies in little more than a week. The un-ambiguous U.S. assessment of the balance of power in the region included a CIA conclusion that Israel 'can maintain internal security, defend successfully against simultaneous Arab attacks on all fronts, launch limited attacks simul-taneously on all fronts, or hold on any three fronts while mounting successfully a major offensive on the fourth.' The Israeli capabilities, another CIA assessment declared, were enhanced because 'the Arab states are hampered by a lack of cohesiveness and by friction among Arab leaders.' Another factor weighed by U.S. intelligence: Egyptian military strength was depleted by the thirty-five thousand troops Nasser had committed to fight alongside the leftist government in Yemen's civil war.

On May 26, in a meeting in Washington with President Johnson, Defense Secretary Robert McNamara, and Rostow, Abba Eban declared that the atmosphere in Israel had become 'apocalyptic,' and that Israel needed a show of support from the U.S.. McNamara assured Eban that three different intelligence groups had in recent days determined that the Egyptian deployments in the Sinai were defensive. The president told Eban that American military experts had unanimously concluded that the Egyptians would not attack, and that if they did, 'You will whip the hell out of them.' As U.S. undersecretary of state

Nicholas Katzenbach would recall, 'The intelligence was absolutely flat on the fact that the Israelis . . . could mop up the Arabs in no time at all.'

The same day, an urgent telegram arrived in Washington from the U.S. embassy in Amman with a personal message from King Hussein. 'USG [United States Government] seriously risking hostility of the entire Arab world and complete loss of influence in the area for the indefinite future by the appearance it has given to Arabs of identifying itself with Israel over the Tiran Straits and related issues,' the message declared. 'USG identification with Israel in this crisis will force America's traditional Arab friends to oppose it in order to survive Arab wrath. It is in fact already questionable, whatever position those who are America's friends might now take, whether their past association with the USG has not made them too vulnerable to survive . . .'

Now came urgent word from Israel. Also on May 26, Dean Rusk, the secretary of state, relayed a message to the president: Israeli intelligence 'indicates that an Egyptian and Syrian attack is imminent. They have therefore requested a U.S. public statement of assurance and support of Israel against such aggression.' 'Our intelligence,' Rusk noted, 'does not confirm this Israeli estimate.'

Events were spinning out of Washington's control. The next day, May 27, the president sent an urgent telegram to Prime Minister Levi Eshkol via U.S. embassy staff in Tel Aviv. 'I have just this afternoon received a most important and private message from the Soviet Union,' the president wrote. 'The Soviets tell me that they have information that you are preparing to take military action against your Arab neighbors, and provoke a conflict which would be fraught with great consequences. They emphasize their commitment to restraint on all sides and the Soviet view that solutions must be found without a military conflict. They tell us that they know the Arabs do not wish a military conflict.' At three o'clock that same morning in Cairo, the Soviet ambassador to Egypt had paid a personal call to Nasser, waking the president to urge him not to go to war.

In Amman, however, there was a growing sense that war was inevitable. On May 28, King Hussein told the Egyptian ambassador to Jordan that he believed Israel was going to launch a surprise attack against Egypt. Two days later, the king flew to Cairo and signed a defense pact with Nasser, stunning onlookers. Only days earlier, the two leaders had been insulting each other, competing for the hearts and minds of the Arab public, as the king secretly pleaded with the U.S. to moderate its position in the region. Now, in joining Nasser, King Hussein had crossed the point of no return.

Hussein had surmised that without an alliance with Nasser, Jordan would be more vulnerable, on the one hand, to an attack from Israel or, on the other, from Palestinians within his own kingdom who would equate any inaction with betraying the Arab cause. Now Hussein was forging a pan-Arab alliance on the eve of battle. He had even agreed to place the forces of his Arab Legion, along with Iraqi, Syrian, and Saudi troops, under the eastern front command of an Egyptian general, Abdul Munim Riad. Riad would operate from a command post in Amman. When the king returned home, he was greeted by throngs of elated Palestinians; the crowds hoisted the king's car and carried it along the street.

In Israel, tension in Prime Minister Eshkol's cabinet had led to a rupture, forcing him to form a unity government with his more hawkish opposition critics. Moshe

Dayan, the commander of Battalion Eighty-nine in 1948 Ramla and Lod, was named minister of defense. The new cabinet dispatched Israel's intelligence chief, Mossad director Meir Amit, on another trip to Washington. He met with McNamara, who was increasingly preoccupied with Vietnam. The American defense secretary listened as the Israeli intelligence chief told him that 'I, Meir Amit, am going to recommend that our government strike.' Amit had come in large part to assess the American reaction to this statement. 'There's no way out,' he recalled telling McNamara. McNamara asked Amit how long a war would last. 'Seven days,' replied the Israeli.

American officials had been considering their own show of force: A U.S.- and British-led convoy of Western ships to steam through the Straits of Tiran to send a signal to Nasser that all nations, including Israel, should enjoy maritime rights of free passage. The plan, however, met with resistance among some U.S. generals, who believed that if an American ship drew fire, the result would be war – only this time, the U.S. would be directly involved. In a world dominated by two nuclear superpowers, there was no telling where that might lead. With scant international support, the convoy plan faded.

All signs continued to point toward war, except that Nasser privately continued to express aversion to it. On May 31, he told former American treasury secretary Robert Anderson, a longtime acquaintance, that he would not 'begin any fight.' The two men discussed a possible visit to Cairo by Hubert Humphrey, the U.S. vice president, and Anderson laid the groundwork for a visit to Washington by Egyptian vice president Zakariya Mohieddin. Two days later, on June 2, Nasser told British MP Christopher Mayhew, that Egypt had 'no intention of attacking Israel.' At the same time, Nasser had made it clear he would not back down from his position on the Straits of Tiran, and on the same day that he pledged to Mayhew not to fire the first shot, Nasser sent an impassioned telegram to President Johnson. At stake, Nasser assured the president, was something more important than the Straits of Tiran or the withdrawal of UN forces. Rather, he said, it was about defending 'the rights of the people of Palestine':

> An aggressive armed force was able to oust that people from their country and reduce them to refugees on the borders of their homeland. Today the forces of aggression impede the Arab people's established right of return and life in their homeland . . . I may ask how far any government is able to control the feelings of more than one million Palestinians who, for twenty years, the international community – whose responsibility herein is inescapable – has failed to secure their return to their homeland. The UN General Assembly, merely confirms that right, at every session.

Nasser repeated his position that 'our forces have not initiated any aggressive act,' but added, 'no doubt, we shall resist any aggression launched against us or against any Arab state.'

On June 3, a new CIA memorandum suggested war was all but certain. 'All reports indicate that the Israelis are still confident of victory,' the report stated, but cited 'the rapidly-growing belief in Israel that time is running out, and that if Israel is not to suffer an ultimately fatal defeat it must very soon either strike or obtain absolutely iron-clad security assurances from the West . . . The Israeli strategy calls for gaining control of the air as the first essential step in the campaign.' In Sinai, the report noted, the Egyptians had set up only 'the rudiments of an air defense system'; nevertheless, 'the Arabs are sniffing blood. So fast and so far does Nasser's band-wagon seem to be rolling . . .'

Still, as Israel sent its troops to the Sinai border, many analysts continued to believe that Nasser's bellicose actions amounted to a bluff for Arab consumption. 'They were meant to be seen as a strong warning, not a declaration of war,' wrote Nasser's confidant, Mohamed Heikal. Some Israelis also doubted Nasser was planning an attack. 'The force initially concentrated in Sinai could not hope of defending the area in the event of war,' an Israeli military intelligence analyst would write in a review of the war published by Israel's Ministry of Defense. 'I do not believe that Nasser wanted war,' Rabin would say later. In his June 2 telegram to Johnson, Nasser welcomed the possibility of a visit to Cairo by Humphrey to discuss the crisis, and, as discussed two days earlier with Robert Anderson, he was preparing to dispatch Vice President Mohieddin to Washington. Mohieddin was to make a 'routine' UN visit in New York, then meet secretly with President Johnson and other administration officials on or about June 7. Administration officials discussed whether they should inform Israel of this secret visit. Nasser held high hopes for the visit: While 'supremely confident,' Anderson reported, the Egyptian president 'earnestly desires friendship of U.S.'

Yet while Nasser privately expressed his preference for a peaceful solution, to the rest of the world the voices coming out of Cairo seemed certain of war and confident of victory. Nasser himself had declared, at a press conference on May 28, 'We are prepared, our sons are prepared, our army is prepared, and the entire Arab nation is prepared.' A broadcast from the Voice of Cairo dared Israel to strike: 'We challenge you, Eshkol, to try all your weapons. Put them to the test, they will spell Israel's death and annihilation.'

To Bashir and his family, words like these meant the enemy would be vanquished and the family would return home. To Dalia and her family, the words meant what they said – annihilation. Whatever their intent, Nasser's choice of words amounted to a monumental gamble. Israeli general Matitiahu Peled would call it 'unheard-of foolishness.' Despite King Hussein's warnings of a preemptive Israeli strike, Nasser was in for the surprise of his life.

At 7:45 A.M. on Monday, June 5, 1967, French-built Israeli bombers roared out of their bases and crossed into Egyptian airspace. Flying below radar, the jets angled toward Egyptian bases in Sinai, the Nile delta, and Cairo. Fifteen minutes later, tanks and infantry of Israel's Seventh Armored Brigade moved west into Gaza and toward the Sinai frontier. The war with Egypt had begun. No action at that hour was taken against Jordan, Iraq, or Syria. At 9:00 A.M., Prime Minister Eshkol sent a message to King Hussein through the chief United Nations observer: 'We shall not initiate any action whatsoever against Jordan. However, should Jordan open hostilities, we shall react with all our might, and the king will have to bear the full responsibility for the consequences.'

A few hours later, Bashir stood up from the plaintiff's table in the Ramallah courtroom. It was late on the morning of June 5, a moment after the young man had come into the courtroom and whispered something important into Bashir's ear.

'Your Honor!' Bashir bellowed. He was surprised how loud his voice sounded. The other lawyer stopped in mid-sentence; everyone in the courtroom stared at Bashir. 'I have just received word that the war has begun on the Egyptian and Jordanian fronts.'

'Stop the proceedings!' exclaimed the judge. 'And someone bring in a radio!'

Bashir left the courtroom in excitement and raced home. On the streets, people were dashing in and out of shops, stocking up on canned food, candles, kerosene, and tape for the windows. Others waited in long lines outside the flour mills. On the sidewalks, men crowded around tables beneath overhead speakers, smoking from water pipes and straining to hear the radio. The city was expectant, not only of war, but of the annual throngs of summer visitors that would flock here after the victory. Nineteen years after the Nakba had transformed Ramallah, the city had again become a summer haven for the Arab world, with twenty-one hotels and an annual musical theater festival attended by families from Libya to Kuwait. During high season, the restaurants would stay open until 2:00 A.M. and reopen two hours later. Preparations for the festival were almost finished, and now it seemed the revelers would mark a more profound celebration: Palestine would again be in the hands of the Arabs.

At home Bashir found Ahmad, Zakia, Nuha, and other siblings transfixed before the radio. Egyptian antiaircraft fire had shot down three-quarters of the attacking Israeli jets, the Voice of the Arabs reported from Cairo. The deep, trusted voice belonged to Ahmad Said, who assured his rapt listeners that the Egyptian air force had launched a counterattack against Israel. Israeli forces had penetrated Sinai, but Egyptian troops had engaged the enemy and taken the offensive. Jordan, the Voice of the Arabs announced, had captured Mt. Scopus, a strategic hill in Jerusalem.

The Arabs were winning, Bashir thought. *The Arabs were winning.* Incredible as it seemed, the family would be going home. Umm Kulthum, the Arab world's most beloved singer and, next to Nasser, the biggest living symbol of Arab unity, would soon be singing in Tel Aviv.

'We thought the victory was in our hands,' Bashir would say thirty-seven years later. 'That we would be victorious and we would be going back home. After nineteen years we really had the very strong feeling that we were going back to our lands, houses, streets, schools – to our lives. That we would get our freedom back, that we would be liberated, that we would get back to the homeland. Sorry to say, that was not the case. It was an illusion.'

By the time Bashir and his family heard the reports of the Egyptian advances, Gamal Abdel Nasser's entire air force lay smoking on tarmacs in Cairo, Sinai, and the Nile delta. Israel's surprise attack of five hundred sorties had destroyed virtually all of Egypt's Soviet-built fighter jets, and now the Jewish state had the sky over Sinai all to itself. During the attack, begun as Egyptian air force command personnel were finishing breakfast and driving to work, the chief of Egypt's armed forces sent a coded message to his counterparts in Jordan, describing early Egyptian victories. Jordanian radar analysts, seeing planes flying toward Tel Aviv, concluded the Egyptian claims were accurate: The intense radar activity, they believed, showed Egyptian jets on the attack, not Israeli fighters returning to base to refuel. Invoking the mutual defense pact, the commander in chief of the Egyptian forces authorized the next step in the plan: the Jordanian offensive against Israel.

By this time, King Hussein had received Prime Minister Eshkol's message promising that Israel would not attack Jordan first and warning of the consequences should Jordan fire the first shot. The king, however, was bound to the pact with Egypt and believed the message from Eshkol was a ploy to help Israel dispense with Egypt first. Only then, Hussein feared, would Israel turn its full military attention to Jordan and the West Bank.

At 11:00 A.M., Jordanian forces began firing long-range artillery toward Israeli suburbs near Tel Aviv and at an airfield at Ramat David. Fifteen minutes later, Jordanian howitzers began firing thousands of shells on neighborhoods and military targets in Jewish parts of Jerusalem. Within an hour, Jordanian, Syrian, and Iraqi fighter jets were slicing into Israeli airspace as Jordanian infantry churned forward toward Israeli positions.

'Brother Arabs everywhere,' promised a broadcast from Jordan, 'the enemy this morning has launched an aggression on our Arab land and air-space.' 'The Zionist barracks in Palestine,' declared Ahmad Said from Cairo, 'is about to be destroyed.' Such triumphal messages would have thrilled Bashir's family and terrified Dalia's; Egyptian claims that its troops had crossed Israel's border and were marching toward the Negev desert actually prompted some Israelis to hang white flags in surrender.

The facts told a different story. By midafternoon of June 5, the air forces of Jordan, Syria, Iraq, and Egypt had all been demolished. Israeli pilots now patrolled the entire region virtually unchallenged and were free to attack Egyptian ground troops in Sinai or Jordanian infantry moving toward

Jerusalem. From this point, the outcome of the war was written. The Six Day War was essentially decided in six hours.

Bashir could hear explosions. The headquarters of the Jordanian army in Ramallah was crumbling under Israeli fire. Then, another series of thunderous booms: the sound of Ramallah's main radio transmitter going down. And two more, ripping into the soccer field at the Quaker School up the road. Bashir and his family assumed these attacks would soon be answered and that reinforcements – Iraqis or more troops from Jordan – would fortify the city. Surely the Arab armies understood the strategic importance of Ramallah, a key transport hub and center of West Bank communications. Army officers, it was said, had been ordered to defend Ramallah at all costs. Soon, however, there would be reports of Jordanian troops wiped out when they tried to reach Jerusalem from Jericho, as Israeli flares lit up the road and fighter jets obliterated an entire infantry battalion. Word would come of desperate fighting in Jerusalem. Some accounts said the Israelis had the Old City completely surrounded. It wasn't clear where the reinforcements for Ramallah would be coming from. Bashir listened to the explosions continuing through the night and into the next day, shaking the city and its confidence.

At noon on Tuesday, June 6, General Riad, the Egyptian in charge of the eastern front forces, sent an urgent message from Amman to his counterparts in Cairo. 'The situation in the West Bank is rapidly deteriorating,' Riad warned. 'A concentrated attack has been launched on all [points], together with heavy fire, day and night. Jordanian, Syrian and Iraqi air forces in position H3 have been virtually destroyed.' Riad had been consulting with King Hussein. The general posed a series of terrible choices to the command headquarters in Cairo: cease-fire, retreat, or fighting for one more day in the West Bank, 'resulting in the isolation and destruction of the entire Jordanian Army.' The cable requested an immediate reply.

Half an hour later, an answer came from Cairo, advising the Jordanians to withdraw from the West Bank and arm the general population. As this reply was coming in, the king sent a telegram to Nasser, underscoring the unfolding calamity on the Jordanian front and asking the Egyptian president for his advice. Nasser replied that evening, repeating the counsel of his men in uniform. The Jordanian army, Nasser urged, should vacate the West Bank while Arab leaders pressed for a ceasefire.

In the light of the early evening of June 6, Bashir stood on the roof of an apartment building in Ramallah, facing south. It was warm and clear but for the dark pillars of smoke rising from the direction of Jerusalem and the haze around the Mount of Olives just to the east. Bashir squinted through the smoke, out past the Amari refugee camp that had grown after 1948 and toward the tower at the Qalandia airstrip, where he had landed from Gaza with his father ten years earlier. There he could see a line of tanks and jeeps moving north. As news of the approaching troops reached the streets below, some Palestinians joyfully began preparing to greet them. They assumed these would be the Iraqi reinforcements. Bashir remained on the roof, his left hand characteristically in his pocket, and fixed his gaze on the road to the south. Slowly, as the tanks came closer, he surmised that they were not Iraqi.

Ramallah fell on the night of June 6 as Israeli ground

forces moved in from the south and west. There was little resistance; eyewitnesses would later say many Jordanian troops had retreated well before the Israelis ever arrived. In some cases, the departing Arab soldiers forgot to leave keys for the weapons storehouses, ostensibly stocked with English rifles for the people of Ramallah to repel the invading Israelis. The Jordanian army's main accomplishment in Ramallah, Bashir would remember wryly, was in urging people to get out of the line of fire. 'The Jordanian army was asking people to go inside their houses,' he said. 'That was the extent of their contribution. We didn't feel that they were really fighting.'

In fact, from Jenin in the northern West Bank to Ramallah, Jerusalem, and Hebron farther south, the Jordanian army was without air cover or radar and defenseless to repeated bombings of its ground troops from Israel's French-built fighter jets. The Jordanians had suffered devastating losses, and because of the constant air attacks they were unable to send supplies or reinforcements to the front lines. By late on June 6, as Israeli troops penetrated the West Bank and stood poised at the walls of the Old City of Jerusalem, King Hussein's forces were in retreat across the Jordan River, to what was left of his kingdom.

By late on June 6, Dalia knew that the war was won. She experienced it not with elation – not yet, since the fighting was still going on – but rather with a sense that a miracle was taking place in Israel. *How could this have happened?* she thought again and again. *Did God save us? How can this be?*

With the news the previous day that Israel had destroyed the Egyptian, Syrian, and Jordanian air forces, Dalia felt a profound relief such as she had never experienced, just as before the war she had never felt such horror. For Moshe and Solia, the feeling tapped something old, from twenty-four years earlier: the moment when they learned that the Bulgarian authorities had suspended the deportation orders for the Jews and that they would not be boarding train cars for Poland.

On the morning of Wednesday, June 7, Bashir and his family woke up to a city under military occupation. Israeli soldiers in jeeps were shouting through bullhorns, demanding that white flags be hung outside houses, shops, and apartment buildings; already balconies and windows fluttered with T-shirts and handkerchiefs.

Bashir was in shock from the surreal and the familiar. Another retreating Jordanian army had been replaced by another occupying Israeli force. *In 1948*, Bashir thought, *we lost 78 percent of our land. And now all of Palestine is under occupation.* The taste was bitter and humiliating. Not only did the Israelis capture and occupy the West Bank and the Gaza Strip, they now held the Egyptian Sinai Peninsula. Perhaps most shocking of all was that East Jerusalem, and the Old City with its holy sites, was now in the hands of the Israelis.

On the evening of June 10, Solia was visiting with Dora and Stella in the addition that had been built onto the house for the two aunts. The women sat at the kitchen table, eating their traditional supper of garlic and Bulgarian cheese, when Dalia burst into the room.

'Get up, get up!' she shouted to her mother and her aunts. 'The war is over!' Moshe heard the commotion and joined them. In the final phase of the war, Israel had captured the Golan Heights from Syria. At 6:30 that evening, the United Nations imposed a cease-fire; the shooting and shelling had stopped. Everyone began jumping wildly, laughing and hugging and kissing one another.

In the evening, Dalia gathered her family and began to dance: slowly at first, arms extended, neck tilted, head back, eyes half-open, loose skirt shifting softly around her. She spun slowly between the walls of Jerusalem stone. Gradually the other women of the family joined Dalia, and they formed a circle, hands on one another's shoulders, moving to the hora, the Israeli national dance. Solia and Dora and Stella and Dalia swayed through the open house, out to the yard, past the jacaranda tree and the lemon tree, laughing and weeping.

As they circled through the yard, Dalia looked up at the night sky and sang: 'David the king of Israel is alive. Alive and present. David is alive . . .' She would always remember this night and its abiding sense of miracle and liberation.

Within a week, refugees began arriving in Ramallah from villages near Latrun. Every villager from Beit Nuba, Imwas, and Yalo had been ordered out of their homes and sent north toward Ramallah; those who tried to return were blocked by a line of tanks and soldiers shooting in the air. Nineteen years earlier, Israeli soldiers commandeering buses had dumped the people of al-Ramla at the edges of these villages as they began their march in the punishing sun to Salbit. Now the villages themselves were emptied and several thousand of the ten thousand residents had taken refuge in Ramallah – a small portion of the more than two hundred thousand Palestinians who would be displaced by the 1967 war.

In Ramallah, life was transformed. The summer theater

festival and countless other plans were canceled abruptly. Israeli soldiers took the place of Jordanian police, and the prisons began to fill with young Palestinian men. Within weeks, the authorities announced a new justice system to be administered by occupation judges sitting in the West Bank. But the Israelis had a problem: Almost no Arab lawyers would come to court. A general strike had rendered the new Israeli courts virtually silent and empty. The strike had been organized, the Israeli authorities would soon learn, by a young West Bank lawyer named Bashir Khairi.

Bashir and dozens of other Ramallah lawyers had begun meeting secretly with clients in private homes. The occupation authorities threatened him and the other organizers with jail time and enticed them with reduced sentences for clients already in prison. 'As long as there's an Israeli flag behind the judge in the courthouse,' Bashir told an Israeli colonel, 'I won't be representing my people.' An Israeli judge told Bashir he would release fifteen Palestinians accused of illegal demonstrations if Bashir simply showed up in court to represent them. Bashir refused, as did almost every other lawyer in similar circumstances: Of the eighty lawyers in Ramallah, Bashir would recount, only five took part in the new system. Now nearly anytime a new trial would be called, the court would be vacant except for the accused and his accusers. Civil matters went underground entirely. People began to resolve their disputes in private, creating an alternative system in the face of a collective enemy.

As the occupation wore on, a sense of calm and clarity began to settle over Bashir. The loss was devastating, but it made one thing clear: Palestinians could rely only on themselves to deliver their own justice. It was clear that the right of return, guaranteed by United Nations Resolution 194, would never be delivered by the UN or the international community. Return was subsequently promised by the Arab states whose armed forces instead were crushed and humiliated. The Arab states still put up a rhetorical front – in the days after the war, they would publicly declare 'no reconciliation, no negotiation, and no recognition' regarding Israel – but these were increasingly taken as empty words by Palestinians.

Strangely, though, in the midst of occupation and the utter failure of the Arab regimes, a sense of freedom was emerging: a notion that the Palestinians were suddenly free to think and act for themselves. In the weeks after the occupation, Bashir began to believe that his people would go back to their homeland only through the sweat and blood of Palestinian armed struggle. He was far from alone in this assessment.

In the wake of the June 1967 war and the Israeli occupation, the pan-Arab movement was in shreds, but the spirit of a Palestinian national liberation struggle was surging. Thousands of young men signed up to become fedayeen – freedom fighters, or, literally, 'those who sacrifice.' Their goal was to 'liberate Palestine' and guarantee the right of return by any means necessary. The ranks of Fatah, led by Arafat and Abu Jihad, swelled, and soon a new organization, the Popular Front for the Liberation of Palestine (PFLP), would be born from an alliance with the pro-Nasser Arab Nationalist Movement. Its leader was Dr. George Habash, the refugee from Lydda.

Across the West Bank and in exile, young men confronted their parents with their plans. Fathers demanded their sons seek the safety of higher education in Cairo or London; one son, a young man named Bassam Abu-

Sharif, asked his father, 'What is a PhD when we have no country?' He did not want to be 'an eternal foreigner, a landless, homeless, stateless, shamed, despised Palestinian refugee.' Bassam, after joining the PFLP, would recall telling his angry father, 'I would rather be in prison in my own country than be a free man in exile. I would rather be dead.'

For now, though, Palestinians would find themselves returning to their homes not in triumph, but simply to ask permission to peer inside.

The great paradox of the occupation was that suddenly historic Palestine was easier to reach than at any time since 1948. Within days of Israel's capture and annexation of East Jerusalem, the boundary that had separated Hussein's Hashemite kingdom from Israel and West Jerusalem became nearly invisible. At the same time, all along the old West Bank-Israel border – also known as the Green Line – Israeli soldiers had been redeployed to other fronts to patrol the vastly expanded occupied territories. Therefore, there were far fewer Israeli soldiers along the Green Line. By late June, it had become easier for Palestinian families to cross into their old homeland and touch the soil and stones of earlier days.

This is how Bashir and his cousins found themselves in the West Jerusalem bus station in the summer of 1967, where they climbed onto the 1965 Royal Tiger and rolled west, past the ruins of old Arab villages, past the husks of burned-out Israeli jeeps covered with bouquets, down the hill to the Latrun Valley, past the cement factory, across the railroad tracks, and into al-Ramla, where a young woman named Dalia was sitting in her yard, staring into the leaves of a jacaranda tree.

Nine

ENCOUNTER

THE BELL RANG, and Dalia, jolted from her contemplation, got up from the veranda and walked through the house to the front door. She picked up a large key and trotted lightly down the path to the green metal gate. '*Rak rega* – just a moment!' Dalia called out, using both hands to raise the heavy key to the lock. She opened the gate partway and looked out from the open space between gate and pillar.

Three men were standing there stiffly in their coats and ties, in the middle of the stifling Israeli summer heat. It was July 1967, a few weeks after the end of the Six Day War. The men appeared to be in their twenties. Dalia knew immediately that they were Arabs.

'*Ken?*' Dalia said. 'Yes?'

The men looked uncomfortable, as if they didn't know what to say now that Dalia had asked them their business. For a moment they remained quiet, but Dalia knew why they had come.

'As soon as I saw them,' she remembered, 'I felt, *Wow, it's them.* It was as if I'd always been waiting for them.'

Now the youngest one, the one with a thin face and large brown eyes, opened his mouth.

'This was my father's house,' said the young man in his halting English. 'And I lived here, too.'

Dalia was ready for what came next.

'Would it be possible,' the young man asked, 'for us to come in and see the house?'

Dalia Eshkenazi knew she had very little time to process this question and respond. Logic dictated she tell the men to come back when her parents were home. If she allowed them to come in, what would that be inviting?

Bashir gazed at the woman. She hadn't responded to his question. Fresh in his mind was the terrible reception Yasser had received at his childhood home only an hour earlier. At least Ghiath, his other cousin, had seen his old house, now converted to a school for Israeli children. This young woman, whoever she was, seemed to be taking her time.

Dalia looked at the three young men. They were quiet and apprehensive. She knew that if she told them to come back later, she might never see them again. Yet if she opened the door, she might not be able to close it. So many thoughts were rushing through her head. She needed to integrate them quickly into a response.

'Yes,' Dalia Eshkenazi said finally to the three Arab men at her gate. She smiled broadly. 'Please, come in.'

Bashir looked at the striking young woman with short dark hair. She was smiling at him, holding open his father's metal gate.

'Please come in,' Bashir thought he heard the woman say. He watched as she turned to walk up the stone path toward the house.

Was this possible? Bashir looked at his cousins. Had the Israeli woman really said to follow her? He stood at the gate, frozen, doubting everything. The men remained planted as the woman disappeared into the house. Bashir looked at Yasser. 'I am sure she said, "You are welcome,"' he told his cousin. A moment later, the woman's head appeared again in the doorway. She was looking at them quizzically.

'Are you sure we can come in?' Bashir managed in his stiff English.

'Yes.' The woman laughed. 'Please, come up the path.'

Bashir would recall stepping gingerly, one stone to the next, taking care not to step on the grass growing between them. He turned back to his cousins, who were still immobile at the gate. 'Follow me,' he said to Yasser and Ghiath. 'Come,' he said. 'Come into my house.'

Dalia stood in the doorway, still smiling as the men came up the path. She knew it was not advisable in the wake of war for a young Israeli woman to invite three Arab men inside her house. This prospect, however, did not unnerve her in the least. Dalia had sensed a vulnerability in these young men, and she was certain they had no intention of harming her. She felt safe.

'Please, give me five minutes,' Dalia told the men. 'Only five minutes.' She wanted the inside of the place to look nice, so that her visitors would have a good image of the house and the people living in it.

Bashir barely heard her. He was taking in the garden: purple and yellow flowers shaped like candles and closed against the sun; the flowering *fitna* tree his mother had told him about, exploding from the branches in brilliant white and yellow; thick, deep red roses from abundant bushes. Behind the house stood a palm tree, its gray tufts rising into broad green leaves far above the roof. In the backyard, he hoped, the lemon tree would still be standing.

Bashir fixed his gaze upon the wooden front door, the one his father had always knocked on when he came home from work, before July 1948, announcing his arrival and bursting through the door as Bashir raced toward him.

What was taking her so long? It had seemed much longer than five minutes. What was she doing? Could she be calling the police? The cousins grew increasingly wary.

Bashir could see the white Jerusalem stone his father had laid with his own hands thirty-one years earlier. If he were standing a bit closer, Bashir could run his fingertips along its cratered surface, its miniature hills and valleys like the landscape of Palestine itself.

'You can come inside now,' the young woman was saying. She had reappeared in the doorway. 'You are welcome. Come in, feel at home.' It was a universal welcome – Make yourself at home; *Mi casa es su casa; Ahlan wa-sahlan; Baruch habah* – yet these particular words seemed especially strange to Bashir as he approached the front door: Feel at home.

The cousins crossed the threshold: Bashir first, followed by Yasser and Ghiath. Bashir took a few careful steps and looked around, standing in silence, breathing in the large open room, exhaling, breathing it in again. It was much as he had pictured it: spare and clean. He would recall feeling as if he were in a mosque; as if he, Bashir, were a holy man.

Dalia would recall leading the cousins through each room, wanting them to feel welcome and comfortable. After the initial tour, she told them to take their time and experience the house as they wished to. She withdrew, watching them with fascination.

Bashir looked like a man in a trance. He floated down hallways and in and out of doorways, touching tile, glass, wood, painted plaster wall, absorbing the tactile feel of every surface.

'And I had a sense that they were walking in a temple, in silence,' Dalia would remember many years later. 'And that every step meant so much to them.'

Bashir stopped in front of the open door to a small bedroom in the corner of the house, near the backyard. He could hear Dalia's voice behind him. 'This is my bedroom,' she said.

'Yes,' Bashir said. 'And it was mine.'

Dalia looked up at the wall above her bed. On it she had tacked a picture of a beaming, blue-eyed Israeli soldier from a cover of *Life* magazine – the archetype of the Israeli Sabra. The soldier was standing chest high in the Suez Canal, his Uzi thrust above his head at the end of the Six Day War. To Dalia the image stood for liberation, for warding off a threat, and for survival. Standing with Bashir in the doorway to the bedroom, she suddenly realized, for the first time, that Bashir might see that poster differently.

Bashir would recall Dalia saying, 'I think you left the house when you were very young. Maybe the same year we came.'

Bashir wanted to explode, to yell, *We didn't 'leave' the house! You forced us out!* Instead he said, 'We haven't been properly introduced. My name is Bashir Khairi. And these are my cousins Ghiath and Yasser.'

Dalia introduced herself and told them she was on summer vacation from Tel Aviv University. She took care not to tell them she was in the officers' training corps for the Israel Defense Forces. This was partly because they were Arabs and she was a Jew; it was also because she had felt, welling up from within her, a surge of *akhrayut*: responsibility, or, literally, an ability to respond to the other. Questions from her childhood returned: What was an Arab house? Who had lived here before? Why did they leave? She realized that these men would have answers. She thought: *Finally I have opened a door that has so long been closed*. Dalia would recall this moment as the beginning of her quest toward understanding.

'And now,' Dalia said, 'will you allow me to treat you as guests? May I offer you something to drink?'

As guests, Bashir thought. *Should a person be a guest in his own house?* 'I don't mind at all,' he said quickly to Dalia. 'Yes, thank you.'

'Let's sit in the garden,' Dalia said, pointing toward the backyard. 'It's very beautiful. What would you like? Lemonade? Turkish coffee?'

The three cousins sat in the sun in the garden. Bashir's eyes were like the lens of a camera, taking in exterior walls, window frames, roofline. He recorded soil, sand, branches, leaves, fruit. He even recorded the blades of grass growing out between the layers of stone on the house. Now his eyes rested on the lemon tree, standing in the corner of the garden.

'I don't think they changed anything in the house,' Yasser said.

'Only the furniture,' Bashir replied.

Dalia came with drinks – Bashir would remember small cups of Turkish coffee; Dalia is certain she served lemonade. 'I hope that this visit gave you some rest,' she said, placing small china cups and saucers – or perhaps it was the glasses of lemonade – before each cousin.

'Of course, of course,' Bashir said.

They made quiet small talk and listened to one another sip. After a few minutes, Yasser stood up. 'I think it's time to go,' he said. Bashir, however, wasn't quite ready.

'Could you give me permission to have another look at the house?' he asked Dalia.

227

She answered with a smile. 'Of course! Feel at home.'

Bashir looked at Yasser. 'I'm going to go for just a minute,' he said.

A few minutes later, Dalia and Bashir were facing each other again at the gate. 'I hope we will meet again,' said Dalia.

'Yes, of course, Dalia,' Bashir said. 'I hope to see you again. And one day you must come to visit us in Ramallah.'

'How will I know where to find you?'

'When you arrive in Ramallah, ask anyone,' said Bashir. 'They will show you to my home.'

The cousins climbed onto the Israeli bus and sat as before, one behind the other. They rode east in silence, exhausted. They had seen their houses; now what? On the way home, there were no surprises and everything looked more familiar. Bashir gazed out the window at nothing, aware of a new burden resting like stones on his chest.

Bashir climbed the concrete steps to the house in Ramallah. He opened the door and found his sisters and brothers, Ahmad, and Zakia all waiting for the returning traveler. In the middle, in a chair at the kitchen table, sat Ahmad. Bashir couldn't bear it. 'I am very tired,' he said. 'The way was long and the story is longer. Let me rest first, and tomorrow I will tell you everything.' It was only 6:00 P.M.

'Sleep, my son,' Ahmad said, his eyes watering. 'Sleep, *habibi*, my dear son.'

In the morning the family was waiting. Bashir took his time, recounting every moment of the journey with his cousins. Everyone pumped Bashir with questions –

everyone, that is, except Ahmad, who remained quiet while the others demanded a replay of Bashir's every step, his every touch of stone. Did the light still stream in through the south windows in the afternoon? Were the pillars on the gate still standing straight? Was the front gate still painted olive green? Was the paint chipping? 'If it still is,' Zakia said, 'when you go back you can bring a can of paint to make it new again, Bashir; you can bring shears and cut the grass growing up along the stone path. How is the lemon tree, does it look nice? Did you bring the fruit? . . . You didn't? Did you rub the leaves and smell them, did your fingers smell like fresh-cut lemons? How were the stones of the house, were they still cool and rough to the touch? . . . What else, Bashir, what else? Please don't leave anything out.'

Throughout the interrogation, Ahmad had been still as a mountain, his eyes watering. Abruptly he stood, pushing back his chair. Tears streaked his face as he left the kitchen and walked down the hallway. All eyes followed Ahmad, but no one dared call him back. He closed the bedroom door.

'God forgive you, my son,' Zakia said. 'You have opened our wounds again.'

In the summer of 1967, conversations like that of the Khairis were taking place throughout the West Bank and Gaza. Hundreds, perhaps thousands of Palestinians had made pilgrimages across the Green Line to childhood homes. They came back burdened with bittersweet accounts of a garden in bloom, of a stone archway with the Arabic script scratched out, of a piano out of tune, of a key that still fit the lock, of wooden doors opened and iron doors slammed shut. It hardly mattered whether a refugee was old enough to remember his home; the landscape and the dream of return were imbibed with mother's milk, so that if there was no memory, there nevertheless seemed to be.

Generations unborn in 1948 spoke the details of neighborhoods in villages destroyed before they were born. For these families there was only the earth itself, and occasionally the rubble of an old cornerstone, to visit and record; yet in Jaffa, Haifa, West Jerusalem, Lydda, and al-Ramla, where the old Arab houses still stood, Palestinians could retrieve tactile proof of their memories: a sprig from an olive tree, a stone from the garden, a handful of figs. Later that summer, Bashir and his younger brother Kamel returned from a second visit to Dalia and the house in al-Ramla; Kamel, despite being only a year old in 1948, swore he remembered the home. The younger brother had accepted a gift of four lemons from Dalia, which he delivered into the hands of his father. Ahmad placed one of them in a glass case in the living room.

Such physical proof of loss only deepened the longing and made even more fervent the wish to go home. The Six Day War may have made the return of the refugees less likely than ever; but to Bashir, his family, and hundreds of thousands of refugees in the camps of the West Bank and Gaza, the sudden nearness of the lost gardens made exile even more intolerable. In the summer of 1967, the dream of return was as ferocious as ever.

In late June 1967, Yasser Arafat and a small band of fellow self-styled revolutionaries snuck across the Jordan River into the Israeli-occupied West Bank. The Palestinian *cadres*, as the fighters were known, wore black and moved through the Jordan Valley at night, evading low-flying aircraft and the spotlights of Israel's patrolling helicopters. Many of the hundreds of *cadres* crossing the river that summer had been trained in Syria; they slung old rifles, Swedish-made machine guns, and Russian-built Kalashnikovs over their shoulders and stuffed land mines, grenades, bullets, and explosive charges into their seventy-five-pound backpacks.

Since New Year's Day 1965, Arafat, Abu Jihad, and other *cadres* from Fatah had been launching small raids into Israel, mostly at military and industrial targets. For the most part, the attacks had had little practical effect. Yet the raids were significant on a psychological level. For Israel, the attacks had rattled a population for whom safety and security were paramount; for Palestinians and the world, in the words of fellow revolutionary Bassam Abu-Sharif, the attacks demonstrated 'that the Palestinian spirit was not crushed . . . that the Palestinian people would never give up, that they would fight with whatever came to hand, by whatever means they could, to recover their dignity and their lost lands, to get justice.'

Still, Arafat knew that a relative handful of young men waging cross-border hit-and-run raids with homemade explosives and old rifles could not actually change the status quo; he wanted to build an insurgency from within Palestine. He led his *cadres* to set up operations to relaunch armed struggle against Israel from the West Bank.

In July 1967, around the time Bashir and his cousins rode the bus to al-Ramla, Arafat traveled in disguise from one West Bank town to another, organizing secret cells to attack across the Green Line. He and his men slept in a network of caves north of Ramallah, much as Sheikh Izzadin al-Qassam had done in the Great Arab Rebellion of the 1930s. Arafat had quickly realized how fast he needed to move. Already the Shin Bet, Israel's domestic intelligence service, had established a formidable network of Palestinian informants whose eyes and ears recorded every revolutionary movement. In exchange the collaborators received money, traveling papers, or leniency for a brother or a father in jail. Each of Arafat's moves was therefore carefully calculated to avoid arrest. The legend of Abu Amar, Arafat's nom de guerre, was built largely on the stories of his narrow escapes: of the time he crawled out a back window as soldiers came through the front door; or when he eluded capture by dressing as an old woman; or when Israeli soldiers arrived at Arafat's cave to find his coffee still steaming on the fire.

Arafat was keenly aware of the power of symbolism. In photographs, the young revolutionary was always in military fatigues and dark glasses, his keffiyeh fashioned painstakingly into the shape of historic Palestine. The iconography and the actions of Arafat, his fellow Fatah leader Abu Jihad, and the other *cadres* invigorated a population disgusted by a second devastating defeat and subsequent occupation. They reinforced the conviction, held by Bashir and thousands of others, that the path to liberation could be determined only by the Palestinians themselves. The Soviet Union was rearming Egypt and Syria after their air forces were reduced to smoking ruins by the Israelis; Syria continued to aid Fatah; but it was increasingly clear to Palestinians that the Arab states would never again join forces to fight Israel. Even if they would, the rhetoric of the Arab leaders was taken as empty talk by Palestinians who felt they had been fooled by such promises of liberation in the past. Palestinians now understood that their painful longing for home would have to be answered from within. Arafat knew this instinctively; he captured his people's imagination with his slogans of 'Revolution Until Victory,' 'In Soul and Blood We Sacrifice for Palestine,' and 'We Shall Return.'

As September arrived in Ramallah, the lawyers' strike showed no signs of waning. Bashir and his fellow attorneys dug in, using the strike to protest both the occupation of the West Bank and the recent annexation of East Jerusalem by Israel. For the Israelis, the annexation would unite both sides of Jerusalem and provide Jews with permanent access to holy sites, including the Temple Mount; for the Arabs of East Jerusalem, whose dream was to have the capital of a future Palestinian state in their midst, 'unification' was a belligerent act by an occupying power. Soon they would see Israeli construction crews building massive 'suburbs' on East Jerusalem lands.

For Arab lawyers working in East Jerusalem, the Israeli annexation carried a huge professional and financial impact that threatened permanent loss of work or, at the very least, the necessity to learn Hebrew and pass the Israeli bar exam, which Bashir and the other lawyers had no intention of doing. Doing so would have implied an acceptance of the occupation and the annexation of East Jerusalem. At that point, though, Bashir believed the occupation of the remainder of the West Bank was temporary and that soon enough he and his fellow lawyers would all be getting back to work. Some signs suggested otherwise: Already, some Israelis, led by the National Religious Party, had begun building settlements in the West Bank, on land they considered part of Eretz Yisrael. Soon, the Israeli military governor would issue a decree that suggested the occupation might last much longer. Military Order 145 authorized Israeli lawyers to take the place of the striking Palestinians. Even before it was implemented, the Israelis began making arrests.

Late on the evening of September 17, 1967, Bashir woke up to the sound of men yelling and fists pounding on the door. 'The Israeli soldiers are surrounding the house!' someone was screaming. Bashir came out of his room and into the glare of floodlights through the windows. 'Open! Open!' Bashir heard the soldiers yelling. He did as he was told. Ten soldiers in battle gear stood at the door. Bashir would recall their faces, black beneath their helmets, and their Uzis pointed at his chest.

'All of you bring your identification,' the one in charge shouted to no one in particular. Bashir brought his ID, and the soldier looked him over. 'You're Bashir,' he said. 'Get dressed and come with me.'

Zakia ran after Bashir as he went to his room to change out of his nightclothes. 'Put on your warm clothes, son,' she said. 'We are at the end of the summer season.'

Bashir spent one hundred days in a Ramallah jail. For much of that time, he was held at the Israel military head-quarters, where officers interrogated him about his activism. 'You are a leader,' they would tell Bashir. They had been following his activities with the striking lawyers and assumed he knew much more. 'Give us details about the resistance.' Each time, his reply would be the same: 'I believe in one thing: Palestine. And I hate one thing: occupation. And if you want to punish me, do it.'

Bashir's arrest was part of a much wider counter-insurgency designed to root out dissidents, guerrillas, and others suspected of plotting attacks on Israeli soil. In late August, Fatah had launched combat operations against

Israel. Some rebels were organized into secret armed cells; others operated as roaming bands of guerrillas, or 'fugitive patrols.' Arafat and his *cadres* were attempting to seize the mantle of Palestinian nationalism and had timed their actions to put pressure on Arab states not to signal any compromise on the right of return with Israel. At their summit meeting in Khartoum in late August, the Arab leaders indeed declared that 'there would be no reconciliation with Israel.'

Yet signs of accommodation with Israel were already emerging from the Arab states. In mid-October 1967, as Bashir sat in jail, a close associate of Egyptian president Nasser wrote a series of highly influential articles advocating a Palestinian state in the West Bank and Gaza – suggesting that the return to old Palestine would not happen. The next month, the United Nations Security Council adopted Resolution 242, calling for 'withdrawal of Israeli armed forces from territories occupied in the recent conflict' in exchange for 'termination of all claims or states of belligerency and respect for and acknowledgement of the sovereignty, territorial integrity and political independence of every State in the area and their right to live in peace within secure and recognized boundaries free from threats or acts of force.'

The resolution called for Arab recognition of Israel in exchange for Israeli withdrawal from Sinai, the Golan Heights, the West Bank, and Gaza. Some hoped the withdrawal from the West Bank and Gaza would lead to an independent Palestinian state; others assumed the land would revert to Jordanian control. In either case, the boundaries would be far different from those outlined by the 1947 UN partition plan. Israel would retain control of 78 percent of historic Palestine, including al-Ramla and Lydda.

Some Arab leaders, including Nasser and King Hussein of Jordan, sent signals suggesting they could support Resolution 242 – Nasser would get the Sinai back, and Hussein hoped that a comprehensive peace could bring calm to his restive kingdom. For most Palestinians in 1967, however, 242 didn't go nearly far enough; their dream still lay in the fight to return to their homes in Palestine. Yet by December 1967, it was becoming clear that Arafat's goal of a mass insurgency was not going to catch fire in the occupied territories. Already, more than a thousand men had been jailed by the Israelis, reducing the ranks of Fatah. Soon Arafat, Abu Jihad, and other leaders would be discussing the need to shift tactics.

On December 11, a few miles from the house in Ramla, Palestinian rebels attacked Israel's national airport. The action was a failure tactically, but it marked the arrival of a new faction in the would-be independence movement: the Popular Front for the Liberation of Palestine. Its leader was George Habash, the refugee from Lydda who had marched through the hills in the punishing heat in July 1948. Habash, who would soon become a permanent fixture on the list of Israel's top enemies, would spark revulsion in Dalia for years to come. For many Palestinians at the time, Habash was a courageous rebel, willing to fight for his people's fundamental rights by any means necessary.

At the end of 1967, Bashir was released from jail. He would report days of interrogation; no formal charges were filed. As he walked free, he would remember later, 'I loved Palestine more than before, and I hated occupation more than ever.'

One clammy gray morning in January 1968, Dalia awoke

in Ramla with Bashir and his family on her mind. For months she had been thinking about Bashir's invitation to visit in Ramallah; today, she hoped, would be the day. Dalia didn't have Bashir's address or telephone number, so she had no choice but to show up in person to accept his invitation. She remembered that Bashir had told her, 'When you get to Ramallah, just ask for the house of Bashir Khairi. Everyone will know.'

Now she had to figure out how to get to Ramallah. The family's two-piston Citroën was not up to the task, and even if it was, Moshe would never have allowed his daughter to go to the West Bank. Dalia decided to call an English acquaintance, Richard, who had been wanting a date with the young woman who bore a strong resemblance to the American film star Natalie Wood. Richard didn't interest Dalia, but he did have a car. And under the circumstances, he was willing to drive Dalia across the Green Line into occupied Palestinian territory.

They set out in late morning, and as they rode east, the Judean Hills, as Dalia knew them, came into sharper relief. The hills were cast in multiple hues of purple; shadows were dappled with thin fingers of light. Dalia recalled the time when she was five, at home with her mother, when she pointed to these same hills, saying, 'Ima, let's go to these mountains.' When Solia told her that the mountains were far away, Dalia took her mother by the hand, saying, 'No, no, if you really want to we can get there. One day, I will get there.' As she approached the mountains of the West Bank, riding toward new ground with the quiet, tense Englishman, Dalia felt a sense of belonging.

The Englishman's car splashed through potholes on the unpaved winter roads of the West Bank. Dalia knew that somewhere on these roads Israeli tanks and jeeps were on patrol, but she and Richard saw mostly a terrain of stony hills, olive groves, and ancient villages growing out of the landscape. They neared Ramallah, driving northeast from Latrun and the empty Arab village of Imwas. Somewhere on the maze of roads north of Beit Sira, they became lost. Children from a nearby village surrounded the car. Dalia felt apprehensive listening to children speaking rapidly in Arabic.

They drove on, traveling down strange and deserted roads in the Israeli-occupied West Bank, still unsure of where they were going.

Six months earlier, in only six days, Israelis had engineered a stunning reversal of their image across the world: from victim to victor and also to occupier. The exhilaration of victory and the public exaltation in Israel and internationally had given way in some quarters to reflections on the brutality of war and the morality of the occupation. One young Israeli writer, Amos Oz, was already calling for a full withdrawal from the occupied territories on ethical grounds. Oz was also part of a team of young kibbutzniks who sought to chronicle the mixed emotions of Sabras, the native-born Ashkenazi Israelis, who were 'dazed by the magnitude of their victory and, no less, shocked by the revelation of what war really is.'

These were Dalia's contemporaries in the Israeli army, and they had been telling Oz and the other chroniclers of their moral ambivalence. On the one hand, almost every soldier saw the war as just – a defense against 'Armageddon . . . of all the things we talked about years ago, when we were kids – about loving our country, about the continuation of Jewish life here in the Land of our Fathers.' On the other hand, many soldiers returned to the kibbutz disturbed by the feeling of having become, in the words of one Sabra, 'just machines for killing. Everyone's face is set in a snarl and there's a deep growl coming from your belly. You want to kill and kill. You've got to understand what things like that did to us. We hated and hated.'

This was a new self-image for the heroic Sabra, whose role had been to show resilience and strength for all of Israeli society. Now, in the wake of the Six Day War, Israelis had a new role – occupier – and it was one few of the kibbutznik soldiers wanted. 'It's an absolutely lousy feeling being in a conquering army,' one soldier told Oz. 'It's a horrible job, really horrible. I'm a kibbutznik. It's not for us. We haven't been brought up to it. We haven't been trained for it.'

Israelis had increasingly seen themselves as a nation of victims, especially since the 1963 trial of Adolf Eichmann in Jerusalem had pulled the Holocaust from the shadows. Now the Sabras, many of whom were children of Holocaust survivors, found themselves confronting an occupied civilian population: mothers pleading with soldiers for the release of their sons; wives, for their husbands; old men bent over sticks, looking with confusion at a battalion passing by and yelling in a language they couldn't understand.

In Ramallah it was just as Bashir had said: As soon as Dalia and Richard pulled up near Manara Square in the heart of the town, they asked a man on the street for the house of Bashir Khairi. The man knew who Bashir was and where he lived. Within minutes, Dalia and Richard were standing at the base of a concrete stairway as a neighbor went up to notify Bashir of his arriving guests.

Bashir, a few weeks removed from an Israeli jail, was in his room when his younger brother Kamel burst in. 'Guess who's here?' Kamel asked excitedly. Bashir knew immediately. He bounded down the stairway to the street. There was Dalia, looking a little nervous, standing beside a tall, stocky, pale fellow who looked even more uncomfortable.

It was cold, and dark skies threatened more rain, but Bashir made no move to invite his guests upstairs. 'I don't know if it's safe for you to come and visit,' he told her. 'Because I've just come out of prison.'

'Why were you in prison?' Dalia asked.

'Because I love my country,' Bashir replied.

Funny, Dalia thought. *I also love my country, and I haven't been imprisoned.* She realized, however, that Bashir's recounting of his incarceration was not meant to display his Palestinian nationalist credentials; rather, he was trying to protect her. Bashir was being watched, and if Dalia came upstairs, she, too, would risk surveillance. The irony was that Bashir was trying to shield Dalia from the eyes of her own army, of which she was now a part. She was faced with a decision, and she came to it quickly: She would not allow anyone to tell her whom she could or could not see. She looked at Bashir's thin, clean-shaven face and his large brown eyes. 'Please,' she said. 'Let us have a visit.'

Upstairs, Bashir led Dalia and Richard to an overstuffed couch in a cold, darkened living room. She was greeted by quiet bustling. Someone rolled in a kerosene heater, and someone else turned on the lamps. Bashir's sisters were darting about, preparing the sitting room for the surprise guests. This was the first time Dalia had seen West Bank women, just as she imagined it was their first look at an Israeli not in uniform.

Bashir introduced his mother, Zakia, who greeted Dalia warmly, and within moments, Dalia would remember, 'things suddenly began appearing on the table: teas, cakes, date pastries, Arabic sweets, Turkish coffee . . .' It was

240

Dalia's first encounter with Arab hospitality, and as more trays and dishes appeared, Dalia was overwhelmed by the generosity.

As warm as the family was, Dalia was struck by how temporary their home felt. She looked around at the couches, the tile floor, and the framed photographs on the wall. Yet something central was missing. Dalia couldn't identify it precisely, but she felt as if the whole family was sitting on its suitcases.

'So,' Bashir began in his hesitant English, 'how are you, Dalia? How is your family? How are you doing at school?'

'I am fine,' Dalia said. 'Fine.'

There was a pause.

Bashir regarded Dalia. He was content to let her determine the course of their conversation. After all, she was his guest. 'You are welcome here, Dalia,' he said. 'I hope you will spend a nice day with us. You are generous and very nice to us.'

Dalia noticed Bashir's sisters whispering and peering at her from around a doorway. These faces held the most beautiful eyes Dalia had ever seen. They seemed to Dalia like the eyes of deer – *enei ayala* in Hebrew, powerful emblems of beauty. Eventually all the family would come out to greet Dalia, except for Bashir's father, Ahmad; apparently, he wasn't home.

Dalia took another deep breath; she had hesitated before posing the question but reminded herself that she had come to Ramallah for the opportunity to learn their story. 'Bashir,' Dalia said, leaning forward, 'I know this is a sensitive issue.' She hesitated. 'It must be very difficult that someone now is living in your house.'

Bashir would have been content to let the conversation remain on the level of 'How are you?' His sense of Arab

241

hospitality dictated that he not challenge a visitor. This, however, was extraordinary. Dalia needed and deserved to be engaged.

'Listen, Dalia,' Bashir said slowly. 'How would you feel to leave your home, all your belongings, your entire spirit, in one place? Would you not fight to get it back with everything you have?'

There were many more details Bashir could have conveyed. He could have told Dalia what the collective Palestinian narrative had taught him: about the Israeli army attacking Lydda and occupying al-Ramla on July 12, 1948; about the soldiers' rifle butts pounding on the doors the next day; about the forced exile of tens of thousands of people from al-Ramla and Lydda; about the nineteen years of an inconsolable longing for home; about the willingness to fight, with your fingernails if necessary, to return. Instead, he stood up suddenly.

'Come, Dalia,' Bashir would remember saying. 'Let me show you something.' Dalia had been trying to engage Richard in the conversation, but the Englishman, looking bored, sighed deeply as Bashir walked toward a glass cabinet in the dining room. Dalia followed Bashir, and the two stood looking through the glass.

'Look at the cabinet and tell me what you see,' Bashir said.

'Is this a test?'

'It is a test. Please tell me what you see in the cabinet.'

'Books, vases, a picture of Abdel Nasser. Maybe some things hiding behind. And a lemon.'

'You won,' Bashir said. 'Do you remember the lemon?'

'What about it? Is there a story?'

'Do you remember when me and my brother came to visit? . . . Yes? Do you remember that Kamel asked you for something as we left? And what you gave him as a gift?'

Dalia was silent for a moment, Bashir would recall. 'Oh, my God. It's one of the lemons from that visit. But why did you keep it? It has been almost four months now.'

They walked from the cabinet and took their seats in the living room.

'To us this lemon is more than fruit, Dalia,' Bashir said slowly. 'It is land and history. It is the window that we open to look at our history. A few days after we brought the lemons home, it was night, and I heard a movement in the house. I was asleep. I got up, and I was listening. We were so nervous when the occupation started. Even the movement of the trees used to wake us. And left us worried. I heard the noise, and I got up. The noise was coming from this room right here. Do you know what I saw? My father, who is nearly blind.'

'Yes,' said Dalia. She was listening intently.

'Dalia, I saw him holding the lemon with both hands. And he was pacing back and forth in the room, and the tears were running down his cheeks.'

'What did you do?'

'I went back to my room, sat in my bed, and I started thinking. Then I started talking to myself until the morning. And I understood why I love him so much.'

Dalia was on the verge of tears herself. She looked at her English friend and tried again to involve him in the conversation. He had begun tapping his feet and looking at his watch. It seemed this would be their only date.

'What would happen if your father came to the house in Ramla?' she asked Bashir.

'He might have a breakdown. He always says he'd have a heart attack before he got to the door.'

'And your mother?'

'And my mother, too. You know what a house means to a wife. She entered the house when she was a bride. And she gave birth in it, too.' Bashir himself was born in that house, nearly twenty-six years earlier.

'We can see ourselves in you, Bashir,' Dalia said. 'We can remember our own history of exile over thousands of years. I can understand your longing for home because of our own experience of exile.' Dalia began considering her notion of Eretz Yisrael (Land of Israel) alongside Bashir's love of Arde Falastin (Land of Palestine).

'And I started expressing my understanding of their sense of exile,' Dalia recalled. 'And that I could understand their longing for their home. I could understand their longing for Falastin through my longing to Zion, to Israel. And their exile I could understand from my own exile. I had something in my collective experience and through which I could understand their recent experience.'

She told Bashir, 'What you have gone through, it must have been a terrible experience.' Dalia was deeply moved and believed she was connecting with her new friend.

Bashir had never been able to understand how another people's ancient longing – their wish to return home from a millennial exile – could somehow be equated with the actual life of generations of Palestinians who lived and breathed in this land, who grew food from it, who buried their parents and grandparents in it. He was skeptical that this longing for Zion had much to do with Israel's creation. 'Israel first came to the imagination of the Western occupying powers for two reasons,' he told Dalia.

'And what are they?' she asked in reply, now feeling her own skepticism grow.

'First, to get rid of you in Europe. Second, to rule the East through this government and to keep down the whole Arab world. And then the leaders started remembering the Torah and started to talk about the land of the milk and the honey, and the Promised Land.'

'But there is good reason for this,' Dalia objected. 'And the reason is to protect us from being persecuted in other countries. To protect us from being slaughtered in cold blood just because we are Jews. I know the truth, Bashir.' Now Dalia was no longer trying to involve her English friend in the conversation. 'I know that my people were killed, slaughtered, put in gas ovens. Israel was the only safe place for us. It was the place where the Jews could finally feel that being a Jew is not a shame!'

'But you are saying that the whole world did this, Dalia. It is not true. The Nazis killed the Jews. And we hate them. But why should we pay for what they did? Our people welcomed the Jewish people during the Ottoman Empire. They came to us running away from the Europeans and we welcomed them with all that we had. We took care of them. But now because you want to live in a safe place, other people live in pain. If we take your family, for example. You come running from another place. Where should you stay? In a house that is owned by someone else? Will you take the house from them? And the owners – us – should leave the house and go to another place? Is it justice that we should be expelled from our cities, our villages, our streets? We have history here – Lydda, Haifa, Jaffa, al-Ramla. Many Jews who came here believed they were a people without a land going to a land without people. That is ignoring the indigenous people of this land. Their civilization, their history, their heritage, their culture. And now we are strangers. Strangers in every place. Why did this happen, Dalia? The Zionism did this to *you*, not just to the Palestinians.'

For Dalia, the love of Zion was not something she felt she could explain quickly to her Palestinian friend. 'For two thousand years we were praying three times a day to return to this land,' she told Bashir. 'We tried to live in other places. But we realized we were not wanted in other places. We had to come back home.'

The two young people stared at each other in silence.

'Okay, Bashir, I live in your home,' Dalia said finally. 'And this is also my home. It is the only home I know. So, what shall we do?'

'You can go back where you came from,' Bashir said calmly.

Dalia felt as if Bashir had dropped a bomb. She wanted to scream, though as his guest she knew she couldn't. She forced herself to listen.

'We believe that only those who came here before 1917' – the year of the Balfour Declaration and the beginning of the British Mandate in Palestine – 'have a right to be here. But anyone who came after 1917,' Bashir said, 'cannot stay.'

Dalia was astounded at the audacity of Bashir's solution. 'Well, since I was born and came here after 1917, that is no solution for me!' she said with an incredulous laugh. She was struck by the total contradiction of her situation: complete disagreement across a seemingly unbridgeable gulf, combined with the establishment of a bond through a common history, in a house where she felt utterly protected and welcomed. At the base of it all, Dalia felt the depth of the Khairis' gratitude for her having simply opened the door to the house in Ramla. 'And this was an amazing situation to be in,' she remembered. 'That everybody could feel the warmth and the reality of our people meeting, meeting the other, and it was real, it was happening, and we were admiring each other's being, so to speak. And it was so tangible. And on the other hand, we were conversing of things that seemed *totally mutually exclusive*. That my life here is at *their* expense, and if they want to realize their dream, it's at *my* expense.'

Dalia looked straight at Bashir. 'I have nowhere else to go, Bashir,' she said. 'I am staying here. The best thing is for you to live and leave us to live, too,' she said. 'We have to live together. To accept each other.'

Bashir stared calmly at his new friend. 'You are living in a place that does not belong to you, Dalia. Do you remember that the Crusaders were in this land for almost two hundred years? But finally they had to leave. This is my country. We were driven out of it.'

'Well, you realize it's also my country,' Dalia insisted.

'No, it's not. It's not your country, Dalia. You stole it from us.'

The word *stole* Dalia experienced as a slap; somehow it was made worse by Bashir's utterly placid demeanor. She sat on the couch, silent, feeling insulted and aggravated.

'You are leaving us in the sea,' Dalia finally said. 'So what do you propose for us? Where shall we go?'

'I'm very sorry, but this is not my problem,' Bashir said quietly. 'You stole our land from us. The solution, Dalia, is very hard. When you plant a tree and it's not the place for it to live, it's not going to grow. We are talking about the future of millions of people.' Bashir then repeated his idea, still prevalent among many Palestinians in the wake of the Six Day War, that Jews born after 1917, or born outside of what was now Israel, would go back to their homeland of origin.

Dalia could hardly believe this was a serious idea. 'No, Bashir, no, we don't have anywhere to go back to.'

'Yes, you can, you can; it can be arranged. You'd be welcomed back.'

'Bashir,' Dalia pleaded, leaning forward, 'don't try to fix one wrong with another wrong! You want to turn us, again, into refugees?' *What am I doing here?* she thought. *What is the point of continuing this conversation?*

Still, she had noticed something: Bashir had never repeated the threats of the Palestinian nationalists to one day take all of Palestine by force. He had never said, We *will* take your house from you – and Dalia had avoided asking him his intentions or his political affiliations. Each had chosen to reside within the contradiction: They were enemies, and they were friends. Therefore, Dalia believed, they had reason to keep talking; the conversation itself was worth protecting. Dalia stood up; Richard seemed immensely relieved as he reached for his coat. 'I think I have stayed here long enough,' she said to Bashir. 'My father must be worried. I have to go.'

Dalia reached for Bashir's hand. 'Really, I enjoyed spending time with you. And I feel that every time I understand more and more than before.'

Bashir's mother and sisters came. Dalia thanked them, and everyone said good-bye. 'You are not a guest in this house, Dalia,' Bashir said. 'It means you have to come again and again, and we're going to do this, too.'

Dalia turned as she reached the door. 'I'm only one person searching for the truth,' she said. 'And I found the thread that's going to take me there.'

Ten

EXPLOSION

THE MORNING OF February 21, 1969, was dry and cold in Jerusalem. A light wind blew down the cobblestone walkway of Ben Yehuda, south across a winter landscape of bare trees and brown grass and down Agron Street, where it swirled around the streetlights on the corner of King George Boulevard. Israel Gefen, veteran of World War II and three Arab-Israeli wars, was running an errand for his wife, a Canadian journalist. Gefen walked into the Supersol market on the corner of Agron and King George just after 10:30 A.M. As he strode past the checkout counters and toward the coolers in the back, Gefen noticed two young men speaking English with what seemed to be South African accents. That was the last thing his mind recorded before the boom.

Gefen was experienced in booms. In the late 1930s, he had joined a secret Jewish resistance on a kibbutz, manufacturing experimental weapons during the Great Arab Rebellion. In 1941, he'd fought in the British army against Rommel in the Libyan desert. His service as an Israeli soldier included the recent Six Day War, the Suez conflict, and what Israelis knew as their War of Independence, when Gefen was part of Moshe Dayan's Battalion Eighty-nine, which stormed Ramla and Lydda in July 1948.

The boom sounded just as Gefen passed the South Africans on his way to pick up a container of frozen lemon juice. As he was thrown upward, as the force of the blast catapulted him back-first through the false ceiling and into the light fixtures overhead, Gefen knew the explosion had come from a bomb.

He slammed hard onto the supermarket floor and looked up to see the two South Africans – it would later turn out that one was actually an Uruguayan – lifeless on the floor. Beside them a woman lay near death; Gefen gazed for a moment into her wide eyes and open mouth. A fourth victim lay on the floor with one eye hanging out of its socket. Gefen thought she, too, was dead; he would later learn the woman had survived.

Gefen looked down at his left leg to see blood spurting from an artery in his ankle. A seeping red patch, the sign of another wound, was growing larger, oozing from his trousers. As he struggled to stand up, he glanced down at his arms and chest and saw that his coat – light brown suede, he would recall – was shredded beyond repair. Gefen glanced at his ankle again and saw the blood coming out as if from a fountain. He pressed his fingers into his groin, putting firm pressure on the femoral artery at the top of his left leg, to stop the flow of blood. He removed his hand; the blood began to spurt again. He stared at his ankle and saw it was nearly severed at the foot.

'On the spot I decided, I don't want to live,' Gefen would remember decades later. 'I felt my ankle was cut off, and after one war and another war, I didn't want to go back to the hospital. I just didn't want to.'

The old soldier looked around. Smoke and dust were settling, the false ceiling dangled crazily from above, and light fixtures, metal tins, and shattered plastic bottles lay amid pools of blood in a chaos on the floor. As the screams of Israeli civilians filled the market, Gefen noticed the familiar wartime smell of gunpowder – mixed, incongruously, with the unmistakable aroma of paprika.

Israel Gefen reconsidered: He didn't want to die anymore. Pressing one hand into the left side of his crotch, he hopped on his right foot toward the exit. Two men emerged through the smoke and hurried him outside and into a barber's chair next door. They told him to wait. After perhaps two or three minutes – it seemed much longer – one of the men reappeared and helped Gefen into the cab of his pickup truck.

'Talk to me,' Israel Gefen told the terrified driver as he raced through the streets of West Jerusalem. The truck darted through red lights, dodging buses, cars, and pedestrians as the driver honked constantly. Gefen wanted the man to keep him awake with conversation; if he passed out, his hand would slip from his groin and the loss of blood would probably kill him. The two men made small talk. A few minutes later, they arrived at the entrance of Jerusalem's Sha'are Tzedek (Gates of Righteousness) hospital. Medics quickly surrounded Gefen and wheeled him toward the emergency ward. It was strange, Gefen thought before passing out: He hadn't been inside this hospital in forty-five years – not since that week in early summer 1922, when he was born.

One day after work, near the end of February 1969, Moshe Eshkenazi walked into the backyard of the house in Ramla, where Dalia was watering the flowers. He had his evening paper, *Ma'ariv*, in his hands. 'Look what's in the papers,' Moshe told his daughter. 'They've been investigating the Supersol bombing in Jerusalem. It says here that your friend Bashir is accused of taking part in this.' He raised his eyebrows.

'Bashir?' Dalia asked incredulously. 'Bashir Khairi of Ramallah?' She walked slowly toward her father, who gazed at her steadily. She would recall the moment vividly thirty-six years later. The operation, the article said, was conducted by the Popular Front for the Liberation of Palestine, a group committed to 'armed struggle,' which Israelis considered another name for terrorism. The PFLP and its leader, the Lydda refugee George Habash, had boasted that their attacks were designed to deprive Israelis of their sense of 'reassurance and security.'

Bashir Khairi in the PFLP? Dalia stood there, the watering can still in her hands. She had opened her home to Bashir and his family, welcoming them whenever they came for a tour of the house and a visit to the garden and the lemon tree. In return she had received warmth and an Arab hospitality she had never experienced before; the family's gratitude to Dalia for simply opening the door came from depths she was only beginning to understand. As the visits had progressed, Dalia had learned more of the history of Bashir's family, especially of the expulsions from Ramla and Lod (Lydda), and Bashir had begun to see that every Israeli was not the enemy. It had seemed to Dalia that a conversation based on common history and mutual interest was not so impossible after all.

Now Dalia came to read the paper over her father's shoulder. Bashir Khairi was accused of involvement in the supermarket bombing and of belonging to an outlawed organization in the West Bank: the Popular Front. The previous July, PFLP guerrillas had commandeered an El Al flight bound to Tel Aviv from Rome, forcing it down in

Algiers and holding the mostly Israeli passengers hostage for nearly six weeks before Israel finally capitulated and released sixteen Palestinian prisoners. Six months later, in December 1968, PFLP operatives attacked another El Al airliner in Athens, killing one passenger. And only two days after the Supersol bombing, a PFLP operation targeted an El Al plane at the Zurich airport, killing one person and wounding four. Dalia had watched the spectacles with burning anger; she had heard the PFLP claims that it wanted to liberate Palestine, which to Dalia simply meant the destruction of Israel and the only home she knew.

Bashir Khairi in the PFLP? Could this be true? The article said Bashir would be tried in an Israeli military court; maybe then the truth would come out. Dalia would try to reserve judgment until the trial. But already she was contemplating a disturbing question: Had she befriended a terrorist?

Bashir Khairi sat in a three-by-five-foot cell with stone walls, iron bars, and a low-watt bulb dangling from the ceiling. He slept on the cement floor, and for six nights he lay in the dark, shivering without bedcovers. Since his incarceration at Sarafand prison – the old British lockup close to al-Ramla – Bashir had developed a high fever and chills; on the seventh day, Bashir remembered decades later, his Israeli jailers brought him a blanket.

'In the interrogation room at Sarafand,' Bashir recounted, 'there was a chair and a table, and on the table was a black *shabbah*,' a hood. 'You put the hood over your head, and they beat you. They beat me on the hands, they choked me with the hood on. Other times they would chain my hands and legs, blindfold me, and unleash the dogs. The dogs would jump on me and pin me back against the wall. I could feel their breath on my neck.' Bashir believed the interrogations were conducted by agents of the General Security Services, or Shin Bet. He would recall the men with a precision and seeming calm of someone remembering a trip to the store the day before. 'Their faces,' Bashir would say quietly. 'To this day I remember exactly their faces.'

After the interrogations came psychological operations. 'In my cell,' he said, 'I would hear shots, and then someone screaming. Then the guards would arrive and bring me outside and show me a hole, and say, 'If you don't cooperate, this is where you'll end up.' Then I would be back in my cell, hearing shooting and screaming. You'd think: *They're killing the people who don't confess.'* The Israeli interrogators wanted Bashir to admit to having played a role in the supermarket bombing and to describe the internal operations of the PFLP so they could put an end to the El Al hijackings. The young lawyer admitted nothing. He refused to confirm any association with the Popular Front. Consequently, he said, the beatings, dog attacks, and psy-ops continued.

This kind of treatment was not exceptional. In 1969, the year Bashir was arrested, little was known outside of the Shin Bet about Israeli treatment of Palestinian prisoners. In 1974, the Israeli human rights lawyer Felicia Langer published a memoir, *With My Own Eyes*, detailing her interviews with prisoners who had endured an 'ordeal of beatings and humiliation.' She described prisoners who showed evidence of blows to the head, hands, and legs; who told of being punched in the face while blindfolded; who arrived for jailhouse interviews in bloodstained shirts; who described hanging from a wall by handcuffs tied to iron bars; who reported interrogations with 'electricity and sticks'; whose feet and hands were bound until they bled.

In one case, Langer wrote, a fifty-two-year-old man with a respiratory disease was interrogated naked, and 'his hands were tied behind his back; a rope was tied to his hands too, and he was lifted in the air thus. His interrogators beat him also now, and after each beating they ordered him to talk, and since he had nothing to say they went on beating him.' Langer also described one prisoner, 'blue from the beatings,' who died, the authorities claimed, after 'he had stumbled and fell down a staircase.'

On one of her jailhouse visits, probably in the spring of 1969, Felicia Langer met Bashir. She would remember a pale man with large eyes who seemed 'barely alive.' 'They beat me very badly,' Langer recalls Bashir telling her, 'until I was barely able to stand up.'

Langer's accounts of abuse and torture would be supported by the Israeli League for Human and Civil Rights, whose director, Israel Shahak, wrote in the foreword to *With My Own Eyes* that 'nobody . . . whatever his political or philosophical opinions, can deny that the cases of persecution, oppression and torture described in this book are not only true in themselves, but are also characteristic of Israeli rule in the occupied territories.'

Three years later, in 1977, the *Sunday Times* of London would publish a detailed investigation of 'allegations of systematic torture by Israel of Arab prisoners.' The *Times* concluded, 'Torture is organized so methodically that it cannot be dismissed as a handful of "rogue cops" exceeding orders. It is systematic. It appears to be sanctioned at some level as deliberate policy.' One of the subjects of the investigation was Rasmiah Odeh, who along with Bashir was jailed in connection with the Supersol bombing. Odeh's father, Josef, whose house was demolished about three weeks after the bombing, described being taken to the prison to witness his daughter's interrogation:

> When they took me back . . . Rasmiah couldn't stand on her own feet. She was lying on the floor and there were bloodstains on her clothes. Her face was blue and she had a black eye . . . They were beating me and beating her, and we were both screaming. Rasmiah was still saying: 'I know nothing' And they spread her legs and shoved the stick into her. She was bleeding from her mouth and from her face and from her end. Then I became unconscious.'

Israel denied the *Times*'s allegations. But the newspaper's five-month investigation concluded that interrogation techniques included 'prolonged beatings' and 'electric shock torture and confinement in specially-constructed cells,' a method that 'removes Israel's practice from the lesser realms of brutality and places it firmly in the category of torture.' The *Times* charged that torture was overseen by all of Israel's security services, including the Shin Bet, military intelligence, and Israel's Department of Special Missions.

The reasons for the torture, the *Sunday Times* reported, were threefold: to extract information; to 'induce people to confess to "security" offenses, of which they may, or may not, be guilty,' so that officials could use those confessions to obtain convictions; and to 'persuade Arabs in the occupied territories that it is least painful to behave passively . . .'

The newspaper found that much of the torture took place 'at a special military intelligence centre whose whereabouts are uncertain, but which testimony suggests is somewhere inside the vast military supply base at Sarafand . . .'

Bashir was at Sarafand, and his family hadn't heard from him in a week. Nuha, his older sister, would recall the day he left with acute clarity thirty-six years later. It was 6:00 in the evening. Nuha had just finished cleaning the house. She was fixing her hair when she heard a loud pounding on the door. An Israeli captain demanded to see Bashir. She told him that he wasn't home. When he comes back, the Israeli captain demanded, he must report to the Muqata – the Israeli military compound in Ramallah. Bashir had done as ordered, and the family hadn't heard from him since. Their efforts to obtain any information had yielded nothing.

A week later, there was another knock on the door. It was the captain again, this time with Bashir. He looked pale and weak. Zakia came from the living room, where she had been entertaining guests. The captain told Bashir not to say a word to anyone. 'His clothes are dirty,' Zakia told the captain. She went quickly to his room and emerged with clean clothes stuffed in a bag.

The soldiers told Nuha to come with them. She got into the jeep with Bashir and drove south; Nuha wasn't sure what they wanted.

'You look tired,' Nuha told Bashir on the road to Jerusalem. 'Did they beat you?'

'Stop!' the captain screamed at Nuha. 'You can't talk to him!'

They arrived at the Muscobia, the Russian compound

that served as an Israeli military interrogation center in Jerusalem. The soldiers brought Nuha into a small room and Bashir into the room next door. Shortly afterward, Nuha would recall, she could hear Bashir's screams. After listening for what seemed an interminable time, she couldn't bear to hear any more and fainted.

Three hours later, the jailers brought her a cup of water. They called her to the next room and opened the door. She saw Bashir, his head bowed, clad only in his underpants. Two men stood on either side of him, wielding sticks.

'Brother,' Nuha said. 'Oh, my brother.' The interrogators then dragged Bashir away and told Nuha to find her way back to Ramallah on her own.

Bashir, by his own account, never admitted any connection to the supermarket bombing. 'I endured the beatings, the hoods, and the dogs. They did not break me.' He denied membership in the PFLP and disavowed any knowledge of its operations.

By now the world knew of the PFLP and the headline-grabbing operations that had terrorized the Israelis. Many Palestinians, still in shock from the defeat and occupation following the Six Day War, had begun to realize that small guerrilla operations alone would not achieve their long-awaited liberation of Palestine. They came to embrace the PFLP's strategy of 'spectacular operations' to reverse years of humiliation and failure and to focus the world's attention on the Palestinian plight. These attacks, combined with the operations of Fatah and other groups, were immensely popular among Arabs, who still saw Israel as illegally occupying Palestine.

'In 1968 a Palestinian *fedayi* could travel right across the

Arab world with nothing more than his organisation card and be welcome everywhere,' Bassam Abu-Sharif, then a member of the PFLP, would recall in his memoir. 'No passport – just the card. Nobody, nobody, in the Arab world then dared raise a voice against a *fedayi* . . .' In the aftermath of the Six Day War, 'the *fedayi* was god.' Many of the guerrilla attacks against Israel were launched from Jordan, and this sharply raised tensions between King Hussein and Israeli leaders and consequently between the king and the guerrilla groups.

In March 1968, in response to the guerrilla incursions, Israeli infantry, tanks, paratroopers, and armored brigades crossed the Jordan River and attacked Fatah positions in the Jordanian town of Karama. The Israeli force, fifteen thousand strong, drew heavy fire from Jordanian and Fatah artillery. Twenty-eight Israeli soldiers died, and the Jordanians captured several Israeli tanks, which would soon be paraded through the streets of Amman. Israel had inflicted more casualties, and it achieved most of its military objectives, but to an Arab world starved for signs of strength, the courage of the guerrillas demonstrated that the Palestinian resistance was genuine. The heroic image of Yasser Arafat, who by most accounts stood under fire to direct his fighters at Karama, grew larger still. The battle of Karama, though in many ways a military defeat, would go down as one of the great symbolic victories in the history of the Palestinian resistance, further enhancing Fatah's image within Jordan. Now King Hussein would find it even more difficult to pressure the guerrillas. On the contrary, in the aftermath of Karama he declared, 'We are all fedayeen.'

From Cairo to Baghdad to Damascus to Amman, thousands of Arabs flooded rebel offices to volunteer in the renewed fight against Israel. Fatah even got its own frequency on Egyptian radio, Arafat was invited to Cairo as a state guest of Nasser, and the ranks of Fatah swelled.

The 'spectacular' operations of the PFLP, meanwhile, began to attract legions of young Europeans, who saw in the airline hijackings a willingness to risk everything to achieve liberation. This was a time not only of cold war, but of revolution, inspired in part by massive and world-wide street protests against the Vietnam War and, in some cases, support of the Vietcong. In the third world, the Vietcong were often seen as freedom fighters and the United States as their oppressors. Similarly, the Palestinian rebels, through the hijackings and other high-profile operations, quickly became identified on the Left with the struggle for revolutionary justice against an occupying power. In the United States, even within much of the Left, and especially among idealistic young Jews who would soon make aliyah to the Holy Land, Israel was still considered the just victor of the recent war. But the surging radical movements in Europe began to feed the Palestinian nationalists with wide-eyed anti-imperialists: Italian, French, Spanish, Greek, and German youths who had become frustrated with the capitalist system and its leaders.

Inspired by Che Guevara and Ho Chi Minh, and by Chairman Mao's admonition to become 'fish in a revolutionary sea,' the European leftists arrived in PLO and PFLP training camps in Iraq, Jordan, Egypt, Lebanon, Algeria, and Yemen. From these connections, 'solidarity committees' sprang up across Europe, doling out financial aid and medical supplies and sending volunteers into the occupied territories.

Soon, infamous revolutionary groups and fugitives

throughout the West became identified with the Palestinian struggle. They included the Venezuelan Communist Ilich Ramírez Sánchez (aka Carlos the Jackal), Andreas Baader and Ulrike Meinhof (leaders of the Baader-Meinhof Gang), and various factions of the Red Brigade: ETA from Spain, the Italian Brigada Rossa, Action Directe of France, and the Japanese Red Army. 'The only language which the enemy understands is that of revolutionary violence,' declared George Habash, 'thereby turning the occupied territories into an inferno whose fires consume the usurpers.' His slogan was 'unity, freedom, vengeance.'

For thousands of Palestinians, the 'spectaculars' brought a sense of power out of defeat and attention to the Palestinian cause as never before. Many Palestinians believed their attacks were against not Israeli civilians, but rather 'soldiers in civilian clothing' in a 'colonial settler regime' that could be mobilized against them in a moment's notice. This was war, the Palestinian rebels believed, and their attacks represented their only recourse to bringing attention to their cause. 'When we hijack a plane it has more effect than if we killed a hundred Israelis in battle,' Habash said. 'For decades world public opinion has been neither for nor against the Palestinians. It simply ignored us. At least the world is talking about us now.' In much of the world, however, the PFLP tactics had turned people against the Palestinians and their liberation movement.

The PFLP operations, moreover, provoked a massive Israeli crackdown. Thousands of Palestinians were jailed, including many who had no knowledge of any guerrilla operations. They were held indefinitely without charge. The PFLP tactics thus became a growing source of tension within the Palestinian nationalist movement, and in February 1969, the same month Bashir was arrested, a new faction broke off from the PFLP, soon to be called the Democratic Front for the Liberation of Palestine. Abu Laila, one of the DFLP founders, believed the 'lunatic actions' of the PFLP against civilians outside Israel had 'smeared the legitimacy of the resistance.' The DFLP leadership also objected to the rhetoric of 'pushing the Jews into the sea' and began to see their struggle as against not Jews, but Zionism. They advocated for coexistence between Arabs and Jews within a single state, where no one would be forced to move. Some within the DFLP even began to talk of Arab and Jewish states existing side by side. Even among some of the radical factions of the Palestinian resistance, the idea of coexistence was gaining ground.

By 1970, however, ideological tensions within the Palestinian movement were minor compared with the antagonistic atmosphere between the Palestinians and King Hussein of Jordan. After the battle of Karama, Fatah and other factions in the Palestinian liberation movement had grown so strong that they became a virtual state within a state in Jordan, turning the capital, Amman, into their 'Arab Hanoi.' Rebels saw the king as coddling the West through his qualified support for a UN compromise, which they feared would scuttle their right of return. Some rebel leaders had labeled the king a 'paper tiger' and threatened to topple him. On September 1, following a Jordanian army shelling of Palestinian refugee camps, the king survived an attack on his convoy that the Jordanians believed was an assassination attempt.

A few days later, with Bashir still in prison and awaiting his long-delayed trial, PFLP fighters staged perhaps the most spectacular operation in the history of the Palestinian resistance. Their plan was to simultaneously hijack three New York-bound airliners from European capitals, thereby maximizing the number of U.S. passengers and the consequent international attention. The airliners would then land in an old British airfield in the Jordanian desert, where the passengers would be held until Israel released Palestinian political prisoners.

PFLP operatives seized two of the flights and directed them toward Jordan. The third attempt was foiled. Leila Khaled, the Palestinian 'queen of freedom fighters,' underwent plastic surgery to hide her identity. She and a fellow PFLP operative posed as a Mexican bride and groom. The attempted hijacking, on an El Al flight from Amsterdam, went awry when the pilot took the plane into a sharp plunge to throw the 'newlyweds' off balance. The 'groom' was shot dead by the Israeli security chief on board; Khaled was taken to a jail in London. However, three days later, when a Palestinian working in Bahrain heard that his heroine queen had been taken prisoner, he single-handedly hijacked a British airliner and ordered the pilot to join the other two planes already on the ground in Jordan. Palestinians would come to know this stretch of desert east of Amman, in Hussein's kingdom, as 'Revolution Airport.'

'I'm sorry,' Bassam Abu-Sharif shouted through his megaphone to the several hundred passengers, standing in the sun in what appeared to be the middle of nowhere, 'we have just hijacked you to the desert in Jordan. This is a country in the Middle East, next to Israel and Syria. We are fighting a just war, a war for the liberation of our country from Israeli occupation. The reason you're in the middle of it is that we want to exchange you for prisoners who were taken in Israel and other countries.'

The list of Palestinian prisoners included the name of Khaled, the 'Mexican bride' whose hijacking operation had unraveled and who sat in jail in London. Khaled would be released in a prisoner-for-hostage exchange, as the direct result of the actions of her admirer. (Bashir's name would appear on another prisoner-exchange list two years later, during a hijacking at the airport near Tel Aviv; the operation ended when Israeli commandos shot and killed the hijackers. Bashir remained in prison.)

After six days, the crisis at 'Revolution Airport' ended with all hostages safe and three charred jumbo jets in pieces on the tarmac, blown up by PFLP fighters to demonstrate their seriousness to the world. Within days, however, King Hussein used the PFLP's spectacle as reason for swift action against all Palestinian factions in the country.

For two weeks in September 1970, civil war erupted as the king's troops engaged PLO, PFLP, DFLP, and other Palestinian factions in fierce battles in the Palestinian refugee camps formed after 1948 and in provincial towns across the desert kingdom. Jordanian troops out-numbered Palestinian guerrillas by more than three to one and had more than nine hundred tanks and armored vehicles, compared with none for the Palestinian side. When Syria crossed the Jordanian border to fight on the side of the Palestinians, the king secretly contacted Israel, asking for air support against the Syrians: a rare personal appeal from an Arab leader to Israel to attack other Arabs. On the ground, especially in the refugee camps, it was Arab against Arab as the Jordanian military unleashed its hardware, killing thousands of Palestinians in the span of eleven days. The month would forever be known to Palestinians as Black September.

On September 26, at the urging of Gamal Abdel Nasser, King Hussein and Yasser Arafat flew separately to Egypt, where they signed a ceasefire agreement. This was to be the last political act of consequence for Nasser. Two days later, the Egyptian leader, still revered across the Arab world despite his central role in one of its most catastrophic defeats, died of a heart attack. Millions of people filled the streets of the Arab capitals, wearing black and sobbing openly, in scene after scene of mass grief. The era of pan-Arab nationalism, of a single hero promising to lead the people to victory over an oppressor, was finished.

Dalia was sickened by the actions of the PFLP. In later years, she would recall her horror at a PFLP-organized attack on the Lod airport, when three members of the Japanese Red Army opened fire with Kalashnikovs, killing twenty-five people, including Christian pilgrims from Puerto Rico. Attacking civilians crossed an ethical line and 'hit a very hard place in me.' At times like these, Dalia understood how someone could feel murderous in response to such attacks.

Between her classes at the university in Tel Aviv, or at home on the weekends, Dalia wondered who these people were and how they thought they could achieve their goals with such extreme tactics. She wondered about Bashir, too. Who was he, really?

Bashir was in jail, a member, according to the Israeli authorities, of the PFLP. It was hard to believe that the same young man who had come to Dalia's door – whose family was received with such warmth in her home – could be part of the Popular Front. She was stunned not because she had considered Bashir a friend, but because she thought the connection was, in some ways, even deeper than that. 'It's beyond friendship, because you didn't choose it,' she would say. 'Israel did not choose to have the Palestinians, and the Palestinians did not choose to have Israelis. It's a given, and that's the most critical point, how one deals with the given.'

Through her encounter with the Khairis, Dalia, now twenty-one years old, had begun to question the stereotypes she was raised with: the stories of mistrust, suspicion, and hatred. 'It was generally believed that an Arab can befriend you, but if their national interest dictates otherwise, they will stab you in the back with a knife,' she said. 'That was a very prevalent thing. One had to fight against that, to prove that it's not true.' Now, Dalia feared, Bashir's perceptions of his own national interest had clashed completely with hers.

At the core of Dalia's faith was the conviction that personal dialogue was the key to transformation. If Bashir was in fact part of the PFLP, if he was connected to the Supersol bombing, it showed that 'personal relationships meant nothing in the face of collective forces. If national interest comes before our common humanity,' Dalia said, 'then there is no hope for redemption, there is no hope for healing, there is no hope for transformation, there is no hope for *anything*!'

One morning as pre-trial preparations dragged on, Ahmad, Zakia, and Nuha Khairi decided to visit Bashir in jail. Prison officials had moved him repeatedly, and now he sat and waited in a cell in al-Ramla. Ahmad's eyesight, always poor, had begun to fail him – it was part of a long, slow decline that would eventually blind him – but as the three Khairis passed through the gates and into the visitors area, he realized where he was. 'Bashir,' Ahmad said when his son was finally sitting in front of him, 'did you notice where this prison is? This is exactly where our olive trees used to be.'

Ahmad said the land had been bequeathed to Khair al-Din al-Ramlawi by the Ottoman sultan in the sixteenth century. The *waqf* land had remained in the family for at least twelve generations, until 1948. Bashir realized the symbolic was also the literal: He was being imprisoned on his own land.

Nuha was constantly worrying about her brother. 'We don't know how long he will be in jail, we don't know what will happen with Bashir,' she would say. 'So many questions, so many uncertainties. He's twenty-eight years old, and still, he's not married. And now he is in prison for I don't know how long. How will this affect his future?'

In 1970, Bashir's trial began at a military court in Lod (formerly Lydda), a few miles from his old home in al-Ramla. His sister Khanom, who was living in Kuwait, had not seen Bashir since his arrest. She came to see him, but there were no family visiting hours during the trial. Bashir's lawyer told her she could pretend to be his assistant, 'just so I could see him. But he told me that I would not be allowed to talk to him and that if I did, there would be consequences.' When the jailers brought Bashir from the courthouse lockup, however, Khanom could not control herself. 'When I saw him, I shouted. I yelled out, "*Habibi Bashir!* My darling Bashir!" I was expelled from the courthouse. But at least I saw him.'

One afternoon during a recess in the trial, Ahmad decided he could no longer stay away from the house in al-Ramla. For more than three years, he had resisted a visit to Dalia and her family, telling his children, 'I would have a heart attack before I reached the front door.' Now, a few minutes removed from the military court and the prison where his son passed his days and nights, Ahmad stood with Zakia and Nuha at the door of the house he had built in 1936. He was barely able to see, but he could make out the figure of a Jewish man in his mid-fifties: Moshe Eshkenazi, from Bulgaria. The two men stood facing each other across the threshold: Ahmad and Moshe, two fathers of the same house.

They went through the house and outside again, to the garden in back. Ahmad walked forward slowly, touching the stones of the house, as Nuha and Zakia helped him along. Moshe invited his guests to sit. Dalia and Solia were out on an errand, soon to return. When they did, as Nuha recalls, Dalia asked all about Bashir. Before leaving, Ahmad asked Dalia if he could take one of the flowers from the *fitna* tree. Dalia told Ahmad, 'You can take it right from the tree.'

Dalia, three decades later, has no such memories; she doesn't believe she was at the house during the Khairis' visit that day, nor does she believe she ever met Ahmad Khairi. She does, however, remember her father telling her about the visit, and especially about what Bashir's father said to Moshe. On this point, her memory is identical to Nuha's.

'There was a lemon tree here,' Ahmad said to Moshe. 'I planted it. Is it still here? Is it still alive?'

Nuha and Moshe rose and stood on either side of Ahmad. They led him slowly to the corner of the garden. Ahmad extended his arms, running his fingers up the smooth, hard bark, over the soft knobs on the tree's base, and along the slender, narrowing branches, until, between his hands, he felt the soft brush of leaves and, between them, a small, cool sphere: a lemon from the tree he had planted thirty-four years earlier. Zakia watched from the table in silence, tears in her eyes.

Ahmad's head was among the lower branches, and he was crying silently. Moshe plucked a few lemons and placed them in Ahmad's hands. The men returned to the table and sat down. Moshe rose again and returned with a pitcher of lemonade, which he poured in silence into waiting glasses.

'It was nice,' Nuha would recall in another century, as a woman in her sixties still in exile in Ramallah. 'Very nice. Of course it was nice! We planted that tree with our own hands. Dalia's family – they were all very kind. But what does that matter? They were the people who took our house.'

Ahmad brought the four lemons back with him to Ramallah. 'As a gift,' Dalia would say. 'And a memory.'

In 1972, Bashir Khairi was sentenced to fifteen years in prison for complicity in the February 1969 bombing of the Supersol market on Agron Street in West Jerusalem and for membership in an outlawed organization, the Popular Front for the Liberation of Palestine. Israeli witnesses and Palestinian informants had testified that Bashir had served as a liaison between the bomb makers and the two members of the PFLP who hid the explosives on the spice rack at the market.

As the judge announced the sentence, Khanom Khairi began to scream. 'Bashir! Bashir!' she cried out as her younger brother locked eyes with her. Nuha was in shock, at the beginning of what she would later describe as a nervous breakdown. The court was in an uproar, and Khanom's enraged cries cut through the din.

Bashir had been expecting the conviction. He stood up and faced the judge. 'I don't recognize this court,' he said. 'I'm innocent.' At no point would Bashir admit any role in the bombing or acknowledge any membership in the PFLP. He considered the entire military trial a 'charade' conducted by an illegitimate government. 'I did not confess,' Bashir would recall in 1998, twenty-six years after his conviction. 'They could not extract a confession from me. They were false accusations. Because if they had been able to prove it, I would have been sentenced to life in prison, not for fifteen years. However, I am Palestinian. I have always hated the occupation. And I believe that I have the right to resist it by the means that are available to me. Yes, at one stage the means were violent. But I understood them. I understood the actions of the Palestinian fighters who were ready to sacrifice them-selves. I still understand them.'

Bashir's co-defendants received harsher sentences: Khalil Abu Khadijeh was sentenced to twenty years; Abdul Hadi Odeh got life. In a separate trial, sisters Rasmiah and Aisha Odeh also received life sentences. 'When the sentences were read out,' Khanom recalled, 'the mother of Abdul Hadi fainted. We all ran towards her and got her water, and someone splashed some perfume on her to wake her up.'

Bashir's aunt Rasmieh left the court and closed herself in her room at home. There she recited the sura of Yassin, from the Koran: 'A sign for them is the night. From it we draw out the day and they are plunged in darkness.'

She repeated the verse forty times.

'We say it has to do with faith and fate,' Khanom said. 'This we believe saved him, in the end.'

The convictions of some of the defendants rested in

part on the testimony of Israel Gefen, the Israeli veteran. The explosion in the spice rack had embedded paprika with such force into Gefen's skin that he had reeked of the stuff for weeks; three years after the explosion, every time he took a bath, he would still find tiny silvers of plastic – from the spice bottles – resting in the bottom of the tub. As for his foot, doctors at the Gates of Righteousness hospital had managed to sew it back to his ankle, but even after several operations it would never be the same. For the rest of his life, on especially cold or hot days, or when he felt especially tired, he would feel again the heat of the blast in his ankle.

After Bashir's conviction, Dalia immediately cut off all contact with the Khairi family. 'I felt very betrayed,' she would recall. Dalia had attached her deepest faith to the unfolding dialogue with Bashir. Now that was shattered, and along with it Dalia's belief in the power of 'person-to-person relationships' to 'touch the deeper humanity that goes beyond all national and political differences – a deeper humanity from which transformative miracles are created.' Dalia's 'natural, inborn faith' dictated that 'together we can find a solution. That was a central component, a central part of my being. That personal relations hold the key for transformation.' Bashir's commitment to his own cause, Dalia believed, meant that he was 'determined that we should "go back where we came from." It meant that we were not wanted here. We were not going to be accepted.' Alongside this anguish, there was a deep sense – more emotional than rational, Dalia would conclude later – that Bashir had confirmed a prejudice inherent to many Israelis: Arabs kill Jews simply because they are Jews.

'Yeah, everything stopped,' she said twenty-six years after Bashir's conviction. 'No contact. It was too much for me.' The door she had opened was closed.

Dalia grew cynical about the future of Arab and Jew living side by side. She became zealous in the defense of Israel and participated wholeheartedly in the nation's defense as an officer in the Israeli army.

When she got out of the service, Dalia plunged into her new work as an English teacher at the Ramla-Lod High School. The school stood adjacent to the Ramla prison, so close that the bricks of the two buildings actually touched.

In September 1972, as Bashir began serving his time, eight Palestinian gunmen snuck into the Olympic village at Munich, shooting two Israeli athletes dead and capturing nine more. In a subsequent shoot-out at a military base with German police, fourteen people died, including all of the Israeli hostages. The gunmen were part of the Black September organization, a splinter group of Fatah born after the civil war in Jordan. One of Black September's first operations, in 1971, had been the assassination of Jordan's prime minister – as revenge for his role in the attack on the Palestinian factions in September 1970. To this day it is not clear whether Black September acted independently in the Munich assassinations or whether Fatah chief Yasser Arafat knew of the operations in advance. At the time, Arafat defended such actions. 'Violent political action in the midst of a broad popular movement,' he declared, 'cannot be termed terrorism.' Many Palestinians agreed. They believed, twenty-four years after the 1948 war, that Israel was occupying their lands and homes and that desperate times required desperate measures: No one would pay any attention to their struggle unless they forced their way onto the international stage. 'Humans must change the world, they must do something, they must kill if needs be,' Habash had declared. 'To kill, even if that means we in our turn become inhuman.'

Israelis responded to the Munich assassinations with air strikes against suspected Palestinian bases in Syria and Lebanon, killing at least two hundred people, including many civilians. Within days, a series of assassinations and maimings rocked the Palestinian movement, part of Israel's Operation Wrath of God. The Israeli general who directed the operation called the assassinations 'politically vital' and said they were driven by 'the old Biblical rule of an eye for an eye.' Operation Wrath of God, however, did not represent an entirely new policy, but rather an intensification of Israeli reprisals in the era of Palestinian hijackings. On July 8, a car bomb had killed revered Palestinian novelist and PFLP spokesman Ghassan Kanafani and his twenty-one-year-old niece as they drove to enroll her at the American University of Beirut.

Two and a half weeks later, Kanafani's PFLP colleague Bassam Abu-Sharif would receive a book-size package in a plain brown wrapper marked INSPECTED FOR EXPLOSIVES.

'Bassam,' the postman called to the young man, 'you've got a present – looks like a book . . .' The young rebel tore off the wrapper and saw he had been sent a book about Che Guevara, one of his longtime heroes. 'Casually,' he would recall in his memoir twenty-three years later, 'I began leafing through the pages to see what it was like . . . Underneath, I saw that the book was hollow. There were two explosive charges in this hollow space, wired to go off when the uncut section of the book was lifted . . .

'I had just lifted it.'

The explosion blew off a thumb and two fingers of Bassam's right hand, broke his jaw apart, smashed his lips and teeth to pieces, opened large wounds in his chest, stomach, and upper right thigh, blinded him in his right eye, and severely impaired his hearing in both ears. Like Israel Gefen, the rebel would be sewn back together and would carry the explosion around with him for the rest of his life. From that day forward, family, colleagues, friends, and visitors would be required to sit close to Bassam Abu-Sharif and shout their greetings, their intimacies, and their questions.

Bashir would spend the next twelve years in several Israeli-run prisons, mainly in Jenin, Tulkarm, and Ramallah. His prison mates were other Palestinian men convicted of armed insurrection, or of membership in banned political groups, or of demonstrating against the occupation, or were simply those who waited for formal charges to be filed against them. In the eighteen years following the Israeli occupation in June 1967, an estimated 250,000 Palestinians – or 40 percent of the adult male population – had seen the inside of an Israeli jail.

Bashir would live the monotonous routine that defined prison life: up at 6:30, prison count, breakfast of one egg or a piece of bread and cheese, a morning of study, a lunch of thin soup, then an afternoon of more study, discussion, and rest. Exercise was discouraged, prisoners would recall, to prevent them from becoming physically stronger.

Fellowship grew from the common experience of incarceration, visceral hatred of occupation, and the dream of return. Prison study groups pored over Hegel, Lenin, Marx, Jack London, Pablo Neruda, Bertolt Brecht, the

Egyptian novelist Naguib Mahfouz, Gabriel García Márquez and his *One Hundred Years of Solitude*, and John Steinbeck's *Grapes of Wrath*. Prison officials carefully screened incoming books to intercept Palestinian nationalist literature, but occasionally some made it through, including the late Ghassan Kanafani's *Return to Haifa*, which prompted renewed discussions about UN Resolution 194. Sometimes a visitor even managed to smuggle in verse from the beloved Palestinian poet-in-exile Mahmoud Darwish.

It was crucial to prison life to find ways to pass the time. The men would listen to Chopin, the great Arabic classical singer Umm Kulthum, and the Lebanese star Fayrouz as they played chess or backgammon on the floor of their cells. They would sit in a big circle, sometimes two or three times a day, to discuss dialectical materialism; the finer points of Soviet versus Chinese Communism; political tensions in Vietnam, South Africa, Rhodesia, or Cuba; Nixon's and Kissinger's ventures in China and the Middle East; the philosophical history of the American Revolution; and the question of Palestine. Often one prisoner would volunteer to study an issue in depth, prepare a paper, and present it at a subsequent meeting. The news of the day came generally from Hebrew-language newspapers, which, over the years, Bashir and his fellow inmates would learn to read.

In the evenings, the prisoners would create their own theater: comedy skits, Shakespeare, Arabic literature, and impromptu compositions about prison interrogations. Other times the men would sing their history: nationalist songs, harvest songs, songs from villages long destroyed; or they would debate whose Palestinian political faction spoke to the people's deepest aspirations and invent new slogans to attach to each faction. Bashir had become a committed Marxist.

Every month, Ahmad would look forward to his prison visit with Bashir. 'He couldn't wait,' Khanom recalled. Many times, however, the night before the visit, Ahmad would break into cold sweats. 'He would get the shakes, like an addiction,' said Khanom. 'And the next day he would be sick and exhausted. And so often he could not go,' leaving Zakia to make the visit without him. On one such occasion, Khanom, who had moved back to the West Bank from Amman in order to visit Bashir every month, told her mother, 'You were very happy to have the baby boy. But life has not been easy with Bashir.'

Zakia said nothing, but when they got to the prison, she teased Bashir with his sister's words. 'Can you believe what your sister is saying about you?' Zakia asked Bashir.

'Bashir was very difficult,' said Khanom. 'When he was in prison we would send him special food, and he would send it back. We sent him clothes, and he refused to wear them. He forbade us from coming in a taxi. All other families came by public transport in buses, and we would refuse to take a bus. He refused to see us several times when we visited him because we had arrived in taxis – he was tough on us. He wanted to be one of the people, and we did not help him in that. So eventually we took the bus.'

During her visits, Khanom noticed that Bashir had become a leader among the prisoners. 'He would always ask us to take something to other prisoners' families,' she said. 'Always he was helping the poor and needy families. He would ask for shoes for this family; clothes and medicine for that family. At the beginning of the school year, he would arrange for books for another family. Every time we visited, he asked us to do this.'

As the years passed, Nuha Khairi marked the events in her life that Bashir, her younger brother, hadn't witnessed: her marriage to Ghiath, their cousin who had made the journey to al-Ramla in 1967; the birth of her first son, Firas, a second son, Senan, and a third, Jazwan; birthdays; anniversaries; celebrations. His brother and sister were moving into middle age, and still Bashir remained in prison.

Khanom consoled herself with the thought that Bashir, her modest, undemanding younger brother, possessed the traits of a Muslim holy man, Omar Ibn Khattab, the second caliph, or successor, to the Prophet Mohammad. Omar Ibn Khattab lived in the seventh century. 'Decent man, disciplined, serious, responsible, a man who knew exactly what he was doing. Every time I read about Khattab, I would think about Bashir.'

For years, Dalia would walk past the Ramla prison on her way to work. Nearly every day, she thought about making contact with Bashir. At least, she thought, she could find out if he was there; indeed, for a time he was. Yet she never inquired about him. Dalia's urge to find out, she would say later, was outweighed by the desire not to know. *Who needs to know all of this?* she would remember thinking. *Why open a wound? Why start all this again?*

Dalia still felt 'grievously betrayed.' For years she had waited for some signal from Bashir, some indication that he was safe and that he was innocent, or sorry.

'Indeed, I was for many years waiting for a letter saying, "I never did this,"' Dalia said, her voice rising. 'Or: "If I did this, I am very, very *sorry*." But I never received such a letter. But I am his friend, yes? Am I his friend or *not*? If I am his friend, he can tell me frankly: "I had nothing whatsoever to *do* with it." And yet he belongs to an organization that puts on its agenda to *destroy Israel*, also through *terror actions* – so-called armed struggle. Bombing buses and so on where also Palestinians are. Where Palestinian *children* can be, because terror is indiscriminate. And *I* can be on one of these buses, *too*!

'I believed he was guilty. I still believe so. And I would be the happiest person on earth to be disabused of this notion.'

At her core, Dalia believed that what Bashir did, if he did it, 'was not an answer. And if it is an answer, it is not an answer I can accept.'

At times, Dalia would consider entering into a new discussion with the family. But then she would remember the Supersol bombing.

In the fifteen years Bashir spent inside Israeli jails, wars would be fought and lost and leaders would rise and be shot down. In 1973, Egypt launched a surprise attack in what came to be known in Israel as the Yom Kippur War. An American president, Richard Nixon, resigned in disgrace, to be replaced by Gerald Ford, and then Jimmy Carter, who spoke of human rights and peace in the Middle East. Civil war broke out in Lebanon, where the Israelis would launch two invasions. In 1974 Arafat addressed the United Nations in New York, to the fury of Israel and thousands of American demonstrators, but to a standing ovation in the General Assembly, where he offered his dream of the 'Palestine of tomorrow,' whereby Arab and Jew would live side by side in a secular, democratic state. The Palestinian movement began to show signs of deep divisions over whether to accept the UN resolution recognizing Israel, which meant a possible end to the dream of return. Bashir and his fellow inmates debated these issues without rest. For Bashir, there could never be compromise on the right of refugees to return to their homes.

Bashir began to draw: first political caricatures, then map after map of Palestine, then more expressive renderings – drawings of uprooted trees, demolished houses, and Palestinians under arrest. One painting he made in the 1970s shows a green-eyed Palestinian peasant woman, one hand on an olive branch and the other holding a torch with the colors of the Palestinian flag. With another prisoner, he passed dozens of hours making a strikingly detailed replica of Jerusalem's Al-Aqsa Mosque, gluing three thousand threads and hundreds of tiny blue and yellow squares of fabric to a Styrofoam base.

As Bashir's Hebrew improved, he began to pressure Israeli prison officials for better conditions: bed frames instead of mattresses on the floors; daily exercise; bigger meal portions, instead of the scant protein and bread that would scarcely nourish a child. Frequently Bashir would organize hunger strikes to protest prison conditions.

'When Bashir was in prison, my father used to fall asleep with the radio in his lap,' Khanom remembered. 'When he heard the prisoners were on a hunger strike, he used to go on a hunger strike with them. We would tell him the strike was over so he would eat, and he would know we were trying to trick him. He would say, "That's not true, they would have announced it on the radio."' It would have been hard to deceive Ahmad on this point; at such times, he went to sleep with the radio on beneath his pillow. 'Bashir had a special relationship with his father, perhaps because he was the firstborn son,' said Khanom. 'They had more than a special relationship, they had chemistry. They adored each other.'

Despite talks with Israeli corrections officials, Bashir reported no changes, other than those outside the walls, which he saw as disastrous.

On November 19, 1977, Egyptian president Anwar Sadat made an unprecedented trip to Jerusalem, signaling his willingness to make a separate peace with Israel despite the continuing opposition of the rest of the Arab world. Two years later, after intense negotiations with U.S. president Jimmy Carter, Sadat and Israeli prime minister Menachem Begin signed the Camp David accords, which ended the state of war between Egypt and Israel. It had been twelve years since the Arab world suffered catastrophic losses in the Six Day War and six years since Egypt had regained a measure of military respect in the Yom Kippur War, or what the Palestinians knew as the October War, of 1973; now, following Camp David, Israel would begin its pullout from the Sinai Peninsula.

For many in the West, in Israel, and in Egypt, Sadat was a hero, a statesman who risked his life to make peace across what Rabin would call the 'wall of hate surrounding Israel'; it was, for supporters, a necessary first step toward a Middle East finally at peace. Indeed, the Camp David accords envisioned a five-year transition to 'full autonomy' for the Palestinians in the West Bank and Gaza. Yet Palestinians were not represented in the Camp David talks, and the accord did not address the dreams that remained central to millions of Palestinians: the right of return and the future of Jerusalem as the capital of an independent Palestinian state.

Many Palestinians, including Bashir, believed the Egyptian president had sold them out by negotiating his own deal and not focusing on a comprehensive settlement involving all the parties. Demonstrations against Sadat and Camp David erupted across the occupied territories. In the coming years, the Begin government would refuse to withdraw from the West Bank and instead intensified Israel's construction of settlements in the territories. Led by Ariel Sharon and the religious parties, the ruling coalition of Begin's Likud government rushed to create new 'facts on the ground,' laying claim to Eretz Yisrael in the West Bank and Gaza. Palestinians were required to present proof of ownership or make way for bulldozers, barbed-wire fences, and Israeli settlers. Palestinians thus came to see their deepest fears realized: They were still stateless, the occupation was becoming more entrenched, and now they would need to go forward without Egypt, their most powerful ally in their decades-long liberation struggle. In the West Bank, Sadat became so despised among Palestinians that he spawned a new word in the Palestinian Arabic dialect: To this day, to be a *sadati* is to be one who is weak, one who capitulates, one who acts cowardly, or, in the words of an old friend of Bashir's, 'someone who is ready to make concessions in exchange for false personal glory.' In 1981, the Egyptian president would pay for his courage, or his cowardice, with his life. On October 6, while watching a military parade with foreign dignitaries, he was assassinated by gunmen from Islamic Jihad in Cairo.

Throughout the late 1970s, Dalia would often sit on her veranda in Ramla after work, gazing out at the Queen Elizabeth roses. During this period, she often felt 'swept into despair by collective forces clashing against each other' and worried that 'my spirit was being crushed by a historic wheel of inevitability.' She wondered if the conflict with the Palestinians would ever end. She knew that each side often seemed to want to wish the other away, but her own attempts to block the Khairi family from her mind were not working. 'Something within me kept pushing,' she wrote years later. 'A little nagging voice wished to figure out why it came to me to be involved in this. People came and knocked on my door, and I chose to open it. Is that door now forever shut? Was that a fleeting opportunity, a passing episode?'

Dalia would recall hours of contemplation about the Khairi family and about the house she lived in, 'which my father bought as "abandoned property from the state." But this house did not belong to the state; it belonged to the family that had built it, that had put its resources into it, that had hoped to raise its children and grow old in this house. I could imagine myself in the Khairis' place.'

Is it either us or them? Dalia thought. *Either I live in their house while they are refugees, or they live in my house while I become a fugitive? There must be another possibility. But what is it?*

Moshe and Solia were growing old. 'I knew that one day,' Dalia said, 'I would inherit that house.'

In the years Bashir spent in one Israeli prison after another – by his count, he moved seventeen times in fifteen years – he would from time to time talk about a young Israeli woman and the door she had opened for his family. 'I told my friends in prison about my visits to the house,' he would recall. 'And what I saw in Dalia. It seemed she was someone different. I would say, "She's open-minded, she's different compared with the other Israelis that I met."'

'I hope,' Bashir would say, 'she is not a lonely candle in a darkened room.'

Yet Bashir would never write the letter Dalia so wanted. He did not confess to his Israeli interrogators, and he was not going to confess to Dalia. Indeed, he maintained his innocence but added, years later: 'We have suffered many massacres. Dawayma. Kufr Qassam. Deir Yassin. In the face of these massacres and dispossessions, if anyone thought that the Palestinians would react as Jesus Christ would have, he is wrong. If I didn't have this deep conviction to the bone marrow in the necessity of hating the occupation, I wouldn't deserve to be a Palestinian.'

In September 1984, having served fifteen years for his conviction in the Supersol market bombing, Bashir Khairi was released from prison. It was one of two truly happy moments Khanom would remember about her brother. The other, she recalled, was when he was born.

Bashir's family was waiting in Ramallah. Brothers and sisters had returned from across the Arab world; they came from Amman, from Qatar, from Kuwait. 'It was like a wedding,' Nuha would recall. 'We prepared the best foods, sweets, flowers, Palestinian flags.'

Israeli officials were adamant that there be no celebration outside the prison walls. 'They said only two or three people should come,' Khanom remembered. 'I made bows for the flowers with the colors of the Palestinian flag, which was illegal at the time. The Israelis did not notice it. But so many people had heard that Bashir was to be released, they gathered around the prison walls to welcome him. When the Israelis saw this, they said we will not let him out. We were there at eight A.M. – they made us wait till after one o'clock. My father and mother were very old and were waiting at home anxiously.'

When Bashir emerged from prison, he was not ready to go home. He went directly to the cemetery. He stood at the grave of Khalil Abu-Khadijeh, his co-defendant in the Supersol trial, who had died in prison. Bashir paid respects with Khalil's family in a quiet, private ceremony. 'Then,' Nuha said, 'he came home.'

The house was full of well-wishers. Relatives from Gaza sent large bags of oranges for the celebration. So many people wanted to see Bashir – schoolchildren, town leaders, family, political activists – that friends had to volunteer to direct traffic in front of the house. 'They did it for Bashir,' Khanom said. 'Mom is cooking, everybody is welcoming.' At first Bashir downplayed the event. 'He did not like the idea of a celebration. "I am not a hero," he said. "I served my time – I did nothing special. No need to celebrate."' But eventually he relented, and the family saw him 'happy, glad, smiling all the time. It was the most beautiful time of my life.'

At home, Bashir had to adjust to life outside of prison. 'He slept on the floor, and he was not used to a bed anymore,' Khanom said. 'He couldn't wear regular shoes, either, because after fifteen years without shoes the size and shape of his feet changed.' More disturbing were the marks of what his family believed was torture. 'When he got out of prison, he had a lot of cigarette burns on his body,' Khanom said. 'When we asked him what they were, he said it was an allergy.'

In December 1984, three months after Bashir's release from prison and forty-eight years after he built the family home in al-Ramla, Ahmad Khairi died. He was seventy-seven years old and had lived nearly half his life in exile.

Later that year, Bashir married his cousin Scheherazade.

When asked, he would say little about the union, except that he knew 'she was the person who would most understand me.' In 1985, their first child was born. In the Arabic tradition, they would name the boy after his grandfather, Ahmad.

That same year, Moshe Eshkenazi died. Solia had died eight years earlier, and now no one lived in the house. 'It was sad,' Dalia remembered. 'All your history is there, it's an empty house, your parents are dead. It was mine now.'

The house was Dalia's, legally. Nevertheless, 'I could not deny that I lived in the house for all those years, while the family that built it had been expelled. How do you balance such realities? How do you confront them and respond to them?

'It was in my hands to do something,' she said. 'It was like the house was telling me a story. More than one story. I had to respond.' She always thought of the crime that had led to Bashir's long sentence. How, she wondered, could she respond in the light of that? Eventually she decided, 'His reaction will not determine mine. I have free choice to think, I have free choice to act, in accordance with my understanding and my conscience.'

Dalia had been thinking of the time when, as a little girl, she had wrenched the star and crescent, the symbol of Islam, from the top of the gate in the house in Ramla and thrown it away. 'It was so beautiful,' she said. 'I wished I could put it back. I was ashamed of what I did.'

One night, as she continued to mull over what to do with the house, the angel Gabriel came to Dalia in a dream. 'He was perched, hovering just there at the top of the gate where the crescent had been,' Dalia said. 'And he was looking at where the symbol was, and he was smiling.

He was blessing the house, he was blessing me, and he was giving a blessing for what I wanted to do with the house.'

In the spring of 1985, Bashir received a message from a Palestinian Anglican priest in Ramallah. His name was Audeh Rantisi. He was originally from Lydda, and he had his own vivid memories of being driven out by force from his home in July 1948.

Rantisi told Bashir that he had just received a phone call from Jerusalem. It was from Yehezkel Landau, Dalia's husband. Yehezkel had explained that Dalia's father, Moshe Eshkenazi, had died and that now, eight years after Solia's death, the house in Ramla was empty. Dalia wanted to meet with Bashir to talk about the future of the house. Would he be willing to meet?

Dalia had been thinking of what she could do. She knew she wanted to act on the basis of two histories. 'I had to acknowledge that this is my childhood home, my parents lived here until they died, my memories are all here, but that this house was built by another family, and their memories are here. I had to acknowledge absolutely all of it.'

Within a month, Dalia and Yehezkel found themselves driving north into the occupied West Bank. They met in the home of Rantisi and his wife, Patricia, next door to the Ramallah Evangelical School for Boys, which Rantisi directed. Bashir was waiting there.

Dalia and Bashir sat facing each other in comfortable chairs in the Rantisi living room. How long had it been? Sixteen years? Eighteen? Dalia was now thirty-seven, with a wedding ring on her finger, and Bashir, forty-three, was also newly married. A tuft of gray hair fell over his forehead. Dalia noticed that his left hand was in his pocket; it always seemed to be.

They exchanged small talk. Was Bashir healthy? How did it feel to walk freely? What were his plans?

Dalia came to the point of their meeting. She had not been able to stop thinking about the house and its history, she explained. This home involved two families, two peoples, two histories. And now, barely a month after Moshe's death, the home was empty. She had been thinking, too, about the endless cycle of pain, retaliation, pain, retaliation. She wondered if there was something she could do to address that and to honor the families' two histories. This was a gesture not just to Bashir, but to the entire Khairi family. *How does one acknowledge the collective wound?* she had asked herself again and again. The heart wants to do something. *The heart wants to move toward the healing of that wound.*

Dalia understood that she could not share ownership of the house with the Khairis, or even transfer the title to their name. Another solution was needed.

'We are open,' Dalia said. 'We are ready to pay reparations for the loss of your property.' She raised the possibility that she sell the house and give the proceeds to the Khairis.

'No, no, no,' Bashir said quickly. 'No selling. Our patrimony cannot be for sale.'

'Then how do you see it, Bashir?' Dalia asked him. 'What shall we do?'

For Bashir, the solution had to be consistent with his rights and his lifelong struggle as a Palestinian. 'This house is my homeland,' he told Dalia. 'I lost my childhood there. I would like the house to provide a very nice time for the Arab children of al-Ramla. I want them to have joy there. I want them to have the childhood that I never had. What I lost there, I want to give them.'

287

Dalia and Yehezkel agreed readily to Bashir's suggestion: The house in Ramla would become a pre-school for the Arab children of Israel. They had other ideas as well, but this was a good start. They would honor Bashir's wishes, though perhaps not the name he suggested for the house his father had built: 'Dalia's Kindergarten for the Arab Children of Ramla.'

'Excuse me,' Patricia Rantisi interrupted gently from the edge of the living room. 'The food is ready.'

Bashir, Dalia, Yehezkel, and Audeh Rantisi rose from their seats to join Patricia at the dinner table. The conversation would continue over the midday feast.

As they prepared to break bread, Dalia and Yehezkel looked across the table at their Arab neighbors and offered a prayer in Hebrew:

> Blessed are You, the eternal One, our God, Ruler of the universe, Who brings forth bread from the earth.

Eleven

DEPORTATION

BASHIR LAY BLINDFOLDED and facedown in an Israeli military van rolling south from the West Bank town of Nablus. His hands were cuffed behind him, his legs shackled and attached by chains to three other prisoners.

His freedom hadn't lasted. Three years after his release from prison, Bashir Khairi was in custody again.

That morning – January 13, 1988 – Bashir and three other men had been taken from their cells at Jneid prison in Nablus and led along the concrete floor toward the prison exit. The action would come as no surprise to the international diplomatic community, the press, human rights lawyers, the Arab world, and the eight hundred Palestinians behind bars at Jneid. The arrest of the four men was part of a broader Israeli crackdown on the suspected organizers of the ongoing disturbances in Gaza and the West Bank, known to Israelis as riots and to the Arab world as the uprising – in Arabic, the intifada.

Five weeks earlier, Gaza and then the West Bank had exploded in demonstrations against Israel's rule. For twenty years, Palestinians living in the Israeli-controlled territories had seen nearly every aspect of public life dictated by an occupying force. Israelis determined school curriculum, ran the civil and military courts, oversaw health care and social services, established occupation taxes, and decided which proposed businesses would receive operating permits. Though the Israelis had allowed the formation of some civil institutions, including trade unions and charities, by the mid-1980s the 1.5 million Palestinians in the West Bank and Gaza seethed under occupation. Israelis controlled the land the Palestinians lived on and guarded access to the streams and aquifers running through and beneath it. They could arrest and imprison Gazans or West Bankers under shifting laws and military regulations not subject to public review. For twenty years, resentment and resistance had built up, and by late 1987, it had reached a point of explosion.

On December 8, 1987, an Israeli vehicle – some accounts claim it was an agricultural truck, others insist it was a tank – veered into a long line of cars carrying Palestinian men returning to Gaza from low-paying day labor in Israel. Four Arabs were killed. The same day, rumors spread that the corpses of the four men had been seized from the Jabalya refugee camp by Israeli troops attempting to cover up evidence that the men had been murdered.

Later, in the Jabalya camp, several thousand people gathered for the funeral, and clashes broke out. The next day, boys and young men began hurling stones at the Israeli soldiers. Hundreds of stones were falling on the troops, and they responded with live fire. A twenty-year-old man, Hatem al-Sisi, was killed; he would be known as the first martyr of the intifada. Quickly the demonstrations spread, first to the rest of Gaza and then to the West Bank, as young men, teenagers, and even boys as young as eight years old hurled stones at the Israeli tanks and troops. Across the West Bank and Gaza, Palestinians declared a general strike, boycotting Israeli goods and calling on 'brother doctors and pharmacists' and 'brother businessmen and grocers' to shutter their shops – out of solidarity with the demonstrators and to make clear that life in the occupied territories would not go on as before. The intifada was born.

Now the image of the Palestinians that splashed across the world's television screens was not of hijackers blowing up airliners or masked men kidnapping and murdering Olympic athletes, but of young people throwing stones at occupiers who responded with bullets. Israel, long portrayed in the West as a David in a hostile Arab sea, was suddenly cast as Goliath.

The intifada, dismissed at first by Israeli defense minister Yitzhak Rabin as an insignificant series of local disturbances, would change the dynamics of Middle Eastern politics. Palestinians would call it the 'Stone Revolution.' One prominent Israeli historian compared it with 'an anticolonial war of liberation'; another called it 'the Palestinian War of Independence.' The question – What kind of independence? – would come to divide the Palestinians in the years to come.

For years the PLO, a coalition of nationalist resistance groups, with Arafat's Fatah at its center, had dominated Palestinian political discourse. Five days into the intifada, however, a new group emerged from the same Gaza refugee camp that had spawned the uprising. It would be called the Islamic Resistance Movement, known by its Arabic acronym, Hamas. Its leader, a crippled, bearded, middle-aged man named Sheikh Ahmed Yassin, had fled with his family from the village of al-Jora in 1948; the village was later destroyed and the Israeli city of Ashkelon built on its rubble.

Hamas favored no recognition of Israel and no compromise on the right of return. The organization sought an Islamic state in all of historic Palestine. Its charter described Jews as conspiring 'to rule the world' and declared that the elimination of Israel would be a historic parallel to the victory of Saladin over the Crusaders eight centuries earlier. Hamas's uncompromising stance on the right of the refugees to return to their homes, and the group's growing role in social welfare programs in the occupied territories, would prove popular. The group was immediately seen as an on-the-ground rival to the PLO, whose leaders, including Yasser Arafat, were in exile in Tunis.

Israel, wanting to weaken Arafat, had initially encouraged the growth of the radical Muslim Brotherhood, whose members had established Hamas. Now Hamas issued fervent denunciations of the 'Zionist entity' and its repression of the intifada.

Palestinian resistance in the intifada went far beyond Hamas or the limited ability of PLO leaders to direct events from Tunis. Much of the resistance was spontaneous, especially in the early months. Local committees sprang up from the grass roots to coordinate demonstrations, plan hit-and-run operations against Israeli platoons, conduct secret classes when the Israeli authorities closed local schools, protest Israeli taxes, remove Israeli products from the shelves of local markets, and form bread, poultry, and sewing cooperatives to replace income when the men could no longer work in Israel. Many families grew 'victory gardens' to replace Israeli supplies of produce, hatched chickens in the shells of old refrigerators, and poured milk into old animal skins, shaking the skins until the milk turned to butter.

The stone was at the heart of the uprising, but some communities engaged in nonviolent civil disobedience. In Beit Sahour, near Bethlehem, thousands of Palestinians, part of a tax revolt against the Israelis, turned in their Israeli-issued ID cards and sat in silent protest at the municipality. Israeli troops dispersed them with tear gas.

At the height of the tax revolt, Dalia rode toward Beit Sahour with a large group of religious Jews. 'They had no representation, and they were being taxed,' Dalia recalled of the Palestinians. Israeli soldiers stopped the group at the checkpoint. They stood before the soldiers, reciting a sura from the Koran about punishment and innocence, reading the Prayer of St. Francis about sowing love where there is hatred, and singing the Hassidic Prayer for Peace:

> May it be Thy will to put an end to war and bloodshed on earth, and to spread a great and wonderful peace over the whole world, so that nation shall not lift up sword against nation, neither shall they learn war anymore . . .
>
> Let us never shame any person on earth, great or small . . .
>
> And let it come to pass in our time as it is written, 'And I will give peace in the land, and you shall lie down and none shall make you afraid. I will drive the wild beasts from the land, and neither shall the sword go through your land.'
>
> God who is peace, bless us with peace!

In the first three weeks of the uprising, twenty-nine Palestinians would die in demonstrations as the Israeli army continued its policy of using live ammunition; soon, facing growing international criticism, Yitzhak Rabin, now defense minister, would shift IDF policy to 'force, might, and beatings,' as soldiers began deliberately breaking the hands and arms of stone throwers. Still, the death toll rose; in the first year of the intifada, at least 230 Palestinians would be shot dead by Israeli troops and more than 20,000 were arrested. Thousands were captured in predawn raids in the refugee camps, as soldiers broke down doors, hauled young stone throwers out of their homes, and loaded them onto buses. Many of the young men and boys would be jailed without charge under 'administrative detention.' Israeli officials closed nine hundred West Bank and Gaza schools; imposed broad curfews that prevented workers from getting to their jobs in Israel; and, despite an international outcry, began to deport to Lebanon the men, including Bashir, who were suspected of organizing the intifada.

Dalia lay in a Jerusalem hospital bed, listening to doctors and nurses discuss the intifada. It was January 1988.

In recent days, the news of the Palestinian uprising had come sporadically: A friend would bring in a newspaper, an orderly would roll in a television, or Dalia would lie on her back and listen to the anguish in the voices of the hospital staff.

Nine months earlier, Dalia had been diagnosed with cancer. After her initial biopsy and treatment, she received four medical opinions strongly recommending more invasive procedures; this treatment, she said, would have involved a hysterectomy. She reluctantly agreed to the procedure, but just days before the surgery, Dalia discovered she was pregnant. She was forty years old. Against the advice of all her doctors, she refused the surgery. They warned her that if she went forward with the pregnancy, she would be risking her life. There was no way to know whether the cancer would come back. 'As a doctor I object,' one of the specialists told her. 'But as a human being, I respect, acknowledge, and admire.'

One evening a few weeks later, Dalia walked to the Old City. She felt elated by her decision to keep her baby and wanted to pray at the Wailing Wall. When she came home she felt intense cramps. In the hospital, doctors told her she had a high-risk pregnancy related to her cancer treatment. She was immediately confined to her hospital bed, twenty-four hours a day. It was in this state that she heard the first news of the intifada.

In early January, Dalia's husband, Yehezkel, arrived at her bedside with the news that Bashir was about to be deported. He was suspected of helping organize the intifada, and it appeared an Israeli military court would order his deportation any day.

'Why don't you do something?' Yehezkel asked.

Dalia thought the question was ridiculous. Do something? She was six months pregnant and struggling to recover from a life-threatening illness. She had been bedridden for months. She could not even rise to go to the bathroom without feeling contractions, and the potent anticontraction medicine was making her tremble.

'Like what?' Dalia asked.

'Maybe you could write about your history,' Yehezkel replied. 'About Bashir and the story of the house in Ramla.'

'No, of course not,' Dalia would remember saying to her husband. 'I don't want to expose myself. I need peace and privacy. I don't want to.'

Yehezkel let the matter drop.

*　*　*

At the Jneid prison on January 13, 1988, as Bashir, Jabril Rajoub, Hussam Khader, and Jamal Jabara walked past the rows of cells, the other prisoners began banging on their bars, shouting, *'Allahu akbar!'* – 'God is great!' – and singing the unofficial Palestinian national anthem, 'Billadi, Billadi, Billadi!' – ('My Homeland, My Homeland, My Homeland!'). As the noise built to an ear-hammering pitch, Bashir and Jabril would recall, Israeli prison guards fired tear gas canisters into the cells, and the yelling and banging gave way to coughing and moaning. As they approached the exit and the noise began to fade, they could hear a few prisoners still shouting: 'Do not deport them! Do not deport them from the homeland!'

The deportation hearing the previous day in an Israeli military court had been swift: Israeli and Arab lawyers for Bashir and the three other prisoners, declaring the proceedings a 'judicial charade' by a court they said lacked legitimacy, had abandoned their attempts to prevent the deportations. 'The game was fixed from the beginning,' said the Israeli human rights lawyer Leah Tsemel at a press conference. In court, the four men were described by the Israeli army as 'among the leaders and instigators' of the disturbances in the West Bank and Gaza. Consequently, the military judge declared, he would approve the deportation order for the four Palestinians, despite objections from many nations, including the United States, and a strongly worded resolution from the United Nations Security Council. The resolution was prompted by the deportation of Bashir, his comrades, and several other groups of Palestinians.

The four men had no idea to where they would be deported. 'You can deport me,' Jabril Rajoub would recall telling the judge. 'But you cannot deport Palestine from my heart. You can deport us, kill us, destroy us. But this will never assure security for you.'

As defense minister, Yitzhak Rabin was a central figure in the deportations of Bashir and his comrades. Only days earlier, Bashir recalled, he had met with Rabin at Jneid prison. The defense minister arrived following complaints from human rights groups about treatment of prisoners. Bashir told Rabin that the conditions in Israeli prisons were not fit for dogs, and that even Haim Levy, the Israeli director of prisons, had said much the same thing. Rabin listened to Bashir's list of prison grievances and said, 'If there will be peace, there will be no problem any more with the prisoners.' Within days, Rabin, who had been part of the Israeli force that expelled Palestinians from al-Ramla and Lydda in 1948, would approve the deportations of Bashir and the three others to Lebanon.

The soldiers pulled Bashir and the three other prisoners from the military van. It was a cold January morning. As Bashir stood on bare ground, he could feel the blast of wind from the blades of a helicopter, and he felt himself being pushed inside. The helicopter began to rise, then swing around to point north. Bashir could not see and had no idea where he was going.

The four men in blindfolds could imagine the lands beneath them. Below, on their left, the shoreline of the Mediterranean snaked north from Jaffa and Tel Aviv toward Haifa and Acca (known to the Israelis as Acre or Acco). Behind them, just inland on the coastal plain, lay al-Ramla and the house Bashir's father had built fifty-two years earlier; beyond, farther east, the Jordan River trickled south from the Sea of Galilee toward the Dead Sea.

Between river and sea – from the old Arab port of Jaffa to the mountains of the West Bank; from the Dome of the Rock in Jerusalem to the fertile warmth of Jericho, one of the cradles of civilization – this crooked finger of land, sixty miles at its widest, was known to most of the world as Israel, the West Bank, and Gaza. To Bashir and the other deportees beside him, all of it was still Palestine.

'I had been in prison six times,' Jabril Rajoub would remember. 'For me, deportation was worse than any of that. I was born in Palestine. My parents, my grandparents, my great-grandparents, and my great-great-grandparents are all from Palestine. My memories are in this country. I feel I am a part of this country. I feel I have a right to live in this country. With my family, with my friends, in my homeland.'

The helicopter crossed Israel's northern border and set down on a road in southern Lebanon. Bashir, Jabril, the two other activists, and the Israeli soldiers guarding them were in the Israel Defense Forces' 'security zone,' a twenty-five-mile south-to-north buffer established in 1982 when Israel invaded Lebanon to crush the PLO. Israel had remained in southern Lebanon ever since, declaring its intent to stop incursions and rocket attacks into the northern Galilee, but the occupation had grown increasingly unpopular, both in Lebanon and at home. Already the conflict was becoming known as 'Israel's Vietnam.'

Bashir stepped beneath the helicopter blades and felt someone take off his blindfold. He could see Jabril and the other two men. The four activists looked out to see two waiting black Mercedes sedans.

An Israeli officer gave Bashir $50 and looked him in the eye. 'If you even try to come back,' he recalled the officer saying, 'we will shoot you.'

The four men climbed into the black sedans driven by masked Lebanese militiamen and sped north, out of the 'security zone' and deeper into Lebanon's Beka'a Valley.

ISRAEL DEFIES UN AND DEPORTS FOUR PALESTINIANS, read a headline in the January 14 edition of the *Times* of London. 'Israel defied the United Nations Security Council openly yesterday and deported four Palestinians to southern Lebanon, as its inner cabinet met to approve even tougher measures to put down the disturbances which are continuing unabated throughout the occupied territories,' the dispatch stated.

The same day, under the headline FOUR EXPELLED SECRETLY, the *Jerusalem Post* reported on its front page that Bashir and the three other activists accused of 'inciting riots in the administered territories' were 'shuttled secretly by helicopter to the northern edge of the Southern Lebanon Security Zone at noon yesterday, without a word of notice to their families or lawyers.' The deportations, the newspaper indicated, were widely denounced around the world as a human rights violation and antithetical to a peaceful solution to the conflict. Even the normally reserved U.S. State Department issued a statement of 'deep regret' about the actions of its ally. Israel's UN ambassador, a young politician named Benjamin Netanyahu, replied that the deportations were 'totally legal' and that the United Nations Security Council could not be a fair arbiter because it 'condones any violence on the Arab side, while condemning all Israeli countermeasures.'

Israeli society was increasingly divided over the deportations, the occupation of southern Lebanon, and the treatment of Palestinians during the intifada. On the Right stood the Likud government of Yitzhak Shamir, which advocated a continuation of the hard-line policy against the Palestinians. Netanyahu, the UN ambassador, had forged many of his own convictions after the death of his brother, Yonatan, during an Israeli raid against a PFLP hijacking in Entebbe, Uganda.

Toward the Israeli political center, representing the conservative wing of the Labor Party, stood Yitzhak Rabin, who, on the eve of Bashir's deportation, had recognized the 'despair' of Palestinian refugees. 'As a soldier, I feel that these people have fought with a courage that deserves respect,' he would tell Mustafa Khalil, the former Egyptian prime minister and an architect of the Camp David accords. 'They deserve to have an entity. Not the PLO, not a state, but a separate entity.' Rabin believed that Israel could not agree to the Palestinians' central political demand – recognition of the PLO as the sole representative of the Palestinian people and to Yasser Arafat as their leader. To do so, Rabin argued, would require Israelis to compromise on the right of return for hundreds of thousands of Palestinian refugees, and that, the defense minister argued, would be 'national suicide.'

At the center of Israel Defense Forces policy under Rabin remained the iron fist: crushing the intifada with military force and deporting PLO and PFLP operatives to Lebanon. Other Israelis, however, had already begun to rethink this logic. In the same January 14 edition of the *Jerusalem Post*, at the back of the paper on the editorial page, a quiet voice emerged amid the international furor over the deportations and the Israeli crackdown in the occupied territories.

The voice belonged to a forty-year-old woman who had grown up in Ramla. Her article was titled 'Letter to a

Deportee.'

'Dear Bashir,' wrote Dalia. 'We got to know each other twenty years ago under unusual and unexpected circumstances. Ever since, we have become part of each other's lives. Now I hear that you are about to be deported. Since you are in detention at present, and this may be my last chance to communicate with you, I have chosen to write this open letter. First I want to retell our story.'

Dalia had initially dismissed Yehezkel's suggestion that she write about her history. Afterward, she would remember, 'an inner voice, an inner conviction' rose up, 'welling up in a wave, saying, *Yes, it's right to do it. You've got to do it.* At that moment it came with the courage. And I knew: Yes, I'm going to be out there.'

Dalia recounted for Israeli readers the story of the Eshkenazis, the Khairis, and the house in Ramla: Bashir's visit to the house after the Six Day War; Dalia's visit to Ramallah and the 'warm personal connection' they established across the gulf of political differences; and her understanding, ultimately, that the house she, Moshe, and Solia moved into in November 1948 was not simply 'abandoned property':

> It was very painful for me, as a young woman 20 years ago, to wake up to a few then well hidden facts. For example, we were all led to believe that the Arab population of Ramla and Lod had run away before the advancing Israeli army in 1948, leaving everything behind in a rushed and cowardly escape. This belief reassured us. It was meant to prevent guilt and remorse. But after 1967, I met not only you, but also an Israeli Jew who had personally participated in the expulsion from Ramla

and Lod. He told me the story as he had experienced it, and as Yitzhak Rabin later confirmed in his memoirs.

'My love for my country,' Dalia wrote, 'was losing its innocence . . . some change in perspective was beginning to take place in me.' She then recounted the 'unforgettable day' of Ahmad Khairi's only visit to the house he had built and the moment when he stood at the lemon tree, tears rolling down his face, as Moshe Eshkenazi plucked a few lemons from the tree and placed them in Ahmad's hands.

Many years later, after the death of your father, your mother told me that, whenever he felt troubled at night and could not sleep, he would pace up and down your rented apartment in Ramallah, holding a shriveled lemon in his hand. It was the same lemon my father had given him on that visit.

Ever since I met you, the feeling has been growing in me that that home was not just my home. The lemon tree which yielded so much fruit and gave us so much delight lived in other people's hearts too. The spacious house with its high ceilings, big windows and large grounds was no longer just an 'Arab house,' a desirable form of architecture. It had faces behind it now. The walls evoked other people's memories and tears.

Dalia described a 'strange destiny' that connected her family to Bashir's. Though the plans for turning the house into a kindergarten and a center for Arab-Jewish dialogue had been long delayed, this 'destiny' was still on her mind. 'The house with which our childhood memories were connected,' she wrote, 'forced us to face each other.' But Dalia then questioned whether genuine reconciliation could be possible across a chasm as wide as the one between herself and Bashir. She recounted Bashir's conviction and prison term in the aftermath of the explosion that killed three civilians in the Supersol market – 'My heart aches for those murdered even now' – and then pleaded with Bashir to transform his politics.

Dalia told Bashir that his support of George Habash and the PFLP – support he had never acknowledged, but which she assumed – represented a 'refusal to accept a Jewish state in even part of Palestine,' a position she said 'will alienate all those Israelis who, like myself, are prepared to support the Palestinian struggle for self determination.'

> People like yourself, Bashir, bear a great responsibility for triggering our anxieties which are well justified, given the PFLP's determination to replace Israel with a 'secular democratic state' and to use terror to achieve this aim.
>
> If you could disassociate yourself from your past terrorist actions, your commitment to your own people would gain true moral force in my eyes. I well understand that terror is a term relative to a subjective point of view. Some of Israel's political leaders were terrorists in the past and have never repented. I know that what we consider terror from our side, your people considers their heroic 'armed struggle' with the means at their disposal. What we consider our right to self-defense, when we bomb Palestinian targets from the air and inevitably hit civilians, you consider mass terror from the air with advanced technology. Each side has an ingenuity for justifying its own position. How long shall we perpetuate this vicious circle? . . .

Dalia then turned to the actions of her own government in deporting Bashir, which she called a 'violation of human rights,' which 'create[s] greater bitterness and extremism among the Palestinians' and allows the deportees 'greater freedom to plan actions against Israel from abroad.' Yet Dalia understood that at the heart of Bashir's deportation was something beyond politics:

You, Bashir, have already experienced one expulsion from Ramla as a child. Now you are about to experience another from Ramallah forty years later. You will thus become a refugee twice. You may be separated from your wife and your two small children, Ahmad and Hanine, and from your elderly mother and the rest of your family. How can your children avoid hating those who will have deprived them of their father? Will the legacy of pain grow and harden with bitterness as it passes down the generations?

It seems to me, Bashir, that you will now have a new opportunity to assume a leadership role. By its intention to deport you, Israel is actually empowering you. I appeal to you to demonstrate the kind of leadership that uses nonviolent means of struggle for your rights . . .

I appeal to both Palestinians and Israelis to understand that the use of force will not resolve this conflict on its fundamental level. This is the kind of war that no one can win, and either both peoples will achieve liberation or neither will.

Our childhood memories, yours and mine, are intertwined in a tragic way. If we can not find means to transform that tragedy into a shared blessing, our clinging to the past will destroy our future. We will then rob another generation of a joy-filled childhood and turn them into martyrs for an unholy cause. I pray that with your cooperation and God's help, our children will delight in the beauty and bounties of this holy land.

Allah ma'ak. May God be with you.

Dalia

Bashir would not read Dalia's open letter for weeks. The morning it appeared in print, he and the three other deportees were well inside Lebanese territory at a PFLP training camp in the Beka'a Valley.

The next day, they were driven in an ambulance operated by Salah Salah, the PFLP leader in Lebanon, to the village of Ksara near the 'security zone' border. The Israelis controlled most of the zone, aided by a force they had financed and organized, the South Lebanon Army, but the area was far from pacified. Hostile villages chafing under the Israeli occupation had spawned the Army of God, or Hezbollah. Their objective was to expel the Israelis from southern Lebanon, to which end they began firing Soviet-made Katyusha rockets into northern Israel.

Israel had occupied southern Lebanon for six years, since its 1982 invasion and attack on Beirut. After Black September in 1970, Arafat's PLO, Habash's PFLP, and other rebel factions had left Jordan and set up operations in Lebanon. From their virtual state within a state, they launched attacks against Israel, just as they had in Hussein's kingdom. Israel funneled tens of millions of dollars to Lebanese Christian militias who were alarmed at the militant Palestinian presence and the rapid growth in Lebanon's Muslim population. The militias fought a proxy war for Israel against the Palestinian factions, but with little success, and in 1982, General Ariel Sharon and his Israeli forces laid siege to Beirut. Tens of thousands of shells rained down on the Lebanese capital as Sharon declared that south Beirut should be 'razed to the ground.' Sharon's central goal was to drive Arafat and the Palestinian forces out of Lebanon and farther away from Israel. PLO forces put up stiffer resistance than expected, but by late July, Arafat and the PLO leadership began to consider the inevitable: evacuation from Lebanon to a safe haven deeper into exile.

On August 21, 1982, the first four hundred Palestinian guerrillas left Lebanon for Cyprus, an island off the Lebanese coast that was divided between Greek- and Turkish-controlled territories. Over the next two weeks, fourteen thousand more would follow them into exile. Arafat himself would quit Lebanon on August 30, boarding a Greek merchant ship under the protective shield of the U.S. Sixth Fleet. By September 1, the PLO would be establishing its third home in exile: Tunisia, the North African nation on the Mediterranean coast, where Arafat and his *cadres* would consider their new options. Left behind in Lebanon were nearly half a million Palestinians living in squalid refugee camps. They had arrived in Lebanon in 1948, fresh with the promise they would be going home 'after fifteen days.' Thirty-four years later, they still taught their children the names of streets in villages long since destroyed. None had been given Lebanese citizenship, which they assured their hosts they didn't want anyway. Their only wish, they insisted, was to exercise their UN-sanctioned right of return.

* * *

Two weeks after PLO forces left, hundreds of Palestinian civilians were slaughtered in the Sabra and Shatilla refugee camps in Beirut. The killings began one day after the murder of Lebanese Christian president Bashir Gemayel, whom the Israelis had hoped to help install as a friendly head of state.

The executioners were Phalangist Christian militias who had entered the camps after Gemayel's death at the encouragement of Ariel Sharon and other Israeli military officers. Their mission, ostensibly, was to root out two thousand militants said to still be in hiding after the departure of the PLO. As Israeli generals and foot soldiers stood by just outside the camps, and the Israeli forces launched night flares to illuminate the militias' search, the Phalangist gunmen began a forty-eight-hour killing spree. Every living creature in the two camps – men, women, babies, even donkeys and dogs – was slaughtered by the Phalangists. It was described in this account by Loren Jenkins in the *Washington Post*:

> The scene at the Shatilla camp when foreign observers entered Saturday morning was like a nightmare. Women wailed over the deaths of loved ones, bodies began to swell under the hot sun, and the streets were littered with thousands of spent cartridges. Houses had been dynamited and bulldozed into rubble, many with the inhabitants still inside. Groups of bodies lay before bullet-pocked walls where they appeared to have been executed. Others were strewn in alleys and streets, apparently shot as they tried to escape. Each little dirt alley through the deserted buildings, where Palestinians have lived since fleeing Palestine when Israel was created in 1948, told its own horror story.

Israeli forces provided bulldozers for the digging of mass graves by Lebanese forces. By Israel's later estimates, at least 700 Palestinians had been slaughtered; one independent international commission put the death toll at 2,750.

The Sabra and Shatilla massacres shocked the world and provoked outrage in Israel, where an estimated four hundred thousand protesters, including Dalia and Yehezkel, filled the streets of Tel Aviv to demand a formal inquiry. It was among the biggest demonstrations in Israel's history. Dalia would recall a day of discussion on the ethics of the Jewish tradition and her feeling of solidarity with the speakers who admonished, 'One does not stand by when such a thing is happening to other people. It's an un-Jewish attitude.'

Five months later, the Israeli Kahan Commission declared that Israel, and Sharon, bore indirect responsibility for the massacres. The commission blamed the defense minister 'for having disregarded the danger of acts of vengeance and bloodshed by the Phalangists against the population of the refugee camps' and recommended that he be dismissed from his post by the Israeli cabinet. Sharon soon began his temporary journey into Israel's political wilderness.

Bashir, Jabril Rajoub, and the two other deportees had arrived in Lebanon without papers. It was January 14, 1988. Like the Palestinians in refugee camps across Lebanon, they were stateless, unwanted by the Lebanese authorities, and determined to return home. Unlike the refugees, their deportations had drawn international attention, which they intended to exploit to the full advantage of the Palestinian cause and the intifada in particular.

Jabril had an idea: What if the four activists found a place to set up tents as close as possible to the southernmost edge of Lebanon? This would be difficult, the four men were told by Salah Salah, their PFLP escort. Movement was highly restricted, and all the men risked arrest by Syria, which was in de facto control of the Lebanese Beka'a Valley. The men would have to move as secretly as possible.

Bashir, Jabril, and their fellow deportees hid in the back of an ambulance driven by Salah Salah. The ambulance snaked through back roads in the Beka'a Valley, toward the village of Ksara, where there was an office of the International Red Cross. The Red Cross would not be pleased to see them, the men were sure, but neither would they be in a position to expel them.

They emerged from the ambulance into a field in front of the Red Cross building. Someone commandeered a tent. Next to it they pitched a Palestinian flag. Within hours, local supporters arrived with more tents, and soon the four celebrated deportees would be at the center of an ever widening group of activists, dignitaries, and the international press. 'I can't remember a night where there weren't at least one hundred people,' Bashir would say.

PLO and PFLP leaders came to see them. The foreign minister of Algeria paid a visit. Lebanese and Syrian officials discussed their status, and the ambassador to South Yemen promised to talk to the Lebanese prime minister and get the four men passports to facilitate their movement.

The occupation was the driving issue for many supporters of the Palestinian cause, whose ranks were growing, even within Israel. For these supporters, the solution was Israel's withdrawal behind the Green Line to its pre-1967 borders and the creation of a Palestinian state on the other side of the line. Some Palestinians were also beginning to believe that this compromise, embodied in UN Resolution 242, was the best way to end the conflict. For Bashir and hundreds of thousands of refugees, however, 'two-four-two' did not go nearly far enough. They still believed in the earlier UN resolution, number 194, which endorsed their right to go back to their homes in what was now Israel.

'The only solution is return,' Bashir told reporters, standing between the tents in the Red Cross field. 'We want to go back to our homeland.' The reporters wanted to know how – given the strength of Israel, the repeated defeats of the Arabs over the decades, and even the growing discomfort of Arab governments in allowing the deportees to speak out from southern Lebanon – this return could ever happen.

'Since there is an Arab decision against having us here,' Bashir replied, 'we demand from the Arabs to give us an aircraft so that we can fly ourselves back into Palestine. And it will be a suicide operation.' Bashir knew full well his demand would never be granted; he was also aware that his comments would be written down by the reporters and might well circulate around the world.

Salah Salah watched Bashir with admiration. Here was a man, Salah thought, who knew how to get the attention of the press but always seemed to stay focused on the larger political question. 'He was analyzing this as an Israeli policy, not as a personal thing,' Salah said. 'He was putting himself out of this. He didn't express his personal pain.' Bashir's style was quiet but forceful. He spoke in emphatic, low tones, rarely smiling. His left hand was characteristically thrust in his pocket, and his right hand, palm down, cut the air like a blade. He was known as passionate and occasionally argumentative in private meetings among the Palestinian political factions, but in public he measured his words, calculating their delivery for maximum effect.

Bashir also knew that the political situation in Lebanon at the time was extremely tense between the elected national leaders and the Syrians, who continued to exercise de facto control on the ground beyond the Israeli security zone. 'Every word was measured,' Salah remembered. 'He was very delicate. Not like Rajoub.'

Jabril Rajoub was the volatile leader of the youth movement of Fatah, the guerrilla group founded by Arafat and Abu Jihad in 1965 and later incorporated as the central organ of the PLO. The young activist had less patience than Bashir with the sensitivities of Syrian-Lebanese politics. One afternoon in early 1988, Salah recalled, after several weeks in the small tent city outside the Red Cross offices, Jabril denounced the Syrians in an angry speech about treatment of Palestinian refugees in the camps.

Salah knew this meant the end of his comrades' time in Lebanon. He arranged to smuggle the four deportees out of south Lebanon to Beirut, and from there got them on a flight to Cyprus. For his trouble, Salah would be picked up by Syrian intelligence and taken to solitary confinement, where over the next eighteen months he would become well acquainted with the harsh justice of Syrian president Hafez al-Assad. 'Salah paid for my speech,' Jabril Rajoub would acknowledge nearly seventeen years later.

* * *

311

In February, several weeks after his deportation from the West Bank to Lebanon and days following his escape to Greek Cyprus, Bashir boarded a plane to Athens. The PLO had come up with a new plan for drawing attention to their plight: *Al-Awda* (*Ship of Return*), which was to sail out of the Greek Cypriot harbor of Limassol and steam toward Haifa. For some the journey would represent the aspirations of Palestinian statehood in the West Bank and Gaza; for others, like Bashir, it would symbolically proclaim the Palestinians' right of return. Some of the passengers would compare the ship to the *Exodus*, the ship of Holocaust survivors that encountered a British blockade when sailing toward Haifa in 1947. On board alongside Bashir would be 130 other deportees and their supporters, including American Jews and Israelis with whom Palestinians had established contact. One of the Israelis had sailed on the original *Exodus*.

In Greece, journalists had joined the several hundred supporters of the Palestinian refugees and deportees. There Bashir met reporters who asked him what he thought about Dalia's 'Letter to a Deportee,' published a month earlier in the *Jerusalem Post*. A reporter gave Bashir a copy. This was the first time he had seen it. He would read it many times in the coming weeks.

Bashir, Jabril, and the two other recent deportees would be remembered as if they were rock stars, showered with praise and affection as the celebrated quartet at the center of the journey. Some Israelis were outraged by the display. One official told reporters that the deportees were 'criminals' trying to 'return to the place of their crime.'

The plan was for the deportees, dignitaries, and activists to stay a night in Athens before traveling to Cyprus to board the ship. Soon, however, word came that the Israelis had pressured the Greek ship owner to break his contract with the PLO. The trip was delayed. Israel was adamant that the ship not sail.

The anxious delegation in Athens heard that the PLO went to another ship line, and a third and a fourth, but that the same thing happened each time: Israeli commercial pressure on each ship's owner would lead to a cancellation. In Athens, the delegation would prepare to leave and then unpack again in an increasingly surreal waiting game. Hilda Silverman, from the small American delegation that was put up in a five-star hotel by the PLO, recalls this period as 'the most bizarre experience in my life. It was like being on another planet. Here we were living in incredible luxury – it's the only time I have ever stayed in a five-star hotel! We were taking walks to the Parthenon during the day, all the time attempting to move this political project forward.'

Finally the PLO decided to buy an old ferry called the *Sol Phryne* and rename it the *Al-Awda*. On February 17, on the eve of the journey, Bashir and the others checked out of the hotel and left for the Athens airport en route to Greek Cyprus. They had barely left the hotel when they heard the news: An explosion aboard the ship had ripped a hole belowdecks. Frogmen, they would later learn, had attached explosive charges to the hull. Just hours before the *Al-Awda* was to sail, it was sunk. 'Unidentified persons' were responsible. Suspicion fell immediately on the Mossad, Israel's spy agency.

Bashir left Cyprus for the exile of Tunis. It was the late spring of 1988. He found a small apartment in the Tunisian capital and spent his days reading, writing, attending political meetings, and thinking about the next move for the resistance. By now it was clear that Bashir's deportation, and that of dozens of others Israel had suspected of organizing the intifada, had done nothing to quell the uprising in the occupied territories.

Not even the assassination of Abu Jihad by an Israeli hit squad that burst into his Tunis apartment after midnight on April 16 could slow the intifada's momentum. The operation to eliminate one of the most beloved Palestinians was overseen by IDF deputy chief of staff Ehud Barak, among others. They considered the co-founder of Fatah a dangerous terrorist and saw him as a puppet master of the intifada from afar. They believed his death would help bring an end to the 'riots' in the territories. If anything, however, the slaying of Abu Jihad had the opposite effect. The intifada grew stronger.

On May 8, 1988, Nuha and Ghiath Khairi paid a visit to Dalia's hospital room in Jerusalem. They had heard from Bashir, who had heard from journalists in Tunis, that Dalia's fragile pregnancy had kept her confined to her hospital bed for the last seven months. Ghiath had called Yehezkel, and they arranged to meet in the Old City and drive back to the hospital.

As they walked into the room, Dalia's eyes were drawn to Nuha, elegant and dignified in her pleated skirt, long-sleeved blouse, and high heels, her reddish-brown hair perfectly done. Nuha's large brown eyes looked directly into Dalia's, and she stood closest to Dalia as they all gathered around the bed. For the last four months, ever since her letter had been published in the *Jerusalem Post*, Dalia had received a stream of visitors, including many reporters and television producers. 'Sometimes it got to be too much for me,' Dalia remembered, but when Nuha and Ghiath arrived, 'I felt an affinity.'

'We have been wanting to visit for a long time,' said Ghiath. They asked about Dalia's health and the baby, and Dalia told them it was scheduled to arrive by cesarean section in two days.

Dalia asked Nuha about the news from Bashir. Nuha said Bashir was now in Amman, but she found it difficult to say anything more, because she didn't want to cry. Ghiath told Dalia that Bashir had written her a response to her open letter and that a journalist, serving as a messenger, would deliver it to Jerusalem soon.

'How is Ahmad?' Dalia asked, referring to Bashir and Scheherazade's boy, who was now three. Hanine, their daughter, was still a baby.

'He is asking for his father,' Nuha said.

'What do you tell him?'

'That the Jews have deported him.'

Dalia would recall imagining what was going through the boy's mind: *Young Ahmad lives with a great enemy, the Jews. The evil that has the power to take his father away from him.* She looked at Nuha, at forty-six still one of the most beautiful women she had ever seen, and thought she recognized, behind her eyes, 'an unforgiving loyalty to the history and suffering of her people.'

Ghiath spoke up. 'In 1967, I went to my father's house. I remember when my father built it. Tell me,' he said, looking at Yehezkel, 'why, why did your people come to our country?'

Yehezkel started to say something, but Ghiath continued: 'Why should it be at my expense?'

'We too felt in exile for all these years,' Yehezkel replied. 'Don't you feel in exile?'

'Yes, I do,' said Ghiath. 'I would rather sleep under a lamppost in al-Ramla than in a palace in Ramallah.'

'Your children were not born in Ramla. Don't they feel the same?'

'Yes, they do feel the same.'

'And their children, will they not feel the same?'

'Yes, indeed they will.'

'So have we,' said Yehezkel. 'Our forefathers and the fathers of our forefathers.'

Dalia, flat on her back in her hospital bed, followed the debate with her eyes. She was struck that Ghiath could not understand her people's longing for the ancient homeland.

'But they were not born here,' Ghiath protested. 'For example, my Jewish friend, Avraham, he and his father and his forefathers were born here. Their family is from Jaffa. He is a true Palestinian.'

So that means, Dalia thought, *that I'm not?*

'It's a different kind of self-understanding,' countered Yehezkel, the religious scholar. 'What are you going to do about that? Why do you think Israelis are afraid of you? We are not as afraid of the entire Syrian army with all its weaponry as we are of you. Why do you think that is?'

Ghiath looked at Yehezkel in amazement. Nuha and Dalia remained silent as Yehezkel continued: 'Because you are the only ones who have a legitimate grievance against us. And deep down, even those who deny it know it. That makes us very uncomfortable and uneasy in dealing with you. Because our homes are your homes, you become a real threat.'

'Why can't we all live in the same state, together

in peace?' said Ghiath. 'Why do we need two states?'

'Then you think you would be able to go back to your father's house?' Yehezkel asked.

Dalia shifted in her bed. 'And what would happen to the people already living in those houses?' she asked.

'They will build new homes for them,' Ghiath replied.

'You mean,' Dalia said, 'they will be evacuated for you to return to your original homes? I hope you can understand why Israelis are afraid of you. Israel will do everything to prevent the implementation of these dreams. Even under a peace plan you will not return to your original homes.'

'What do we want? Only our rights and to live in peace.'

'Justice for you is receiving back what you lost in 1948. But that justice will be at the expense of other people.'

Ghiath looked at Dalia. 'Bashir told me that you said to him in 1967 or 1968, "The expulsion was a mistake. But another mistake will not correct this one."'

'I really said that so many years ago?'

'Why do you need a state of your own? And if you do need one, why could you not have gone to Uganda, or to another place, many years ago? How many Arabs are there now in the USA? Do they demand a state of their own in the USA?'

Dalia said, 'I'm not going to explain to you what the yearning for Zion means to us. I will just say that because you see us as strangers in this land, that is why we are afraid of you. You should not think that I myself am free of fear. I have a good reason to be afraid: The Palestinian people as a collective have not accepted the Jewish home in this land. Most of you still consider us a cancerous presence among you. I struggle for your rights despite my fears. But your rights have to be balanced against our

317

needs for survival. That is why you cannot be satisfied. For you, every viable solution will always be lacking in justice. In a peace plan, *everybody will have to do with less than they deserve.*'

No one spoke for a few moments. It was getting late, and Nuha and Ghiath had to get back to Ramallah.

Ghiath looked across Dalia's hospital bed and said to Yehezkel, 'May you have a son!'

Nuha looked at Dalia and said, 'They only dream of sons. Everyone.'

Ghiath, undeterred, continued, 'And may he think like you, Yehezkel.'

'I am a Jew and a Zionist, and if he thinks like me, he will be a Jew and a Zionist!'

By now everyone was laughing, and Ghiath said, to more laughter, 'I will give him Islamic books to read, and you never know what your son will think!'

They prepared to leave. Yehezkel would drive Ghiath and Nuha back to Nablus Gate at the Old City, to catch a taxi back to Ramallah.

Nuha leaned close to Dalia and took her hand. 'May you bear a healthy child,' she said. *'Ehsh'Allah.'* God willing.

Two days later, on May 10, 1988, Raphael Ya'acov Avichai Landau was born by C-section in Misgav Ladach (Upholder of the Poor) hospital in Jerusalem. 'It was considered a feat by the whole hospital crew,' Raphael's mother, Dalia, remembered nearly seventeen years later. It seemed all the doctors and nurses wanted to share with Dalia and Yehezkel in the celebration of their son. His very name – Raphael – meant 'God's healing.' Dalia had spent months in her hospital bed. She was hooked to intravenous drips and beeping machines that would constantly monitor her condition. Now, she held a healthy baby boy in her arms.

Outside her hospital room – to the north in Ramallah and Jenin, to the south in Bethlehem and Hebron, to the east in Jericho, to the west in Gaza – the intifada showed no signs of letting up. Perhaps, Dalia hoped, there could be an answer in compromise, like the UN resolution that would honor the Palestinian rights to self-determination while acknowledging Israel's own right to exist in peace with her neighbors. She knew this would not give Bashir everything he longed for or demanded. *Yet, after all this time, she thought, must not each of us be willing to compromise?*

By late 1988, as Bashir continued his exile in Tunis, signs of a widening political gap in the Palestinian movement were becoming more apparent. Arafat, it seemed, was considering a monumental political compromise. Although the PLO chairman had not publicly announced his support of negotiations with Israel and the two-state solution, there were enough hints to worry people like Bashir who remained focused on the right of return.

Arafat believed that the intifada had opened the door to a Palestinian state and that moving through the door would carry a price. At his side in Tunis was Bassam Abu-Sharif, the former hard-line PFLP activist. As early as 1979, when Egypt signed its peace deal with Israel, Bassam had begun to grow disillusioned with George Habash and what he saw as the Popular Front's uncompromising position on Israel. 'Why pretend we could defeat Israel by force of arms?' he would recall. 'If that wasn't possible, why not face reality and deal?'

In late 1988, the former PFLP spokesman, who still

carried deep scars from the letter bomb that had blown up in his face sixteen years earlier, was working alongside Arafat to tap the 'incredible opportunity' provided by the intifada. Both men knew they were taking a huge risk. Arafat had long been a fighter for the return of the refugees through the liberation of all of historic Palestine, and he knew that recognizing Israel would create ruptures with other Palestinian factions, which would decry this step as a sellout. Yet with signs that the cold war was winding down, Bassam sought out Habash, his former boss and leader of the PFLP.

'Dr. George,' Bassam told Habash on the eve of a U.S.-Soviet summit in June 1988, 'Reagan and Gorbachev are going to meet in Moscow. They have to discuss hot spots – Central America, the Middle East. The Palestinians must be there with their political plan.' No longer would it be realistic, Bassam argued, for the Palestinians to demand a return to all the lands between the Jordan River and the Mediterranean. 'Look, from river to sea is not accepted,' Bassam told Habash. 'The world community cannot swallow this. It would mean the elimination of Israel. That is a line that people cannot go over.' The next month, July 1988, King Hussein cut all judicial and administrative ties with the West Bank, 'in deference to the PLO,' further paving the way for a future independent state on the land his grandfather, Abdullah, had annexed nearly four decades earlier.

The need for compromise with Israel became even more clear to Bassam on December 7, when Gorbachev announced that the Soviet Union would sharply reduce its military presence in Eastern Europe. Now the Soviet satellites would be allowed to choose their own destiny. Bassam knew that the Palestinian political factions, long supported by the Soviet Union, would soon be cut loose as well. The time to act was now, Bassam believed, and it had to be on the basis of 'a two-state solution' as envisioned by many supporters of UN Resolution 242.

In mid-December 1988, Arafat flew to Geneva, where the UN General Assembly had called a special meeting after the PLO chairman had been barred from entering the United States. On December 14, a year after the start of the intifada, Arafat announced for the first time his unconditional support for 242, which included recognition of Israel's right 'to live in peace within secure and recognized boundaries free from threats or acts of force.' Arafat also renounced 'all forms of terrorism, including individual, group, and state terrorism.' This was sufficient for U.S. secretary of state George Shultz, who announced that the United States would open a dialogue with the PLO. The United States, however, continued to oppose a Palestinian state. Nevertheless the U.S. recognition would lead to the so-called Madrid talks, which in turn would lead to Oslo. The road to compromise was open.

Bashir was not happy. If the Palestinians accepted 242, he knew, they would have to accept Israel's right to exist. And if they accepted Israel and the 'solution' of two states, what would happen to Bashir's right of return to al-Ramla, in the state now known as Israel? What would happen to the dream of hundreds of thousands of others from Haifa and Jaffa and Lydda and West Jerusalem; from the Galilee and the Negev desert – people who were refugees across the Arab world and beyond? The dream of return had been part of Bashir's very identity – part of the Palestinian identity – for four full decades. Bashir insisted on the rights conveyed him by UN Resolution 194. For nearly his whole life, he had watched Israel deny his right to come home while it accommodated waves of Jews from the Middle East, Ethiopia, Argentina, and the Soviet Union. Bashir felt that he had not spent more than half his adult life in prison, enduring humiliation, torture, statelessness, and now deportation, for a compromise like the one Arafat seemed to be considering. One of Bashir's colleagues would tell of a heated discussion around this time between Bashir and Arafat, but Bashir would not speak of it, or of his disagreements with other Palestinian leaders, or of strategy for the movement. This was even true for his family; they knew little of the specifics of his political work. 'It is all a big secret to us,' Khanom said. Behind closed doors within the Palestinian movement, however, Bashir had a reputation for speaking his mind. 'He dared to say he was against a policy of negotiating under the conditions of the United States,' a former comrade would remember. 'He showed unity in public. But when it was just Palestinians together, he was very strong in defending his vision. He didn't sugarcoat anything.'

Bashir was not alone. Even members of Arafat's own organization turned against him. In August 1989, Fatah, the mainstream PLO faction co-founded by Arafat, endorsed renewed armed struggle against Israel.

In the fall of 1989, Salah Salah, Bashir's PFLP comrade from the Lebanon tent camp, arrived in Tunis after eighteen months of solitary confinement in a Syrian prison. Bashir knew well what prison could do to a man, but still, he was shocked when he saw his emaciated friend. 'Suffice it to say,' Salah would recall, 'that I went into prison at seventy-five kilos [165 pounds], and I came out at fifty-four [119 pounds].'

Bashir and Salah became neighbors in Tunis, each in his own small apartment. Often they would prepare meals together; Bashir would encourage his friend to eat as much as he could. They played chess and backgammon, smoked their water pipes, and strategized about the future of Palestine and their struggling liberation movement.

Some afternoons Bashir and Salah would sit quietly in the sun, planning and reminiscing in their garden chairs. From time to time, Bashir would tell Salah about Dalia and the house in al-Ramla. 'He would show me documents in a file he carried with him,' Salah recalled. 'The file had clippings and personal letters,' including the letter from Dalia.

Bashir had read the clipping from the *Jerusalem Post* many times. He was moved by Dalia's public acknowledgment of the expulsions from al-Ramla and Lydda (Lod); of her declaration that 'the feeling has been growing in me that that home was not just my home' and that 'the lemon tree which yielded so much fruit and gave us so much delight lived in other people's hearts too.' Yet Bashir was also struck by Dalia's references to his 'past terrorist actions' and her admonishment that he transform his politics and embrace nonviolence. How ironic, he thought, that he had first read her letter only hours before 'unknown persons' had blown up the *Al-Awda*, which was to make a peaceful journey to Palestine.

For months, Bashir had been thinking of the best way to respond to Dalia. He had something important to tell her, something that in the twenty-one years he had known her, he had never revealed.

* * *

Dalia doesn't remember exactly where she was when she received Bashir's letter or even who brought it to her. Perhaps it was delivered by a journalist coming to Jerusalem from Tunis; perhaps it was carried to her by a friend of Bashir's or an Israeli peace activist.

The letter had been translated from the Arabic; it was typed on single-spaced pages and stuffed into a thick envelope. Seventeen years later, Dalia still has the letter, along with the original in Arabic, in Bashir's hand. 'Dear Dalia,' the letter began.

It's true that we got acquainted as you mentioned in your letter in exceptional and unexpected circumstances . . . And it's true that after we got acquainted, each one of us has become part of the life of the other. I don't deny that what I've sensed in you, Dalia, of morality, sensitivity and sensibility, left a deep impact in me that I cannot ignore. There was even a sixth sense that was telling me that in this human being that I got acquainted with lives an alert living conscience that will one day express itself.

Your letter that came in the period of my exile from my land, from the land of my country, Palestine, after our dialogue, conversations and acquaintance had become the talk of the press in the media, and even the talk of all the people whose consciousness was moved to recognize the truth of what's really happening and to reassess what happened.

Allow me first to express my affection and respect as well as appreciation of your courage to write to me, and your courage to present the ideas contained in your letter. Please allow me to present my respect to your husband Yehezkel Landau, who I have a lot of appreciation for . . .

Bashir's letter, Dalia saw, reflected the many hours of conversation the two had had before Bashir went to prison in 1969: tremendous personal warmth that somehow bridged a chasm of anguish and mistrust. He told her that he had spoken of her to 'my comrades' many times while 'living in the graves of the living dead while I was spending my sentence – fifteen years of the prime of my youth' in prison – a sentence, he insisted, that was 'for no reason except for my being a freedom fighter who had fallen in love with his homeland and was committed to his cause.'

Now Dalia read as Bashir countered her suggestion that any of his actions had 'planted hatred,' as she had suggested in her open letter. Rather, he wrote, 'the Zionist leadership has planted hatred in the souls of one generation after another.'

He who plants barley, Dalia, will never reap wheat. And he who plants hatred can never reap love. That leadership has planted hatred in our hearts, not affection. It has destroyed all human values the day it destroyed our childhood, our existence, and our right to live on the soil of our homeland. Your change, Dalia, and your new perspective was attained through research and investigation. And your ability to see things the way they are in reality, not the way they were told to you.

We were exiled by force of arms. We were exiled on foot. We were exiled to take the earth as our bed. And the sky as a cover. And to be fed from the crumbs of those among the governments and international organizations who imparted their charity. We were exiled but we left our souls, our hopes and our childhood in Palestine. We left our joys and sorrows. We left them in every corner,

325

and on every grain of sand in Palestine. We left them with each lemon fruit, with each olive. We left them in the roses and flowers. We left them in the flowering tree that stands with pride at the entrance of our house in al-Ramla. We left them in the remains of our fathers and ancestors. We left them as witnesses and history. We left them, hoping to return.

Dalia read on as Bashir challenged her description of his actions as terrorist: 'You cannot equate the struggle of the people for liberation and independence and self-determination,' he wrote. 'You cannot equate that with aggression, expansionism and oppression of the other.' As for his trying a nonviolent approach, as Dalia had urged in her open letter, Bashir wrote:

Dalia, I have tried to go back to Palestine on board the Ship of Return (*Al-Awda*), following Gandhi's road. I did not carry a missile or a bomb ... I was carrying my history and my love for my homeland. But what was the result, Dalia? The ship was sunk before it sailed. It was sunk while it was docked in a Cypriot port. They sunk it so that we would not return ... Why aren't we given our right to return? Why are we prevented from determining our future and establishing our state? Why am I exiled from my homeland? Why am I separated from my children, Ahmad and Hanine, from my wife, from my mother, from my brothers and sisters, from my family?

'I want you to hear something new, Dalia,' Bashir continued.

Do you know, Dalia, that in 1948, with childhood innocence, I played with one of the booby-trapped toys that were scattered by the Zionists – Stern, the Haganah and Irgun? The gifts of the terrorist Zionist organizations to the children of Palestine . . .

The family was in Gaza, Bashir explained, late in 1948, shortly after arriving from Ramallah. Bashir, Nuha, and other brothers and sisters had been playing in the dirt yard outside their cement-block house. They saw something gleaming in the sun. It was bulbous, with a wick protruding. It looked like a lantern. The children brought it inside. Bashir held the new toy as the other children gathered around. A clay water jug stood on the kitchen counter; one of the children bumped into it, and it crashed to the floor. The other children scattered. Bashir was left alone with the toy in his hands. Suddenly there was an explosion.

The booby-trapped toy exploded in my left hand to crush my palm, to scatter my bones and flesh. And shed my blood, to blend it with the soil of Palestine, to embrace the lemon fruits and the olive leaves, to cling to the dates and the flowers of the *fitna* tree.

In the explosion in Gaza, six-year-old Bashir lost four fingers and the palm of his left hand.

Who is more entitled to a reunion, Dalia? Sharansky, the Russian who doesn't have a cultural linguistic historic attachment to Palestine? Or the Palestinian Bashir, who is attached to Palestine with the language, culture, history, family and the remains of my palm that I left in

327

Palestine? Does not the world owe me the right to reunite myself, to reunite my palm with my body? Why do I live without my identity and without my homeland while my palm remains in Palestine?

Dalia stared at the page in amazement. She was astounded. How could she have known Bashir for twenty-one years and not know he was missing his left hand? Slowly it came to her: His hand was always in his pocket. It was always hidden – hidden so well, she never knew she never saw it. Now Dalia realized: She had only ever seen the left thumb, hitched over the top of the pocket. It looked so natural.

Since she was a girl, Dalia had carried the gift of empathy – for the children of Holocaust survivors, the Sephardic classmates at her school, and the Arabs, like Bashir, who once lived in Ramla. On each occasion, she had struggled to enter someone else's experience through the faculty of her own imagination. She thought of six-year-old Bashir, missing a hand in the Gaza of 1948.

Dalia realized that for nearly all his life, Bashir had blamed the Zionists for placing booby-trapped 'toys' in the sands of Gaza in order to maim Palestinian children. 'I was amazed at the intensity of his perception that Zionism was this incredibly evil manifestation and that this was his experience,' she reflected. But she was a child of Zion, the 'mountain of God.' 'There was no way I could accept this description of the Zionists, my people, me, as being the expression of darkness. To me Zion is an expression of my very ancient longing, for me it's a word that symbolizes a harbor for my people and our collective expression here. And for him, it's a regime of terror. Something that's an obligation to fight. And to resist in every way. Because for him if Zionism is a reign of terror, then terrorism is an appropriate answer!'

Dalia's voice was rising. She paused and gathered herself before speaking again: 'And I say that I cannot afford to fight one wrong with another wrong. It doesn't lead *anywhere*!'

Bashir had neared the end of his letter. 'I don't want to overburden you, Dalia,' he wrote.

> I know how sensitive you are. I know how you hurt. I don't wish you any pain. All that I wish is for you and me to struggle together with all of the peace and freedom loving people for the establishment of a democratic popular state. And to struggle together to bring the idea of the Dalia child care center to life. And to struggle with me for my return to my old mother, to my wife and my children, to my homeland, to struggle with me to reunite me with my palm, my palm that has blended with every grain of Palestinian soil.
>
> Yours with respect, faithfully,
> Bashir

Dalia sat quietly for a long time, 'quite shaken,' gazing at the letter. She tried to enter the psychological reality of the person who wrote it. Bashir was making an appeal for Dalia to help him unite with his homeland. By what means? she kept asking herself. Dalia had long heard Bashir's proposal that the land of Israel and Palestine be transformed into a single democratic secular state for all the people of historic Palestine. She believed, however, that a single state would mean the end of Israel, and for this reason she could not endorse Bashir's idea or his belief in the right of Palestinians to return to their old homes. It was true that Dalia had offered to return her house to Bashir, or at least to find some way to share its legacy, but she would go to great lengths to explain that this was a personal choice, not to be understood as an endorsement of a broader right of return for the Palestinians. It seemed inevitable that Bashir and Dalia would never reconcile their differences.

In September 1989, shortly after she received, read, and reread Bashir's letter from Tunis, Dalia drove out of Jerusalem, where she now lived, up the smooth, curving highway toward the crest of Kastel, the hilltop where the Haganah won a key battle to control the road in her country's War of Independence; past the stone minarets of the mosque of the Arab village of Abu Ghosh; down the hillside as the mountain walls closed in at Bab al-Wad, the Gate of the Valley; past the burned carcasses of Israeli army trucks and jeeps blown up in past battles and now adorned with wreaths; through the valley of Latrun; past the old familiar cement factory; and finally to the bump of the railroad crossing at the outskirts of Ramla. Dalia was back in her hometown.

It was time to move forward with the plan to honor the common history of the Khairi and Eshkenazi families. Dalia drove past Ramla City Hall – an Arab house that once belonged to Sheikh Mustafa Khairi – and parked outside the office of the city's cultural center on Weizmann Street, where she soon found herself shaking hands with a young Arab man named Michail Fanous.

The Fanous family history in Ramla went back

centuries. Michail's father, Salem, a Christian minister, had been held as a prisoner of war by the Israeli army after the occupation of al-Ramla in 1948. Salem Fanous had accepted imprisonment in the POW camp as God's will, but he would not tell his children about it until decades later, a few days before his death. He told Michail, 'Christianity is love. I didn't want you to hate the Jews. They are your neighbors.'

'His lands were taken away,' Michail recounted. 'He woke up to a different life, a different culture, a different reality. He was in jail for nine months. And he felt a stranger in his own home. And all the time he was talking about Jesus. And he never had hatred for all the people who hurt him. It's amazing.'

Michail had spent much of his thirty years trying to reconcile his identity as a Christian Palestinian citizen of Israel. He had grown up with the Zionist narrative, which for an Arab boy was inherently confusing. When his classmates insisted the other Arabs had fled Ramla like cowards, Mikhail would shout, 'No, they didn't, just ask my father!'

During the early 1970s, Michail had attended junior high in the West Bank and understood what it meant to be a Palestinian living under occupation. Later he returned home to attend Ramla-Lod High School and tried anew to fit into his Zionist surroundings. He even tried to embrace the Zionist narrative for a time while rising to the presidency of the student body in Ramla's nearly all-Jewish high school. Of the 850 students, only 6 were Arabs. In his senior year, he was told he would be ineligible to attend military training camp with his Jewish schoolmates. Michail realized this was simply because he was an Arab. He began to understand why people would refer to him as a 'demographic problem' in Israel.

By 1989, Michail Fanous had been elected to the Ramla City Council – only the second Arab since 1948. His platform was based on antiracism and on advocating for the rights of the Arab minority in Israel, which made up nearly 20 percent of the population.

Minutes after Dalia arrived in the Ramla cultural center, she and Michail were deep in conversation. At first it seemed the other Israelis at the meeting had been uncomfortable with the subject, but soon neither Dalia nor Michail was paying them much attention. Dalia told Michail her story and the story of the house built in 1936 by Ahmad Khairi – the home that had been at the center of her life and of Bashir's.

Michail's wish was to serve the Arab population of Ramla as best he knew how; perhaps, it occurred to him, just as it occurred to Dalia, they could work together to share their two dreams. Each wanted do something for the Arab population and provide a place where Arab and Jew could meet.

Dalia proposed that Michail be the Christian Arab partner in an enterprise that would give witness to the history of Arab and Jew. It would include a kindergarten for the Arab children of Ramla and a center for Arab-Jewish coexistence.

'Here is someone telling me my story,' Michail recalled thinking at the time. 'It's a story of 1948, and of one people finding a home and another losing his home. It could not happen one without the other.'

He looked at Dalia and said: 'We can dream together.'

In October 1991, the first four Arab kindergarten

CHAPTER

children walked through the doors Ahmed Khairi had framed and secured fifty-five years earlier. This was the beginning of Bashir's dream: to bring joy to the Arab children of al-Ramla. Soon the mission would expand, incorporating the vision of Dalia, Yehezkel, and Michail: to be a place of encounter between Arab and Jew.

They would call it Open House.

Twelve

HOPE

BASHIR SAT IN the shade near the eastern end of the Allenby Bridge, which connected the kingdom of Jordan to the land of his birth. It was April 1996, a warm spring morning in the Jordan Valley. Bashir and his sister, Khanom, were resting on a bench outside the Jordanian passport control building, waiting to cross. Finally a bus arrived. Bashir, Khanom, and the other passengers climbed on and rode past military sentry posts and through a series of checkpoints and razor-wire fences. The bus crossed the bridge and over the narrow trickle of the once great Jordan River – diminished by upstream dams and diversions to a weed-lined ditch separating Hussein's kingdom from the West Bank. Anyone foolish enough to jump from the East Bank to the West would be more likely to get shot than wet.

The Allenby Bridge was named after the British general who led his troops into Palestine in 1917 at the beginning of the British Mandate. After eight decades of rule by British, Jordanian, and Israeli forces, the bridge was now under limited control of the newly formed Palestinian Authority. The partial autonomy was a result of the Oslo peace accords, symbolized by the handshake between Israeli prime minister Yitzhak Rabin and PLO chairman Yasser Arafat on the White House lawn in September 1993.

The intifada had convinced Rabin to begin discussions with a 'Palestinian entity', and after the 1991 Gulf War, the two sides began negotiations. Rabin, however, had still refused to recognize the PLO, and consequently the negotiations had stalled. The two sides then began the secret talks at Oslo, where the initial agreements called for limited Palestinian self-rule and a gradual Israeli pull-out from the occupied territories. In exchange, Arafat, in a letter to Rabin, promised to 'renounce the use of terrorism and other acts of violence' and 'discipline violators'.

'Mr. Chairman,' Rabin wrote in response to his long-time nemesis, 'the Government of Israel has decided to recognize the PLO as the representative of the Palestinian people . . '. For decades, Rabin had sworn Israel would never do this.

The mutual pledges were intended to mark the beginning of the end of the occupation and lead, the Palestinians hoped, to a sovereign state of Palestine. Israeli troops would 'redeploy' from Gaza and Jericho, then other West Bank cities; Palestinians would hold free elections for a president (according to the Palestinians) or chairman (according to the Israelis) and a legislative council; and the Palestinian Authority, supported by funds from European governments, the United States, and private donors, would take responsibility for education and culture, health, social welfare, taxation, and tourism. These initial steps in a five-year 'transitional period' were to lead to final status negotiations over the more difficult issues of Jerusalem, control of water, settlements, and, most important for Bashir and many others, the right of return.

In the first days after Oslo, plans for even limited self-government were immensely popular with Palestinians.

When Arafat returned to Gaza in July 1994, delirious throngs welcomed him as a conquering liberator. Tangible symbols of sovereignty – the freedom to wave the Palestinian flag or Arafat's mailing, on January 1, 1995, of the first letter bearing a Palestinian stamp – seemed the beginning of something larger and more profound.

By early 1996, hundreds of PLO officials and former Palestinian fighters had begun to return from their exile in Tunis and cross back into the West Bank and Gaza. Each individual had been approved by the Israelis during lengthy amnesty discussions. On the bridge, unseen behind the Palestinian police in their olive green uniforms, Israeli military officers peered through one-way glass, carefully monitoring the crossings.

The bus carrying Bashir and Khanom pulled up at a terminal built by Israel to process Palestinians and Israelis in separate wings. The Palestinian wing was managed by a Palestinian deputy who reported to an Israeli director-general. Israel, according to the Oslo agreements, 'remains responsible during the interim period for external security,' including 'throughout the passage' of the border terminals.

Bashir and Khanom got off the bus and entered the Palestinian wing, where a Palestinian policeman stood beside a Palestinian flag. Next to him stood an Israeli soldier. The terminal was packed with people awaiting family reunions: aged women in flowing white head scarves and dark, ankle-length dresses, their heavy purses slung over their shoulders; gray-haired men in keffiyehs and neckties; teenagers in jeans and sneakers; balding middle-aged men in business suits, toting briefcases and cell phones the size of shoes. They all waited in long lines to pass through the metal detectors. It was remarkably quiet, given the crowds and the impending reunions. People pointed to their luggage so it could be placed on a conveyor belt for inspection; beyond the metal detectors, Bashir could see opened suitcases atop the customs tables, where Israeli security officials were carefully examining clothing, books, newspapers, brushes, and toothpaste tubes.

Bashir and his sister waited their turn. By now the rest of the family would have gathered just a few feet away, on the other side of the exit doors. Bashir had been gone for eight years, but even in exile, he had dreamed of a different kind of return. For him, this return was marked by the deep flaws of the Oslo process. Oslo represented concessions by the Israelis to allow the exiled to come back to the West Bank and Gaza, but it also implied acceptance by the Palestinians that return to the rest of Palestine was no longer attainable. For many former fighters and activists in the Palestinian political factions, the journey back to Palestine was therefore marked by deep ambivalence. Nowhere during the Oslo negotiations or their resulting agreements, Bashir noted, was there any mention of Resolution 194, the 1948 UN mandate for return of the refugees. Rather, the basis of negotiations was the later resolution, 242, which called for withdrawal of Israeli troops from the occupied territories. This was what led to the 'land for peace' equation: a Palestinian state on a part of Palestine, in exchange for Palestinian acceptance of Israel. For many Palestinians, including Arafat, it was time to make hard political sacrifices. Some Palestinians, including Bashir, felt the sacrifices they had already made were on behalf of a national liberation for all of old Palestine; this compromise, if it meant giving up the right of refugees to return, represented capitulation.

Worse for some Palestinians was that Oslo had placed the refugee question, along with key issues of East Jerusalem as the Palestinian capital, and control of water in the West Bank and Gaza, to final-status negotiations at some unknown future date, while Israel maintained control in the present.

As Bashir waited in line to pass through security there was an inherent tension between his dream and the Palestinian reality – a tension Bashir preferred not to talk about: As a result of Oslo, Bashir would soon be seeing his mother, his wife, and his two small children. He would be in Palestine for the first time since his deportation to Lebanon in 1988. But he would not be all the way home in al-Ramla.

A security guard pulled Bashir aside. They had some questions, Khanom recalled, and she watched her brother disappear into a room while she waited.

Several hours later, Bashir and Khanom walked through the clouded glass doors at the western end of the terminal and into the open air of the West Bank, where Zakia, Nuha, Scheherazade, and the children, and many of Bashir's friends were waiting.

They had traveled from Ramallah. It was like the time in 1984, when Bashir was released from prison – except that for at this reunion, twelve years later, Ahmad was gone. As before, Bashir didn't want a big celebration. 'He was overwhelmed,' Khanom remembered, but 'he was very happy.'

'It was like a second wedding,' said Nuha. 'My mom prepared food, many friends came. With Bashir there were many more sad days than good days. And this was for sure a significant day in the history of the family.'

Bashir's first days back in Ramallah were bittersweet. Arafat's embrace of Oslo, together with his pledge to control 'terrorism and other forms of violence', had begun to pit the champion of Palestinian liberation against the disparate Palestinian factions that had grown increasingly unsettled about Oslo. To them, accepting Oslo represented a surrender of 78 percent of historic Palestine; even the West Bank, Gaza, and East Jerusalem, which represented the other 22 percent, Israel didn't seem prepared to hand over. Already the Israeli government had announced plans for thousands of new housing units in East Jerusalem, which the Palestinians envisioned as their capital, and Israeli construction crews were building new 'bypass' roads to better facilitate the travel of settlers from the West Bank to Israel. These plans were being undertaken within the Oslo framework, and many Palestinians worried that the new facts on the ground would permanently alter their chances for a viable, sovereign state. These fears were made more acute with the sudden surge in political violence and assassination, which had begun less than six months after the famous handshake on the White House lawn.

On February 25, 1994, a medical doctor and American settler named Baruch Goldstein walked into the Cave of the Patriarchs, part of the Ibrahimi Mosque in Hebron, where Bashir had received his *aqiqa* ceremony in 1943. The settler from Brooklyn pulled an M-16 from beneath his coat and opened fire, killing twenty-nine Palestinians praying in the mosque. Survivors pummeled him to death. Six weeks later, Hamas, the militant Islamic organization, abandoned its strategy of attacking only Israeli military targets. On April 6, a car bomb exploded in the Israeli town of Afula, killing six Israeli civilians. Hamas claimed responsibility. A communiqué declared the attack was revenge for those who died in the Hebron massacre.

The cycle of pain and retaliation had returned. Suicide bombers recruited by Hamas and Islamic Jihad blew themselves up in Netanya, Hadera, Jerusalem, Tel Aviv, and occupied portions of the Gaza Strip, killing dozens of Israelis; Hamas leaders claimed each attack on civilians was a direct response to Israeli attacks that killed Palestinian civilians.

Israel bulldozed the houses of suicide bombers' families and rounded up hundreds of suspected co-conspirators. Prisoners, according to Human Rights Watch, reported 'sleep deprivation, hooding, prolonged standing or sitting in unnatural positions, threats, beatings and violent whiplashing of the head . . . Applied in combination, these methods often amount to torture.' Many of the suspects were later released without charge.

Arafat condemned each suicide attack and, under pressure from Israel and the United States, ordered the arrest of suspected members of militant groups. Hundreds of young Palestinian men were in Palestinian jails, many by order of a secret Palestinian military court for state security established under the Oslo framework. In the first year of the court, several men died during interrogations; many Palestinians accused Arafat of doing the dirty work for Israel. The chairman responded to criticism by closing several newspapers and detaining prominent Palestinian human rights advocates. Edward Said, the Columbia University professor and leading Palestinian intellectual, wrote that 'Arafat and his Palestinian Authority have become a sort of Vichy government for Palestinians.'

Anger at Arafat deepened as he began granting favors to

loyalists who had come with him from Tunis. The chairman himself continued to live modestly, but some of his longtime cohorts in exile built mansions in Gaza, all the more striking for their juxtaposition against the squalor of the refugee camps on one of the most crowded places on earth. One of the mansions, estimated to cost $2 million, was built for Mahmoud Abbas, known as Abu Mazen, who would later succeed Arafat as the leader of the Palestinians. 'This is your reward for selling Palestine,' a graffiti artist scrawled on the mansion stones. The poor of the refugee camps, whose young men formed the basis of the resistance to Israeli rule and whose casualties during the intifada numbered in the thousands, now chafed under the rule of the elite of Tunis. 'Every revolution has its fighters, thinkers, and profiteers,' one Gazan would say. 'Our fighters have been killed, our thinkers assassinated, and all we have left are the profiteers.' The conservative Gazans were stunned at the appearance of seaside nightclubs with belly dancers and alcohol catering to the wealthy arrivals from the diaspora. It was not uncommon to see a black Mercedes with VIP plates streaking through a red light in Gaza City, leaving donkey carts literally in its dust.

For ordinary Palestinians who supported Oslo in principle, the end of the occupation was paramount. Oslo II, signed in Washington in September 1995, mandated three phased troop withdrawals from West Bank cities and towns and a division of the West Bank into three areas. Palestinians would be given control of most West Bank cities (Area A), including Ramallah, Nablus, and Bethlehem, while Israel would retain full control around military posts and settlements (Area C). Israeli forces would withdraw from Area B, where many of the

Palestinian villages were located; the new, lightly armed Palestinian police force, whose total numbers were to reach thirty thousand, would have no jurisdiction over Israelis in the area, and Israel retained the right to reenter 'for defense against external threats including the overall security of Israelis and settlements.' For the average Palestinian in the refugee camps and cities, the withdrawal of Israeli troops and tanks would bring immense change to daily life. Anyone moving from town to town in the West Bank, however, still faced military checkpoints and the confusion of traveling through multiple jurisdictions. A map of the West Bank after Oslo II resembled a series of scattered islands, and critics of Oslo, whose numbers were growing, worried that the map resembled a fractured vision of a truncated Palestinian state.

By October 1995, polls showed that support among Palestinians for the 'peace process,' and all it represented, had plummeted to 39 percent.

Israelis weren't much happier. The wave of suicide bombings had traumatized the country, and many people believed that as a result of the concessions Rabin was making in the Oslo process, the country was less secure. The bombings increased pressure on Rabin to suspend the talks entirely and to crush Hamas. He declared that 'Arafat will deal with Hamas,' because the Palestinian leader was not restrained by democratic institutions like 'Bagatz and B'tselem' – a reference to Israel's high court of justice and its prominent independent human rights organization. On the contrary, critics charged: Arafat, far from cracking down, was essentially putting revolving doors on Palestinian jails – letting people out shortly after they were brought in. Rabin raised the prospect of 'total separation' between Israel and the Palestinians, in order to curb the bombings, and Israeli citizens began talking about the advantages of a wall between the two peoples.

Rabin was coming under repeated attack from Benjamin Netanyahu, his rival from the Likud Party, who declared the prime minister had agreed 'not to talk with the PLO, not to give up territory during this term of office, and not to establish a Palestinian state. He is breaking all these promises one by one.' Netanyahu, who aspired to be prime minister himself, was a relentless critic of Oslo. He believed that the plan to arm thousands of Palestinian police, and to allow the PLO *cadres* to return to the edge of Israel, was absurd. The 1994 Nobel Peace Prize, awarded to Rabin, Arafat, and Israeli foreign minister Shimon Peres, did little to blunt such criticism. If anything, the image of a longtime enemy of the state onstage with the two Israeli leaders only fueled the attacks. In 1995, Netanyahu accused Rabin of helping to establish 'the Palestinian terrorist state.' Religious settlers formed the sharpest edge of the opposition. Many believed God had given the Jews the land of Judea and Samaria, known to others as the West Bank. Some extremist rabbis called Rabin a *rodef*, or violent aggressor, who they believed was about to negotiate away their God-given home. A poster circulated showing Rabin in a doctored photo, wearing a Nazi uniform. For a growing number of Israelis on the religious Right, Yitzhak Rabin was an enemy of the state.

Dalia was stunned that anyone in Israel would use the memory of the Holocaust to manipulate people's minds. 'It was ugly,' she remembered thinking. 'This was murderous. Where are the limits of freedom of speech? I understood that the battle for compromise in Israel was going to be very difficult.' Still, she remained hopeful of the prospects for peace. Despite the carnage of the suicide bombers, she believed historical change was taking place among her people. Rabin, the old warrior, had shown the courage to accept a dialogue with the PLO and his former sworn enemy Arafat. Dalia, despite her own mistrust of Arafat, believed that each side had taken steps to create space for the other. 'If we make space for that other, then it truly helps us make it possible to weave together a reality that is much more splendid than the reality we can envision alone.' She was heartened by the news of more Israeli troop withdrawals from the West Bank and the early signs of sovereignty for her Palestinian neighbors. She saw these as the first steps toward equality for the Palestinians, a concept she had been considering for decades, since the day in 1967 when she opened the door to Bashir and his cousins.

At Open House, now in its fifth year in the house in Ramla, Dalia and Yehezkel had seen more willingness among Israelis to engage in Arab-Jewish dialogue. The summer peace camps with Arab and Jewish children were suddenly popular, and Yehezkel believed 'the whole co-existence approach,' which he and Dalia had advocated for years, 'was legitimized in the eyes of Jews.' Dalia, for her part, would remember how she had concluded her letter to Bashir seven years earlier: 'I pray that with your cooperation and God's help, our children will delight in the beauty and bounties of this holy land.'

On November 4, 1995, Dalia thought these dreams were still possible. It was a Saturday, the Jewish Sabbath (Shabbat), and she had spent all day and the previous evening in a convent run by the Sisters of Zion in the Old City, sharing a Shabbat meal and talking about the possibilities of Open House. The convent was part of the church known as Ecce Homo, 'Behold the Man,' the words Pilate used in denouncing Jesus Christ. The church's Lithostrotos, or smooth stone pavement, is said to be the place where Jesus stood when he was condemned.

From the higher levels of the convent, Dalia looked out at one of the most magnificent panoramas in Jerusalem: the glittering of the Temple Mount, or al-Haram al-Sharif, the holiest place in Jerusalem for both Muslims and Jews; the gray dome of the twelfth-century Church of the Holy Sepulchre, perhaps the most sacred site in all of Christianity; the rooftops of ancient stone homes with their clustered steel antennae reaching upward; Mt. Scopus to the north; and beyond that, the mountains of the West Bank, which Dalia knew as the Judean Hills, part of biblical Judea and Samaria. Dalia believed that Israel had to give up the settlements in those lands and that thousands of Jews would have to move. Even though this was part of what she, too, considered the biblical land of Israel, for centuries it had also been home to other people. Hard as it was, Dalia believed, each side in this conflict had to give up something precious.

That evening, November 4, as Dalia was preparing to leave the Old City to return home, Yehezkel and Raphael went for supper across the apartment hallway with Aunt Stella, who had moved from Ramla after Dalia's parents died. An hour west, in Tel Aviv, Yitzhak Rabin was at a rally at Kings of Israel Square, where one hundred thousand Israelis had gathered in support of peace with the Palestinians. The prime minister – who had fought against the Arabs in 1948, 1956, and 1967; who had authorized 'might, force, and beatings' against Palestinian youths in the intifada; and who for years had opposed recognition of the PLO – addressed the crowd:

> I was a soldier for twenty-seven years. I fought as long as there was no prospect of peace. I believe that there is now a chance for peace, a great chance, which must be seized ... I have always believed most of the nation wants peace and is prepared to take risks for peace. And you here, who have come to take a stand for peace, as well as many others who are not here, are proof that the nation truly wants peace and rejects violence. Violence is undermining the foundations of Israeli democracy. It must be rejected and condemned, and it must be contained. It is not the way of the state of Israel.

The crowd began to sing, and someone handed Rabin a page containing the lyrics of a song, 'Shir l'Shalom,' which conveyed the sorrows of the dead speaking from underground to instruct the living. It was written in 1969, two years after the Six Day War, and it had become the anthem of the Israeli peace movement. Rabin sang along:

> Nobody will return us
> from the dead dark pit.
> Here, neither the joy of victory
> nor songs of praise
> will help.
>
> So sing only for peace,
> don't whisper a prayer,
> it's better to sing a song for peace
> with a great shout!

As the rally ended, the prime minister folded the page of lyrics, slipped them into his shirt pocket, and walked toward his motorcade.

At about the same moment, Dalia was getting into a taxi and riding down the Via Dolorosa, the path Christ traveled with his cross. She rode out of the Old City through the eastern entrance at Lion's Gate, facing the Mount of Olives. The Arab driver turned west, and at a stoplight they encountered another taxi driver, who shouted through his window: 'Rabin has been shot!' Dalia was confused; she couldn't digest the words. *This isn't possible*, she thought. *It can't be.* The driver sped toward West Jerusalem. 'Oh, my goodness,' he told Dalia in Hebrew. 'I have no radio!' At each light they signaled to other cars and asked, 'What happened, what happened?'

'Maybe it's not true,' said the driver, trying to reassure Dalia. 'How could this be true?'

Twenty minutes later, the taxi pulled up at Dalia's four-story apartment building. She dropped her heavy bag on the floor of the lobby and raced up the stairs, where Yehezkel, Raphael, and Stella were fixed on the television screen. The reporter for Israel Channel One was outside the hospital, surrounded by thousands of others, reporting on 'rumors of Rabin's condition.' Soon it was confirmed: Yitzhak Rabin was dead. He had been shot at point-blank range by a twenty-year-old religious law student, Yigal Amir. 'I acted alone,' Amir told police, 'and on orders from God.' Rabin's blood, Israel would soon learn, had seeped through his shirt pocket and soaked the page of the peace anthem.

Dalia watched the television screen as people started falling into one another's arms, their bodies shaking with sobs. She stayed up until the morning, completely bewildered. 'There was an immense sense that something was lost. This was a man who had gone through tremendous change. I heard him myself, at a Memorial Day talk in Israel.' Enough of the struggle for war, Dalia remembered Rabin saying. Enough bereavement. Now we have to struggle for peace. This is the most challenging of all wars – the war for peace. Over and over, Dalia asked herself, 'Who could have thought that terror would hit home in such a way?'

Yehezkel recalled experiencing a familiar, sickening feeling he had felt three times as a teenager growing up in the States in the 1960s, with the assassinations of President Kennedy, his brother Bobby, and Martin Luther King Jr.

'That was really the turning point,' Yehezkel said. 'It destroyed any chances for accommodation, at least for a long time. I remember thinking in subsequent years, *If Rabin had lived, would he and Arafat have worked something out?*

'I don't know.'

Neither did Dalia. 'Had he been alive, I don't know if he could have brought his entire people along with him. But I felt terribly hurt,' she said, crying. 'I felt that good people that could make a difference – they don't stand a chance.'

Bashir remembered Rabin's words to him when the two met at Jneid prison, just before Bashir's deportation to Lebanon: 'If there will be peace, there will be no problem anymore with the prisoners.' Bashir, however, did not share Dalia's optimism that Rabin would have brought a just peace to the region; neither did he think Arafat was doing that. He continued to believe there could be no peace, no justice, without the Palestinian right of return, which, for Bashir, remained limited to modest, symbolic gestures.

It was a warm Friday morning in the summer of 1999, according to Lamis Salman, a young Arab woman who grew up in Israel. She was a teacher at Open House, the kindergarten for the Arab children of al-Ramla. Lamis was returning from a trip to the store to purchase drinks when she saw a middle-aged man gazing at the children at play in the yard of Open House. He appeared to be in his fifties – short, with a slight paunch and a tuft of gray hair that fell over his forehead. Standing beside him were two other adults about his age, and two young men. The man spoke to Lamis in Arabic, introducing himself, his sister and brother-in-law, and his two nephews.

'He came in secret. Nobody knows how he got there,' Lamis recalled. 'He asked about Dalia.' Lamis and the other Arab teachers working at Open House were excited about the man's sudden appearance, but at least one of the Israelis there was alarmed. She considered him an intruder, a former criminal who had come illegally – no matter that he may have lived there decades earlier.

Lamis watched Bashir as he gazed at the kindergartners. They stood with the other Arab teachers in the garden, talking about politics, and life in Ramallah, and in al-Ramla. 'He was missing the home,' Lamis said. 'The land and the house and al-Ramla. He didn't talk about it, but I could see it in his eyes.'

In the summer of 2000, Arafat found himself across the table from a new Israeli prime minister, Ehud Barak, at Camp David, the White House retreat. Yitzhak Rabin, whom Arafat still liked to call 'my partner' in the 'peace of the brave,' had been buried for nearly five years. His successor, Shimon Peres, had been defeated in a tight election race by Benjamin Netanyahu following a new wave of suicide bombings in the spring of 1996. Three years later, Barak, the Labor Party candidate and former chief of the Israel Defense Forces, had in turn defeated Netanyahu in what amounted to a referendum on Oslo: The Israelis believed an agreement with the Palestinians was their best chance for long-term security. In July 2000, two months after Israel ended its occupation of Lebanon, Barak, Arafat, President Bill Clinton, U.S. secretary of state Madeleine Albright, National Security Advisor Sandy Berger, and teams of negotiators spent two weeks at Camp David in search of a historic final agreement with the Palestinians.

Clinton was deeply involved in many of the discussions. On July 15, five days into the negotiations, the president attended a meeting of the border negotiating committee. Israelis revealed a map identifying what they said was 92 percent of the West Bank as land for a demilitarized Palestinian state, with settlements and Israeli military outposts remaining on 8 percent of the land. The Palestinians would be compensated with additional lands inside Israel, but less than the amount they were being asked to give up. The 92 percent figure did not include land that Israel had already annexed for Jewish neighborhoods in East Jerusalem and other lands in the Jordan Valley, over which Israel intended to maintain control for at least ten years.

For the Palestinians, the percentage on the table from the Israelis, whatever it amounted to, was carving into the little of Palestine that remained for them. They argued that in accepting Oslo and Israel's existence, they had already conceded the other 78 percent to the Jewish state, and they weren't prepared to give up any more of what was left. Clinton's influential Middle East negotiator, Dennis Ross, thought little of these 'old arguments about the settlements being illegal and the Palestinians needing the 1967 lines,' calling such positions 'the same old bullshit.' This point of view apparently influenced the president, who also considered these positions to be Palestinian intransigence. At one point, Clinton demanded that chief Palestinian negotiator Ahmed Qurei (also known as Abu Ala) produce an alternative map as a counterproposal to the Israelis' idea. 'My map,' replied Abu Ala, one of the architects of the Oslo accords, 'is the map of June 4, 1967' – the day before the Six Day War and Israeli occupation.

'Sir,' Clinton said pointedly to Abu Ala, his voice rising to a shout, 'I know you'd like the whole map to be yellow. But that's not possible. This isn't the Security Council here. This isn't the UN General Assembly. If you want to give me a lecture, go over there and don't make me waste my time. I'm the president of the United States. I'm ready to pack my bags and leave. I also risk losing a lot here. You're obstructing the negotiation. You're not acting in good faith.' With that the president rose and, accompanied by Secretary of State Albright, stalked out of the room.

'We strode dramatically out,' Albright recalled in her memoirs, 'at precisely the moment a downpour began. It was either get wet or forfeit the drama of our exit, so we went and got drenched.'

Over the next two days, Clinton met with Arafat at least eight times. The president reiterated the land-for-peace proposals, approved in advance by Barak, in which the Palestinians would be allowed to establish a capital in the Arab outskirts of East Jerusalem and to have a combination of sovereignty, 'guardianship,' and 'functional autonomy' over parts of the Old City. They would be given control over some religious sites, but not full autonomy over the Haram al-Sharif, the third most sacred place for Muslims across the world.

As for refugees, Clinton promised a 'satisfactory solution.' The right of return, however, would be limited to the Palestinian state in the West Bank and Gaza – not to the part of old Palestine that was now Israel. Instead the United States would offer a massive aid program, in the tens of billions of dollars, to resettle and rehabilitate the refugees – now numbering more than five million, many in refugee camps in Lebanon, Jordan, Syria, the West Bank, and Gaza.

'I have great respect for you, Mr. President,' Arafat responded, according to Palestinian negotiator Saeb Erekat, 'but your proposals are not a basis for a solution.'

President Clinton banged his fist on the table and shouted at Arafat: 'You are leading your people and the region to a catastrophe. Barak presented proposals, but you take them and pocket them.'

'I came here representing Arabs, Muslims, Christians around the world,' Arafat told them. 'I came to make peace and won't accept that you or anyone else put me down in history as a traitor.' Arafat still saw himself as the leader of a national liberation movement and after thirty-five years in the PLO didn't want to be remembered for giving up important parts of East Jerusalem. Arafat knew the importance of the Haram al-Sharif to Muslims around the world and that therefore it would be impossible for him to concede even partial sovereignty over the site to the Israelis, even if it was also the site of the Temple Mount.

He also refused to concede the right of return at Camp David, even though, for many Palestinians and Israelis alike, by accepting Oslo and a two-state solution, he had essentially done so already. But Arafat knew the importance of the issue to millions of refugees, and he still sought room to maneuver.

That night, Arafat told the Palestinian delegation to pack up and prepare to leave Camp David. Late in the evening, the president came to the porch of Arafat's cabin and saw the delegation's luggage stacked neatly in preparation for departure. 'Won't you change your mind?' the president asked. He prevailed on the Palestinian leader to stay until he returned from a four-day trip to Japan. 'I will go to G-8 meeting on Wednesday, and I will ask them to provide the support you need for your state,' Clinton told the Palestinian leader. 'What I ask you to do is make a principled compromise on Jerusalem. It is not everything you want, but it's the price you have to pay.'

The president returned to Camp David on July 23, and the next day, he pressed Arafat one last time. At a meeting with Albright, Berger, CIA director George Tenet, and Palestinian negotiators Abu Ala and Saeb Erekat, Clinton proposed a 'sovereign presidential compound' for Arafat inside the Muslim quarter of the Holy City. The proposal would still not grant full autonomy to the Palestinians over the Haram al-Sharif, and Arafat rejected it. 'So there will be a small island surrounded by Israeli soldiers who control the entrances,' he said. 'This is not what we are asking for. We are asking for full Palestinian sovereignty over Jerusalem occupied in 1967.'

Bill Clinton lost his temper. 'You have lost many chances,' the president told Arafat, echoing former Israeli foreign minister Abba Eban's slogan that the Palestinians never miss an opportunity to miss an opportunity. 'First in 1948 . . . now you are destroying yourselves in 2000. You have been here fourteen days and said no to everything. These things have consequences. Failure will mean the end of the peace process. Let hell break loose and live with the consequences. You won't have a Palestinian state and you won't have friendships with anyone. You will be alone in the region.'

Arafat did not budge. 'If anyone imagines that I might sign away Jerusalem, he is mistaken,' the Palestinian chairman told the president. 'I am not only the leader of the Palestinian people, I am also the vice president of the Islamic Conference. I will not sell Jerusalem. You say the Israelis move forward, but they are the occupiers. They are not being generous. They are not giving from their pockets but from our land. I am only asking that UN Resolution 242 be implemented. I am speaking only about 22 percent of Palestine, Mr. President.'

Clinton continued to press Arafat to compromise on Jerusalem. Arafat, however, knew that Muslims around the world expected the Palestinians to be custodians of the Haram al-Sharif and therefore that no Palestinian could sign away sovereignty. He knew that if he did, he might not live long enough to see any agreement implemented. 'Mr. President,' he said to Clinton, 'do you want to come to my funeral? I would rather die than agree to Israeli sovereignty to Haram al-Sharif.'

Moments later, Arafat told the president: 'I respect you very much, and I realize that you are affected by the Israeli position. I have led my people's revolution. The siege of Beirut was easier on me than the siege of Camp David. The revolution is easier than peacemaking.'

Barak was also furious with Arafat. He had gone further

than any Israeli prime minister to make peace. Arafat, by contrast, 'did not negotiate in good faith' and never intended to come to any agreement. 'He just kept saying "no" to every offer, never making any counterproposals of his own,' Barak told Israeli historian Benny Morris. Arafat, Barak said, believed Israel 'has no right to exist, and he seeks its demise.' This became the prevailing view in the United States and Israel: that in rejecting Israel's 'generous' offers, the PLO chairman alone was to blame for the failure at Camp David.

Many other observers, including diplomats present at Camp David, believe the reasons for the summit's failure were far more complex and were partly the result of American favoritism toward the Israeli side and deficient understanding of the Palestinian perspective. All of this was exacerbated, according to these critics, by poor American preparation and rivalries between Madeleine Albright's State Department and Sandy Berger's National Security Council, which resulted in what American insiders called a 'dysfunctional' negotiation conducted by 'too many poobahs.'

A strong retort to the Clinton-Barak analysis came from Robert Malley, part of the Clinton team at Camp David, and Hussein Agha, a veteran Arab political analyst and former negotiator on the Palestinian side, who argued in a series of articles that such analysis failed to take into account the Palestinian point of view. 'For all the talk about peace and reconciliation, most Palestinians were more resigned to the two-state solution than they were willing to embrace it,' Malley and Agha wrote. The path to Camp David, after all, had begun in the secret discussions at Oslo, and those had emerged from the 1991 Gulf War, when Arafat had sided with Saddam Hussein's

Iraq. What much of the world viewed as historical concessions by Arafat at Oslo, many Palestinians looked upon as terms of surrender by the man who stood against the United States and its allies. 'They were prepared to accept Israel's existence, but not its moral legitimacy,' Malley and Agha wrote of the Palestinian delegation at Camp David. 'The notion that Israel was "offering" land, being "generous," or "making concessions" seemed to them doubly wrong, in a single stroke both affirming Israel's right and denying the Palestinians'. For the Palestinians, land was not given but given back.'

Some accounts maintain that the apparent Israeli offer of 92 percent, when factoring additional land deductions in East Jerusalem and the Jordan Valley, actually amounted to far less, and that Israel would have retained sovereignty over airspace, aquifers, 'settlement blocs' in the West Bank, and a 'wedge' of Israeli land between East Jerusalem and the Jordan River that would have divided Palestinian territory. In essence, this critique holds, Palestine would have been not a state, but an 'entity' broken into several parts, with limited sovereignty and little control of its own resources. Even for those Palestinians willing to achieve a historic compromise, this was not an acceptable outcome to decades of struggle and sacrifice.

Malley and Agha criticized the U.S. team for its 'exaggerated appreciation of Israel's substantive moves' and its acute sensitivity to Israel's domestic politics, 'a reaction that reflected less an assessment of what a 'fair solution' ought to be than a sense of what the Israeli public could stomach. The U.S. team often pondered whether Barak could sell a given proposal to his people, including some he himself had made. The question rarely, if ever, was asked about Arafat.' As for Barak offering more to the Palestinians than any other Israeli leader, Malley wrote in the *New York Times*, 'The measure of Israel's concessions ought not be how far it has moved from its own starting point; it must be how far it has moved toward a fair solution.'

Two months after Camp David, at eight o'clock on the morning of September 28, 2000, Likud Party leader Ariel Sharon arrived in the Old City at the most contested religious site in Jerusalem. It was known to Jews as the Temple Mount and to Muslims as the Haram al-Sharif. Control of the site was a crucial element in the failure of the Camp David summit two months earlier. Sharon, disgraced in the wake of the 1982 massacre of Palestinians at Sabra and Shatilla refugee camps in Lebanon, had returned from his journey in the Israeli political wilderness. He served as minister of infrastructure in the Netanyahu government, a position he used to help expand the settlements in the West Bank. Now, as the top opposition leader in the Israeli Knesset, Sharon was sending a message about Israeli sovereignty at a place Muslims consider the third most holy in Islam: To them, what the Israelis call the Temple Mount, with its Western (or Wailing) Wall, is the Haram al-Sharif ('Noble Sanctuary'), a large complex of Muslim holy places that include the Dome of the Rock and the Al-Aqsa Mosque. Sharon's move was a political challenge to Barak, his Labor Party rival, and Netanyahu, who had pledged to contest the Likud Party leadership. Under Israeli law, Sharon had a right to visit the Temple Mount, and for security, Barak, as prime minister, authorized some 1,500 Israeli police to accompany Sharon to the contested East Jerusalem site.

The next day, at the end of Friday prayers at Al-Aqsa Mosque, large crowds of Palestinians began throwing stones at Israeli soldiers. Most of the demonstrators were young men and teenage boys, and none fired weapons, according to later investigations. Israeli troops opened fire with live ammunition, killing four Palestinians.

Barak and other Israelis charged that Arafat had planned the new intifada as part of a 'grand plan' of terror and violence after the failure at Camp David. Over the next eight weeks, however, nine times more Palestinians were killed than Israelis, and the disparity in rates of wounded civilians was higher still. Israel blamed this on Palestinians seeking 'moral high ground by deploying children to stand in front of men with machine guns who fire at Israelis.' Numerous fact-finding teams found such cases to be the exception, not the rule. Later, however, Palestinian resistance would indeed grow more violent, as Fatah's militia, Tanzim, led by Marwan Barghouti, carried out attacks against Israeli troops. Palestinians looked to Israel's pullout from Lebanon, driven by what they considered Hezbollah's resistance, and saw a parallel in the West Bank and Gaza.

By October, the uprising had spread to Arab communities within Israel, including Nazareth and other villages in the Galilee. Palestinians within Israel made up nearly 20 percent of the population. Violent clashes between these 'Israeli Arabs' and police left thirteen Palestinians dead. On the Israeli Right, talk returned of a disloyal 'fifth column' of Arabs who might have to be expelled from Israel. Other prominent Israelis, including the tourism minister, Rehavam Zeevi, advocated an increasingly popular idea: 'transferring' all Palestinians out of the West Bank to Jordan and returning Eretz Yisrael to the

Jewish people. The deaths of the Palestinian citizens of Israel also provoked an outcry within Israeli society, and a national investigative committee headed by an Israeli supreme court justice put the police behavior under high-profile scrutiny.

As mistrust grew throughout the divided country, Dalia and Yehezkel found themselves on an island at Open House: They were amazed at the outpouring of emotion from Arab citizens who began talking openly about their own family stories from 1948. 'Suddenly, Arabs opened up with statements of pain,' Yehezkel recalled. 'Liberal, well-meaning Israelis who thought they were building cultural bridges and alliances were forced to confront the fact that there were endemic problems and injustices in Israeli society that required much more than cross-cultural encounter and coexistence activity. It required social and political transformation on a societal scale.' That same fall, Dalia, Yehezkel, Michail, and other Open House supporters were approached by a member of the Israeli Knesset to participate in a national think tank to improve the conditions of Arabs in Israel.

Yet the polarization in Israel was taking its toll. Elsewhere, Yehezkel noted, reconciliation groups were shutting down, their work made virtually impossible by the tensions within the country. Israeli television showed repeated images of two soldiers being lynched by an angry mob in Ramallah and their mutilated bodies being dragged triumphantly through the streets. Israel, Yehezkel said, was 'more polarized than at any time since 1948 – probably because their hopes had been raised so high' – by Oslo – 'and then dashed.'

Israelis still wanted an agreement with their longtime enemies but were growing increasingly inclined to support Sharon in the upcoming 2001 elections. In

December 2000, three months into the Al-Aqsa intifada, Barak and Israeli negotiators met intensively with Arafat and the Palestinian team in the Egyptian resort town of Taba. By all reports, the two sides were much closer to an agreement than they had been at Camp David, with progress on Palestinian sovereignty in East Jerusalem and even movement, however slight, on the right of return.

On January 1, 2001, a suicide bomber struck in Netanya, injuring more than forty Israelis. It was three weeks before the end of Clinton's second term and a month before Israelis would choose between Barak and Sharon. Barak briefly suspended the Taba discussions but said he would send representatives to Washington if the Palestinian leader put an 'end to terror . . . We truly have deep doubts about the seriousness of his intentions.' The talks came closer still, and at one point the two sides appeared close to an actual agreement. In the end, they foundered, in part on the issue of right of return. 'We cannot allow even one refugee back on the basis of the "right of return,"' Barak would say. 'And we cannot accept historical responsibility for the creation of the problem.'

As time ran out, the Taba discussions collapsed, and Sharon was elected by a landslide.

Bashir awoke to the sound of loud banging. It was a familiar sound, and Bashir, now fifty-nine years old, walked quickly to the door, sensing what he would find: Israeli soldiers surrounding the house. He estimates there were two hundred of them. It was 5:30 A.M. on August 27, 2001.

'Why are you making so much noise?' Bashir asked angrily of the officer in charge, his left hand thrust in his pocket. 'You'll wake up all the sleeping people! Who do you want?'

'We want Bashir Khairi,' the officer replied.

'I am Bashir.'

'We want you. If you move, we will shoot you. You people make trouble for us.'

'Who is "you"?' Bashir asked.

'You, PFLP.'

'I'm not PFLP,' Bashir insisted.

The soldiers surrounded Bashir and escorted him into a waiting olive jeep. He was taken to a tent prison outside Ramallah surrounded by barbed wire and patrolled by soldiers and dogs. The moment he arrived, he spotted some men playing chess and went to join them.

The same day, Israeli helicopters fired two missiles into the Ramallah headquarters of the PFLP, killing the organization's leader, Abu Ali Mustafa, also a prominent member of the PLO and a friend of Bashir's. Mustafa was the highest-ranking target killed to date in an Israeli policy of assassination of Palestinian militants.

Revenge for Abu Ali Mustafa's death was taken in October, when Rehavam Zeevi, the Israeli minister of tourism who advocated expelling Palestinians from the West Bank, was shot twice in the head after finishing breakfast at the Hyatt Hotel in Jerusalem. The PFLP claimed responsibility, and Sharon vowed to launch 'a war to the finish against the terrorists.'

Six weeks later, on Monday December 3, Ariel Sharon returned from a meeting with President Bush in Washington and declared war on the Palestinian Authority. It was nearly three months after September 11 and eight weeks since the United States launched the invasion of Afghanistan. Sharon pledged his solidarity with the U.S. war on terror. Over the previous two days, a car bomb and three human bombs had exploded in Jerusalem and Haifa, killing 25 Israelis and wounding 229.

At dusk on Monday, American-made F-16 fighter jets and Apache helicopter gunships unleashed a barrage of rockets and missiles on Palestinian Authority headquarters and police buildings in Gaza and the West Bank, bombing the Palestinian airport and Arafat's helicopters in Gaza and rocketing a Palestinian fuel depot, from which a massive cloud of smoke rose over the Gaza coast. Israeli tanks rolled into towns across the West Bank, reoccupying the territories. On December 13, following new suicide bombings, Israeli shells slammed into the Voice of Palestine, toppling the antenna and taking out the station. Helicopter gunships shelled Arafat's Ramallah offices, leaving only part of the compound standing. Arafat, a statement from Sharon's cabinet declared, was 'irrelevant.' The man who had driven Arafat out of Lebanon twenty years earlier was now intent on dismantling his Palestinian Authority. All but officially, Oslo was dead.

In February 2002, Arafat published an appeal on the op-ed page of the *New York Times*, declaring that 'the Palestinians are ready to end the conflict' and have a 'vision for peace . . . based on the complete end of the occupation and a return to Israel's 1967 borders, the sharing of all Jerusalem as one open city and as the capital of two states, Palestine and Israel. It is a warm peace,' Arafat added, 'but we will only sit down as equals, not as supplicants; as partners, not as subjects; as seekers of a just and peaceful solution, not as a defeated nation grateful for whatever scraps are thrown our way.' Sharon and his cabinet were unmoved. They believed Arafat was orchestrating much of the violence and that he never intended to make peace at Camp David. In late February, the Israel Defense Forces launched additional rocket attacks on Arafat's headquarters in Gaza and in Ramallah, where he was now confined; the Ramallah compound, or Muqata, was reduced largely to rubble. The Palestinian leadership declared that 'our people will continue their steadfast resistance until the military occupation and settlers are kicked out, to ensure the freedom, independence, and dignity of our people.' Arafat, whose support had been dwindling, enjoyed a sudden surge in popularity. A tattered Palestinian flag fluttered from amid the smoking ruins.

In some areas, Israeli reoccupation of the West Bank met with little Palestinian resistance. Occasionally resistance was peaceful: In Ramallah, doctors at the Arab Care hospital sat down in front of Israeli tanks approaching the casualty ward. When Israel attacked Jenin in April, however, gunmen from the Jenin refugee camp fired back, and a major battle ensued. Israeli soldiers abandoned their armored vehicles and chased the gunmen down the narrow alleys of the Jenin refugee camp, where Palestinian fighters hid, waiting to ambush them. In response, armored IDF bulldozers plowed into the camp, demolishing more than 130 homes, shops, and refugee offices and burying some people alive under the rubble. At least fifty-two Palestinians were killed, twenty-two of them civilians. Twenty-three Israeli soldiers died in the fighting. The uprising was crushed, but in the process the fighters from Jenin became heroes among Palestinians. In Ramallah, where resistance to the reoccupation had been light, a joke circulated: A Muslim woman walks past a group of men on the street. Her head scarf is tied loosely, and her hair is exposed.

'Fix your *hijab*,' one of the men admonishes. 'There are men here.'

'Oh, is that so?' she replies. 'Why, did the Israelis lift the curfew in Jenin?'

In the summer of 2002, Sharon intensified a policy of demolishing Palestinian houses in the occupied territories – a policy initiated by the British during the Great Arab Rebellion of the 1930s. The Israeli policy was carried out against families of suicide bombers and other militants; for 'military purposes,' primarily in Gaza; and against Palestinian residents of East Jerusalem who had built without the permits Israel required of them. Human rights groups estimated that between ten thousand and twenty-two thousand Palestinians lost their homes as a result of the policy and hundreds of acres of their olive groves and other crops were uprooted as part of a military strategy to improve the nation's security.

A growing number of voices in Israel rose in protest. One of the most prominent belonged to a young Israeli sergeant, Yishai Rosen-Zvi, an observant Orthodox Jew and son of the late dean of Tel Aviv University Law School. 'I won't take part in a siege enforced against hundreds of thousands of people, including women and children,' Sergeant Rosen-Zvi declared in a letter to a superior officer. 'I won't starve entire villages and prevent their residents from getting to work each day or to medical check-ups; I won't turn them into hostages of political decisions. A siege against cities, like bombing raids from helicopters, does not stop terror. It is a sop to placate Israel's public, which demands "Let the IDF win."' Israel's policies, the young 'refusenik' declared, were creating 'nurseries of terror.'

* * *

Just before 7:00 A.M. on November 21, 2002, Nael Abu Hilail crept through tall grass and up a hillside toward the West Jerusalem neighborhood of Kiryat Menachem. Abu Hilail was twenty-three, from the West Bank village of Al Khader, near Bethlehem. He wore a bulky coat, which, if pulled tight, would have revealed a large bulge around his midsection.

A few blocks away, Raphael Landau was leaving the fourth-floor apartment where he lived with his parents, Dalia and Yehezkel. It was a school day; Raphael, fourteen years old, slung his heavy book bag over his shoulder and trotted down the stairway and toward his bus stop.

Nael Abu Hilail boarded the number 20 bus at about 7:00 A.M. It was filled with commuters, mostly working-class Jews and immigrants, and children traveling to school. At 7:10 A.M., the bus rolled to a halt at the Mexico Street stop in Kiryat Menachem. The doors opened, and more workers and students began to board. At that moment, Abu Hilail reached under his coat and detonated the bomb he had strapped to himself. The explosion ripped the bus apart, sending human limbs flying through the gaps where the windows had been. A man's torso toppled out of the bus and onto the street, where it lay amid shattered glass and the hot screws released by the detonated bomb. Children's schoolbooks and sandwiches were scattered about.

At 7:20, the phone rang in the Landaus' apartment. Dalia and Yehezkel were asleep; Yehezkel had just returned from a trip to the States and was still contending with jet lag. Yehezkel answered to hear the worried voice of his friend Daniel, calling from his home just west of Jerusalem.

'I just wanted to make sure you're all right,' Daniel said.

'I heard on the radio that a bus had exploded near your home, on Mexico Street.'

Raphael's bus, Yehezkel knew, had just passed through the neighborhood. He hung up and rushed to the television, where he learned that the explosion occurred on a municipal bus, the number 20 line, not on the school bus Raphael rode. As he watched the live scene on Israeli television, his immense relief turned to horror. A dead man's blood-smeared arms hung outside the bus window. Rescue workers in white masks and gloves were lining up bodies in a row of black plastic bags along Mexico Street. Someone had covered the torso with a blue-and-white-checkered blanket. Eleven people were dead, Yehezkel would learn; four of them were children. Ambulances were rushing most of the forty-nine injured Israelis to the hospital.

Reporters in Bethlehem found Abu Hilail's father, Azmi, who told them he considered his son a martyr. 'This is a challenge to the Zionist enemies,' he said.

The next day, Prime Minister Sharon ordered Israeli troops back into Bethlehem, where they reoccupied the city, imposed a military lockdown, conducted house-to-house arrests, and blew up five homes, including the house where Nael Abu Hilail had lived with his parents and siblings. Since Sharon had come to power less than two years earlier on a pledge to increase Israelis' security, bombers had struck Israel nearly sixty times; this was nearly twice the number of attacks of the previous seven years. Sharon's spokesman blamed Arafat and the Palestinian Authority for the attacks, saying that 'all our efforts to hand over areas, and all the talk about a possible cease-fire, that was all window dressing because on the ground there was a continuous effort to carry out as many terrorist activities as possible.'

Arafat condemned the suicide bombing, saying civilians 'are normal people who are living their daily lives, and targeting them is a condemned act ethically and politically.' The bombings, he added, make even 'legitimate resistance' to the occupation look like 'blind terrorism.'

With the Israeli incursion into Bethlehem, the military reoccupation of all major West Bank towns except Jericho was complete.

The bus had exploded during the Jewish celebration of Chanukah, which is marked by the lighting of candles on eight consecutive nights. One night after the bombing, Dalia visited the bus stop at Kiryat Menachem and met a neighbor, a teenager whose eight-year-old brother and grandmother had been killed in the explosion. The old woman had been accompanying her grandson to school. 'His friends were with him,' Dalia remembered of the teenager. 'All very silent. Just being.' They struck a flame and repeated the Chanukah prayer: 'Blessed are You, our God, master of the universe, Who has sanctified us with His commandments and commanded us to light the candle of Chanukah.'

In the coming days, Dalia and Yehezkel made regular trips to the bus stop, where residents and visitors had erected a shrine of candles, wreaths, newspaper clippings, photos of the dead, prayer books, handwritten poems, and letters. Alongside the expressions of grief were signs promising to avenge the killings: 'No Arabs, No Terror'; 'O People of Israel! This will not end until we cry out a great cry!!! And only then, God will hear and answer us'; 'The way to true peace: If someone comes to kills you, thwart him by killing him first!'

*   *   *

The day after the attack, an Arab resident living near the Landaus was stabbed in the back by three Jewish youths. A Palestinian bakery down the road was stoned by an angry mob and its glass cases smashed. For several nights, police were called in for protection, and Yehezkel came to the baker's family to show his solidarity and to try to reason with the group's leaders. They insulted him and questioned his Jewishness. 'I could share their anger over the incessant terror attacks,' Yehezkel wrote later in the Jewish magazine *Tikkun*, 'but I vehemently rejected their racist and hateful attitudes . . . My heart has broken many times as I confronted the deeply painful reality of my fellow Israelis, including my Jerusalem neighbors, being overwhelmed by fear, anger, and grief.'

The 'toxic atmosphere' of the intifada and the suicide attacks propelled Yehezkel toward a new kind of reconciliation work. Especially in the wake of 9/11, he believed his calling was in addressing what he considered a 'global spiritual crisis.' Healing, he said, 'has to come from within *and* without, and my leverage point is from without.' He began spending more time in the States and eventually took a position at the Hartford Seminary, where he continued his interfaith work. 'It was increasingly clear,' he said, 'that I was meant to be here, at Hartford, and Dalia was meant to be there,' in Jerusalem.

Dalia watched as other families left Israel, seeking safe haven in Europe, the United States, or Australia. 'Many people are leaving Israel to find a place of safety elsewhere, to protect their children,' Dalia wrote in her journal in the late fall of 2002. 'But isn't that what our enemies want? Yet, on the other hand, Raphael too could have been on that bus. What is the responsible thing to do under the circumstances? There are many people in Israel who have no family or friends in other parts of the world. They do not have the luxury of the choices that I have here. Am I going to abandon them?'

Dalia made her decision. 'My choice is to stay here,' she wrote. 'I will not be able to look myself in the face if I leave when it gets difficult. I am going to stay present for the pain, and for the hope. I am an integral part of it all. I am part and parcel of this complexity. I am part of the problem because I came from Europe, because I lived in an Arab house. I am part of the solution, because I love.'

Thirteen

HOMELAND

E<small>L</small> A<small>L</small> FLIGHT 551 approached Sofia airport from the
south, swooped low over the Balkan Mountains, and
set down in the Bulgarian capital. It was twilight on July
14, 2004. Jews of Bulgarian descent peered out through
the airliner windows. Most were residents of Israel returning to their birthplace or that of their parents. Many were
children. Some were coming back for the first time.

Dalia Eshkenazi Landau stepped slowly down the
portable stairway, grasping the handrail and adjusting
the large red bag slung over her shoulder. She walked in the
fading light to the small terminal building, built during
Communist times. Dalia had not stood on Bulgarian soil
since October 26, 1948, nearly fifty-six years earlier. On that
day, Moshe's brother, Jacques, and his wife, Virginia, had
come to the Sofia railway station to bid farewell to the
family as they set off for the new state of Israel.

Dalia pulled her suitcase off the belt, rolled it past the
Bulgarian customs officers, and scanned the line of faces
in the waiting hall just beyond. She was looking for a man
about her age whom she had never met: Maxim, the son
of Jacques and Virginia. During Communist times,
Jacques, despite his high rank in the Party, was always
required to leave his children at home when visiting his

brother in Israel. Consequently Maxim, though a fierce defender of the Jewish state, had never been there and didn't know what his cousin looked like. He had come dressed all in white and held a sign in Bulgarian bearing Dalia's name. Virginia, now eighty-three years old and widowed, was at home, awaiting the reunion.

Three days later, after emotional meetings with Virginia, Maxim, and other relatives she had never met, Dalia rode in a taxi leaving Plovdiv, Bulgaria's second-largest city, toward a monastery in the Rhodope Mountains. In the backseat beside her sat Susannah Behar, whose father had been the rabbi of Plovdiv in March 1943 and who had waited out the hours with hundreds of other Jewish families in the Plovdiv school yard. At that same moment six decades earlier, Dalia's parents were in Sliven, several hours to the east. 'My mother thought, *This is the end,*' Dalia told Susannah.

The yellow Fiat snaked up the two-lane road and along the Chepelare River through thick pine forest. Susannah, eighty-three years old, looked out the window, telling Dalia she had nearly escaped the school yard on that March morning to join the Partizan fighters roaming these same hills. If she had, Dalia suggested, perhaps she would have met Uncle Jacques Eshkenazi, who had escaped the work camps to join the Partizans fighting the pro-Fascist government of King Boris.

The taxi arrived at Bachkovo, the Bulgarian Orthodox monastery built in the late twelfth century, burned to the ground by the Ottomans, and rebuilt again in subsequent decades. Dalia and Susannah got out and walked past the stalls of vendors selling rugs, buffalo yogurt, and religious trinkets. They passed under the broad eaves of a two-hundred-year-old lotus tree and toward their destination.

Inside, Dalia and Susannah walked under a low arch and into a room adorned with flowers, chandeliers, and centuries-old Christian frescoes painted on the walls. Hundreds of candles burned from every corner of the room. At first they couldn't see what they had come for. Then Dalia realized she was standing right beside them: the marble tombs of Kiril and Stephan, the Orthodox bishops who had vigorously fought Bulgaria's attempts to deliver the nation's Jews to the Nazis in 1943. Recently, Yad Vashem, Israel's Holocaust memorial, had declared the two Christian bishops 'Righteous among the Nations for saving Jews during the Holocaust.' Trees, in memory of the two bishops, were planted in the 'Forest of the Righteous.'

Dalia touched her fingertips to the marble, first of Stephan's tomb, then of Kiril's. Her lips were moving silently. Later she would try to find the words in English for her feeling of *hityakhadoot*: being alone and intimate with the soul of another and making space in your heart for that soul.

Dalia approached a bearded priest, who smiled and handed her candles. She lit them and prayed some more. Susannah stood in the center of the room, holding her unlit candles and gazing upward at the slowly rotating crystals of an antique chandelier.

Near the end of her pilgrimage, a few days before she returned to Israel, Dalia sat on a wooden bench in the back of the Sofia synagogue. Considered one of the most beautiful in the Balkans, it was unlike any synagogue Dalia had been in. Moorish arches rose to domed ceilings of dusky blue, with stars of painted gold. A magnificent chandelier, imported a century ago by train from Vienna, hung by heavy chains from wooden beams high overhead; it was said to weigh eighteen thousand pounds. Dalia gazed at a spot in the front of the synagogue, just before the ark, where Theodor Herzl had addressed fervent Zionists in 1896 and where her own parents had stood for their marriage forty-four years later. Dalia imagined the moment: her mother in white, ravishing, with raven hair flowing over her shoulders; her father, stiff and nervous in his suit, a future life of responsibility weighing heavily on his shoulders.

Sixty-four years later, their daughter sat quiet and still on the synagogue bench, thinking of the possibilities.

Bashir was struggling with the propane heater he had rolled in to warm his guests. Repeatedly he clicked the button to ignite the pilot light, but every time he released it, the flame went out. It was an early winter's day in 2004. Bashir kept pressing the button with his right index finger, until finally, after many clicks, the fire ignited; tiny waves of heat began to fill the room. He flashed a momentary, toothy smile and rose to offer his guests cookies and sweet Arabic tea.

The previous year, Bashir had been released from the Ramallah jail where he had spent more than a year beginning in August 2001. He had lost count of the number of times he'd been imprisoned, but it was safe to say that Bashir, now sixty-two years old, had spent at least a quarter of his life in a cell. This time, Bashir said, he was not convicted of anything, or charged, or even questioned. He had spent most of his 'administrative detention' playing chess and trying to keep warm in the outdoor tent prison.

A friend had told a story of the day Bashir left jail.

Israeli prison officials required that he sign a pledge not to commit any future acts of terror. What Israel called terror, however, Bashir often saw as legitimate resistance. He did not accept the legitimacy of the Israeli justice system, and he had never been told why he was in jail; consequently he refused to sign the document. 'If you don't sign,' the guard said, 'we will send you back.' Bashir told the guard to send him back. It was then, according to Bashir's friend, that the Israeli guard asked Bashir for a favor: Could he wait there a few minutes to make it *appear* to the other guards that he was cooperating? This could solve both men's problems. Bashir, suppressing a smile, agreed, and a few minutes later he was released.

Or so the story went; Bashir would not talk about it. 'Whenever I go into the prison I feel as though I'll never leave,' he would say. 'And every time I leave I feel as though I've never been there.'

Bashir's reluctance to confirm the story of his release was not simply a matter of refusing to humanize his Israeli jailer; it was instead part of a broader reticence to evoke memories or feelings. There were times when a visitor could detect emotion – in the hardening of his expression, the arching of his eyebrows, and the flush of his face when he talked about the Palestinian resistance; in the softness of his voice when he spoke about the *fitna* or lemon trees in the garden of the house in al-Ramla; in his smile or the narrowing of his eyes, when he talked about Dalia. But he was uncomfortable discussing politics in detail, or personal relations with his family, or memories from his childhood. The one memory that seemed most powerful, and least discussed, involved the loss of his hand. His thumb was forever hooked over his pocket, making the hand look normal; visitors or friends might go for months, or even years, before they learned that his hand was missing, and invariably they would learn of the tragedy from someone else. 'Bashir, why don't you get an artificial hand?' his cousin Ghiath once said when the two young men were studying law in Cairo. 'His face turned *this* color,' Ghiath said, grabbing his purple shirt. 'The incident made him complicated.'

Bashir returned to the sitting room with a tray of cookies and a teapot with three tiny glasses. He wore pressed gray slacks, a gray V-neck sweater, and a blue windbreaker, and he sat beside a bookshelf filled with Arabic literature and political thought and two volumes in English: *The Age of Reason* and *The Age of Enlightenment*. Gamal Abdel Nasser's image stared down from the white walls, alongside a black-and-white framed photograph of the house in al-Ramla. The picture was taken in the 1980s, around the time Bashir was deported to Lebanon, and showed the one-story home with its fourteen layers of white Jerusalem stone and a television antenna on the roof. A large palm tree grew out of the frame. Two beat-up cars were parked in front. Children were walking past the gate Ahmad Khairi had placed there in 1936.

Ahmad's son spooned three teaspoons of sugar into his steaming glass, and as he stirred, he asked his visitors what was on the agenda for today, one of many days of long interviews. The visitors had just returned from al-Ramla, and Bashir sat expressionless as he heard the new Israeli names of his old streets. Omar Ibn Khattab, the street named after the second caliph, whom Khanom liked to compare to Bashir, was now called Jabotinsky, named after a founding father of the Israeli right wing. 'Do you have any idea,' he asked after a while, 'how it feels that you can go there and I can't?' In fact, Bashir found it

375

difficult to go even to Amman, where he wanted to visit Khanom, Bhajat, and other family but was unable to get the necessary permits from the Israelis. 'I really miss Bashir very much,' Khanom had told a visitor to Amman. 'He is not able to come to Amman. He is in his prison again, in Ramallah. An open prison, a big prison. I am now getting old, and I'm not able to go there very much.'

Bashir rose again and returned with photocopies of the family tree – encircled names in Arabic script with arrows and dates going back four centuries – from Khair al-din al-Ramlawi through fifteen generations to the twenty-first-century Khairi diaspora in the West Bank, Jordan, Saudi Arabia, Qatar, Canada, and the United States. Khairis across the globe, Bashir said, still have claims to the *waqf* lands of Khair al-din, in what is now Israel. 'There are documents from the Ottoman period,' Bashir said, his left hand in his pocket. 'You can go to the Islamic law court in Istanbul to find these documents.'

For many Palestinians like Bashir, such claims, grounded in a 1948 United Nations resolution, remained paramount; for others they were less important than ending the occupation, now in its thirty-eighth year. Since the outbreak of the second intifada, more than 550 Palestinians under the age of eighteen had been killed. This was five times the number of Israelis of that age. One of the most recent victims was Iman al-Hams, an unarmed thirteen-year-old Palestinian girl. She was shot and killed by an Israeli officer, who then, according to accounts from his fellow soldiers, fired a stream of bullets into her body. Dozens of the deaths were of children under ten years old; thirteen were babies who died at checkpoints as their mothers gave birth. 'With horrific statistics like this, the question of who is a terrorist should have long since become very burdensome for every Israeli,' an Israeli columnist wrote. 'Who would have believed that Israeli soldiers would kill hundreds of children and that the majority of Israelis would remain silent?'

Daily humiliation was unavoidable for Palestinians traveling out of their own town or village. Bashir himself had been waiting for months for the Israeli authorities to grant him the permission to travel to Jordan for medical treatment. Numerous reports documented ambulances denied passage at checkpoints. Other Palestinians endured lengthy waits in long lines at muddy, potholed crossings or on foot at the checkpoint turnstiles. In one incident, a young Palestinian man on his way to a violin lesson was told by Israeli soldiers to take out his instrument and 'play something sad' before he was allowed to pass. For many Israelis, the incident evoked memories of Jewish violinists forced to play for Nazi officers at concentration camps, and it created a national outrage. Many of the commentators believed the checkpoints were essential for protecting Israel from suicide bombers, but they believed the humiliation of the young Arab violinist, Wissam Tayem, had undercut Israel's moral authority and disgraced the memory of the Holocaust.

For Palestinians, the effects of the intensifying occupation fueled a growing rage and sharpened the debate about the best course of political action. The disagreements were pronounced, even within Bashir's own family.

'If you want to get the land back,' Ghiath Khairi was saying, 'we will need generations and generations. An entire cycle of history. A new balance of power.' Ghiath was at home in Ramallah, sipping a cola in the family's living room. Ghiath was a few years older than his cousin

Bashir; he had left al-Ramla shortly after Bashir in 1948; he had attended law school in Cairo with Bashir in the early 1960s; he had traveled back to Ramla with Bashir and cousin Yasser on the bus in 1967; he had married Bashir's sister Nuha after Bashir's imprisonment for the Supersol bombing. The couple had three children.

After all the suffering he had witnessed, of his cousin and of others around him, Ghiath had adopted what he considered a patient and practical attitude. 'I can't draw the map of the world in two hundred years,' he said. 'Before one hundred years there was no Soviet Union. Two hundred years ago, Ottoman troops were in Vienna. Before two hundred years, there was nothing called Germany. Who is to say what the next hundred years will bring? Now Israel rules America. But I don't know what happens after one hundred years. It is the Israeli opinion that for the time being I cannot go back. So I yield up: I don't plan for coming generations. We can't do anything.'

Nuha sat erect on the couch across from Ghiath. 'We have the right to go back to our homeland,' she said. 'We can't be scattered all over. And meanwhile, they [Israelis] come from all over to live in our home.' She crossed her arms. 'Someone has to convince America of our right of return. Everybody should go back to his house. What about us these last fifty-six years? Whoever cares about us? Everybody cares only about them. They should go back where they came from. Or they could go to America. There's plenty of space there.'

'These are dreams, *dreams*!' Ghiath exclaimed.

'This is justice,' Nuha replied. 'And the solution.'

Ghiath would not back down. The problem of the day, he believed, was not return, it was the occupation. 'Every day, every night, the Israelis are coming here,' he told his guests. 'We went to a wedding last week, and the Israelis arrested the groom! Nevertheless, George Bush says Sharon is a man of peace. This is a joke, my dear sir. We are *les misérables*. We can't do anything! We are weak, and they are strong, and because we are weak, we should never have made this intifada. I don't believe in it. Hamas named it the 'Al-Aqsa intifada'. The PLO named it the 'intifada for the liberation of Palestine'. Israel named it the 'intifada of the security wall'. And who succeeded?'

'The Israelis,' Nuha said quietly.

'The intifada brought us this wall,' Ghiath proclaimed. He shrugged. 'I'm a practical person. Since I can do nothing, I'm sad for nothing. If what you want does not happen, want what happens.'

Ghiath no longer believed that radical Palestinian politics served the people's interests. 'In 1984, a few months before Bashir was released, I went to the prison,' he said. 'I said, "Look, Bashir. You spent fifteen years in an Israeli prison. Now, Bashir, it is enough for you."'

Bashir looked at his older cousin. He made something clear: He would never give up his right of return or his intention to fight for it by any means necessary. 'I told him, "You are talking nonsense,"' Ghiath recalled.

'I'm very proud of being Bashir's sister,' Nuha said. 'I believe in resistance. The way the Israelis are treating us today, we can't sit silent.' She paused and looked at her husband. 'I wish you were like Bashir.'

'I will *never* be like Bashir,' Ghiath replied. He turned to his guests. 'There is a competition between me and Bashir,' he said with a little smile. 'And we are cousins.'

Nuha reached for the television remote. *The Bold and the Beautiful* flickered on the screen, with subtitles in Arabic.

'We have to go back to our homes,' she said.

Dalia sat in the passenger seat of the rental car, staring straight ahead and trying to look casual, as if she, too, were a journalist and that it was normal for her to cross the Israeli military checkpoint heading north from Jerusalem to Ramallah. In fact, it was forbidden for Israeli civilians to travel to the occupied territories, and Dalia knew she risked being turned back. The soldier, however, checked only the driver's American passport, and surprisingly, the gamble paid off: Dalia was through the checkpoint and on her way to Ramallah. This was Qalandia, where Bashir and Ahmad had landed in the plane from Gaza in 1957; where, a decade later, Bashir had spotted the Israeli tanks from his rooftop in Ramallah.

'Oh, my God,' Dalia gasped. To her left, a long line of vehicles pointed south, nearly frozen in place. Young Palestinian men and boys passed between the cars, offering gum, cactus fruit, cucumbers, kitchen utensils, and soap to frustrated, immobile drivers. 'The Palestinian duty-free,' said Nidal Rafa, the Palestinian journalist who was accompanying Dalia.

Just behind the cars and the hawkers stood the subject of Dalia's exclamation: a towering curtain of concrete, stretching out of sight to the north. This was Israel's 'security barrier' separating the West Bank from Israel and, in some cases, the West Bank from itself. Construction for the barrier had begun in 2002 and would include six thousand workers digging trenches, stringing razor wire, erecting guard posts, laying concrete, and installing tens of thousands of electronic sensors. Part wall, part electrified fence, the construction project would cost $1.3 billion, or more than $3 million per mile. 'The sole purpose of the fence,' Israel declared, 'is to provide security' in response to 'the horrific wave of terrorism emanating from the West Bank.'

'They are building the wall,' said Nidal, 'so they don't have to look into our eyes.'

Palestinians called the barrier the 'apartheid wall' and accused Israel of grabbing more land in the West Bank under the guise of security. The barrier did not follow the 1967 border, or Green Line, and in some cases it carved deep into West Bank lands to incorporate settlements. In the summer of 2004, the UN's International Court of Justice in The Hague ruled, 'The construction of such a wall accordingly constitutes breaches by Israel of its obligations under the applicable international humanitarian law.' The court suggested Israel was creating a 'fait accompli' on the ground by annexing West Bank lands in lieu of a political settlement. Israel rejected the court's ruling, declaring, 'If there were no terror, there would be no fence.' Further, Israel said, the international court had no jurisdiction in the matter. The White House concurred, saying the UN court was not 'the appropriate forum to resolve what is a political issue.' John Kerry, the Democratic presidential candidate, called the barrier 'a legitimate act of self-defense' and said it 'is not a matter for the International Court of Justice.'

The rental car bumped along potholed roads, passed under a banner welcoming visitors to Ramallah, went left at the first traffic light, and stopped near a shop selling Palestinian crafts. Dalia got out and waited at the entrance to the building. Nidal, who would translate for Dalia, stood beside her.

'You go first,' Nidal said.

'No, please, you first,' Dalia said. 'Let me hide a little bit. It's been seven years.' They walked up the stairs.

Bashir stood waiting at the second-floor landing.

Bashir and Dalia stood in the hallway outside Bashir's office and shook hands for a long time, smiling broadly and looking straight into each other's face. '*Keef hallek?*' Bashir said. 'How are you, Dalia?'

Dalia handed Bashir a white paper bag with green lettering in Hebrew. 'A little lemon cake, Bashir,' she said.

Bashir led Dalia into his office, and they faced each other again, still standing. 'How is Yehezkel?' Bashir asked in English. 'And Raphael? How is your son?'

'Raphael is sixteen now. He's in high school. He likes computers. And I heard Ahmad is eighteen and going to Harvard!'

'It's only for four years.'

'The years mean nothing to him,' Dalia remarked, looking at Nidal. 'He was fifteen years in prison.'

Bashir nodded; his silver hair matched his steel-framed glasses. He wore khaki pants and a khaki windbreaker. 'Now I'm getting old,' he said. 'I'm sixty-two.'

'The gray looks good on him,' Dalia said. 'Tell him, Nidal. Good, wonderful!' As Nidal translated, Bashir's face turned red.

Bashir had been smiling from the moment Dalia arrived; now his face changed. 'I'm eager to see you, but I was very afraid for you. Especially with the news of each day. The wall, the arrests, the house demolitions, the way it is. The situation is not quiet. You can see people tense. You never know what could happen.'

Bashir had not expected Dalia, or he would have received her at his house. When she hadn't confirmed, he explained, and given the difficulty of passing the

382

checkpoints, he had assumed she wasn't coming.

There was a pause; Bashir disappeared for a moment to heat water for tea, and then the two old friends moved into padded chairs across a coffee table in the tiled, spare office.

'Everything's all right?' Bashir asked.

'What shall we say?' Dalia replied. 'I cannot answer this question.'

'Is Raphael doing well in school?'

'Yes.'

'Of course, this is natural. He comes from his father and you.'

Dalia rubbed her hands together and looked around the office. On the wall to her left was a picture of Abu Ali Mustafa, the PFLP and PLO official assassinated by Israeli helicopter rockets in 2001.

'Was he a friend?' Dalia asked after a long pause.

'Yes, a good friend. He was killed by two rockets from an Apache.'

Bashir got up for a moment and returned with steaming Styrofoam cups of tea. The subject turned to prison. Dalia wanted to know if Bashir was in Ramla when she was teaching high school next door in 1971.

'Maybe I was there, in solitary confinement,' Bashir replied. 'I was there less than one year. I was in seventeen prisons.'

'So you were moving around. Getting the grand tour. A prison tourist!' Dalia laughed uncomfortably. 'Did any of the guards treat you well?'

'There was a Romanian guard. He was a good guy.'

Bashir looked at his watch. Dalia knocked over her teacup, splashing herself and looking flustered.

'Don't worry! Don't worry!' Bashir exclaimed as Dalia mopped herself with a tissue.

'The Romanian guard,' Bashir continued, 'he kept letters from my nephew because the warden was coming to confiscate them.'

'Didn't you tell me once that Rabin came to visit the prison?'

Yes, Bashir said, it was when he was at Jneid prison near Nablus, before he was deported to Lebanon. Bashir was the prisoners' representative. 'I told Rabin that even Haim Levy' – the prisons commissioner – 'said that a dog couldn't live in these conditions.'

'It's interesting that he would come as minister of defense to sit with the prisoners,' Dalia remarked.

'I was a prisoner. He was minister of defense. Nothing changed.'

Dalia was thinking of Rabin and Oslo. 'But Bashir – don't you think that someone like that, who did something to change – made some progress, as much as he could in changing his position, to move a little bit – to make a compromise and extend his hand to your people . . . ?' Her question was left unfinished.

Bashir leaned forward. 'For Palestinians it didn't change the daily life. It went from bad to worse. I didn't go back to al-Ramla. We don't have our independent state, and we don't have our freedom. We are still refugees moving from one place to another place to another place to another place, and every day Israel is committing crimes. I can't even be on the board of the Open House. Because I'm Palestinian, not Israeli. If somebody comes yesterday from Ethiopia but he's Jewish, he will have all the rights, when I'm the one who has the history in al-Ramla. But for them I'm a stranger.'

Dalia's arms were folded tightly across her chest. She unfolded them and took a breath.

'Bashir. Maybe I have no right to say what I'm going to say. We need to make sacrifices if both of us are to live here. *We need to make sacrifices.* And I know it is not fair for me to say that. I know. I mean, you cannot live in your house in Ramla. I know it's not fair. But I think we do need to strengthen those people who are willing to make some compromise. Like Rabin, who paid with his life. And so for your own country, you need to strengthen the hand of those who are ready to make a compromise and ready to make space for us here. By not accepting the state of Israel or by not accepting the state of Palestine, I think none of us has a real life here. Israelis don't have a real life here, either. But if you're not okay, we're not okay. And if we're not okay, you're not okay.'

Dalia took another long breath. She slipped off her sandals and tucked her feet beneath her on the office chair. 'I was passing through the checkpoint today,' she said. 'I could see the wall – it is like a wall in the heart. You said you're in your prison here in Ramallah. Who am I to say that people like you who find themselves in a situation like this, that they need to sacrifice so much, so that my people will have a place? I mean, it's unfair, I understand, from your point of view. But you know from me from the past, how attached I am to the state of Israel. And how can I even ask you to make space for this state? But if I knew or if we knew that you could make space for the state of Israel, first of all in your heart, then we could find a solution on the ground. How much less threatened my people would feel. I say this understanding that I don't even have a right to ask you for this. I'm just asking this. That is my plea.'

As Nidal translated, Dalia and Bashir gazed across the room at each other, not smiling, not frowning, not blinking, eyes locked. The lemon cake sat forgotten in the white bakery bag on the table. A refrigerator hummed in the next room, and the voices of children at play drifted through the window.

'You, Dalia, remember thirty-seven years ago, when we first met; when I came to visit you,' Bashir said finally. 'And since then there have been more settlements, land confiscations, and now this wall – how can there be any solution? How can there be any Palestinian state? How can I open my heart, as you say?' For Bashir, of course, the solution was not simply dismantling the wall and making a Palestinian state on 22 percent of old Palestine; it remained 'having one state, and all the people who live in this one state are equal, without any consideration of religion, nationality, culture, language. Everyone is equal, has equal rights, has the right to vote and choose his own leadership.' At the core of this solution was return.

Bashir's views were supported by many Palestinians, but they stood on one side of a divide that had grown since Oslo. He was among those considered unrealistic and fixated on what his cousin Ghiath would consider an impractical dream. In recent years, however, a movement based on return had grown up in the Palestinian diaspora, from the refugee camps to young, more affluent Palestinians in Europe and the United States, who had been raised with the stories of villages long since destroyed. Bashir believed the right of return was both sacred and practical. Like an increasing number of Palestinians opposed to Oslo-type solutions, he believed that without return, the conflict will be eternal. 'And it will be a tragedy for both people,' he told Dalia.

Bashir believed 'it's the strong who create history,' but his years in prison and in exile had helped forge a longer-range view. 'We are weak today,' he said. 'But we won't stay this way. Palestinians are stones in a riverbed. We won't be washed away. The Palestinians are not the Indians. It is the opposite: Our numbers are increasing.'

The children's voices seemed loud through the open window. 'Dalia,' Bashir said, 'I really wanted to welcome you properly, in my house. I really didn't want to open this subject. This tragedy.'

Dalia's chin rested in her palm, and she was squinting intently at Bashir. 'If you say everything is all Palestine and I say everything is the whole land of Israel, I don't think we'll get anywhere,' she said. 'We share a common destiny here. I truly believe that we are so deeply and closely related – culturally, historically, religiously, psychologically. And it's so clear to me that you and your people are holding the key to our true freedom. And I think we could also say, Bashir, that we hold the key to your freedom. It's a deep interdependence. How can we free the heart, for our own healing? Is this possible?

'Where I live is very close to the Green Line,' Dalia continued. 'On the other side is the West Bank, and I can see the mountains from my window. And I love these mountains, it's like I feel that these mountains are in my heart. My ancestors lived on the Judean Hills. I'm not saying it's the same thing, don't get me wrong. I'm just saying there needs to be a compromise.'

Dalia had long believed in Einstein's words – that 'no problem can be solved from the same level of consciousness that created it.' For Dalia, the key to coexistence lay in what she called 'the three A's': acknowledgment of what had happened to the Palestinians in 1948, apology for it, and amends. Acknowledgment was, in part, to 'see and own the pain that I or my people have inflicted on the

Other.' But she believed this must be mutual – that Bashir must also see the Israeli Other – lest 'one perpetuate the righteous victim syndrome and not take responsibility for one's own part in the fray.' Through this acknowledgment, she and Bashir could act 'as mirrors through which our own redemption can eventually grow.' As for amends: 'It means that we do the best we can under the circumstances towards those we have wronged.' But for Dalia this could not involve a mass return of refugees. Yes, she believed, the Palestinians have the right of return, but it is not a right that can be fully implemented, because the return of millions of Palestinians would effectively mean the end of Israel.

For Bashir, as for many Palestinians who still believed in the right of return, this reasoning made little sense: How could you have a right, but not be able to exercise it? Perhaps after more than half a century, many refugees, in the end, would choose not to return to the site of their old villages, or move back into their old homes, but Bashir believed this should be *their* choice, not anyone else's. 'Our right of return is a natural human right,' Bashir said. 'The Israelis created this problem, and they can't place more burdens on us to solve it.'

For Dalia, the solution lay in two states, side by side – much as they had existed prior to the Six Day War in 1967, except that now alongside Israel would rise a peaceful, independent, Palestinian state. The Palestinians would have their right of return, but it would be limited to only a part of old Palestine.

Bashir believed the solution lay rather in 1948 and the long-held dream of return to a single, secular, democratic state. Bashir had always understood Dalia's gesture of sharing the house in al-Ramla, and making it into a kindergarten or Open House for the town's Arab children, as an acknowledgment of his right of return, and, by extension, of the rights of all Palestinian people, as enshrined by the UN, to go back to their homeland. Dalia, on the contrary, saw Open House, with its programs of encounter between Arabs and Jews, as the result of one choice made by one individual. 'It's not an overall solution and it's not a political statement,' she would say. 'It was something that destiny had in store for me. I simply feel that, yes, as a member of the Jewish people I have the right to assume some responsibility for our history in this land . . . and also for the injustice we caused another people.' This was her personal decision, Dalia would make clear, and not one that should be required of other Israelis.

Dalia leaned toward Bashir. 'I also feel the whole land is in my heart, and I know the whole land is in your heart,' she told him. 'But this mountain will be Palestine. I know it will, I can feel it. And I want to come and visit. As a respectful visitor. To visit the people of that mountain that I love so much.'

'It's touching what you are saying, Dalia,' Bashir said. 'That you look at this mountain and have this feeling. And you in this case are unique. But when you see the reality on the ground, and the Israeli politicians and how they deal with things, and when they see such a mountain, or such a land, they think of house confiscation, they think of settlements, they think of more settlers to come and to live . . . That is the reality today. And this is what is very difficult to understand. I wish more people were like you.' *I wish*, Bashir had written Dalia sixteen years earlier, *there had been a forest of Dalias*.

Dalia had always resisted being singled out as the 'good

Israeli' among the 'bad'; she pleaded for Bashir to show her 'that you really care and you really feel for my people. I have this need personally from you. From you, Bashir, who was born in my home. In your home. In our home. Not just for me, not just for Dalia. Because I know you care for me. And you know I care for you. Right? For you and your family . . . and you know that I care for the Palestinian people. And I also need to know that you care for my people. Because that would make me feel so much safer. Then we could move on. We could create a reality together.'

Bashir looked again at his watch; he was late for an appointment. 'We couldn't find two people who could disagree more on how to visualize the viability of this land,' Dalia said, standing and slipping on her sandals. 'And yet we are so deeply connected. And what connects us? The same thing that separates us. This land.'

Bashir was standing now, and he took Dalia's hand again. 'I was afraid for you to come here,' Bashir said.

'I wanted to come,' Dalia replied.

They stood between the padded office chairs and looked at each other, shaking hands and smiling.

'Expect me any day, Dalia,' Bashir said, still grasping her hand. 'I am forbidden to go to Jerusalem. But expect that one day, I will show up at your door.'

Bashir released Dalia's hand, waved good-bye from the landing, and went back into his office. Dalia walked slowly down the single flight of stairs toward the street in Ramallah.

'Our enemy,' she said softly, 'is the only partner we have.'

Fourteen

THE LEMON TREE

IN 1998, the fiftieth anniversary of the War of Independence and the Catastrophe, the lemon tree died. It had been bearing fewer lemons in the years leading up to its death, and by the spring of 1998, two shriveled, hard-shelled lemons lay on the ground, the only physical evidence the tree had ever borne fruit.

'This is the nature of things; things just die on this planet,' Dalia said at the time. 'Trees die standing.' For a couple of years, the teachers of the Arab kindergarten at Open House would hang balloons and ribbons on the branches to help the children discern one color from another. The ribbons fluttered in the wind, and it appeared the lemon tree had been replaced by a Christmas tree. Eventually a storm came and blew the tree down, leaving only a thick, gnarled stump.

Dalia hoped that one day Bashir, Khanom, Nuha, Ghiath, and other Khairis could return to the house in Ramla to plant another lemon tree, as a sign of renewal.

On January 25, 2005, as a full moon rose over the coastal plain just east of the Mediterranean Sea, Dalia walked with a group of Arab and Jewish teenagers to a corner of the garden at the house in Ramla. In their hands was a sapling of a lemon tree. A cone of earth in the shape of a bucket clung to the sapling roots. 'It looked so fragile,' Dalia said.

It was Tu B'shvat, the day the Jewish sages call the holiday of the new year for trees, and one of the Jewish teenagers had spontaneously suggested that this would be the perfect day to plant a new lemon tree.

'For years I was postponing this to wait for the Khairis,' Dalia said. 'And at that moment, the holiday of the trees, it felt so right, and yes, it's a new generation. And now the children will plant their tree in their house.' She said she did not want to stand in the way of the children who had chosen that day, the Jewish holiday, to plant a new lemon tree in the old garden of Ahmad Khairi.

Dalia's hands, and the hands of the Arabs and Jews, lowered the sapling into a hole beside the old stump. They all went to the kitchen and brought a pail of water, and everyone gently tamped down the soil.

'I felt that the Khairis were not there, so there was something missing,' Dalia recalled. 'But that empty space was filled up with all these children. The trunk was there, very beautiful. Just by it, we planted a new sapling. I couldn't just let the past stay like that. Like a commemoration stone, the kind you put in a graveyard. The pain of our history.

'This dedication is without obliterating the memories. Something is growing out of the old history. Out of the pain, something new is growing.

'I wonder how they will take it,' Dalia said of the Khairis. 'I felt it was right.' Also, she said, 'It meant moving on. It meant it's the next generation now that's going to create a reality. That we are entrusting something in their hands. We are entrusting both the old and the new.'

In the end, the decision of what to plant, and when, and where, was Dalia's. Bashir, when he heard about it by telephone from Ramallah, said he was pleased. Perhaps some day, he said, he would be back home in al-Ramla, and on that day, he would see the tree for himself.

ACKNOWLEDGMENTS

THE LEMON TREE would have never come to life without the support, insight, and generosity of eyewitnesses, scholars, archivists, journalists, and editors in the United States, Bulgaria, Israel, the West Bank, Jordan, and Lebanon.

I am indebted to the archivists at the American Jewish Joint Distribution Committee, in Queens, New York, and Jerusalem; the Central Zionist Archives and Israel State Archives in Jerusalem; the Institute for Palestine Studies in Beirut and Washington; the National Archives in Washington; the Lyndon Baines Johnson Library in Austin, Texas; and the National Archives of Bulgaria in Sofia, where Vanya Gazenko spent hours tracking down Jewish records from the 1940s.

Portions of the manuscript were reviewed in various drafts by scholars, writers, editors, and other colleagues across a range of disciplines and perspectives. I am grateful for the insight and comments of Polia Alexandrova, Nubar Alexanian, Lamis Andoni, Naseer Aruri, Hatem Bazian, Sophie Beal, George Bisharat, Matthew Brunwasser, Mimi Chakarova, Frederick Chary, Lydia Chavez, Hillel Cohen, Dan Connell, Beshara Doumani, Haim Gerber, Daphna Golan, Patricia Golan, Cynthia Gorney, Jan

Gunnison, Rob Gunnison, Debra Gwartney, Debbie Hird, Adam Hochschild, Alon Kadish, Bashir Khairi, Dalia Landau, Vicki Lindsay, Nur Masalha, Benny Morris, Moshe Mossek, Nidal Rafa, Tom Segev, Elif Shafak, Hani Shukrallah, Nikki Silva, Sami Sockol, Allan Solomonow, Salim Tamari, John Tolan, Kathleen Tolan, Mary Tolan, Sally Tolan, Tom Tolan, Sarah Tuttle-Singer, Anthony Weller, and Gosia Wojniacka. Some readers commented on multiple drafts, and I am especially grateful to the Tolan readers and to Julian Foley, Erica Funkhouser, and Rosie Sultan for their dedication to word and narrative.

Research and reporting for this book was conducted in six languages, only two of which – English and Spanish (close to Ladino, the language of Sephardic Jews) – I speak. For the work in Arabic, including translations of texts and interpreting, I thank Lamis Andoni, Naseer Aruri, Raghda Azizieh, Mahmoud Barhoum, Hatem Bazian, Lama Habash, Senan Khairi, Nidal Rafa, and Mariam Shahin. For the Bulgarian, Polia Alexandrova and Matthew Brunwasser helped immensely. For the Hebrew texts and interviews, I was lucky to work with Ora Alcalay, Ian Dietz, Patricia Golan, Boaz Hachlili, and Sami Sockol. Among those colleagues, I want to especially thank my old friend Patti, who among other things found me old soldiers, old buses, and great old newspapers; Polia, whose work from Sofia to Kyustendil to Plovdiv to Varna was unfailingly generous, thorough, and professional; Nidal, whose enthusiasm, dedication, journalistic passion, and knowledge of the landscape transformed my experience in Jerusalem and the West Bank and whose work in Amman (along with that of Mariam Shahin) proved vital for enriching the book. To each of you, I'm more grateful than you know.

In Boston, I learned of many initial contacts from the Bulgarian and Bulgarian-Jewish communities there. Thanks to Kiril Stefan Alexandrov, Iris Alkalay, Jennifer Bauerstam, Anne Freed, Roy Freed, Assya Nick, George Nick, Vladimir Zlatev, and Tanya Zlateva. Thanks also to Peter Vassilev for putting me in touch with his mother, Marie, in Sofia.

In California, two people merit special mention. Julian Foley, who not so long ago was my student at the University of California, Berkeley, Graduate School of Journalism, was suddenly reviewing my writing, and her insights into early and subsequent drafts were unfailingly on the mark. At the National Archives, Julian also unearthed vital documents on the period immediately after July 1948. Sarah Tuttle-Singer did substantial book and periodicals research at the University of California and eventually took the job of lead fact-checker, tracing the source for literally thousands of quotes, historical events, and moments of family history. Sarah also provided comments on several drafts of the manuscript and assembled the book's bibliography. Her tasks were daunting, and she delivered thorough work with grace and goodwill. She was assisted by Sara Dosa, who came to us late in the process and proved a big help at a crucial time.

I spoke with hundreds of people during the course of the research, and their names are too numerous to mention here. I would, however, like to single out a few whose generosity and clarity helped take the book into new territory. They include Susannah Behar in Plovdiv and Vela Dimitrova in Sofia and Kyustendil, Bulgaria; Sharif Kanaana, Firdaws Taji Khairi, Nuha Khairi, and Ghiath Khairi in Ramallah; Khanom Khairi Salah in

Amman; Ora Alcalay, Moshe Melamed, Moshe Mossek, and Victor Shemtov in Jerusalem; Israel Gefen in Tel Aviv; Yehezkel Landau in Cambridge, Massachusetts, and Hartford, Connecticut; and most of all, Bashir Khairi in Ramallah and Dalia Eshkenazi Landau in Jerusalem. Dalia's willingness to interview her cousin Yitzhak Yitzhaki, late in the process, and to translate and fax me those transcripts and other materials, added much to the book.

This book began its life as a radio documentary, and I am grateful to Danny Miller, the executive producer of Fresh Air, for giving The Lemon Tree its first home outside of Israel and Palestine. The radio program generated more response than all of the many dozens of NPR programs I had done over the years combined, and this, along with the urging of friends like Joe Garland, Anthony Weller, Dan Connell, and Alan Weisman, convinced me to transform the story into print.

The book was written in multiple venues over a two-year period. My thanks go to the staff of the Mesa Refuge, a retreat in Pt. Reyes, California; to the people of the Villa Sagona at the Sea Gardens in Varna, Bulgaria; to Kevin Kelley, who provided a guest room, and great company, at his home in Canada's Gulf Islands; and to Nubar, Rebecca, and Abby Alexanian, whose support (including Abby's West Gloucester studio) was immeasurable, especially at the final days of writing.

Toward the end of the writing, I began to refer to the book as a living, sentient being: at times a benign presence, at others a demanding taskmaster. Many could attest to my virtual disappearance for weeks at a go, and during these times I was lucky to have understanding friends and colleagues. To Alan Weisman, Jonathan Miller, and Melissa Robbins, my colleagues in Homelands Productions: Thank you for your patience. To Nubar Alexanian and Vicki Lindsay, friends always throughout the writing: You understand. To Dean Orville Schell and all my colleagues at the Graduate School of Journalism, who supported this work with their eyes, ears, and encouragement (none more so than Mimi Chakarova, Lydia Chavez, Cynthia Gorney, and Rob Gunnison): It's an honor to work with you.

My agent, David Black, believed in me and the possibility of *The Lemon Tree* beyond the radio documentary; Karen Rinaldi of Bloomsbury brought passion to the book from the first moment and never wavered; Bloomsbury editor Kathy Belden was patient, clear-eyed, precise, and a pleasure to work with. It wouldn't be possible to have a better, more supportive team than these three. To the rest of the team at Bloomsbury, including many people I haven't even met – thank you.

To the friends in Bulgaria, Israel, and the Arab world who fed me, found me places to rest, and provided a few laughs and rays of hope between the painful moments of history, big and small: I'm grateful.

For Lamis, who opened up worlds, and the Andoni family, who showed me the generosity and warmth of an Arab family: I will always be grateful. Thank you, Margaret, Reem, Jack, Wido, Tala, Lana, Nabil, Missy, Laila, Charlie, and Michael.

To my brother, Yam, and all the aforementioned Tolans, to Tolan spouses, nephews, and nieces: I love you all.

Finally, to Bashir Khairi and Dalia Eshkenazi Landau, who sat with me dozens of times over hundreds of hours, listening to the smallest questions, sometimes with disbelief ('How do I know what color my tie was in July 1967?'), I can only say: In more ways than one, this book would not have existed without you. *Alf shukran. Toda roba.*

Thank you.

BIBLIOGRAPHY: WORKS CITED

Archives

American Jewish Joint Distribution Committee Archives. Queens, New York, and Jerusalem, Israel.

Broadcast Archives of the British Broadcasting Corporation. London.

The Central Zionist Archives. Jerusalem, Israel.

Israel State Archives. Jerusalem, Israel.

Institute for Palestinian Studies Archives. Beirut, Lebanon.

Lyndon Baines Johnson Library Archives. Austin, Texas.

Kibbutz Na'an Archives. Kibbutz Na'an, Israel.

National Archives of Bulgaria. Sofia, Bulgaria.

National Archives of the United States. Washington, D.C.

National Library of Bulgaria. Sofia, Bulgaria.

Palestinian Association for Cultural Exchange. Ramallah, West Bank.

Electronic Sources (Including Online Media)

'A Small Revolution in Ramle.' Ha'aretz. http://www.haaretz-daily.com/ hasen/pages/ShArt.jhtml?itemNo=337040 &contrassID=2&subContrassID=5&sbSubContrass ID=0&listSrc=Y.

'Background of the Repatriation and Land Exportation Schemes and the Laws Purporting to Justify Israel's Actions.' http://www.badil.org/ Publications/Legal_Papers/ cescr-2003-A1.pdf.

Bard, Dr. Mitchell. 'Myth and Fact: The Creation of Hamas.' *United Jewish Communities: The Federations of North America*. http://www.ujc.org/content_ display.html?ArticleID=114644.

Bodendorfer, Gerhard. 'Jewish Voices About Jesus.' Jewish-Christian Relations. http://www.jcrelations.net/en/?id=738.

'Count Folke Bernadotte.' Jewish Virtual Library. http://www.jewishvirtuallibrary.org/jsource/biography/Bern adotte.html.

'Giuliani: "Thank God That George Bush Is Our President."' CNN. http://www.cnn.com/2004/ALLPOLITICS/08/30/ giuliani.transcript/index.html.

'Gregorian-Hijri Dates Converter.' June 7, 2005. http://www.rabiah.com/ convert/convert.php3.

'Hezbollah Fires Rockets into Northern Israel.' CNN. http://www.cnn.com/WORLD/9603/israel_lebanon/30/.

'Interview with Defense Minister Arens on Israel Television – 8 May 1983.' Israel Ministry of Foreign Affairs. http://www.mfa.gov.il/MFA/Foreign+Relations/Israels+ Foreign+Relations+since+1947/1982–1984/111+Interview+ with+Defense+Minister+Arens+on+Israe.htm.

'Israel 1948–1967: Why Was King Abdullah of Jordan Assassinated in 1951?' Palestine Facts. http://www.palestine-facts.org/ pf_1948to1967_abdulla.php.

'Israeli Army Blows Up Palestinian Broadcasting Center.' CNN. http://archives.cnn.com/2002/WORLD/meast/01/18/mideast .violence.

'Israeli West Bank Barrier.' Wikipedia.http://en.wikipedia.org/ wiki/Israeli_West_Bank_barrier.

'Israel Sends Letter to UN Protesting Hezbollah Attack.' Ha'aretz.http://www.haaretz.com/hasen/pages/ShArt.jhtml?-itemNo=436197&contrassID=13.

'John Kerry: Strengthening Israel's Security.' Jewish Virtual Library. http://www.jewishvirtuallibrary.org/jsource/US-Israel/kerryisrael.html.

'Knowledge Bank: Profiles – Gamel Abdel Nasser.' CNN. http://www.cnn.com/SPECIALS/cold.war/kbank/profiles/nasser.

'Lebanese Mortar Lands in Northern Israel.' http://archives.tcm.ie/breakingnews/2005/08/25/story217788.asp.

Meron, Ya'akov. 'Why Jews Fled the Arab Countries.' http://www.freerepublic.com/focus/f-news/956344/posts.

'Moroccan Jewish Immigration to Israel.' http://rickgold.home.mindspring.com/Emigration/emigration%20statistics.htm.

'Moroccan Jews.' http://www.usa-morocco.org/moroccan-jews.htm.

Pappe, Ilan. 'Were They Expelled? – The History, Historiography and Relevance of the Palestinian Refugee Problem.' http://www.nakbainhebrew.org/library/were_they_expelled.rtf

'PLO Founder Killed by Israeli Missile Attack.' News.telegraph. http://www.telegraph.co.uk/news/main.jhtml?xml=/news/2001/08/28/wmid28.xml.

'Progress Report of the United Nations Mediator on Palestine Submitted to the Secretary-General for Transmission to the Members of the United Nations.' UNISPAL. http://domino.un.org/UNISPAL.NSF/0/ab14d4aafc4e1bb985256204004f55fa?OpenDocument.

'Progress Report of the United Nations Mediator on Palestine.' UNISPAL. http://domino.un.org/UNISPAL.NSF/0/cc33602f61b0935c8025648800368307?Open Document.

Remnick, David. 'Profiles: The Spirit Level: Amos Oz Writes the Story of Israel.' *The New Yorker* http://www.newyorker.com/fact/content/?041108fa_fact.

Shlaim, Avi. 'Israel and the Arab Coalition in 1948.' Cambridge University Press. http://www.fathom.com/course/72810001.

'The Law of Return 5710 (1950). Knesset.http://www.knesset. gov.il/laws/special/eng/return.htm.

'The Making of Transjordan.' Hashemite Kingdom of Jordan. http://www.kinghussein.gov.jo/his_transjordan.html.

'The Separation Barrier in the West Bank.' B'tselem. September 2005. http://www.btselem.org/Download/Separation_Barrier _Map_Eng.pdf.

'Water and the Arab-Israeli Conflict.' http://www.d-n-i.net/ al_aqsa_intifada/collins_water.htm.

'Why Did Arabs Reject the Proposed UN GA Partition Plan Which Split Palestine into Jewish and Arab States?' Palestine Remembered. http://www.palestineremembered.com/Acre/ Palestine-Remembered/Story448.html.

Yacobi, Haim. 'From Urban Panopticism to Spatial Protests: Housing Policy, Segregation, and Social Exclusion of the Palestinian Community in the City of Lydda-Lod.' 2001. http://www.lincolninst.edu/ pubs/dl/622_yacobi.pdf.

Zureik, Elia. 'Palestinian Refugees and the Peace Process.' http://www.arts.mcgill.ca/MEPP/PrrN/papers/Zureik2.html.

Newspaper and Magazine Articles in Print

'2 Die, 8 Wounded in J'lem Terror Outrage at Supersol.' *Jerusalem Post*, February 23, 1969.

Amos, Elon. 'War Without End.' *New York Review*, July 15, 2004.

'Anglican Clergyman, Surgeon, Among Those Held in Terrorist Round-Up.' *Jerusalem Post*, March 4, 1969.

Bellos, Susan. 'Supersol Victims Buried; Allon Promises Vengeance.' *Jerusalem Post*, February 24, 1969.

Bilby, Kenneth. 'Israeli Tanks Take Arab Air Base at Lydda.' *New York Herald Tribune*, July 11, 1948.

————. 'Israeli Units Cut Way into Ramle, Lydda Surrender of

Both Reported in Cairo.' *New York Herald Tribune*, July 12, 1948.

Currivan, Gene. 'Arabs Encircled at Vital Highway, Surrender Lydda.' The *New York Times*, July 12, 1948.

————. 'Curb Arabs, Count Bids UN; Israeli Force Wins Ramleh.' The *New York Times*, July 13, 1948.

Feron, James. 'Bomb Explosion in Jerusalem's Largest Supermarket Kills 2, Injures 9.' The *New York Times*, February 22, 1969.

————.'Israel and Arabs: Tensions in the Occupied Territories.' The *New York Times*, April 28, 1968.

'First Sabotage Attempt on Supersol Failed.' *Jerusalem Post*, May 14, 1969.

'"Front" Chief Says Terrorism Against Israel to Continue.' *Jerusalem Post*, March 5, 1969.

'Houses of 9 West Bank Terrorists Demolished.' *Jerusalem Post*, March 11, 1969.

Safadi, Anan, and Malka Rabinowitz. 'Major Terror Gang Seized.' *Jerusalem Post*, March 6, 1969.

'Supersol Blast Suspects Held in Round-up of 40.' *Jerusalem Post*, March 2, 1969.

'Supersol Crime Reconstructed.' *Jerusalem Post*, March 3, 1969.

'Supersol.' *Jerusalem Post*, February 23, 1969.

'Supersol Reopens; Business as Usual.' *Jerusalem Post*, February 24, 1969.

Journals and Journal Articles

Abu Hadba, Abdul Aziz, ed. *Society and Heritage* 32 (1998).

Abukhalil, As'ad. 'George Habash and the Movement of Arab Nationalists: Neither Unity Nor Liberation.' *Journal of Palestine Studies* (1999).

Abu Sitta, Salman. 'Special Report of Badil: Quantification of Land Confiscated inside the Green Line.' *Annex to Follow-Up Information Submitted to the Committee for Economic, Social and Cultural Rights* (2000).

Alpher, Joseph, and Khalil Shikaki. 'Concept Paper: The Palestinian Refugee Problem and the Right of Return.' *Middle East Policy* 6 (1999): 167–189.

Bruhns, Fred C. 'A Study of Arab Refugee Attitudes.' *Middle East Journal* 9 (1955): 130–38.

Busailah, Reja-E. 'The Fall of Lydda, 1948: Impressions and Reminiscences.' *Arab Studies Quarterly* 3 (1981): 123–51.

Christison, Kathleen. 'Bound by a Frame of Reference, Part II: U.S. Policy and the Palestinians, 1948–1988.' *Journal of Palestine Studies* (1998).

Friedman, Adina. 'Unraveling the Right of Return.' *Refugee* 21 (2003).

Gilmour, David. 'The 1948 Arab Exodus.' *Middle East International* 286 (1986): 13–14.

Hanafi, Sari. 'Opening the Debate on the Right of Return.' *Middle East Report: War Without Borders* 2–7.

Hanieh, Akram. 'The Camp David Papers.' *Journal of Palestine Studies* 2 (2001): 75–97.

Khader, Hassan. 'Confessions of a Palestinian Returnee.' *Journal of Palestine Studies* 27 (1997).

Khalidi, Walid. 'Selected Documents on the 1948 Palestine War.' *Journal of Palestine Studies* 27 (1998): 60–105.

Lebanese Center for Documentation and Research, ed. 'Political Violence in the World: 1967–1987.' *Chronology Bibliography Documents*, Vol. 1. Beirut: 1988.

Lesch, Ann M. 'Israeli Deportation of Palestinians from the West Bank and the Gaza Strip, 1967–1978.' *Journal of Palestine Studies* 8 (1979): 101–31.

Macpherson, Rev. James Rose, trans. *Palestine Pilgrims Text Society* 3 (1895).

————. *Palestine Pilgrims Text Society* 5 (1895).

————. *Palestine Pilgrims Text Society* 6 (1895).

————. *Palestine Pilgrims Text Society* 8 (1895).

Middle East International (various biweekly issues, 2003–2005).

Morris, Benny. 'Operation Dani and the Palestinian Exodus from Lydda and Ramle in 1948.' *Middle East Journal* 40 (1986): 82–109.

————. 'The Causes and Character of the Arab Exodus from Palestine: The Israel Defense Forces Intelligence Branch Analysis of June 1948.' *Middle Eastern Studies* 22 (1986): 5–19.

Munayyer, Spiro, and Walid Khalidi. 'Special Document: The Fall of Lydda.' *Journal of Palestine Studies* 27 (1998): 80–98.

Palestine-Israel Journal of Politics Economics and Culture 9, no. 4 (2002). *Narratives of 1948*. East Jerusalem: Middle East Publications, 2002.

'Palestinian Refugees of Lebanon Speak.' *Journal of Palestine Studies* 26 (1995): 54–60.

Said, Edward. 'A Changing World Order.' *Arab Studies Quarterly* 3 (1981).

Social, Cultural, and Educational Association of the Jews in the People's Republic of Bulgaria 14 (1983).

'Special Document: Israel and Torture.' *Journal of Palestine Studies* 9 (1977): 191–219.

Tamari, Salim, ed. *Jerusalem Quarterly* File (2003).

Yost, Charles. 'The Arab-Israeli War: How It Began.' *Foreign Affairs* (January 1968). Vol. 46, no. 2.

Published Articles and Pamphlets

'Deportation of Palestinians from the Occupied Territories and the Mass Deportation of December 1992.' Jerusalem: Israeli Information Center for Human Rights in the Occupied Territories (B'Tselem), 1993.

'Aufruf/Ma'amar: Article.' Hulda Takam Archive, 1947 or 1948.

Masalha, Nur. 'The 1967 Palestinian Exodus.' *The Palestinian Exodus 1948–1998*. Ghada Karmi and Eugene Cotran, eds. London: Ithaca Press, 1999.

Mossek, Moshe. 'The Struggle for the Leadership Among the Jews of Bulgaria Following Liberation.' *Eastern European Jewry – From Holocaust to Redemption, 1944–1948*. Benjamin Pinkus, ed. Sede Boqer, Israel: Ben-Gurion University Press, 1987.

Paounovski, Vladimir. 'The Anti-Jewish Legislation in Bulgaria During the Second World War.' From *The Jews in Bulgaria between the Holocaust and the Rescue*. Sofia: Adasa-Pres, 2000.

Pappe, Ilan. 'Were They Expelled?: The History, Historiography and Relevance of the Palestinian Refugee Problem.' *The Palestinian Exodus 1948–1998*. Ghada Karmi and Eugene Cotran, eds. London: Ithaca Press, 1999.

Government Publications

A Survey of Palestine: Prepared in December 1945 and January 1946 for the Information of the Anglo-American Committee of Inquiry. Jerusalem: The Government Printer, 1946.

Great Britain. Labour Middle East Council, Conservative Middle East Council, Liberal Democratic Middle East Council. Joint Parliamentary Middle East Councils Commission of Enquiry – Palestinian Refugees, Right of Return. London, 2001.

Israel. State of Israel. Government Year Book 5714 (1953–1954). Government Printer.

Palestine and Transjordan Administration Reports 1918–1948 (vols. 5, 6, 10, and 16), archive editions, 1995.

Ramla City Council Minutes. Ramla, Israel, 1949.

United Nations. United Nations Relief and Works Agency (UNRWA). *UNRWA: The Long Journey* 45 (1993).

United Nations. United Nations Special Committee on Palestine. Report on Palestine: *Report to the General Assembly by the United Nations Special Committee on Palestine*. New York: Somerset Books, 1947.

Media

Journey to Jerusalem. Ivan Nichev, director. Videocassette. Bulgarian National Television, 2003.

The Lemon Tree. Sandy Tolan, producer. NPR's *Fresh Air*, 1998.

The Optimists: The Story of the Rescue of the Bulgarian Jews from the Holocaust. Jacky Comforty, director. Videocassette. New Day Films, 2001.

Troubled Waters. Sandy Tolan, producer. A five-part series for NPR's *Living on Earth*. Portions aired on NPR's *Weekend Edition*, 1997.

Unpublished Works

Alkalay, Iris. 'My Father's Three Bulgarias.'

Chapple, John. 'Jewish Land Settlement in Palestine' (unpublished paper), 1964.

'The Jewish Community in Plovdiv: History, Style of Living, Culture, Traditions, Place in the Life of the Town.'

Krispin, Alfred. 'The Rescue of the Jews in Bulgaria: A Closely Kept Secret. Recollections of a Bulgarian Jew.'

Books

Abdul Hadi, Mahdi F. *Palestine Documents Volume II: From the Negotiations in Madrid to the Post-Hebron Agreement Period*. Jerusalem: PASSIA, 1997.

Abdulhadi, Faiha, ed. and compiler. *Bibliography of Palestinian Oral History (with a Special Focus on Palestinian Women)*. Al-Bireh, West Bank: Palestinian National Authority Ministry of Planning and International Cooperation, 1999.

Abu Nowar, Maan. *The Jordanian-Israeli War: 1948–1951: A History of the Hashemite Kingdom of Jordan*. Reading, U.K.: Ithaca Press, 2002.

Abu Hussein, Hussein, and Fiona McKay. *Access Denied: Palestinian Land Rights in Israel*. London: Zed Books, 2003.

Aburish, Said K. *Arafat: From Defender to Dictator*. London: Bloomsbury, 1998.

Abu-Sharif, Bassam, and Uzi Mahnaimi. *Best of Enemies*. Boston: Little, Brown & Co., 1995.

Ajami, Fouad. *The Dream Palace of the Arabs: A Generation's Odyssey*. New York: Vintage Books, 1998.

————. *The Arab Predicament: Arab Political Thought and Practice Since 1967*. Cambridge: Cambridge University Press, 1992.

Almog, Oz. *The Sabra: The Creation of the New Jew*. Translated by Haim Watzman. Berkeley, Calif: University of California Press, 2000.

Amad, Adnan, ed. *Israeli League for Human and Civil Rights*. Beirut: Neebii.

Anidjar, Gil. *The Jew, the Arab: A History of the Enemy*. Stanford, Calif.: Stanford University Press, 2003.

Armstrong, Karen. *Jerusalem: One City, Three Faiths*. New York: Ballantine Books, 1996.

Aruri, Naseer. *Dishonest Broker: The Role of the United States in Palestine and Israel*. Cambridge, Mass.: South End Press, 2003.

————. *Palestinian Refugees: The Right of Return*. London: Pluto Press, 2001.

Avineri, Shlomo. *The Making of Modern Zionism: The Intellectual Origins of the Jewish State*. New York: Basic Books, 1981.

Avishai, Bernard. *Tragedy of Zionism: How Its Revolutionary Past Haunts Israeli Democracy*. New York: Helios Press, 2002.

Bahour, Sam, and Alice Lynd, eds. *Homeland: Oral Histories of Palestine and Palestinians*. New York: Olive Branch Press, 1994.

Bar-Gal, Yoram. *Propaganda and Zionist Education: The Jewish National Fund 1924–1947*. Rochester, N.Y.: University of Rochester Press, 2003.

Bar-Joseph, Uri. *The Best of Enemies: Israel and Transjordan in the War of 1948*. London: Frank Cass, 1987.

Bar-Zohar, Michael. *Beyond Hitler's Grasp: The Heroic Rescue of Bulgaria's Jews*. Holbrook, Mass.: Adams Media Corporation, 1998.

Barouh, Emmy. *Jews in the Bulgarian Lands: Ancestral Memory and Historical Destiny*. Sofia: Inernational Center for Minority Studies and Intercultural Relations, 2001.

Bauer, Yehuda. *Out of the Ashes*. Oxford: Pergamon Press, 1989.

Begley, Louis. *Wartime Lies*. New York: Ballantine Books, 1991.

Bennis, Phyllis. *Understanding the Palestinian-Israeli Conflict*. Orlando, Fla.: TARI, 2002.

Ben-Sasson, H. H., ed. *A History of the Jewish People*. Cambridge, Mass.: Harvard University Press, 1976.

Bentwich, Norman. *Israel: Two Faithful Years, 1967–1969*. London: Elek Books Ltd., 1970.

Benvenisti, Meron. *Intimate Enemies: Jews and Arabs in a Shared Land*. Berkeley, Calif: University of California Press, 1995.

————. *Sacred Landscapes: The Buried History of the Holy Land Since 1948*. Berkeley, Calif.: University of California Press, 2000.

Bishara, Marwan. *Palestine/Israel: Peace or Apartheid – Prospects for Resolving the Conflict*. New York: Zed Books, 2001.

Bisharat, George Emile. *Palestinian Lawyers and Israeli Rule:*

Law and Disorder in the West Bank. Austin: University of Texas Press, 1989.

Braizat, Musa S. *The Jordanian-Palestinian Relationship: The Bankruptcy of the Confederal Idea*. London: British Academic Press, 1998.

Brenner, Lenni. *Zionism in the Age of Dictators*. London: Croom Helm, 1983.

————. *The Iron Wall: Zionist Revisionism from Jabotinsky to Shamir*. London: Zed Books, 1984.

Bucaille, Laetitia. *Growing Up Palestinian: Israeli Occupation and the Intifada Generation*. Princeton, N.J.: Princeton University Press, 2004.

Carey, Roane, and Jonathan Shainin, eds. *The Other Israel: Voices of Refusal and Dissent*. New York: The New Press, 2002.

Chary, Frederick B. *The Bulgarian Jews and the Final Solution, 1940–1944*. Pittsburgh: University of Pittsburgh Press, 1972.

Childers, Erskine B. *The Road to Suez: A Study of Western-Arab Relations*. London: Macgibbon & Kee, 1962.

Cleveland, William. *History of the Modern Middle East*. Boulder, Colo.: Westview Press, 1994.

Cohen, Aharon. *Israel and the Arab World*. Boston: Beacon Press, 1976.

Cohen, David, compiler. *The Survival: A Compilation of Documents 1940–1944*. Sofia: 'Shalom' Publishing Centre, 1944.

Cohen, H. J. *The Jews of the Middle East, 1860–1972*. Jerusalem: Israel Universities Press, 1973.

Cohen, Michael J. *Palestine and the Great Powers: 1945–1948*. Princeton, N.J.: Princeton University Press, 1982.

————. 'The Anglo-American Committee on Palestine, 1945–1946.' *The Rise of Israel*, vol. 35. New York: Garland

Publishing, Inc., 1987.

————. 'United Nations Discussions on Palestine, 1947.' *The Rise of Israel*, vol. 37. New York: Garland Publishing, Inc., 1987.

————. 'The Recognition of Israel, 1948.' *The Rise of Israel*, vol. 39. New York: Garland Publishing, Inc., 1987.

Connell, Dan. *Rethinking Revolution: New Strategies for Democracy and Social Justice: The Experience of Eritrea, South Africa, Palestine, and Nicaragua.* Lawrenceville, N.J.: Red Sea Press, 2001.

Constant, Stephan. *Foxy Ferdinand: 1861–1948, Tsar of Bulgaria.* London: Sidgwick & Jackson, 1979.

Crampton, R. J. *A Short History of Modern Bulgaria.* Cambridge: Cambridge University Press, 1987.

Darwish, Mahmoud. *Memory for Forgetfulness: August, Beirut, 1982.* Translated from the Arabic by Ibrahim Muhawi. Berkeley, Calif.: University of California Press, 1995.

Dayan, Yael. *Israel Journal: June 1967.* New York: McGraw-Hill, 1967.

El-Asmar, Fouzi. *Through the Hebrew Looking-Glass: Arab Stereotypes in Children's Literature.* Vermont: Amana Books, 1986.

————. *To Be an Arab in Israel.* London: Frances Pinter Ltd., 1975.

Einstein, Albert. *About Zionism: Speeches and Letters.* Translated and edited with an introduction by Leon Simon. New York: Macmillan, 1931.

Elon, Amos. *A Blood-Dimmed Tide: Dispatches from the Middle East.* New York: Columbia University Press, 1997.

————. *The Israelis: Founders and Sons.* Tel Aviv: Adam Publishers, 1981.

————. *Jerusalem: City of Mirrors.* Boston: Little, Brown & Co., 1989.

Enderlin, Charles. *Shattered Dreams: The Failure of the Peace Process in the Middle East, 1995–2002*. Translated from the French by Susan Fairfield. New York: Other Press, 2003.

Eshkenazi, Jacques, and Alfred Krispin. *Jews in Bulgarian Hinterland: An Annotated Bibliography*. Translated from the Bulgarian by Alfred Krispin. Sofia: International Center for Minority Studies and Intercultural Relations, 2002.

Eveland, Wilbur Crane. *Ropes of Sand: America's Failure in the Middle East*. London: W. W. Norton & Co., 1980.

Farsoun, Samih K. *Palestine and the Palestinians*. Boulder, Colo.: Westview Press, 1997.

Feiler, Bruce. *Abraham: A Journey to the Heart of Three Faiths*. New York: William Morrow, 2002.

————. *Walking the Bible: A Journey by Land Through the Five Books of Moses*. New York: William Morrow, 2001.

Finkelstein, Israel, and Neil Asher Silberman. *The Bible Unearthed: Archaeology's New Vision of Ancient Israel and the Origin of Its Sacred Texts*. New York: Simon & Schuster, 2001.

Flapan, Simha. *The Birth of Israel: Myths and Realities*. New York: Pantheon Books, 1987.

Frances, Samuel. *Recuerdos Alegres, Recuerdos Tristes*. Sofia: Shalom, 2000.

Friedman, Thomas L. *From Beirut to Jerusalem*. New York: Anchor Books, 1995.

Gaff, Angela. *An Illusion of Legality: A Legal Analysis of Israel's Mass Deportation of Palestinians on 17 December 1992*. Ramallah: Al-Haq, 1993.

Gefen, Israel. *An Israeli in Lebanon*. London: Pickwick Books, 1986.

————. *Years of Fire*. London: Ferrington, 1995.

Gelber, Yoav. *Palestine 1948: War, Escape and Emergence of the Palestinian Refugee Problem*. Brighton: Sussex Academic Press, 2001.

Gerner, Deborah. *One Land, Two Peoples: The Conflict over Palestine*. Boulder, Colo.: Westview Press, 1994.

Gharaibeh, Fawzi A. *The Economies of the West Bank and Gaza Strip*. Boulder, Colo.: Westview Press, 1985.

Glubb, Sir John Bagot. *A Soldier with the Arabs*. London: Hodder & Stoughton, 1957.

Green, Stephen. *Taking Sides: America's Secret Relations with a Militant Israel, 1948–1967*. London: Faber & Faber, 1984.

Gresh, Alain. *The PLO, the Struggle Within: Towards an Independent Palestinian State*. Translated from the French by A. M. Berrett. London: Zed Books, 1988.

Grossman, David. *Sleeping on a Wire: Conversations with Palestinians in Israel*. Translated by Haim Watzman. London: Picador, 1994.

Groueff, Stephane. *Crown of Thorns*. Lanham, Md.: Madison Books, 1987.

Grozev, Kostadin, et al. *1903–2003: 100 Years of Diplomatic Relations Between Bulgaria and the United Sates*. Sofia: Embassy of the United States of America in Bulgaria, 2003.

Haddad, Simon. *The Palestinian Impasse in Lebanon: The Politics of Refugee Integration*. Brighton: Sussex Academic Press, 1988.

Hashavia, Arye. *A History of the Six-Day War*. Tel Aviv: Ledory Publishing House, n.d.

Heikal, Mohamed. *Secret Channels: The Inside Story of Arab-Israeli Peace Negotiations*. London: HarperCollins Publishers, 1996.

Herzog, Chaim. *The Arab-Israeli Wars: War and Peace in the Middle East*. New York: Vintage Books, 1982.

Hillel, Shlomo. *Ruah Kadim*. Jerusalem: 'Idanim, 1985.

Hillenbrand, Carole. *The Crusades: Islamic Perspectives*. New York: Routledge, 2000.

Hiro, Dilip. *Sharing the Promised Land: A Tale of Israelis and*

Palestinians. New York: Olive Branch Press, 1999.

Hirsch, Ellen, ed. *Facts About Israel.* Jerusalem: Ahva Press, 1999.

Hirst, David. *The Gun and the Olive Branch: The Roots of Violence in the Middle East.* New York: Thunder's Mouth Press/Nation Books, 2003.

Hroub, Khaled. *Hamas: Political Thought and Practice.* Washington, D.C.: Institute for Palestine Studies, 2000.

Idinopulos, Thomas A. *Weathered by Miracles: A History of Palestine from Bonaparte and Muhammad Ali to Ben-Gurion and the Mufti.* Chicago: Ivan R. Dee, 1998.

Janik, Allan, and Stephen Toulmin. *Wittgenstein's Vienna.* New York: Simon & Schuster, 1973.

Jayyusi, Salma Khadra, ed. *Anthology of Modern Palestinian Literature.* New York: Columbia University Press, 1992.

Kallen, Horace Meyer. *Zionism and World Politics: A Study in History and Social Psychology.* Garden City, N.Y.: Doubleday, Page & Co., 1921.

Kamhi, Rafael Moshe. *Recollections of a Jewish Macedonian Revolutionary.* Sineva, Bulgaria: 2001.

Kanaana, Sharif. *Folk Heritage of Palestine.* Israel: Research Center for Arab Heritage, 1994.

————. *Still on Vacation!: The Eviction of the Palestinians in 1948.* Jerusalem: SHAML – Palestinian Diaspora and Refugee Centre, 2000.

Karmi, Ghada. *In Search of Fatima: A Palestinian Story.* London: Verso, 2002.

Karsh, Efraim. *Fabricating Israeli History: The 'New Historians.'* London: Frank Cass & Co., 1997.

Khalidi, Rashid. *Palestinian Identity: The Construction of Modern National Consciousness.* New York: Columbia University Press, 1997.

Khalidi, Walid, ed. *From Haven to Conquest.* Beirut: Institute for Palestine Studies, 1971.

————. *Before Their Diaspora: A Photographic History of the Palestinians, 1876–1948*. Washington, D.C.: Institute for Palestine Studies, 1991.

————. *From Haven to Conquest: Readings in Zionism and the Palestine Problem Until 1948*. Beirut: Institute for Palestine Studies, 1971.

————, with Kamal Abdul Fattah, Linda Butler, Sharif S. Elmusa, Ghazi Falah, Albert Glock, Sharif Kanaana, Muhammad Ali Khalidi, and William C. Young. *All That Remains: The Palestinian Villages Occupied and Depopulated by Israel in 1948*. Washington, D.C.: Institute for Palestine Studies, 1992.

Kirkbride, Sir Alec. *From the Wings: Amman Memoirs, 1947–1951*. London: Frank Cass, 1976.

Koen, Albert. *Saving of the Jews in Bulgaria, 1941–1944*. Bulgaria: State Publishing House, 1977.

Kossev, D., H. Hristov, and D. Angelov. *A Short History of Bulgaria*. Translated by Marguerite Alexieva and Nicolai Koledarov. Sofia: Foreign Languages Press, 1963.

Lamm, Zvi. *Youth Takes the Lead: The Inception of Jewish Youth Movements in Europe*. Translated from the Hebrew by Sionah Kronfeld-Honig. Givat Haviva, Israel: Yad Ya'ari, 2004.

Langer, Felicia. *With My Own Eyes*. London: Ithaca Press, 1975.

Lockman, Zachary. *Comrades and Enemies: Arab and Jewish Workers in Palestine, 1906–1948*. Berkeley, Calif.: University of California Press, 1996.

Lowenthal, Marvin, ed. and trans. *The Diaries of Theodor Herzl*. New York: Dial Press, 1956.

Lustick, Ian. *Triumph and Catastrophe: The War of 1948, Israeli Independence, and the Refugee Problem*. New York:

Garland Publishing, Inc., 1994.

Maksoud, Clovis (introduction). *Palestine Lives: Interviews with Leaders of the Resistance*. Beirut: Palestine Research Center and Kuawiti Teachers Association, 1973.

Masalha, Nur. *Expulsion of the Palestinians: The Concept of 'Transfer' in Zionist Political Thought, 1882–1948*. Washington, D.C.: Institute for Palestine Studies, 1992.

————. *Imperial Israel and the Palestinians: The Politics of Expansion*. London: Pluto Press, 2000.

Mattar, Philip. *The Mufti of Jerusalem*. New York: Columbia University Press, 1988.

Miller, Ylana N. *Government and Society in Rural Palestine, 1920–1948*. Austin, Texas: University of Texas Press, 1985.

Milstein, Uri. *History of Israel's War of Independence, Vol. IV: Out of Crisis Came Decision*. Translated from the Hebrew and edited by Alan Sacks. Lanham, Md.: University Press of America, 1998.

Minchev, Ognyan, Valeri Ratchev, and Marin Lessenski, eds. *Bulgaria for Nato 2002*. Sofia: Open Society Foundation, 2002.

Minns, Amina, and Nadia Hijab. *Citizens Apart: A Portrait of the Palestinians in Israel*. London: I. B. Taurus & Co., 1990.

Morris, Benny. *1948 and After: Israel and the Palestinians*. Oxford: Clarendon Press, 1994.

————. *Israel's Border Wars, 1949–1956: Arab Infiltration, Israeli Retaliation, and the Countdown to the Suez War*. Oxford: Clarendon Press, 1993.

————. *Righteous Victims: A History of the Zionist Arab Conflict, 1881–2001*. New York: Vintage Books, 2001.

————. *The Road to Jerusalem: Glubb Pasha, Palestine and the Jews*. London: I. B. Tauris, 2002.

Musallam, Sami, compiler. *United Nations Resolutions on Palestine, 1947–1972*. Beirut: Institute for Palestine Studies, 1973.

Mutawi, Samir A. *Jordan in the 1967 War*. Cambridge: Cambridge University Press, 1987.

Neff, Donald. *Fallen Pillars: U.S. Policy Towards Palestine and Israel Since 1945*. Washington, D.C.: Institute for Palestine Studies, 1995.

Oren, Michael B. *Six Days of War: June 1967 and the Making of the Modern Middle East*. New York: Ballantine Books, 2003.

Oz, Amos. *In the Land of Israel*. Translated by Maurie Goldberg-Bartura. San Diego, Calif.: Harcourt Brace & Co., 1993.

Pappe, Ilan. *A History of Modern Palestine: One Land, Two Peoples*. Cambridge: Cambridge University Press, 2004.

Patai, Raphael. *The Arab Mind*. New York: Charles Scribner's Sons, 1973.

Pearlman, Moshe. *The Army of Israel*. New York: Philosophical Library, 1950.

Pearlman, Wendy. *Occupied Voices: Stories of Everyday Life From the Second Intifada*. New York: Thunder's Mouth Press/Nation Books, 2003.

Podeh, Elie. *The Arab-Israeli Conflict in Israeli History Textbooks, 1948–2000*. Westport, Conn.: Bergin & Garvey, 2002.

Pryce-Jones, David. *The Face of Defeat: Palestinian Refugees and Guerillas*. London: Weidenfeld & Nicolson, 1972.

Quigley, John. *Palestine and Israel: A Challenge to Justice*. Durham: Duke University Press, 1990.

Reeve, Simon. *One Day in September: The Full Story of the 1972 Munich Olympic Massacre and Israeli Revenge Operation 'Wrath of God.'* New York: Arcade Publishing, 2001.

Rogan, Eugene L., and Avi Shlaim, eds. *The War for Palestine:*

Rewriting the History of 1948. Cambridge: Cambridge University Press, 2001.

Ross, Dennis: *The Missing Peace: The Inside Story of the Fight for Middle East Peace*. New York: Farrar, Straus & Giroux, 2004.

Roy, Sara. *The Gaza Strip: The Political Economy of De-Development*. Washington, D.C.: Institute for Palestine Studies, 1995.

Sacco, Joe. *Palestine*. Seattle, Wash.: Fantagraphics Books, 2001.

Said, Edward. *Out of Place: A Memoir*. New York: Alfred A. Knopf, 1999.

————. *Peace and Its Discontents: Essays on Palestine in the Middle East Peace Process*. New York: Vintage Books, 1995.

————. *Politics of Dispossession: The Struggle for Self-Determination, 1967–1994*. New York: Vintage Books, 1995.

Samara, Adel, Toby Shelley, Ben Cashdan, et al., contributors. *Palestine: Profile of an Occupation*. London: Zed Books Ltd., 1989.

Salti, Ramzi M. *The Native Informant and Other Stories*. Colorado Springs, Colo.: Three Continents Press, 1994.

Sayigh, Yezid. *Armed Struggle and the Search for State: The Palestinian National Movement, 1949–1993*. Oxford: Clarendon Press, 1997.

Schleifer, Abdullah. *The Fall of Jerusalem*. London: Monthly Review Press, 1972.

Segev, Tom. *One Palestine Complete: Jews and Arabs Under the British Mandate*. New York: Metropolitan Books, 1999. Translation copy, 2000.

————. *1949: The First Israelis*. New York: Free Press, 1986.

Shapira, Avraham, ed. *The Seventh Day: Soldiers' Talk About the Six Day War*. London: Andre Deutsch Ltd., 1970.

Shehadeh, Raja. *Strangers in the House: Coming of Age in*

Occupied Palestine. South Royalton, Vt.: Steerforth Press, 2002.

Shemesh, Moshe. *The Palestinian Entity 1959–1974: Arab Politics and the PLO.* London: Frank Cass, 1996.

Shlaim, Avi. *The Iron Wall: Israel and the Arab World.* London: Penguin Books, 2000.

————. *War and Peace in the Middle East: A Concise History Revised and Updated.* London: Penguin Books, 1995.

Singer, Howard. *Bring Forth the Mighty Men: On Violence and the Jewish Character.* New York: Funk & Wagnalls, 1969.

Slyomovics, Susan. *The Object of Memory: Arab and Jew Narrate the Palestinian Village.* Philadelphia: University of Pennsylvania Press, 1998.

Sprinzak, Ehud. *Brother Against Brother.* New York: Free Press, 1999.

Stein, Kenneth. *The Land Question in Palestine, 1917–1939.* Chapel Hill, N.C.: University of North Carolina Press, 1984.

Steinberg, Milton. *The Making of the Modern Jew.* Lanham, Md.: University Press of America, 1976.

Swedenburg, Ted. *Memories of Revolt: The 1936–1939 Rebellion and the Palestinian National Past.* Minneapolis, Minn.: University of Minnesota Press, 1995.

Swisher, Clayton E. *The Truth About Camp David: The Untold Story About the Collapse of the Middle East Peace Process.* New York: Nation Books, 2004.

Tamir, Vicki. *Bulgaria and Her Jews: The History of a Dubious Symbiosis.* New York: Sepher-Hermon Press, Inc., for Yeshiva University Press, 1979.

Tavener, L. Ellis. *The Revival of Israel.* London: Hodder & Stoughton, 1961.

Tavin, Eli, and Yonah Alexander. *Psychological Warfare and Propaganda: Irgun Documentation.* Wilmington, Del.:

Scholarly Resources Inc., 1982.

Teveth, Shabtai. *The Tanks of Tammuz*. London: Weidenfeld & Nicolson, 1968.

Todorov, Tzvetan. *The Fragility of Goodness: Why Bulgaria's Jews Survived the Holocaust*. Translated from the French by Arthur Denner. Princeton, N.J.: Princeton University Press, 1999.

Tyler, Warwick P. *State Lands and Rural Development in Mandatory Palestine, 1920–1948*. Brighton, U.K.: Sussex Academic Press, 1988.

Vassileva, Boyka. *The Jews in Bulgaria 1944–1952*. Portions translated from the Bulgarian by Polia Alexandrova. Sofia: University Publishing House, St. Kliment Ohridski, 1992.

Yahya, Adel H. *The Palestinian Refugees, 1948–1998: An Oral History*. Ramallah: Palestinian Association for Cultural Exchange, 1999.

Yablonka, Hanna. *Survivors of the Holocaust: Israel After the War*. New York: New York University Press, 1999.

SOURCE NOTES

The seed for this book was a forty-three-minute radio documentary I produced for National Public Radio's *Fresh Air* in 1998 on the fiftieth anniversary of the 1948 Arab-Israeli war. All else flowed from there. A radio program weaving two voices speaking to each other is one matter; transforming that pure narrative into a book rich with family stories and historical context is something else entirely. My challenge was to retain the simplicity and tone of the documentary while simultaneously writing a history book in disguise – and making it feel, all the while, like a novel.

This book is entirely a work of nonfiction. While many of the events described happened decades ago, their retelling is based on interviews, archival documents, published and unpublished memoirs, newspaper clippings, and primary and secondary historical accounts.

In rare cases, in chapters 2 and 3 only, I have described an event based on multiple interviews with family members who are recounting family oral history or who describe the customs of the family that would have led to the events described. The gathering of the Khairis to celebrate the finishing of the house is one such example, from chapter 2 – and in each case that I rely on such family oral history, rather than actual eyewitnesses or documents, I have indicated so in the text or the source notes.

Crucial, and more controversial, moments in each family's history rely strictly on the aforementioned documents and eye-witness accounts.

In some cases old memories clash: Nuha Khairi, for example, specifically recalls Dalia being at the house in al-Ramla on the day her father, Ahmad, came to the door in 1969; Dalia is certain she was not there that day. In such cases I describe both the conflict in memory and the common ground of agreement. Dalia and Bashir also differ, and agree, on places and times each was present: Where there is difference in memory or argument, I either eliminated the portions that didn't match or noted them.

Dalia and Bashir have reviewed the manuscript for accuracy, as have numerous scholars and experts, both Israeli and Palestinian. In addition, the manuscript has undergone a rigorous, months-long fact-checking process, overseen by Sarah Tuttle-Singer and me, in which thousands of facts were checked against interview transcripts, historical texts, memoirs, archival documents, and other material. Any mistakes that may remain are, of course, my responsibility.

Chapter 1

This chapter is based mainly on interviews with Bashir al-Khairi and Dalia Eshkenazi Landau in 1998, 2003, 2004, and 2005 and on Bashir's memoir, *K'afagat Thakirq* (*Heartbeat of Memory*), portions of which were translated from the Arabic by Nidal Rafa.

Bashir's memoir describes him standing before a mirror but does not say where he stood. However, Ya'acov Haruzi, long-time worker for Egged, the Israeli national bus line, who worked in the Jerusalem terminal and has become an unofficial historian for the company, confirmed that the only mirrors in the station were in the restrooms and that there were porcelain basins there; and Bashir, in a fact-checking session in August 2005, corroborated this, as well as his action (nudging tie and so on) in front of the mirror.

Bashir's questions to himself at the bus station, his comparison to visiting a long-lost lover, and his cousin's interjection ('The bus is leaving!') come from his memoir and interviews.

The walk across the old boundary to the West Jerusalem bus station comes from interviews with Bashir and his cousin Ghiath Khairi.

The description of the bus station comes from Haruzi. Dalia does not remember bars in the ticket windows in Jerusalem in 1967, but Haruzi insists they were there.

The description of the bus comes from brochures in the Egged archives, corroborated with a tour of the Egged bus 'museum,' actually a big parking lot south of Tel Aviv, where helpful Egged employees led me to the type of bus that was used on the Jerusalem-Ramla line in 1967.

The description of Dalia sitting at her table comes from her memory, as does her description of Ramla during this period, both before and after the Six Day War.

The description of life for Dalia's parents, Moshe and Solia, during the 1940s in Bulgaria comes from numerous interviews and archival research in Sofia, Tel Aviv, Jerusalem, and Queens, New York. See notes for chapters 3 and 5 for specific documentation.

The description of how the Israelis described the departure of the Arabs from Ramla, in particular that they 'ran away,' comes from interviews with Dalia and with Sami Sela (in Rishon Letzion) and Esther Pardo, M. Levy, Mordechai Egenstein, and Michail Fanous (in Ramla). Specific language is cited in Elie Podeh's *The Arab-Israeli Conflict in Israeli History Textbooks, 1948-2000.*

The description of Bashir's ride, where he and his cousins sat, and what he was thinking on the journey comes from his memoir and my interviews with him. Additional details and corroboration come from Ghiath Khairi.

The route the bus took comes from Bashir's memory. One reader insisted that Israeli buses did not pass through Latrun in July 1967, and it is possible the route instead went through what is now the Israeli town of Modi'in, but Bashir specifically recalled passing through Latrun, so I left it in.

The description of Abu Ghosh as a village that 'collaborated with the enemy' is written through Bashir's eyes and memory as he rode toward Ramla. Further corroboration of the Arab attitude toward Abu Ghosh and the village supplying 'small quantities of ammunition' to a nearby Jewish settlement can be found in Benny Morris's *1948 and After*, p. 258.

Description of the burned vehicles along the roadside comes from personal observation and interviews with Bashir and can be found in numerous printed and online accounts (see, for example, 'The Road to Jerusalem' from the online site Jewish Virtual Library, www.jewishvirtuallibrary.org/jsource/vie/vieroad.html). Dalia's memory of what she was doing and thinking that day comes from several interviews and correspondences.

The bus ride and the cousins' impressions of Ramla after they got off the bus, including the story of the butcher Abu Mohammad and the trips to cousin Yasser and cousin Ghiath's old homes, come from Bashir's memoir and from interviews with Ghiath and Bashir.

Bashir distinctly remembers pressing the bell. He described it in his memoir and in a 1998 interview with me.

Chapter 2

Dimensions and cut of the stone come from my own observation and measurements. Not all of the stones for the house were uniformly cut to the same size. Ahmad's attire as he stood in the field, his placing of the first stone, and his being accompanied by relatives and workers is described in interviews with his descendants, in particular Bashir's sisters Nuha and Khanom, who said their father would never venture outside without his fez and tie. The description of the house building comes from Bashir, Nuha, and Khanom and from a contemporary builder of traditional Palestinian stone homes, Ali Qumbar. 'They cut it from the mountains here,' Qumbar said in an interview. 'Even though it's rough, it's soft to the touch. The whole idea of building a house like this – it's nice. It's optimistic. The land, the holy stone. It's coming from here.'

Qumbar also confirmed, as did Bashir and his cousin Ghiath, that it is customary for the owner of the house to lay the first stone before the other workers begin to build the rest of the house.

Population figures for Ramla in 1936 are gleaned from *A Survey of Palestine, Vol. I*, p. 151. My figure of 11,000 is conservative. The population of Ramla in 1931 is given as 10,347, including five Jews, while the 1944 population was more than 15,000.

The origin of Ramla's name comes from *The Encyclopedia of Palestinian Cities*, portions translated from the Arabic by Hatem Bazian; and from Shimon Gat, PhD, of the neighboring kibbutz of Na'an, whose doctoral dissertation in Hebrew is on the ancient history of Ramla.

Crop and tonnage numbers come from *A Survey of Palestine, Vol. I*, p. 320; from the al-Ramla district section of *All That Remains*, pp. 355–426; and from hand-scrawled reports from the municipality of Ramla, provided by Yonatan Tubali, the longtime city manager of Ramla.

The story of Khair al-Din is part of the Khairi family history, traced painstakingly on handwritten family trees and passed down through the generations. Bashir and Ghiath each told me the story of Khair al-Din. Dr. Sharif Kanaana, the Palestinian folklorist, confirmed the method of *waqf* land distribution.

The Ramla quarter, the Khairis' life in it, and Ahmad's decision to build his house outside the quarter was described by Khanom Khairi, one of Bashir's older sisters, in an interview conducted by my colleague Mariam Shahin with questions submitted from me. (Khanom's married name is Salah, but for clarity in these notes, I continue to use Khairi.)

Sheikh Mustafa Khairi's patriarch status is confirmed in interviews I did with numerous family members, including with his daughter-in-law Firdaws Taji Khairi in Ramallah. Her married name is Khairi, and she is mentioned hereafter as Firdaws Taji for the purpose of clarity. Sheikh Mustafa's standing with the British comes from colonial British records housed at the University of California at Berkeley. One set, *Political Diaries of the Arab World*, consists largely of confidential periodic reports sent by commissioners and subcommissioners in Palestine to His Majesty's government in London. The reports from the southern district commissioner in November 1938 (*Political Diaries, Vol. 3, 1937–1938*) refer to Sheikh Mustafa as the 'very able mayor' of Ramla.

Description of the restiveness among the British, the Arabs, and the Jews in the 1930s, and the subsequent Arab Rebellion (described later in the chapter), is based on multiple sources, including Ted Swedenburg's *Memories of Revolt*, Tom Segev's *One Palestine, Complete*, Khairi family interviews, and the aforementioned bound British records, upon which many of the details of the conflict are based. See the bibliography for other titles or the following text for specific citations.

The text of the Balfour Declaration is online at http://www.yale.edu/lawweb/avalon/mideast/balfour.htm. Arthur Balfour, the British foreign secretary, had seen the endorsement of a Jewish homeland as a 'way to bring Jewish forces over to our side in America, the East, and elsewhere.' As for the Arabs, Balfour would declare in 1919, 'Zionism, be it right or wrong, good or bad, is rooted in age-old traditions, in present needs, in future hopes, of far profounder import than the desires and prejudices of the 700,000 Arabs who now inhabit that ancient land.' (Quotes in Morris, *Righteous Victims*, pp. 74–76).

Ahmad's decision to consult with Sheikh Mustafa about the financing of the house is confirmed by Bashir and Ghiath as part of the family's oral history.

The story of Mr. Solli comes from the interview with Khanom Khairi in Amman, as do the stories of Khairi and Ramla co-existence with surrounding Jewish communities at various times in the 1930s and 1940s. Another source for understanding such coexistence, sporadic as it was, is Zachary Lockman's *Comrades and Enemies: Arab and Jewish Workers in Palestine, 1906–1948*. The British records also described relations between the Arab and Jewish communities, but usually as separate entities under British rule.

The ancient history of the city, including its mosque and aqueduct, comes from the aforementioned *Encyclopedia of Palestinian Cities*, with additional material and confirmation from Dr. Gat. The content of the caravans was described by Dr. Hatem Bazian of UC-Berkeley, in an interview.

The quote about Ramla by the early Islamic traveler Muqaddasi can be found in 'Description of Syria, Including Palestine, Circa 985,' p. 32, printed by the Palestine Pilgrims' Text Society in London in 1896. Muqaddasi confirms that at the time, Ramla was the 'capital of Palestine.'

The reference to British foxhunting, some 950 years after Muqaddasi traveled to Ramla, can be found in 'Palestine: 1920–1923,' by W. F. Stirling, in *From Haven to Conquest*, p. 230.

Population and Jewish immigration figures are derived from *A Survey of Palestine, Vol. I*, p. 149 and p. 185. These are official figures; actual numbers, which would include all illegal immigration from Europe, may have been higher. In 1936, more than two-thirds of the immigrants were Polish and German.

For an extensive analysis of land sales from Arabs to Jews, see Kenneth Stein's *The Land Question in Palestine, 1917–1939*. Stein points out that many of the land sales to Jews were by non-Palestinian Arabs, though many were not: During the 1920s and early 1930s, driven largely by economic need, many 'notables' of Palestine sold land to Jews. These sales were a major factor in tensions that led to the Arab Rebellion, and that would ultimately weaken the nationalist movement of Palestine's Arabs. Stein (p. 70) writes, 'At a time of feverish anti-Zionist and anti-British sentiment, Palestinian Arab land sales to Zionists showed that individual priorities were equal to or more important than an emerging national movement.' Nevertheless, as early as 1911, Arabs of Palestine were warning against land sales (see Morris, *Righteous Victims*, p. 62). Swedenburg, in *Memories of Revolt*, writes that land sales were'of such major concern to the national movement in the thirties, so serious in fact that the Mufti launched vigorous public campaigns against the notorious Palestinian land agents, and branded them as heretics . . .' The estimate of thirty thousand landless peasant families (by 1931) comes from Doreen Warriner's *Land and Poverty in the Middle East*, Royal Institute of International Affairs, London, 1948, pp. 61–2, as cited by Hirst, *The Gun and the Olive Branch*, p. 198 and p. 230. Hirst writes (p. 198), 'They lived in squalor. In old Haifa there were 11,000 of them crammed into hovels built of petrol-tins, which had neither water-supply nor rudimentary sanitation. Others, without families, slept in the open . . . It should be noted that despite the land sales by Arabs, the total land owned by Jews in Palestine on the eve of the war of 1948 was 7 percent (John Chapple, *Jewish Land Settlement in Palestine*, cited in Walid Khalidi's *From Haven to Conquest*, p. 843).

Swedenburg's *Memories of Revolt* is an excellent source for the Arab Rebellion. See p. 78 on the arms-smuggling operation (also mentioned in *A Survey of Palestine*, p. 33). Details on Sheikh al-Qassam come from Segev, *One Palestine Complete*, pp. 359–363; *A Survey of Palestine*, Vol. I, p. 33, and *Vol. II*, pp. 594–95; *Memories of Revolt*, p. 12 and p. 104; and *Palestine and Transjordan Administrative Reports*, Vol. 6, p. 20. More than six decades later, Sheikh Qassam's martyrdom would be remembered by operatives of Hamas, who would build crude rockets in his name and fire them into Israeli settlements in Gaza.

See *Palestine and Transjordan Administrative Reports*, Vol 6. pp. 19–39, for the sequence of events of the Arab Rebellion. Additional details from *Memories of Revolt*, pp. 30–32, 126, and 130. The account of the assault on the bathing British troops comes from *Palestine and Transjordan Administrative Reports*, Vol. 6, p. 30. The importance of the keffiyeh, or traditional male Palestinian head scarf, is mentioned in *Memories of Revolt*, p. 30. The quote about 'frequent detonations and crashes of falling masonry' is from a judgment by British justice Michael F. J. McDonnell and is quoted in 'The Town Planning of Jaffa, 1936' (as cited in *From Haven to Conquest*, pp. 343–47). This appears to be the beginning of a policy of house demolitions against rebels and their families.

Impressions of Zakia Khairi and the family's lifestyle, as well as the festival at Nabi (Prophet) Saleh, come largely from Khanom Khairi. Khanom and Firdaws Taji discussed the political pressure Sheikh Mustafa was under; additional details about that can be gleaned from the *Political Diaries of the Arab World, Palestine and Jordan*, Vol. 3, p. 394.

Chaim Weizmann's 'forces of the desert' remark is quoted in Philip Mattar's *The Mufti of Jerusalem*, p. 100. Details of the Wednesday market come from interviews with the Palestinian folklorist Dr. Sharif Kanaana and from Widad Kawar, who has a large collection of embroidery, pottery, metalwork, jewelry, and textiles in her Amman home. The centerpiece is the collection of traditional dresses worn by rural Arab women of Palestine. Once disdained by the Arab elite as fit only for the *fellahin*, or peasantry, the dresses and their bodices have in exile come to symbolize solidarity with the Palestinian cause.

Details of the Khairi family meals, and Ahmad's social life at the *diwan*, were described by Khanom Khairi. The *arguileh*, or water pipe, has many other names, including *narguileh*, *shisha*, *hookah*, and hubbly-bubbly.

The strike by the Arab Higher Committee was suspended on October 11, 1936, and is documented in a timeline in Walid Khalidi's *Before Their Diaspora*. Work resumption is described in *Palestine and Transjordan Administrative Reports*, Vol. 6, p. 48. Lord Peel's attire is described by Segev in *One Palestine Complete*, p. 401. Peel's letter to London appears in the *Political Diaries of the Arab World*, Vol. 2, p. 681.

The Peel Commission report was formally titled *Palestine Royal Commission Report* and appears in its entirety in *Palestine and Transjordan Administrative Reports*, Vol. 6, pp. 433–850. On p. 835 (or p. 389 of the original report), the commission recommends an 'Exchange of Land and Population.' It cited the 1922 exchange of Turkish and Greek populations as precedent.

One Palestine Complete, p. 402, describes the Jewish reaction to Peel. Arab reaction is noted in *Before Their Diaspora*, p. 193, and Yeshua Porath's *The Palestinian Arab National Movement: From Riots to Rebellion*, Vol. 2, 1929–1939, pp. 228–32.

Theodor Herzl's quote about 'the penniless population' comes from his diary entry of June 12, 1895, from *The Complete Diaries of Theodor Herzl*, translated by Harry Zohn. The same year, Israel Zangwill, a British Zionist leader, argued that Jews 'must be prepared either to drive out by the sword the tribes in possession as our forefathers did or to grapple with the problem of a large alien population, mostly Mohammedan and accustomed for centuries to despise us' ('Israel Zangwill's Challenge to Zionism,' by Hani A. Faris, in the *Journal of Palestine Studies* 4, no. 3 [Spring 1975]: 74–90). Zangwill also said, 'If we receive Palestine, the Arabs will have to "trek."' A generation later, Chaim Weizmann, who would become the first president of Israel, suggested in the wake of Arab riots in Palestine that an 'exchange of populations could be fostered and encouraged' to allow Arabs 'to flow into neighboring countries' (*The Letters and Papers of Chaim Weizmann, Vol. 14*, p. 69, as cited in Masalha, *Expulsion of the Palestinians: The Concept of 'Transfer' in Zionist Political Thought, 1882–1948*).

Ben-Gurion's 'transfer cause' quote comes from his diaries of July 1937 and was translated for me by the Israeli journalist Sami Sockol. His 'I support compulsory transfer' remark was made on June 12, 1938, and is quoted in Morris (*Righteous Victims*, p. 253). Segev's *One Palestine Complete*, pp. 399–406, analyzes the Zionist reaction to Peel and its support of the concept of transfer. A broad overview of the transfer idea comes from Nur Masalha, a Palestinian scholar at St. Mary's College at the University of Surrey in London who worked from original documents in Hebrew from Israeli archives. A similar approach comes from a sharply different political perspective: that of Rabbi Dr. Chaim Simons, a West Bank settler and curator of *A Historical Survey of Proposals to Transfer Arabs from Palestine, 1895–1947*, a large collection of Zionist writings on transfer

that can be found online at www.geocities.com/CapitolHill/
Senate/7854/transfer.html. (The Zangwill 'trek' quote is cited at
www.geocities.com/CapitolHill/Senate/7854/transfer07.
html.) A briefer overview of transfer and Zionism comes from
Ilana Sternbaum's 'Historical Roots of the Idea of Transfer,'
www.afsi.org/OUTPOST/2002OCT/ oct7.htm.

Other Zionists, like Albert Einstein and Martin Buber,
advocated coexistence with the Arab population and opposed
any transfer plans. See Stanley Aronowitz in 'Setting the Record
Straight: Zionism from the Standpoint of Its Jewish Critics,'
www.logosjournal.com/issue_3.3/ aronowitz.htm.

The resumption of the Arab Rebellion and the British crack-
down are chronicled in *Political Diaries of the Arab World, Vol. 3*,
pp. 39–49. The air attack on rebel bands was documented in an
article in the *Times* of London, October 3, 1938, as cited by
Hirst, p. 215. Shukri Taji's sale of land is documented by
Kenneth Stein in *The Land Question in Palestine, 1917–1939*, p.
171 and p. 238. Most of the sales were from 1922 and 1936.
Stein cites original documents now housed in the Central
Zionist Archives. The quote about Sheikh Mustafa comes from
Political Diaries of the Arab World, p. 352. The political difficulties the mayor faced, the respect he commanded, and his attire
are all documented by his admiring survivors, including Firdaws
Taji and Khanom Khairi. Where exactly Sheikh Mustafa stood
between the nationalists and the elites, or 'notables,' is not clear.
While some family members say Mustafa and his sons may have
gone so far as to aid the rebels, Mustafa's membership in the
National Defense Party, run by the 'notable' Nashashibi family,
would have subjected him to strong criticism from the nationalists and the rebels. The nationalists considered
the 'notables' to be collaborators with the Zionists, and many
were assassinated by Arab rebels. I explored these ideas in an
interview with Hillel Cohen, author of *Shadow Army*:

Palestinian Collaborators in the Service of Zionism: 1917–1948 (in Hebrew). Sheikh Mustafa's daughter-in-law, Firdaws, says his departure to Cairo in 1938 was 'for health reasons,' but rebel threats would have been more likely to force him into his brief exile. Fear of recrimination would also have prompted Mustafa's proclamation, upon his return, that he would focus exclusively on municipal affairs. All this may also help explain why Sheikh Mustafa was replaced as mayor in the mid-1940s.

Discussion of the White Paper comes from various sources, including *Memory of Revolt*, p. xxi. Zionist reaction to the White Paper, including Ben-Gurion's 'Satan himself' quote, is documented in *One Palestine Complete*, pp. 440–41. Arab casualty figures are cited in *From Haven to Conquest*, p. 846.

News events of the day Bashir was born come from the *New York Times* and the *San Francisco Chronicle* editions of February 16 and 17, 1942. The British high commissioner's monthly telegram is printed in *Political Diaries of the Arab World, Vol. 6, 1941–1942*, pp. 437–40. In closing, the commissioner noted new political recruiting efforts on both Arab and Jewish sides. 'This development has its potentialities for mischief,' the commissioner wrote, 'and is being carefully watched.'

Chapter 3

Dalia Eshkenazi grew up with the story of the wallet, as passed down by her father, Moshe. She was not yet born when the event in question took place, in 1943. The story, in its general outlines, is confirmed by Dalia's aunt Virginia, who in 2004 was eighty-two years old and living in Sofia. It is possible, of course, that some of the actual details were different or that the police officer used different words, but the gist of the story seems beyond question.

Bulgaria's political history in the 1940s, in particular the nation's treatment of the Jews, is conveyed in Frederick Chary's 1975 account, *The Bulgarian Jews and the Final Solution*. Chary also reviewed this chapter, and chapter 5, for accuracy. Additional details come from Guy Haskell's 'From Sofia to Jaffa'; Michael Bar-Zohar's *Beyond Hitler's Grasp: The Heroic Rescue of Bulgaria's Jews*; *Jews in the Bulgarian Lands: Ancestral Memory and Historical Destiny* (Emmy Barouh, ed.); *Saving of the Jews in Bulgaria: 1941–1944*, a 1977 account of the State Publishing House of the Bulgarian Communist Party; Tzvetan Todorov's fascinating combination of original essays and translated texts, *The Fragility of Goodness*; and *The Survival: A Compilation of Documents, 1940–1944*, large portions translated from the Bulgarian by journalist Polia Alexandrova. This history was more fully understood through dozens of interviews with Bulgarian Jews in Israel and on three trips to Bulgaria in 2003 and 2004. Polia did most of the translating for those interviews, as well as of original documents in the Bulgarian National Archives and the National Library, both in Sofia.

Bulgaria's alliance with the Axis powers is described on p. 3 of *The Bulgarian Jews and the Final Solution*. On p. 66 it describes the labor camps, which were also recalled by Dalia's cousin Yitzhak Yitzhaki in an interview Dalia conducted and sent to me by fax. Additional description is in Bar-Zohar, pp. 46–48, and Tamir, *Bulgaria and Her Jews*, pp. 176–77. Dalia and Virginia also recount the family stories of the work camps from Moshe and Jacques. The camps were at times brutal, but generally not on the scale of other parts of Europe: Moshe, Dalia was told, was excused after he developed a serious ear infection.

The figure of forty-seven thousand Bulgarian Jews comes from correspondence with Chary. (Many others have used the round figure of fifty thousand.)

The story of Susannah Shemuel Behar and her family comes from interviews I did with her in Plovdiv. The family details could not be corroborated separately, but her story fits credibly into the larger narrative of Bulgarian Jews in March 1943. The story of Moshe and Solia Eshkenazi waiting in Sliven with Solia's parents, the Arroyos, was passed down to Dalia by her parents over the years. Her aunt Virginia and cousin Yitzhak also confirm this. Additional confirmation comes from Dr. Corinna Solomonova of Sliven, who was eighteen years old in March 1943. Dr. Solomonova referred to Solia as 'Solche' (SOUL-chay), a Bulgarian diminutive, and said she had worked as a seamstress. Moshe and Solia were 'for certain' in Sliven in March 1943, she said. Dr. Solomonova also recalls receiving her own letter from the Bulgarian Commissariat for Jewish Questions:

> It reported that on the 10th of March we have to appear in a specific elementary school. We have to appear at 8 a.m. with only a little baggage. The letter was dated around the 7th of March. In our family we began to sew backpacks for everyone. We were very worried because we knew we were going to German camps in which they killed Jews. We knew about that because our [Gentile] friends listened to radio programs [from Radio Moscow and the BBC]. Jewish radios had been confiscated. We knew we were going to the death camps.

Details on the Law for the Defense of the Nation are taken from numerous sources, including *The Bulgarian Jews and the Final Solution*, pp. 35–46 and 24–25 (regarding the link to the Nuremberg laws), and, to a lesser extent, *Beyond Hitler's Grasp*, pp. 27–40. Additional background is culled from more than twenty interviews with Jews still living in Bulgaria and additional Jews in Israel who are old enough to recall the details.

Yitzhak Yitzhaki's memories were recounted in interviews with Dalia, which she transcribed for me.

The quote from Bayazid II is confirmed by Turkish scholar Elif Shafak of the Near Eastern Studies Department at the University of Arizona in Tucson.

Bulgarian revolutionary history is documented in R. J. Crampton's *A Short History of Modern Bulgaria*. The details of Levski can be found in a paper, 'The Bulgarian Policy on the Balkan Countries and National Minorities, 1878-1912,' by the Bulgarian scholar Vladimir Paounovski. Levski as the 'George Washington of Bulgaria' is confirmed by Chary. Though he is a founding father of Bulgaria, the comparison stretches only so far: He was hanged by the Turks in Sofia several years before Bulgaria's liberation, and did not live to see the free state he had imagined. Levski is said to have been sheltered by Jews in Plovdiv during the nineteenth-century struggle for Bulgarian independence. In the early 1940s, his name was invoked in protests against the Fascist laws against the Jews; the Communist regime that followed considered him a 'leader of the Bulgarian national-liberation revolutionary movement'; and in the early postwar period, according to Moshe Melamed, a Bulgarian Jew and former Israeli ambassador to Mexico, 'Levski' brand cigarettes were among the most popular in Bulgaria.

The testimonies against the Law for the Defense of the Nation come from *The Survival*. Additional documents, including the statement of the Bulgarian Writers' Union, the Lawyers' Union, and the open letter to the National Assembly Deputies, are from *Fragility*, pp. 45-53.

The October 1942 quote from the Nazi authorities in Berlin comes from *Saving of the Jews in Bulgaria*, chapter 7, p. 3. Further details on Belev's powers come from *The Bulgarian*

Jews and the Final Solution, pp. 35–46. Dannecker's arrival in Sofia is documented in *Beyond Hitler's Grasp*, pp. 59, 63–75. The Dannecker-Belev Agreement is printed in its entirety in *The Bulgarian Jews and the Final Solution*, pp. 208–10. The destination points of the February 22 memo is documented in *Survival*, p. 71. The 'private' and 'extremely important' memo appears in *Survival*, p. 206. Belev's note to Gabrovski about maintaining secrecy is taken from N. Greenberg, *Documents, Central Consistory of the Jews in Bulgaria, 1945*, pp. 8–11, and is referenced in Emmy Barouh's 'The Fate of the Bulgarian Jews During World War II,' which appeared in *Bulgaria for NATO 2002*.

The story of Liliana Panitsa appears in many accounts, including *The Bulgarian Jews and the Final Solution*, p. 91, and *Beyond Hitler's Grasp*, pp. 77–86. An original source for both accounts is the testimony of Buko Levi from the postwar Protocols of the People's Court Number 7, V, 1498. Additional reference to Panitsa and Levi is in Vicki Tamir's *Bulgaria and Her Jews*, p. 198. The suggestion that Belev and Panitsa were lovers was made to me in several interviews and appears in various published accounts, most prominently *Beyond Hitler's Grasp*. Bar-Zohar's conclusions go further than others have been willing to go, and some remain skeptical that she was as devoted to him as Bar-Zohar suggests. However, Buko Levi's son, Yohanan, told me in a telephone interview that Belev and Panitsa were indeed lovers and that Buko's testimony at Yad Vashem, the Israeli Holocaust museum, makes that clear. In any case, Yohanan Levi told me, 'She was the one who saved us. I can't express the gratitude that we owe her.'

The story of the optician and the bribe is told by Bar-Zohar (p. 104), Chary (p. 91), and Tamir (p. 198). The description of Kyustendil comes from personal observation and from interviews with Kyustendil natives, including Vela Dimitrova, Sabat

Isakov, and my colleague at the Graduate School of Journalism at UC-Berkeley, Kyustendil native Mimi Chakarova. The initial fears in Kyustendil are recounted vividly in the excerpted memoir of Asen Suichmezov (*Fragility*, pp. 132–36) and in interviews with Isakov and with Violeta Conforty, who told the story of the Macedonian leader Vladimir Kurtev and the party at Belev's house.

The description of the Jews in the train cars traveling through Bulgaria on the way to Treblinka was recounted in numerous interviews, including with Yitzhak Yitzhaki. Metropolitan Stefan's memories of this appear in *Fragility*, p. 126. The story of Mati Braun, the locket of hair, and the photo album was retold by her old friend Vela Dimitrova. It is not clear how many Bulgarian Jews knew, by 1943, of the atrocities elsewhere in Europe, but it is clear from my dozens of interviews, from the Eshkenazi family oral history, and from written statements by Bulgarian religious leaders that terrible stories were being carried across the Bulgarian border. Mati survived the war, but Vela heard that soon after, she moved to Israel. She didn't come back for her album, and Vela never saw her again.

The mobilization of the Jews of Kyustendil comes largely from Chary's account, pp. 92–93 (especially on Yako Barouh), and from Violeta Conforty, who recalls the arrival of Vladimir Kurtev in Kyustendil and his warnings to the Jewish community there.

Description of Suichmezov and the journey comes from interviews with Dimitrova, Conforty, and Isakov. Suichmezov's recollections, including the pleas of the Jews, come from the aforementioned memoir excerpts.

The description of the events in the school yard in Plovdiv comes from Susannah Behar, with additional details provided from interviews with other Jewish eyewitnesses in Plovdiv, including Berta Levi and Yvette Amavi. Kiril's defense of the

Bulgarian Jews is well documented, including by Chary (pp. 138–39) and Bar-Zohar (pp. 126–27, 169–70).

The story of Kiril's pledge to lie on the railroad tracks comes from an interview with a woman named Beba of Plovdiv, who was ten years old at the time. Susannah is skeptical of this and maintains that as an older eyewitness, who was at the school from the beginning of the day, her recollection is more reliable than that of a child's. 'You know how kids make up stories,' she said. Bar-Zohar (p. 126) goes further than either account, suggesting that Kiril, in his robes and heavy cross, managed to climb the fence, challenging the Bulgarian authorities to 'try to stop me!' Neither Beba, Susannah, nor any of the other Plovdiv eyewitnesses I spoke with recalls such a thing.

Susannah's recollection of the contingency plan to join the Partizans in the Rhodope Mountains has an echo in the story of Dr. Corinna Solomonova, the friend of Solia Arroyo Eshkenazi's family in Plovdiv. 'I was only eighteen,' she told me. 'I had a wonderful family. I had a proposition from the Partizans to go to the mountains with them and not go to the camps. I had received their offer. I had no intention of going to the concentration camps.'

The portrait of Peshev is drawn largely from the interview I did in Kyustendil with his niece Kaluda Kiradzhieva. Additional details are taken from Gabriel Nissim's biography of Peshev, *The Man Who Stopped Hitler*. Further insight into Peshev, and especially the importance of his actions, can be found in Todorov's essays in *Fragility*, especially pp. 35–40. Peshev himself explores his political philosophy in his memoir, excerpted in *Fragility*, pp. 137–83.

Suichmezov's actions in Sofia are described in his memoir (excerpted in *Fragility*, pp. 134–36). The initial meeting between Suichmezov and Peshev is also described by Peshev in *Fragility*, p. 160. Peshev describes the earlier pleas of a fellow MP, about the 'defeated, desperate, powerless people,' on p. 158 of *Fragility*, and on p. 159 he describes his moment of decision, perhaps the single most important moment in the entire story of the rescue of the Bulgarian Jews. The tense moments in the parliament building are described in both men's memoirs (*Fragility*, pp. 136 and 161–62), by Chary (pp. 94–96) and Bar-Zohar (pp. 113–24). Suichmezov's memoir is the source for the quotes from Peshev and Colonel Tadger.

The moment in the school yard when the Jews were set free was described by Susannah Behar and the other eyewitnesses mentioned earlier. The late notice, confirmed by printed accounts, provides insight into the state of communications in 1940s Bulgaria as well as, perhaps, into the reluctance of some members of the Commissariat for Jewish Questions to swiftly carry out Gabrovski's orders.

Metropolitan Stefan's letter imploring the king is part of his memoir, excerpted in *Fragility*, p. 127. The letter by Peshev and his fellow deputies appears in its entirety in *Fragility*, pp. 78–80. The deportation plans along the Danube is documented on p. 143 of *The Bulgarian Jews and the Final Solution*.

To this day, there remains a fierce debate about the role of King Boris in the 'saving' of the Bulgarian Jews. Did the king stop the deportation of Bulgaria's Jews to Poland out of concern for his Jewish citizens? Or did the foxlike ally of Hitler, after the Nazi devastation at the battle of Stalingrad, sense that the end was coming and keep the Bulgarian Jewry intact to avoid charges of genocide?

The fact that the Germans believed the order to suspend the deportations came from the 'highest place' has led many to believe that Boris himself approved this, but Chary, who has probably spent more time studying this issue than anyone, disagrees. 'It is very unlikely that Gabrovski would have talked to the king,' Chary wrote me. 'The king did not like him and furthermore had removed himself from the issue of deporting the Jews at this point.' Bar-Zohar, on the other hand, states flatly that 'the king had acted at the eleventh hour, and the deportation had been thwarted' (p. 128, *Beyond Hitler's Grasp*). He argues the king reversed his policy in March 1943 and essentially decided to stand with the Jews of Bulgaria. Many others are skeptical of this, including Jacky Comforty, producer with Lisa Comforty of the acclaimed documentary *The Optimists: The Story of the Rescue of the Bulgarian Jews from the Holocaust*, and Todorov, who writes in *Fragility*, pp. 19 and 23:

It is impossible to take the king's words at face value . . . His actions were guided by self-interest, or rather, by what he saw as Bulgaria's interests . . . What motivated him was national interest as he understood it, not humanitarian principles. Small countries have to come to terms with great ones. Hitler had the power; thus some of his demands had to be accepted.

The quote about 'ideological enlightenment' comes from *Saving of the Jews in Bulgaria*, chapter 10, p. 16.

The idea behind Tzevtan Todorov's title, *Fragility of Goodness*, is that if one event had transpired differently, if one person had not acted or had acted in some other way – even, indeed, if King Boris had not joined the Axis powers, thus prompting the Germans into a brutal occupation of Bulgaria – the outcome for the Bulgarian Jews could have been completely different. I agree.

Chapter 4

This chapter is grounded in dozens of documents, books, and firsthand accounts, including multiple interviews with Dalia's and Bashir's families; interviews with numerous eyewitnesses to

443

events in Ramla, Lydda (Lod), and Jerusalem in 1947 and 1948; published accounts from historical figures of the day and other eyewitnesses; original documents from the Central Zionist Archives and the archives at Kibbutz Na'an; and numerous secondary sources, including books by Israeli and Arab scholars who base their work in the archives.

The *aqiqa* ceremony was described by Khanom Khairi, Bashir's older sister, who was an eyewitness to the event. Details of the ceremony were verified by Islamic scholar Hatem Bazian of UC-Berkeley. The young Bashir was recalled by Khanom and Nuha Khairi in 2004 interviews in Berkeley and Amman, respectively. The 'sweeten your teeth' saying is a familiar one in Palestinian culture. It was translated by my colleague Nidal Rafa.

Sheikh Mustafa's worries are chronicled in the British high commissioner's monthly telegram, which is printed in *Political Diaries of the Arab World*, Vol. 6, 1941–1942, pp. 437–40.

Discussion of the Jewish refugees from the DP camps, and the debate over Britain's acceptance of additional refugees to Palestine, is in Morris (*Righteous Victims*, pp. 180–84); Neff (*Fallen Pillers*, pp. 30–34); Cohen (*Palestine and the Great Powers*, pp. 113–14); and Hirst (pp. 238–39). The story of the *Exodus* is told by Hirst (p. 239), Morris (p. 183), and Cohen (pp. 254–57).

The internal politics in the Jewish community of Palestine (known as the Yishuv) immediately after World War II is described in *Righteous Victims*, pp. 173–84; *One Palestine Complete*, pp. 468–86; Avi Shlaim's *The Iron Wall*, pp. 22–27; and Ehud Sprinzak's *Brother Against Brother: Violence and Extremism in Israeli Politics from Altalena to the Rabin Assassination*, pp. 38–40. The King David explosion is mentioned in *The Road to Jerusalem: Glubb Pasha*, Palestine and the Jews, where Benny Morris puts the death toll at eighty;

Segev, in *One Palestine Complete*, p. 476, says there were 'more than ninety' deaths; the Jewish Virtual Library (www.jewishvirtuallibrary.org/jsource/History/King_David.html) and Walid Khalidi's *Before Their Diaspora* both cite a death toll of ninety-one. An insight into the British view of the Jewish military capacity can be found in *Palestine and Transjordan Administrative Reports, Vol. 16*, p. 496.

British troop strength and the accompanying quote are taken from p. 498 of *Palestine and Transjordan Administrative Reports, Vol. 16*. The 'wholesale terrorism' quote comes from the same volume, p. 496.

The pressures on Britain at the end of the colonial era and how this contributed to their quitting Palestine a year after quitting India were pointed out to me by Tom Segev in his comments on an early draft of my manuscript. The arrival of the UN fact-finding team, known as the United Nations Special Commission on Palestine, or UNSCOP, is mentioned in *Righteous Victims*, pp. 180–84, and in Segev, pp. 495–96.

Palestinians' concerns about the potential fate of Arabs in a Jewish state and their desire for a one-state solution come from several sources, including an interview with the Palestinian scholar Naseer Aruri. The fractured nature of Palestinian society in 1947, particularly in the wake of the Arab Rebellion, is discussed in Rashid Khalidi's *Palestinian Identity*, pp. 190–92; Yoav Gelber's *Palestine 1948*, pp. 31–33; and Ilan Pappe's *A History of Modern Palestine*, pp. 119–20. Further corroboration of Palestinian-Arab disunity on the eve of war was provided by Hillel Cohen, author of *Shadow Army: Palestinian Collaborators in the Service of Zionism: 1917–1948* (in Hebrew), and Michael J. Cohen, professor at Bar-Ilan University, in *Palestine and the Great Powers, 1945–1948*. 'It was never easy for the outsider,' wrote former Israeli intelligence officer David Kimche and his brother Jon in their 1960 book, *Clash of Destinies*

(p. 42), 'and especially for the governments of Europe and the United States, to be sure which was the valid expression of the Arab mood: the publicly voiced determination to fight against the Jewish aspirations in Palestine, or the privately uttered assurance that some kind of amicable arrangement was quite possible . . .'

A more recent source for the disconnection between the Arab states' words and their private interests is Rogan and Shlaim's *The War for Palestine: Rewriting the History of 1948*, a collection of essays by Arab, Israeli, and Western scholars. Shlaim, an Israeli scholar and Oxford professor, also details Abdullah's November meeting with Golda Meir, representative for the Jewish Agency, in his book, *The Iron Wall: Israel and the Arab World*. Shlaim writes (p. 30):

> Abdullah began by outlining his plan to preempt the mufti, to capture the Arab part of Palestine, and to attach it to his kingdom, and he asked about the Jewish response to this plan. Mrs. Meir replied that the Jews would view such an attempt in a favourable light, especially if Abdullah did not interfere with the establishment of a Jewish state, avoided a military confrontation, and appeared to go along with the United Nations.

Jon and David Kimche essentially confirm this account.

The text of United Nations General Assembly Resolution 181, better known as the 'partition resolution,' is printed in its entirety in volume 37 of *The Rise of Israel*, a thirty-nine-volume collection of original documents edited by Michael J. Cohen. The UN minority report, completed on November 11, 1947, is printed in *From Haven to Conquest*, pp. 645–95, with the key provisions on pp. 694–95. The map for this proposed federal state can be found on the interleaf between pp. 204 and 205 in

Report on Palestine: Report to the General Assembly by the United Nations Special Committee on Palestine.

The British intent to quit Palestine on May 15, 1948, is confirmed in *Palestine and Transjordan Administration Reports, Vol. 16*, p. 490.

Many accounts, citing the 44 percent of historic Palestine that was set aside for an Arab state, calculate that therefore the remaining 56 percent was for the Jewish state. However, 1.5 percent of the land would have been set aside for the city of Jerusalem and the immediate surrounding area, including Bethlehem, under a demilitarized international trusteeship administered by the UN. (See *Report on Palestine*, pp. 187–91, for the Jerusalem proposal.)

The citrus and grain percentages were calculated by Harvard scholar Walid Khalidi and printed in *Before Their Diaspora*, p. 305. The figures on Jewish population and land ownership come from John Chapple, *Jewish Land Settlement in Palestine*, referenced in *From Haven to Conquest*, p. 843. Population figures for Arabs and Jews in the proposed states are listed in *Report on Palestine*, p. 181.

The UN vote was the result in part of an intense lobbying effort by Zionists from the United States and Palestine to secure the necessary support. In a memo to his Foreign Office (*The Rise of Israel*, Vol. 37, p. 213), British diplomat Harold Beeley describes the 'active' Zionist lobbyists who persuaded the United States to 'use its influence with Governments which were for one reason or another dependent on it, and which if left to themselves would either vote against partition or abstain,' including Haiti, the Philippines, and Liberia, all of which voted for partition after previously announcing their intention to oppose it.

According to a secret U.S. State Department memo dated December 15, 1947, Gabriel Dennis, the Liberian secretary of state and UN delegate, complained of a 'high-pressure election-eering job, in which . . . the Liberian Minister at Washington had received a warning that unless Liberia voted with the American Delegation in favor of partition, the minister could expect no further favors for his country from Congress' (*Rise of Israel*, Vol. 37, p. 197). The UN representative of the Philippines reported receiving a radiogram from his president instructing a vote in favor of partition. The diplomat found the incident 'exceedingly unpleasant,' especially in light of the public stance against partition that he had already taken (*From Haven to Conquest*, pp. 723–26).

The chief advocate for the Arab side was Sir Muhammad Zafrulla Khan, who was described admiringly by Michael Comay, a prominent Zionist leader, as 'a powerful champion . . . undoubtedly one of the ablest and most impressive delegates present from any country.' Comay, head of the New York office of the Jewish Agency and later Israel's UN delegate, wrote in a 'strictly confidential' letter that Khan 'and some of the other Arab spokesmen were badly hampered by the refusal of the Palestine Arabs to consider making any concessions or talking in conciliatory terms. But for this we may have had an even more difficult time as many delegations supported the partition scheme with the greatest reluctance . . .'

A crucial factor in swaying the reluctant parties toward partition, Comay wrote, had been a delay in the vote over the Thanksgiving holiday, during which time 'an avalanche descended upon the White House' (*The Rise of Israel*, Vol. 37, pp. 185–192). President Harry Truman would write later in his memoirs: 'I do not think I ever had as much pressure and propaganda aimed at the White House as I had in this instance' (*Fallen Pillars: U.S. Policy Towards Palestine and Israel Since 1945*, p. 50).

Rejection of the plan by the Arab states is mentioned in numerous sources, including on p. 8 of Maan Abu Nowar's *The*

Jordan-Israeli War, 1948–1951. Walid Khalidi, the Palestinian scholar, writes on pp. 305–06 of *Before Their Diaspora*:

> The Palestinians failed to see why they should be made to pay for the Holocaust . . . why it was not fair for the Jews to be a minority in a unitary Palestinian state, while it was fair for almost half of the Palestinian population – the indigenous majority on its ancestral soil – to be converted overnight into a minority under alien rule in the envisaged Jewish state according to partition.

To Jews around the world, on the other hand, the vote 'was Western civilization's gesture of repentance for the Holocaust, that the establishment of the state of Israel in some way represented the repayment of a debt owed by those nations that realized they might have done more to prevent or at least limit the scale of Jewish tragedy during World War II' (*Palestine and the Great Powers*, p. 292). The celebrations of Dalia's relatives following the UN vote are described by her cousin Yitzhak Yitzhaki. Victor Shemtov, a Bulgarian Jew who would later become a member of the Israeli Knesset, recalls dancing in the streets of Haifa, even though his political party, the leftist Mapam, had professed its support for a single binational state.

The proposal for a 'Jewish commonwealth,' known as the 'Biltmore Program,' had called for 'the establishment after the war of a Jewish state in Palestine that would stretch from the river Jordan to the Mediterranean' (*Palestine and the Great Powers*, p. 8). However, Benny Morris writes in *Righteous Victims* (pp. 168–69) that with Biltmore 'the possibility that the state would be established in only part of Palestine was implicit.'

Ben-Gurion's 'stable basis' quote comes from his *War Diary, Vol. 1*, p. 22, and is cited in *Expulsion of the Palestinians*, p. 176.

Ben-Gurion's remarks may appear to some as a precursor to

a policy of expulsions. One could also argue that he simply meant that many more Jews would have to be brought into the new Jewish state to increase the percentage of the Jewish majority; indeed, the Zionist leader promoted the aliyah of millions of European and later Middle Eastern Jews after World War II. Expulsion and aliyah are not mutually exclusive concepts, however, and Ben-Gurion's own support for forced 'transfer' is perhaps most clearly understood in his memorandum 'Outlines of Zionist Policy' from October 1941, when he wrote: 'Complete transfer without compulsion – and ruthless compulsion at that – is hardly imaginable' (*Righteous Victims*, pp. 168–69).

Yitzhak Yitzhaki, the cousin of Dalia's mother, Solia, recalled the events of November 29 and 30, 1947, in an interview. The bus attacks in Ramla and the three-day strike are mentioned in Yoav Gelber's *Palestine 1948*, p. 17; Walid Khalidi's chronology of events in 1947 and 1948 from *Before Their Diaspora*, p. 315, includes the strike as well as Arab plans to mobilize troops. Khalidi's chronology can be searched online at www.qudsway. com/Links/English_Neda/PalestinianFacts/Html_Palestinian/ hpf8.htm.

Egypt's boast about occupying Tel Aviv is from *The War for Palestine: Rewriting the History of 1948*, p. 155. The book outlines other prewar promises, including the Iraqi prime minister's call for a coordinated Arab military campaign and the specter of an oil embargo against the Western powers (p. 131), which the Saudis opposed (*Clash of Destinies*, pp. 79–80).

The Kimche brothers describe the arrival of recruits fresh from the DP camps and their determination to fight for a new state (*Clash*, pp. 13–14) and refer to a 'new Zionism emotionally supercharged by catastrophe' (p. 20) as an underrated factor in the war to come. The Haganah battle plans, including the establishment of regional field commands and mobile brigades, coalesced in Plan Dalet (Hebrew for the letter D), which is described in detail in Chaim Herzog's *The Arab-Israeli Wars*, pp. 32–34. Israeli historian Uri Milstein, in his multivolume *History of Israel's War of Independence*, writes that an objective of Plan D 'was control over Jewish settlement blocs beyond the borders. This constituted one stage in the execution of the secret plan, the final phase of which would be all of *Eretz-Yisra'el* [including at least all of historic Palestine] as a Jewish state' (*Vol. IV*, p. 185). Part of Plan D stated:

These operations can be carried out in the following manner: either by destroying villages (by setting fire to them, by blowing them up, and by planting mines in the debris) . . . In case of resistance, the armed force must be wiped out and the population expelled outside the borders of the state.

[This is printed in Y. Slutzky's 1972 book, *The Book of Hagana* (Hebrew), vol. 3, pp. 1955–559, and is cited in Israeli 'new historian' Ilan Pappe's article 'Were They Expelled?' and on the pages of MideastWeb.org, an Israeli organization promoting coexistence between Arabs and Jews: www.mideastweb.org/pland.htm.]

Ben-Gurion's quote on the boundaries of the state comes from his memoirs. The violence described in the 'early 1948' paragraph is chronicled in Michael J. Cohen's *Palestine and the Great Powers*, pp. 300–10, and Khalidi's *Before Their Diaspora*, pp. 316–18. During this same time, Zionist leaders continued to fight on the political front in Washington. Chaim Weizmann, who would become the first president of Israel, met with President Truman in the days following the vote when U.S. support for implementing the partition plan appeared to be wavering; indeed, Zionist leaders thought Truman was preparing to reverse U.S. policy. Weizmann said, 'The choice for our people, Mr. President, is between statehood and extermination' (*From Haven to Conquest*, pp. 737–43).

The attack on Hassan Salameh's headquarters was described by Israeli historian Uri Milstein on pp. 263–64 of *History of Israel's War of Independence, Vol. IV*; Spiro Munayyer, an Arab native of Lydda, in 'The Fall of Lydda,' *Journal of Palestine Studies* (Summer 1998): 80–98; and Khanom Khairi. Milstein mentions seventeen deaths; Munayyer, an eyewitness, recalled thirty dead and 'bits of human anatomy hanging from trees.' Khanom recalls going to the site the next day with her nationalist teacher in solidarity with the ex-mufti's fighters, most of whom were Iraqi.

The death of Abd al-Qader al-Husseini, the ex-mufti's other main commander in Palestine, was perhaps the Arabs' most devastating single loss in the fighting, and it marked a turning point for the official war to come. The fall of the charismatic Husseini, the 'bravest and most aggressive leader' on the Arab side (*Clash of Destinies*, p. 98), at the hill at Qastal (or Castel, or Kastel) is described in detail in Milstein's *Vol. IV* on pp. 306–10.

The massacre by Irgun and Stern Gang militias at Deir Yassin, in the minds of Palestinians, is the most infamous of the entire conflict. Michael J. Cohen, on pp. 337–38 of *Palestine and the Great Powers*, describes 'the atrocity of Deir Yassin':

> The village had made a nonaggression pact with the Hagana and had abided by it strictly. The Hagana had intended to take over the village in any case, later, to prevent it falling into the hands of irregular bands. But on April 9, an IZL-Lehi [Irgun-Stern Gang] force attacked the village and reduced all resistance, ruthlessly and indiscriminately. The result was the massacre of some 245 villagers, men, women

and children, many of whom were first paraded through the streets of Jerusalem, then taken back to the village and shot.

Reports of rape at Deir Yassin are quoted by Morris (*Righteous Victims*, p. 208). The report of Assistant Inspector General Richard Catling, the British officer who investigated the Deir Yassin massacre, declares, 'There is . . . no doubt that many sexual atrocities were committed by the attacking Jews. Many young school girls were raped and later slaughtered. Old women were also molested. Many infants were also butchered and killed . . . I also saw one woman who gave her age as one hundred and four who had been severely beaten about the head with rifle butts. Women had bracelets torn from their arms and rings from their fingers, and parts of some of the women's ears were severed in order to remove earrings.' *Report of the Criminal Investigation Division*, Palestine Government, No. 179/110/17/GS, 13, 15, 16 April, 1948, as cited by Hirst (*The Gun and the Olive Branch*, p. 250).

Numerous sources describe how this massacre induced many Palestinians to flee their homes and villages, with the understanding they would return in weeks or at most months. Benny Morris, in *Righteous Victims*, p. 209, quotes Israeli military intelligence as saying Deir Yassin was 'a decisive accelerating factor' in the flight of the Arabs. Gelber, in *Palestine 1948*, p. 116, and Nur Masalha, author of *The Expulsion of the Palestinians*, in an interview with me, each said that the massacre was important but less of a factor than others have estimated. In my view, after a decade of interviewing dozens of refugees in the UN camps in the West Bank, Gaza, and Lebanon, it is clear that Deir Yassin had a tremendous impact in creating panic and inducing flight in the spring of 1948. Many refugees, especially those in Haifa and the Galilee who fled north into

Lebanon, believed they would be coming back 'within fifteen days.'

Debate has raged for decades over whether, beyond the fear of 'another Deir Yassin,' most of the seven hundred thousand Palestinians who left their homes in 1948 fled or were driven out by force and whether Arab leaders told them to leave (sometimes via broadcasts) or were the victims of a coordinated, preplanned Zionist operation. This question is too complicated to address here, save for a few important details:

The long-standing and persistent rumor that Arab commanders promulgated orders for villagers to leave (via radio and other means) was discredited in an extensive investigation by Walid Khalidi published in the *Arab Journal* of summer 1968 and numerous subsequent corroborations (see Morris, *1948 and After*, p. 18). Anecdotally, some villagers told me (decades later, in Lebanese refugee camps) they had been urged to temporarily evacuate their homes by local leaders, and at least one Jewish leader, Shabtai Levy, the mayor of Haifa, pleaded with the Arab population to remain. According to Morris in 'The Causes and Character for the Arab Exodus from Palestine,' an Israeli military intelligence analysis of June 1948 ascribed 70 percent of the exodus by June 1 to the 'operations . . . and their influence' of the IDF and dissident Jewish militias like the Irgun. Only 5 percent of the villages were emptied, according to the analysis, as a result of Arab orders to local villagers to leave (*1948 and After*, pp. 84–102).

Yitzhak Yitzhaki's account of the attack on Mt. Scopus conforms to the historical descriptions of that attack, which is described by Milstein in *Vol. IV*, p. 387, and by Morris in *Righteous Victims*, p. 209:

The shooting continued for more than six hours, the Arabs eventually dousing the armored buses with gasoline and setting them alight. When the British finally intervened, more than seventy Jews had died. Deir Yassin and the death of Abd al-Qadir had been avenged.

The story of relations between Lydda's leaders and Dr. Lehman of Ben Shemen appears in Munayyer's 'The Fall of Lydda' (*Journal of Palestine Studies*, p. 85) and was confirmed by Alon Kadish, coauthor with Avraham Sela, of *The Conquest of Lydda* (Hebrew) in an interview in June 2004.

The Bedouin fighters were recalled in the interview with Khanom Khairi and by Lydda native Reja'e Busailah in his article, also called 'The Fall of Lydda' (*Arab Studies Quarterly 3*, no. 2: 127–28). Abdullah's promise to defend Arab lives is mentioned in *The Jordan-Israeli War*, p. 56. The stories of poor coordination among Arab forces comes from *Clash of Destinies*, p. 82:

> The Arab leaders . . . did not confide their respective plans to each other. There was no coordination between their armies or their commands. The Military Committee of the Arab League existed only on paper and it exercised authority over none of the Arab armies. The Egyptians told neither Abdullah nor the Syrians how they proposed to act; the decisions of the Arab commanders of Syria, Iraq, Lebanon and Transjordan . . . were not conveyed to General Glubb [the British commander of Abdullah's Arab Legion].

The fall of Jaffa (known to the Arabs as Yaffa and the Israelis as Yafo) and the arrival of the refugees in the Lydda/Ramla area is described by Munayyer on p. 87.

I first heard the story of Khawaja Shlomo in 1998 in the Amari refugee camp near Ramallah from an Arab native of

Na'ani, while working on an unrelated story. Six years later, I was able to verify it with Dr. Shimon Gat, whose PhD is on ancient Ramla and who as a lifelong resident of Kibbutz Na'an has become its unofficial historian. The horse rider's real name, Gat told me, was Moshe Ben Avraham of Kibbutz Na'an, and he worked for the intelligence arm of the Haganah. 'Quite possibly, he was concerned' about the Arab villagers, Gat said. But he speculated that, given Ben Avraham's work with the Haganah, the ride into Na'ani in May 1948 was likely part of a military psychological operation to induce villagers to flee. Two of Ben Avraham's children, Ruthie and Boaz, also confirmed the story of their father's journey (by telephone during my visit with Gat), though one of them suggested he went to Na'ani on foot, and the other thought he might have ridden on horseback, but not in his pajamas. A similar psy-op, or whispering campaign, this one in the Galilee in early May 1948, was described by Allon himself: 'I gathered all of the Jewish mukhtars [kibbutz leaders], who have contact with Arabs in different villages, and asked them to whisper in the ears of some Arabs, that a great Jewish reinforcement has arrived in Galilee and that it is going to burn all of the villages of the Huleh. They should suggest to these Arabs, as their friends, to escape while there is still time . . . The tactic reached its goal completely.' (*Ha Sepher Ha Palmach*, Vol. 2, p. 286, as cited by Hirst, p. 267).

The scene in Ramla in mid-May and the Khairi family's continuing worries are described by Khanom, with additional description by Firdaws Taji Khairi.

On May 13, Chaim Weizmann sent a letter to President Truman, praising him for 'your inspiration,' which 'made possible the establishment of a Jewish state, which I am convinced will contribute markedly toward a solution of world Jewish problems, and which, I am equally convinced is a necessary preliminary to the development of lasting peace among the peoples of the Near East.'

Ben-Gurion's declaration of the Israeli state the next day, in front of the national council of Palestinian Jewry assembled at the museum in Tel Aviv, is described in detail in *Clash of Destinies* on p. 155. Chaim Weizmann sent a letter to U.S. president Truman asking him to 'promptly recognize the Provisional Government of the new Jewish state,' and on May 15, he obliged. Both letters appear in *Rise of Israel, Vol. 38*, pp. 163–65.

Benny Morris (*Righteous Victims*, pp. 218–35) provides details of the Arab attacks at the official beginning of the war in May 1948. Walid Khalidi (*Before Their Diaspora*, pp. 310–13) describes Haganah operations prior to May 15 in Jerusalem and near Ramla. The Irgun-Arab fighting in Ramla and the Arab defense of the city from May 15–19 are described by several sources, including Firdaws Taji as eyewitness and participant; *Haboker* newspaper reports; and Israeli military intelligence reports dated May 28 and June 19, 1948, in which it is made clear that Hassan Salameh's Iraqi troops were among the defenders of the city. According to the May report, Irgun attacks included fighters whose 'Sten guns didn't work' and whose 'level of professionalism is extremely low and is far from what is demanded by regulations.'

The *Haboker* article described al-Ramla as 'the focal point of this campaign as it lays in the middle of the route to Jerusalem and its conquest will greatly improve the military balance in the whole area.' Benny Morris, in 'Operation Dani and the Palestinian Exodus from Lydda and Ramle [Ramla] in 1948,' *Middle East Journal* 40, no. 1 (Winter 1986), describes the broader strategic objective as 'relieving the city of Jerusalem and the road to it of enemy pressure.'

The urgent cables of al-Ramla's leaders, invoking another

possible slaughter on the scale of Deir Yassin, are referenced by Morris in *The Road to Jerusalem*, p. 173, from an Israel Defense Forces mobile (Alexandroni) brigade report. Pleas to King Abdullah are cited on p. 108 of Glubb's memoir, *A Soldier with the Arabs*. Abdullah's warning to Glubb ('any disaster suffered') is quoted in Maan Abu Nowar's *The Jordan-Israeli War, 1948–1951*, p. 93. The quote from Radio Jerusalem comes from Busailah's account (*Arab Studies Quarterly*, p. 129). Glubb describes his initial forces in Jerusalem on p. 114 of *A Soldier with the Arabs*, and the attack on p. 115, where he also quotes 'a Jewish writer' describing the siege of Jerusalem through Israeli eyes.

David Ben-Gurion described the Arab-Israeli war of 1948 as '700,000 Jews pitted against 27 million Arabs – one against 40' (*War Diaries*, p. 524, quoted in Flapan's *The Birth of Israel: Myths and Realities*). Chaim Herzog, in a letter to President Truman, said the Israelis were outnumbered '20 to 1.' Israeli commander and president Chaim Herzog, in his *Arab-Israeli Wars*, described the conflict as 'a Jewish population of some 650,000 ranged against a Palestinian Arab population of approximately 1.1 million, supported by seven Arab armies from across the borders' (p. 11). These kinds of comparisons were often based on Arab population or troop strength of the entire armed forces of the Arab states that entered Palestine/Israel in May 1948, but do not reflect that numbers of the Arab forces actually engaged in battle in 1948. In *Clash of Destinies*, the Kimche brothers estimate that total strength of the invading Arab armies was twenty-four thousand, compared with thirty-five thousand for the Haganah, with the Arab armies initially possessing 'greater firepower.' Benny Morris, in *1948 and After*, pp. 14–15, adds:

> The atlas map showing a minuscule Israel and a giant surrounding Arab sea did not, and, indeed, for the time

being, still does not, accurately reflect the true balance of military power in the region ... Jewish organization, command, and control ... were clearly superior to those of the uncoordinated armies of Egypt, Syria, Iraq, and Lebanon.

U.S. officials of the day also didn't consider the Arab forces to be the juggernaut depicted by Ben-Gurion, Weizmann, and Herzog. On May 12, three days before the official start of the war, Secretary of State George Marshall received a telegram from the American embassy in London (*Rise of Israel, Vol. 38*, p. 155):

Mufti, and Arab Governments for various reasons do not show signs of assuming significant roles in the next few weeks, although Iraq and Egypt might arrange to fire a few token shots just to be able to say they have done so ... if Abdullah should attack Jews he will confine himself to token forays ...

Glubb, in *Soldier with the Arabs*, pp. 96–97, describes the Arab Legion's intention only to 'occupy the central and largest area of Palestine allocated to the Arabs by the 1947 partition.' The sense that some Jewish leaders had that Abdullah reneged on their unwritten agreement is conveyed by Shlaim in *The Iron Wall*, p. 32, and by Herzog in *The Arab-Israeli Wars*, p. 47. The attack on the Etzion bloc is described by the Kimche brothers in *Clash of Destinies*, p. 140, and by Morris in *Righteous Victims*, p. 214:

Villagers shouting 'Deir Yassin, Deir Yassin' poured through the breach. The remaining defenders laid down their weapons and walked, hands in the air, into the center of the compound. There, according to one of the few survivors, the villagers (and perhaps some legionnaires as well) proceeded to mow them down. In all, about 120 defenders, 21 of them women, died that day. Of the 4 survivors, 3 were saved by Arabs.

The ramifications of the Arab Legion's move into Jerusalem, which in the end represented far more than 'token forays,' are discussed by Shlaim in *The Iron Wall*, p. 32, and by Morris in *Righteous Victims*, p. 221 and p. 225. Morris (p. 225) points out that Jerusalem 'had been designated an international zone and therefore lay outside the tacit nonaggression agreement concluded by Golda Meir and Abdullah.'

The Kimche brothers describe the plight of Jewish residents of Jerusalem during the Arab onslaught (*Clash of Destinies*, p. 186). Israeli attacks on the Arab neighborhoods of Jerusalem are described by Walid Khalidi·in *Before Their Diaspora*, p. 340. Other accounts of Arab life in Jerusalem come from Ghada Karmi's memoir, *In Search of Fatima*, pp. 79–128, and in my 1998 interviews with Hala and Dumia Sakakini, daughters of the prominent Jerusalem Arab, Khalil Sakakini.

Glubb's initial reluctance to enter Jerusalem is discussed in *The Jordan-Israeli War*, p. 93; his concern that additional troops would thin Arab Legion lines elsewhere is on p. 113 of *A Soldier with the Arabs*.

The patriotic songs are described by Reja'e Busailah in the *Arab Studies Quarterly* article, p. 129.

The defeat of the Irgun forces on May 19 is chronicled in the aforementioned Israeli intelligence report, which also commented: 'The commanders give the impression that they don't know how to organize such a large body of men against such a serious and complicated target as Ramla. They lack proper training and knowledge of military tactics.'

Within days, the Irgun forces would be integrated into the command of the Haganah and would become part of the Israel Defense Forces.

Ahmad's decision to send the family to Ramallah and the journey the children took were described by Khanom Khairi.

The death of Hassan Salameh and the pall it cast was recalled by Firdaws Taji in an interview and by Munayyer in his 'Fall of Lydda' article, pp. 88–90.

The maneuvering before the June truce, Count Bernadotte's arrival in Amman, and Glubb's reluctance to send more than a token force into Ramla and Lydda are described by Glubb on pp. 141–43 of *A Soldier with the Arabs*. The Arab Legion, considered the most professional of all Arab forces in Palestine, was, at 4,500 troops (*Clash of Destinies*, pp. 161–62), also among the smallest.

The decision not to attack Ben Shemen is described by Glubb on p. 142 of *Soldier with the Arabs* and by Bromage in a letter to Maan Abu Nowar on pp. 147–48 of *The Jordan-Israeli War*.

The truce period and the arms embargo are described in *A Soldier with the Arabs*, pp. 142–153; *The Road to Jerusalem*, pp. 171–72; *The Jordan-Israeli War*, pp. 195–200; and on p. 34 of *From the Wings*, the Amman memoirs of British representative Sir Alex Kirkbride, who quoted Abdullah complaining about his 'not very desirable friends.' Additional factors may have contributed to the arms and ammunition shortage facing Transjordan after the truce: Glubb (p. 166) also mentions Egyptian seizure of a Transjordan-bound ammunition shipment. It is not clear how Glubb's claim squares with evidence of British pressure on Abdullah not to break the embargo. (See Gelber, *Palestine* 1948, p. 160.)

The sinking of the *Altalena* is recounted in *Brother Against Brother*, pp. 17–32. Israel's ability to break the arms embargo is described on pp. 204–05 of *Clash of Destinies*. The weapons included artillery, Messerschmitt fighter aircraft, Czech-made Beza machine guns, and millions of rounds of ammunition in a 'shuttle service of arms and planes to Israel' from the 'Haganah's main base in Europe.'

Glubb describes Abdullah's position vis-à-vis war, the Arab League, and the end of the truce on pp. 151–52; see also *The Road to Jerusalem*, p. 175. The 'don't shoot' quote comes from *A Soldier with the Arabs*, p. 150.

Israel Gefen was eighty-two years old and in possession of a vivid recollection of detail when I interviewed him. The details of the weaponry conform with the matériel secured by Israel in the aforementioned Czech arms shipments; additional details were verified by Alon Kadish, coauthor of *The Conquest of Lydda*. Gefen and Kadish confirmed the firing rate of the machine guns.

Kadish also provided me with the first name of Dr. Ziegfried Lehman, who was recalled only by his last name in Spiro Munayyer's account of the Ben Shemen story ('Fall of Lydda,' p. 85). Interestingly, the Kimche brothers note (*Clash of Destinies*, p. 74) that Ben Shemen was not simply a peaceful settlement before the outbreak of the war; it was used as a training site for the Haganah.

The battle plans for 'mobility and fire' employed by Dayan were described to me by Alon Kadish, who said that Dayan had heard about the tactic of overwhelming force from an American tank commander during a trip to the United States. This plan and the account of Dayan's trip to the United States were confirmed in an interview with Yohanan Peltz, who was for part of 1948 Dayan's second in command.

Newspaper accounts of the attack on Lydda corroborate and in some cases expand on the description by Gefen; details are in the July 11 and July 12 editions of the *New York Herald Tribune*, the *Chicago Sun Times*, and the *New York Times*. Additional details are described by Yoav Gelber in *Palestine 1948* on p. 159 and by Benny Morris in his 1986 article in the *Middle East Journal*, 'Operation Dani and the Palestinian Exodus from Lydda and Ramla in 1948,' pp. 82–109, and in his *1948 and After*, pp. 1–4. The attack was part of Operation Dani, one side of what Kadish described as a 'pincer movement' hitting Ramla and Lydda (including the airport) from two sides, cutting it off from Arab Legion positions to the east. The direction of Dayan's convoy was described by Kadish in the 2004 interview and in *Clash of Destinies*, pp. 227–28.

The next morning, July 12, an incident occurred that would help shape events of the coming forty-eight hours. Israeli army units had entered Lydda after Dayan's Battalion Eighty-nine (conversation with Kadish, June 2004). Most of the civilian population of Ramla and Lydda remained, and shooting had died down in both towns. Just before noon, three Arab Legion armored cars appeared along the border between Ben Shemen and Lydda (*A Soldier with the Arabs*, pp. 161–62). Apparently they were there on a scouting mission. But the Israelis, and Arabs of Lydda, thought the cars were the advance guard of a counterattack. Fighters in Lydda began sniping from the buildings (*1948 and After*, p. 1). One eyewitness I interviewed recalls someone from Lydda throwing a hand grenade, which he believes killed several Israeli soldiers. It was, everyone thought for a moment, the beginnings of an uprising, but it didn't last long. 'Soon it became apparent that the armoured cars were unsupported,' Glubb would write in *Soldier with the Arabs*, p. 161. The trucks and their soldiers were 'obliged to withdraw.'

Israeli troops opened fire. Eyewitnesses I interviewed who claim to have been inside a mosque at the time recall indiscriminate machine-gun fire (interview with Abu Mohammad Saleh Tartir, Amari refugee camp, December 2003). When the shooting stopped, about 250 people were dead, including many unarmed men in the Dahmash mosque. Four of the dead and about twenty of the wounded were Israelis. Morris, on p. 1 of *1948 and After*, referred to what happened in Lydda as a 'slaughter'; Gelber, the Israeli historian, called it a 'massacre' and 'probably the bloodiest throughout the war' (*Palestine 1948*, p. 162); numerous Palestinian sources also call it a massacre and focus on the deaths at the mosque, which may have exceeded eighty.

According to Firdaws Taji, word of the killings in Lydda spread quickly to Ramla, prompting discussions of surrender and flight.

The actions of Dr. Rasem Khairi are described by Firdaws Taji. The aerial bombing of Ramla on July 9 and 10 is described by Firdaws and corroborated by Morris in his review of military archives in 'Operation Dani,' *Middle East Journal*, p. 86. One communiqué referred to the 'great value in continuing the bombing,' as it was, in Morris's words, 'designed to induce civilian panic and flight,' which Gefen, in his interview with me in June 2004, reported seeing from his convoy: 'Soon after, every path leading to the east ... people walking, children, women, people with bundles ...'

Firdaws Taji, in an interview, described leaflets dropped from the air by Israeli planes, as did Busailah in the *Arab Studies Quarterly* article, p. 133, and Morris in the *Middle East Journal*, p. 76.

The condition of the towns of Ramla and Lydda were described by Firdaws Taji and in interviews with current and former Arab citizens of Lydda (now the Israeli city of Lod), including Adla Salim Rehan at the Amari refugee camp in Ramallah and Mohammad Saleh Tartir of the Lydda Society at Amari. Khanom Khairi described Sheikh Mustafa's emergency trip to secure bullets in Transjordan.

The state of the defenders of Ramla is described by Taji and

Reja'e Busailah (*Arab Studies Quarterly*, pp. 127-35). Writing more broadly about the Palestinian Arabs during 1948, the Kimche brothers stated:

> The local Arabs, who had only the haziest of notions concerning the strength of the Jews, knew even less about the nature of their own forces . . . No one told the Palestinian Arabs in their villages – until it was too late – that the Arab countries were not fulfilling all they had promised and that many of the weapons they had sent were old, decrepit and useless. (*Clash of Destinies*, pp. 81-82)

Sheikh Mustafa's desire to keep Ramla residents from fleeing is described by Firdaws Taji Khairi, who recalls a series of meetings on the elegant patio of her father-in-law-to-be. The chaos of people going back and forth between Ramla and Lydda is described by Taji and by Busailah. Busailah also reports the urgent telegrams and the promises of a 'flood of gold' and is a source for the surrender talk and the Bedouins' departure. Glubb writes about the departure of the Arab Legion in *Soldier with the Arabs*, as does Abu Nowar in *The Jordanian-Israeli War*, p. 206.

The account of Sheikh Mustafa sending his son to Kibbutz Na'an is also from Khanom Khairi. Alon Kadish told me his understanding was that some of the 'notables' of the town were actually trying to leave when intercepted by Israeli troops and taken to the kibbutz to sign the surrender documents. The surrender terms and signature were taken from a copy of the original document in Hebrew and translated by Israeli journalist Ian Dietz. Copies of the surrender were provided by Yonatan Tubali, city manager of Ramla, and by Hava Enoch, the archivist at Kibbutz Na'an.

Galili B's quote on Ben-Gurion's orders to 'evacuate Ramla'

come from his handwritten note, which is deposited in the Na'an archives. Kadish, whose book was published by the Israel Defense Forces, confirms that the populations of Lydda and Ramla were expelled. David Kimche, former Israeli intelligence officer and coauthor of *Clash of Destinies*, wrote that 'Lydda fell on July 11th and its Arab population of 30,000 either fled or were herded on to the road to Ramallah. The next day, Ramla also surrendered, and its Arab population suffered the same fate. Both towns were sacked by the victorious Israelis.' The Israeli historian Gelber, in *Palestine 1948*, writes that 'Yigal Alon [commander of the Palmach, or Israeli army] had ordered that all males of military age be detailed as prisoners-of-war and the rest be deported across the lines.' Morris, in *1948 and After*, p. 2, and 'Operation Dani' (*Arab Studies Quarterly*, p. 91), cites Israeli military communiqués issued from Dani headquarters, including the order by Rabin. A similar order, Morris writes, was issued shortly afterward. For a detailed discussion of the July 1998 expulsions from al-Ramla and Lydda, with extensive citation from Israeli military and civilian archives, see Morris's *The Birth of the Palestinian Refugee Problem Revisited*, pp. 423-436.

Firdaws Taji's recollections of soldiers yelling, 'Go to Abdullah,' are echoed in perhaps a dozen interviews I have done with 1948 Arab residents of al-Ramla and Lydda, many of whom now live in the Amari refugee camp in Ramallah; Reja's Busailah also mentions this in the *Arab Studies Quarterly* article, p. 140.

Shitrit's arrival in the al-Ramla/Lydda area is mentioned in Tom Segev's *1949: The First Israelis*, pp. 26-27; Morris's article in *Middle East Journal*, pp. 92-93; and Gelber's *Palestine 1948*, p. 161.

Rabin recalled the meeting with Ben Gurion in his memoirs. Although this portion was censored in its Hebrew version, the translator, Peretz Kidron, later published the memoirs in English and leaked the quote to the *New York Times*. (See the *New York Times*, October 23, 1979.) Gelber, in *Palestine 1948*, p. 162, challenges Rabin's interpretation, arguing that 'Ben-Gurion's habit was not 'waving' his orders but formulating them clearly and expressing them verbally or in writing ... Ben-Gurion might have waved his hand to get rid of a fly.'

Yigal Allon's strategy for using the expelled populations of Ramla and Lydda to clog the roads and prevent the Arab Legion from retaking the towns is outlined in the *Palmach* 67 (July 1948): 7–8 (in Hebrew, reference provided by Alon Kadish, coauthor of *The Conquest of Lydda*).

The newspaper quotes from Currivan and others are from the July 12 and July 13 editions of the *New York Herald Tribune* and the *New York Times*. The recollections of men who boarded the buses come from Michail Fanous, in an interview in Ramla, who heard the story from his father, and from Mohammad Taji, also of Ramla.

The heat of mid-July 1948 in the central plain of Israel/Palestine is mentioned by Glubb on p. 162 of *A Soldier with the Arabs* and by Busailah in his *Arab Studies Quarterly* report, p. 142. Evidence that thousands had already left al-Ramla and Lydda by July 14 comes from numerous interviews with eyewitnesses, including Mohammad Taji, Firdaws Taji, Abu Mohammad Saleh Tartir in the Amari refugee camp, 1998 interviews with the Reverend Audeh Rantisi, and Busailah, p. 140.

The items the Khairis and others of al-Ramla left behind come from numerous interviews with family members and other former and current residents of Ramla and Lydda and years of observation and visits with Palestinians in the West Bank, Lebanon, Gaza, and Jordan.

Numerous interviews I have done over the years, including with the late Reverend Audeh Rantisi of Lydda, describe the confiscation of rings and other gold jewelry by Israeli soldiers on the outskirts of the towns. Morris, in the *Middle East Journal* article, pp. 97–98, reports, 'In general, the refugees were sent on their way unmolested,' but adds that in July 1948, Israeli cabinet minister Aharon Cohen alleged that Israeli troops 'at the checkpoints on the way out of Lydda had been "ordered" to 'take from the expelled Arabs every watch, piece of jewelry or money . . . so that arriving completely destitute, they would become a burden on the Arab Legion.' The extent to which this happened is not clear, but it is consistent with interviews and other written accounts.

The account of the Taji and Khairi families' flight and the landscape they crossed comes from Firdaws Taji and is echoed by numerous other interviews, including those with Mohammad Taji, Abu Mohammad Saleh Tartir, and Rantisi. A similar account is given by Busailah, p. 141.

The 'donkey road' reference is from an interview with Khamis Salem Habash of al-Ramla, the details of whose journey during the same period are consistent with Firdaws Taji's. The description of cactus and Christ's thorn near al-Ramla during this period comes from various sources, including Israeli landscape architect Ya'acov Golan. The actual distance the group traveled is unclear, though it is certain the people of Ramla did not journey as far as Busailah and the others from Lydda.

The figure of thirty thousand refugees and the terrain they crossed come from estimates by Glubb (*A Soldier with the Arabs*, p. 162) and from Ben-Gurion's diary of July 15, 1948 (quoted in Segev's *1949*, p. 27). Morris (*Middle East Journal, p. 83)* and Kadish (interview with me, June 2004) estimate that there were between fifty thousand and sixty thousand Arabs in the two towns of Lydda and Ramla in July 1948, including refugees who had arrived from Jaffa and nearby villages. ('Maybe thirty-four thousand [in Ramla and Lydda combined] without refugees,'

Kadish told me. 'So you're talking about fifty-five to sixty thousand people.') Postwar Israeli figures for the Arab populations of both towns are fewer than five thousand; hence it appears Ben-Gurion and Glubb's figure of thirty thousand refugees is reasonable, if not conservative.

Ben-Gurion's 'demanding bread' quote comes from *1949*, p. 27.

Ramallah's past as a Christian hill town is understood through numerous interviews and documents, including an interview with Nicola Akkel in Ramallah and Palestinian scholar Naseer Aruri in Boston.

That tens of thousands of refugees were in Ramallah in mid-July is verified by U.S. government cables, including one dated August 12, 1948, and sent from the American consulate in Jerusalem to the State Department in Washington. That the refugees were already thinking of return is documented in dozens of interviews with refugees in camps in the West Bank and elsewhere, including in Ramallah. Morris, in his *Middle East Journal* article, p. 98, included the account of Shmarya Guttman, an officer in the Palmach and a resident of Kibbutz Na'an, who described the walk of the refugees:

A multitude of inhabitants walked one after another . . . We tried to make things as easy as possible for them. Occasionally you encountered a piercing look from one of the youngsters walking in the stream of the column, and the look said: 'We have not yet surrendered. We shall return to fight you.'

Chapter 5

This chapter is grounded primarily in two kinds of sources: original documents from archives, and interviews with

Bulgarian Jewish immigrants to Israel in 1948 and those in Bulgaria who remember the preparations for the journey. I interviewed more than fifty people for this chapter and examined documents at the American Jewish Joint Distribution Committee (JDC) archives in Queens, New York; at the Bulgarian National Library and the Jewish section of the Bulgarian National Archives, both in Sofia; and at the Central Zionist Archives and JDC archives in Jerusalem.

The description of the railway station comes from interviews in Bulgaria with Virginia Eshkenazi, the widow of Moshe's brother, Jacques; from several interviews with Bulgarian Jews in Israel, including Moshe Melamed, who at twelve years old was in the railway station on the same day for the same journey described herein, and has a photographic memory; and from Moshe Mossek, another Bulgarian Jew who traveled to Israel at about the same time in 1948 and who read this chapter and verified the accuracy of the description of the emigration process.

The description of Solia and Moshe comes from old family photos and from Dalia, who assured me that her mother always wore a hat for such occasions; that Solia's hair would 'absolutely' have been worn loose over her shoulders and never tied back; and that her father would have undoubtedly held the family's identity papers. Dalia's parents told her about the straw basket they kept her in and that she slept for nearly the entire journey.

Dalia, by the way, was born 'Daizy' and would not change her name until age eleven. In Bulgaria, her father was known as Mois and her mother as Solia (and occasionally by the diminutive 'Solche').

The story of how Moshe and Solia met, including Moshe's bold prediction of marriage, comes from Eshkenazi family oral history, as told to Dalia by her parents.

The description of the lines and emigration forms is extrapolated from Boyka Vassileva's *The Jews in Bulgaria*, summarized and large portions translated from the Bulgarian by journalist Polia Alexandrova. These descriptions were further verified by Moshe Mossek. The figure of 3,694 Bulgarian Jews comes from the ship's seventy-four-page manifest for the *Pan York*, the ship that the Eshkenazis and other Bulgarians were soon to board, housed at the Family Research Department of the Central Zionist Archives.

The Bulgarian Jews' unique history in Europe is documented throughout the text and source notes for chapter 3.

The date of the *Pan York*'s trip is verified in 'General Letter No. 1102' from Fred Baker in the JDC's offices in Sofia to the European headquarters in Paris and from the JDC archives in Jerusalem and is corroborated by Melamed.

Boris's death in 1943 (on August 28, at 4:22 P.M.) is described by Stephane Groueff in *Crown of Thorns*, p. 372. Groueff and others describe it as 'mysterious': Boris died of a heart attack just two weeks after a meeting with Hitler that went poorly, and the timing prompted speculation that Boris had been poisoned. However, Frederick Chary, author of *The Bulgarian Jews and the Final Solution*, is skeptical. 'After his return from the führer's headquarters,' Chary points out, 'the king went for a week's holiday to Cham Koria, his retreat in the Rila mountains; on one day he climbed Mousalla – the highest peak in the Balkans' (p. 159).

The early history of Zionism in Bulgaria comes from Vladimir Paounovski's article in *Etudes balkaniques*, 1997, No. 1-2, titled 'The World Zionist Organization and the Zionists in Bulgaria According to Newly Discovered Documents.' Paounovski, who is also the director of the Jewish Museum in Sofia, wrote of the discovery of nine letters and two telegrams written in German that explore relations between Bulgarian

Zionists and their counterparts in the World Zionist Organization. Herzl's *Orient Express* quote comes from his diary of June 17, 1896, and can be found in *The Diaries of Theodor Herzl* (Lowenthal, ed.), p. 142. Herzl's 'bandy legs' quote comes from *The Jewish State*.

It has often been said that Herzl became a Zionist because of the anti-Semitic trial of Alfred Dreyfus, a French Jew in Paris. Herzl himself wrote that his belief in the necessity of a separate homeland for the Jews came from his experience as the Paris correspondent for the Viennese newspaper *Neue Freie Presse*, covering the so-called Dreyfus affair (Lowenthal, Herzl's *Diaries*, p. xviii). Shlomo Avineri, in *The Making of Modern Zionism*, writes (pp. 92-93) that 'the Dreyfus Affair was correctly understood by Herzl as only the dramatic expression of a much more fundamental malaise.'

Lowenthal, however, wrote in his introduction that Herzl's witness of the Dreyfus affair as a reporter was different from his later recollections (pp. xviii-xix). Other chroniclers of Herzl's life, including Lenni Brenner, in *Zionism in the Age of the Dictators*, believe he took the wrong message from the Dreyfus affair altogether, because the Dreyfus case 'aroused a huge surge of Gentile support', including from 'kings', the 'socialist movement', and 'the intellectuals of France'. An additional factor in the rise of political Zionism were pogroms in Russia – particularly, Morris points out (*Righteous Victims*, pp. 16-17 and pp. 24-25), those in 1891-92 and 1903-06.

Herzl's 'holy ark' and 'calm demeanor' quotes come from his diary entry of June 30, 1896 (*Diaries*, pp. 170-71).

The prewar Zionist newspapers are housed at the Bulgarian National Library. That the Arabs 'did not figure in these discussions' is corroborated by Bulgarian Jewish archivist David Koen of Sofia, who also recalled the 'land without people' quote.

The closing of the Zionist newspapers is documented by Vicki

Tamir (*Bulgaria and Her Jews*, pp. 170–72). Evidence of the regrouping of the Zionist papers can be found in documents of the Jewish 'consistory' offices, located in the Bulgarian National Archives. The bulk of this material comes from folder 622–1 and includes many documents that describe an attempt to restore Jewish life, reestablish Jewish schools, and reassimilate Jews into Bulgarian society. Additional documentation comes from Boyka Vassileva's *The Jews in Bulgaria*.

The question of immigration to Israel comes from both Dalia and Virginia Eshkenazi.

The devastation of the Bulgarian landscape is described by Crampton in *A Short History of Modern Bulgaria*, pp. 128–29; Tamir in *Bulgaria and Her Jews*, p. 216; and Chary in *The Bulgarian Jews and the Final Solution*, p. 169. Crop failures, hunger, and inflation are mentioned by Yehuda Bauer in *Out of the Ashes*, pp. 276–80.

Ben-Gurion's arrival in Bulgaria in December 1944 is described by Vassileva and in Ben-Gurion's diaries. The visit is also the subject of Moshe Mossek's article 'The Struggle for Leading the Jews of Bulgaria,' translated from the Hebrew by Boaz Hachlili. The Ben-Gurion 'task of the moment' quote and the response of 'aliyah!' comes from Vassileva.

Yitzhak Yitzhaki (born Isaac Isaakov) recalled in an interview his return from the work camp, his army duty after Bulgaria's liberation by the Soviet Red Army, and his emigration to Palestine.

Ben-Gurion's impressions of Bulgaria, his longer-term strategy, and the quote about the five thousand pairs of shoes come from the Mossek article and from an interview with Mossek.

Documents on trade relations can be found in the Central Zionist Archive (CZA) in Jerusalem (s31/43/1,2,3). The telegram formalizing trade relations, also from the CZA documents, was dated October 7, 1947.

Documentation of postwar funds sent to Bulgarian Jews by the JDC comes from Yehuda Bauer's *Out of the Ashes*, p. 179; from Vassileva's *The Jews in Bulgaria*; and from the CZA and Bulgarian National Archives documents listed previously.

The JDC's support for the Jewish community in Bulgaria, including local cooperatives, comes from documents found in JDC archives in Queens (e.g., 45/54 169). Relations between the JDC and the Jewish Agency are clear from the JDC archives, including in a memo from Charles Passman to M. W. Beckelman on November 10, 1948, discussing the need to 'prepare the necessary bill for the Jewish agency.' The JDC's ties with the Mossad are also seen in numerous JDC documents, including one letter dated December 16, 1948, from the JDC's Jerusalem archives (Box 11 C) stating, 'The Mossad will refund to us all that we will spend for the food . . . for the boats leaving from Bulgaria.'

Tensions between Bulgarian Jewish Communists and Zionists come from numerous sources, including JDC and CZA documents (especially folder 25/9660), postwar Bulgarian Jewish publications in the National Library in Sofia, and interviews. The aliyah as a 'false Zionist fantasy' comes from the Mossek article.

The Zionists as 'reactionaries' quote and accounts of the Fatherland Front and World Zionist Organization meetings come from Vassileva. The initial steps to return Jewish property came from a March 1945 law and are documented in Chary, *The Bulgarian Jews and the Final Solution*, p. 178.

The punishments meted out by the new Communist-led government are documented in Tamir's *Bulgaria and Her Jews*, p. 223. The sparing of Peshev is explored in chapter 7 of Gabriele Nissim's *The Man Who Stopped Hitler*, pp. 165-89. The figure of 2,138 executions is listed in *Bulgaria and Her Jews*, p. 285, footnote 588, quoting official figures of the

People's Court; Tamir (p. 223) believes the figure is closer to 3,000.

Dimitrov's return to Bulgaria is documented in his memoirs and in Crampton's *A Short History of Modern Bulgaria*, p. 153. Additional discussion of Dimitrov and Jewish property is in Chary, p. 182. His two decades in the Kremlin are mentioned by Tamir on p. 224. The strategy of the Communist leadership and its replacement of private ownership with collectives are documented in the Mossek article.

The celebrations of Sofia Jews comes from documents in the Central Zionist Archives in Jerusalem (folder 25/9660).

The birth of Dalia (then Daizy), and her father's excitement, was recalled by Virginia Eshkenazi. Dalia was told by her parents that they had hoped for a child; Virginia remembered her beauty and quiet manner.

Dimitrov recorded the February 18, 1948, meeting with Stalin in his diary. Bulgaria's vice premier and interior minister were also present.

The 'boundless appreciation' and 'satisfaction' quotes come from letters found in the Bulgarian National Archives, folder 622–1 of the Central Consistory of the Jews in Bulgaria. That Jacques Eshkenazi, a committed Communist, would have adopted the same stance is confirmed by Dalia. The consolidation and control of the Zionist groups under the Communist umbrella is confirmed by Mossek, Vassileva, and by Chary on p. 182.

The 'chain reaction' of emigration was described in several interviews with Bulgarian Jews in Israel and Bulgaria, notably Moritz Assa, a Communist who did not wish to emigrate but who saw most of his family, friends, and many of his neighbors do so. The names and professions of the immigrants are taken from a 128-page list in folder 622–1 of the Jewish Consistory in the National Archives in Sofia. The 'psychosis' quote is from Assa.

The early emigration of five merchant marine ships, the average of $40 per person for the passage on the ships, and the Bulgarian government's need of hard currency are all documented in JDC's Queens archives, collection 45/64, file 4201. The figure of 750 people on five ships is confirmed in a confidential memo, dated September 5, 1948, to JDC offices in New York. The use of the Bulgarian merchant marine is mentioned in a similar memo, dated August 30.

The 'first big operation' is documented by Vassileva, chapter 4, pp. 110–26. She also mentions the tests of immigrants for various diseases, which were becoming a major concern in the new Jewish state. The precise number of Bulgarian Jews comes from the ship's manifest, cited earlier. The date of the departure from the Sofia rail station is confirmed in General Letter No. 1205 (JDC Jerusalem archives, Box 11C) and in an October 29, 1948, letter to the JDC offices in Paris.

The route of the train was described in detail by Moshe Melamed.

The 'four steps in Israel' quote was recalled by David Koen. There are other translations of this. According to Rabbi Maller of Temple Akiba in Culver City, California, the saying is as follows: 'Anyone who walks four cubits [about six feet] in the land of Israel is certain of receiving a place in the world to come.' This expression comes from the Talmud, Tractate Ketubot.

Herzl's political journey into Zionism and his actual trips to convince the imperial powers that a Jewish state was in their interest are documented in Herzl's *Diaries*. Additional insight into Herzl is given by Allan Janik and Stephen Toulmin in their 1973 book, *Wittgenstein's Vienna*. The authors portray Herzl as a member of the Viennese cultural elite who was 'first, last, and always a dandy'; he insisted 'that frock coats be worn at the first Zionist International conference in Basel.'

Some of Herzl's initial discussions of the Zionist idea were in

1895 with Baron Maurice de Hirsch. The two men talked of Hirsch's funding of Jewish settlements in Argentina (*Diaries*, pp. 13–28). Zionist hostility to the Uganda idea is documented, among other places, in Avineri's *The Making of Modern Zionism*, p. 110. Chaim Weizmann's 'fit the gem' quote comes from *The Letters and Papers of Chaim Weizmann*, *vol. 1*, *series B*, *paper 24* and is taken from Masalha's *Expulsion of the Palestinians*, pp. 5–6.

The arrival of the train at the Dalmatian coast of the Adriatic was remembered by Moshe Melamed. The figure of four thousand tons of crates, and their storage in the synagogue in Sofia, comes from a May, 9, 1949, confidential memo (JDC Queens archives, 45/64/2970).

The arrival at the port of Bakar and the lights of the *Pan York* were recalled in interviews in Israel with Melamed, Mossek, and Sami Sela.

Description of the *Pan York* comes from '*Pan Crescent and Pan York*' (the ships also known as 'the *Pans*') and can be found online at www.jewishvirtuallibrary.org/jsource/Immigration/pans.html.

The ship's supplies are listed in a memo sent by JDC's Bulgaria director Fred Baker to the JDC offices in Paris (general letter 1102). Melamed adds this from the journey: 'They brought very bad soup. We kept throwing it up. And we ate more.'

The idea of a binational state and discussion of Brit Shalom is from *The History of Zionism*. Additional background can be found online atwww.kehillasynagogue.org/KehillaMEPeace/Document_III.html. Buber's 'two peoples' quote comes from a talk he gave on Dutch radio in June 1947, which is reprinted in 'A Land of Two Peoples' by Buber with Paul R. Mendes-Flohr. It can be found online at www.one-state.org/articles/earlier/buber.htm. Buber, while promoting coexistence, also made clear in the speech that he believed the Arab love of homeland was less significant than that of the Jews: It 'is more passive among the Arabs . . . dimmer, simpler and more inchoate than that of the Hebrew pioneers.'

The history of Mapam comes from an interview with Bulgarian Jew and former Israeli Knesset member Victor Shemtov, who was active in the party in the 1940s. Additional details on Gromyko's stance can be found in Cohen's *Israel and the Arab World*, pp. 202–04.

The lights of Haifa and Carmel were described in interviews. The lyrics of 'Hatikva' were translated by Sarah Tuttle-Singer.

The processing of the arriving Bulgarian immigrants was described by Sela, Mossek, and Melamed, who recalled that 'one hand gave me a sandwich, another sprayed DDT on my head.' Additional details on the processing can be found in Tom Segev's account in *1949: The First Israelis*, pp. 95–116.

Moshe's restlessness and his discovery that Jews could sign up to move to 'a place called Ramla' was described to Dalia during her childhood and confirmed by Melamed, who was in the same group of immigrants in the Pardes Hannah camp.

Chapter 6

This chapter is grounded primarily in interviews, both with members of the Khairi and Taji families and with other eye-witnesses to the events of late 1948 and early 1949; written accounts from additional eyewitnesses; declassified State Department, United Nations, and Red Cross memos and telegrams from the National Archives in Washington, D.C.; and additional primary and secondary accounts in various books, brochures, and reports.

The arrival in Ramallah is described by Firdaws Taji, second cousin of Bashir, who would also become Mustafa's daughter-in-law. Additional description comes from an interview with eyewitness Abu Issam Harb; Palestinian folklorist, Dr. Sharif

Kanaana; and a telegram sent from the American consul in Jerusalem on August 12, 1948, housed in the National Archives.

The telegram, with its vivid language, gives a sense of how Ramallah felt to international observers and relief workers in the late summer of 1948:

SANITATION PRACTICALLY NONEXISTANT ... NO WATER AVAILABLE FOR BATHING OR LAUNDRY. SICK NOT ISOLATED. COMPLETE LACK OF ORGANIZATION APPARENT ... MEDICINES LIMITED TO LITTLE MORE THAN ASPIRINS, 20 SUSPECTED CASES TYPHOID HAVE BEEN 'SENT BACK TO SLEEP UNDER THE TREES' ... NIGHTS BECOME VERY COLD MID SEPTEMBER AND RAINS START SOON AFTER ...

Ahmad's trips and the family's location near the Quaker School were described in interviews with Bashir, Nuha, and Khanom Khairi.

Conditions in the camps are described in various documents from the National Archives in Maryland, including a September 16, 1948, declassified draft report to the UN General Assembly sent to U.S. secretary of state George Marshall on September 17 (hereinafter referred to as the September 17 report).

Refugees strapping gold to their bodies comes from interviews with refugees in the Amari camp near Ramallah and Reja'e Busailah's 'The Fall of Lydda' (*Arab Studies Quarterly 3*, no. 2: 141). Bashir verified the refugees' hauling water and hawking sweets; Dr. Kanaana, the folklorist from Bir Zeit University, recounted the tensions between refugees and local residents and the taunts of the locals. The story of the sugar-coated nuts appears on p. 147 of 'The Fall of Lydda.'

The impression of men 'shocked into silence' and sitting idly on burlap sacks comes from the interview with Abu Issam Harb.

The harvest times for particular crops were verified by Kanaana, as was the role of women during the time. The relief supplies, their sources, and their modest aim of preventing starvation are listed in the September 17 report. The scouring of trash bins is mentioned on p. 44 of *The Palestinian Refugees: 1948–1998 (An Oral History)*, edited by Adel H. Yahya.

Bernadotte's telegrams and the 'human disaster' quote come from the September 17 report, as does the estimate of refugees who fled or were driven out. Bernadotte's 'ghastly' quote comes from the *Progress Report of the UN Mediator on Palestine General Assembly, Official Records*, Third Supplement, No. 11 (A/648), Paris, 1948, p. 200, as cited by Hirst, p. 276. See also Bernadotte's *To Jerusalem*, p. 200, as cited by the official Web site of the Swedish government, http://www.sweden.se/ templates/cs/ BasicFactsheet_4198.aspx. The anger of the refugees in 1948 is clear from numerous interviews and is recalled by Glubb in his memoir, *A Soldier with the Arabs*, pp. 163–64, where he also recalls the spitting and 'worse than Jews!' remark. Additional mention of these events, including the demonstrations, is in Morris's *Road to Jerusalem*, pp. 178–79; see also Gelber's *Palestine 1948*, p. 163 and pp. 172–73. The 'five times their numbers,' 'Admittedly,' and 'what else could I have done?' quotes all come from *Soldier with the Arabs*, p. 164.

Abdullah's apparent contact with Sheikh Mustafa, including the 'shall I bring them?' and 'stay where you are' exchange, is part of Khairi family oral history, as described here by Samira Khairi.

Abdullah's kingdom under siege is described in many accounts of the time, including in *From the Wings*, the memoirs of Alec Kirkbride, pp. 47–50, which also describes the apparently imminent 'bloodbath' and the king striking a refugee on his head.

Glubb, in *Soldier with the Arabs*, pp. 164–66, describes his personal upbraiding in the wake of the loss of al-Ramla and Lydda, at a mid-July meeting of the king and his ministers in Amman. Arab Legion troops strength is listed at forty-five hundred by Glubb in *A Soldier with the Arabs*, p. 92, though on p. 90 he writes of '6,000 in 1948.' Morris (*Righteous Victims*, p. 223) estimates the force at eight thousand.

British refusal to resupply the Arab Legion is documented in Gelber, *Palestine 1948*, p. 160, citing British cable traffic.

The 'little prospect' quote comes from a July 29, 1948, air gram sent from the American embassy in Cairo to Secretary of State Marshall in Washington, from declassified material retrieved from the National Archives. The Ben-Gurion and Sharett quotes come from Meron Benvenisti's *Sacred Landscapes*, p. 150. Israeli confirmation of this position is corroborated in an August 1948 'Note on the Refugee Problem in Palestine,' submitted by A. Katznelson, the head of Israel's delegation to the International Red Cross Conference. The *'not one of them has been deported'* quote comes from that note.

It should be noted that a few Israeli officials did argue for the return of Arab refugees, in varying numbers. At one point, Israel told the U.S. ambassador it was willing to receive one hundred thousand refugees out of a total of more than seven hundred thousand who had fled or were driven out, provided this would resolve the refugee problem. Neither Arab governments nor the refugees would have accepted such a proposal; in any case, the prevailing sentiment in Israel was set against return. (See Segev, *1949*, pp. 28–34.)

The report citing the 'Controlled American Source' is in the Cairo air gram cited previously.

The description of Arab POW conditions comes from interviews with Labib Qulana, Mohammad Taji, and Michail Fanous, all Arabs of Ramla. Additional recollections are in Fouzi el-Asmar's memoir, *To Be an Arab in Israel*, p. 23.

Confirmation comes from minutes of the first meeting of the City-Council of Israeli Ramla, provided by Yonatan Tubali, longtime city manager of Ramla. Military restrictions on Arabs of Israel, including martial law, are described by Segev in *1949*, pp. 47–51.

That the first group of Jewish immigrants would not arrive until November 1948 is confirmed by original documents from Tubali and by Yablonka in *Survivors of the Holocaust*, p. 24, citing documents in the Israel Defense Forces archives. Physical description of doors ajar and belongings spilling out comes from recollections by the first Israeli immigrants to Ramla of their arrival in the town, including M. Levy and Moshe Melamed, and from an October 1948 memo from a field officer in Ben Shemen to the Israeli Custodian of Abandoned Properties (Israeli State Archives document 15a/49/27/12), from which the 'Men of Battalion 89' quote is also taken.

The crossing of the front lines by Arab villagers back to their old lands is documented in kibbutz and state archives cited by Benny Morris in 'The Harvest of 1948 and the Creation of the Palestinian Refugee Problem,' pp. 239–56 of *1948 and After*. The 'must be destroyed' quote from Yadin is on p. 248; 'additional 1,000 dunams' is on p. 255; 'Every enemy field' is on p. 248.

The Cizling quote is taken from an Israeli cabinet meeting of July 21, 1948, as cited by Segev in *1949*, p. 31.

The continuing refugee crisis in mid-September is described in a report from the American Officers Consul General and sent by telegram from Jerusalem on September 25, 1948. The amount and type of nations' contributions to the relief efforts is from the September 17 report cited earlier.

Bernadotte's advocacy of a division of Palestine between Israel and Transjordan is documented in appendix C of Abu Nowar's *The Jordan-Israeli War: 1948–1951*, pp. 451–55.

Bernadotte's assassination is described by Glubb on p. 182 of *A Soldier with the Arabs* and by Sprinzak in *Brother Against Brother*, pp. 40–48. Sprinzak also details Shamir's involvement and the planning of the operation, describing it (p. 42) as 'the result of a long and careful plan.' The Stern Gang detentions are described by Herzog on p. 88 of *The Arab-Israeli Wars*. See also Avishai, *The Tragedy of Zionism*, p. 183. Accusations of truce violations are found in Herzog (p. 88) and Mohamed Heikal's *Secret Channels*, p. 97.

The need for thousands of tents and blankets was mentioned in the September 25, 1948, telegram from the American consul. The story of refugees lighting fires in their tents comes from Yahya's *Palestinian Refugees: 1948–1998 (An Oral History)*, p. 45.

Recollections of the early Khairi abodes in Gaza come from interviews with Bashir and Nuha Khairi. The Gaza figures of population and density and the 'hardly surprising' quote come from the September 28, 1951, 'Report of the Director of the United Nations Relief and Works Agency for Palestine Refugees in the Near East' (General Assembly official records, sixth session, supplement no. 16, A/1905), available on the UNISPAL Web site (United Nations Information System on the Question of Palestine, online at domino.un.org/unispal.nsf).

Recollections of 'constant shelling' are from interviews with Bashir. Incursions are mentioned from an Israeli perspective by Gelber (Palestine 1948, pp. 212–13) and from an Arab point of view by Heikal (Secret Channels, p. 81). Yezid Sayigh's *Armed Struggle and the Search for State* examines the political rivalries among Arab states, especially between Egypt and King Abdullah of Jordan, on pp. 13–16. Sayigh mentions Abdullah's ambitions and his April 1950 'Act of Union' between Jordan and the West Bank (that is, annexation of the West Bank) on pp. 41–42; Heikal discusses this from an Egyptian perspective in *Secret Channels*, pp. 82–86.

Sayigh discusses the formation of UNRWA on p. 4 and p. 43 of *Armed Struggle and the Search for State*. The materials of the camp structures as well as the rations are described in the 'Report to the Director of the United Nations,' cited previously.

Ahmad's and Zakia's work was described by Nuha and Bashir, who recalled the work-for-rations barter arrangement.

The time and manner of Sheikh Mustafa's death was recalled by Khanom Khairi and verified by Bashir. The preparation of his body under Islamic custom, and the difficulty of doing so in exile, is verified by Muslim scholar Hatem Bazian of UC-Berkeley, who adds:

It is rather difficult for a family not to be able to directly be engaged in preparing the body for the funeral since it is part of Islamic practices that the men of the family are to oversee and participate in washing the dead body and then help in the process of wrapping. Also, the family can see the dead body before the washing takes place as well as offer prayers and recite Qur'an at that time. Also, immediate family members at this time might want to make sure that the body is sprayed with the favorite perfume, so much so that some people write in their wills what type to be used in keeping with the example of the Prophet. All these must have been a source of pain to the family.

The armistice agreements are mentioned by Gelber, p. 298, and Sayigh, p. 4 and p. 58. Abdullah's assassination is mentioned in Heikal, pp. 85–86, and Glubb, pp. 277–78.

The 'shabby and ragged' quote comes from the previously mentioned UN 'Report to the Director.'

The conditions and routines of the Gaza schools, and the schooling in shifts, were recalled by Bashir, Nuha, and Ghiath

Khairi. The 'Palestine is ours' poem appears in A. L. Tibawi's article, 'Visions of the Return: The Palestine Arab Refugees in Arabic Poetry and Art,' *Middle East Journal*, Vol. 17, no. 5. Late Autumn 1963, pp. 507-526. The reality of right of return transforming into a long-term dream was described by Bashir. The frustration of the refugees and the 'irritable and unstable' quote are from the 1951 UN 'Report to the Director.' The Israeli 'doing the refugees a disservice' quote is cited in Daniel Dishon, *Middle East Record* 5 (1969-1970): 399.

The frustration of the Palestinians under Egyptian control is documented by Sayigh, pp. 14-15 and p. 44. The growth of banned political groups can be understood in Sayigh, pp. 49-51, and in Sara Roy's *The Gaza Strip: The Political Economy of De-Development*, p. 69. The 1951 UN 'Report to the Director' is the source of the 'demonstrations and small riots' quote. Roy (p. 69) is a source for the Sharon attack on el-Bureij refugee camp. Roy describes fifty killed; other accounts range from nineteen (*Al-Ahram Weekly*, August 21-31, 2005) to forty-three (Azmi Bishara in Arabic Media Internet Network, September 4, 2003 (http://www.amin.org/eng/azmi_bishara/2003/sept04.html). Sharon describes the Bureij raid on p. 273 of Benny Morris's *Israel's Border Wars: 1949-1956*. Sayigh (pp. 61-62) and Shlaim (*The Iron Wall*, pp. 123-29) cover general tensions between Egypt, Israel, and the Gaza Palestinians.

The hope in Nasser was expressed by Bashir; Nasser's background, including his roots as the son of a postal worker, are discussed by Heikal on pp. 88-90. Nasser and pan-Arabism are discussed by Sayigh, pp. 29-33, and Heikal, pp. 110-11.

Heikal, a close aide to Nasser, relays a fascinating and little-known part of the story: the near intervention of Albert Einstein. 'Einstein felt sorry for Palestinians who had been dispossessed by the Jews, just as he had been by the Nazis,' Heikal wrote.

He asked me to convey a message to the Egyptian leadership [Nasser] expressing his wish to serve as a catalyst for peace . . . The message was delivered as requested and discussed within Nasser's inner circle. Einstein's stature and the way he framed his approach made a negative reply difficult, but the taboo [against Arab leaders' recognition of Israel] was overwhelming in its power. The only solution was to make no reply, with all the discourtesy which silence implied. (*Secret Channels*, pp. 94–97)

Chapter 7

This chapter was built from interviews with the original Israeli inhabitants of Ramla; from founding documents of Israeli Ramla provided by city manager Yonatan Tubali; from the *Israel Government Year Book* for 1950 and its vast storehouse of state figures and official declarations; from 1948 and 1949 military reports housed in the Israeli State Archives; from secondary sources such as Meron Benvenisti's *Sacred Landscapes*, which rely on archival material; and from personal recollections and family oral histories, as conveyed in more than a dozen interviews with longtime residents of Ramla, especially Dalia.

The date of November 14, 1948, is on a handwritten list of the first Jewish families to arrive in Ramla provided to me by Yonatan Tubali, Ramla city manager, and confirmed by Moshe Melamed, former Israeli ambassador to Mexico, who was twelve years old when he arrived in Ramla on November 14, 1948 with his family. Melamed remembers being in one of 'two or three' buses to arrive that day. However, there may have been more buses; Yablonka, on p. 24 of *Survivors of the Holocaust*, cites 'Reports of Military Administration Ramlah and Lydda' in describing 'the arrival in Ramlah of a group of 300 people' on November 14. The makeup of the early immigrants is listed by

NOTES FOR PAGES 166-193

Yablonka on p. 24 and confirmed in an interview with Tubali. Dalia is certain that she and her parents were in that first group.

The Jewish Agency's early presence in Ramla was recalled in numerous interviews, including with Melamed:

[The Jewish Agency] told us, Here is Ramla. Every family gets one room in a house. My parents left me with the luggage next to the bus. And they said, We'll go to look for a house. I stayed on the street with the luggage, and my parents came back fifteen to twenty minutes later and they said, This is your room . . .

It is highly likely that Dalia's parents, arriving with the same group, underwent the same process, and Dalia confirmed this from family history.

It is possible that Moshe and Sofia would have heard fighting between Israelis and Egyptians to the south of Ramla, according to Melamed; during this time, the Israelis were gaining the upper hand in fighting with the Egyptians over the Negev, and Egyptian forces were increasingly confined to defending a small slice of land known as the Gaza Strip. (See Gelber's *Palestine 1948*, pp. 199–219.)

State supplies provided to the early immigrants were recalled in interviews with Tubali, Levy, Melamed, and others. A broader sense of the austerity measures can be found in the 1950 *Israel Government Year Book* (English-language edition), pp. 198–202. The 'custodian' office responsibilities are described in the 1950 *Year Book*, p. 134. Dalia recalled living on 'K.B. Street' and the fact that her parents had a signed agreement with the state; such agreements are confirmed on p. 134 of the 1950 *Year Book*. The role of 'naming committees' is described in detail by Meron Benvenisti in *Sacred Landscapes*, pp. 11–27, and in correspondence from Melamed to me.

The items hauled away in trucks are listed in Israeli State Archives document 15a/49/27/12. The quote about belongings of 'absentee owners' being 'liquidated' is from p. 134 of the 1950 *Year Book*.

The children's experience was recalled by Moshe Melamed.

Work in the early years of Israeli Ramla was described in numerous interviews in Ramla, including with Mati Braun, Labib Qulana, M. Levy, Esther Pardo, and Melamed, who would soon find work, at age fourteen, as a bank clerk. The difficulty of making the harvest is described by Benvenisti in *Sacred Landscapes*, p. 164.

The figures on jobs and the kinds of work and businesses established by Jewish immigrants to Ramla come from hand-written records unearthed by Yonatan Tubali.

One prominent Israeli writer who reviewed the manuscript cautioned me: 'I would avoid [using] Arab ghetto and any other alluded comparison to the persecution of the Jews' during the Holocaust. However, the term *sakne* has been widely used in Ramla and elsewhere by Israelis since at least 1949 and understood to be interchangeable with the word *ghetto*, and thus I am using it here.

Dalia vividly remembers the image of steaming bowls of soup being left behind by the fleeing Arabs.

The laws and ministries forged during the first Knesset are listed in the *Israel Government Year Book* for 1950 on pp. 59–71.

Ben-Gurion's 'four-year plan' was announced in the July 12, 1949, edition of the *Palestine Post*. His 'ingathering' quote comes from the 1950 *Year Book*, p. 29. The figures of Bulgarian Jews who emigrated and those who stayed vary slightly. Chary, one of the world's authorities on Bulgarian Jews, uses a total figure of forty-seven thousand; others say forty-eight thousand or even fifty thousand. Some figures suggest that only three thousand Jews remained in Bulgaria. Whatever the numbers, the speed and volume of the Jewish exodus from Bulgaria was astonishing even to those who planned and executed it. On April 11, 1949, Fred Baker, the JDC director for Bulgaria, wrote to European headquarters in Paris: 'Over a six months period 35,000 persons emigrated plus 7,000 persons prior to Octover [*sic*] 1948. It would appear that the maximum of 4,000 Jews will remain in Bulgaria. I think that you will agree that it was impossible to foresee this gigantic emigration movement in a relatively short span of time.'

The pressure on Ramla for work was underscored to me by Avraham Shmil, longtime director of the Ramla office of the Histadrut labor federation. The demonstration in Tel Aviv is mentioned in Segev's *1949*, p. 131. The criminal court and its first defendants are mentioned in a July 13, 1949, article in the *Palestine Post*. The Ministry of Police quote comes from the 1950 *Year Book*, p. 183.

The changing of the street names was recalled by Mohammad Taji, a lifelong resident of Ramla and one of the few Muslims in the city whose family did not flee in 1948.

The minutes of the first City Council meeting, which include the figure of 1,300 Arabs, were provided by Tubali. The POW status of the Arab men of Ramla and Lydda is described in interviews with Mohammad Taji, Labib Qulana, and Michail Fanous, all Arabs of Ramla, and is recalled in Fouzi el-Asmar's memoir, *To Be an Arab in Israel*, p. 23.

The plowing under or other destruction of the Arab fields and groves is described in detail by Morris on pp. 239–56 of *1948 and After*, and by Benvenisti, *Sacred Landscapes*, p. 165.

The letter from 'S. Zamir' comes from the Israeli State Archives (RL 5/297, September 15, 1948) and was translated by Ian Dietz. The Arabs' confinement under martial law has been previously sourced above; see Segev's *1949*, pp. 47–51, and

Nadia Hijab's *Citizens Apart: A Portrait of Palestinians in Israel*, pp. 30–33. The desire to 'transfer' additional Arabs can be seen in a meeting of the secretariat of the ruling Mapai party (the precursor to the current-day Labor Party), quoted by Segev on pp. 46–47 of *1949*, where the 'fifth column' fears are also mentioned. For more on 'transfer' as a political and military strategy, see 'Yosef Weitz and the Transfer Committees, 1948–1949' in Morris's *1948 and After*, pp. 103–58, and Nur Masalha's *The Expulsion of the Palestinians: The Concept of 'Transfer' in Zionist Political Thought, 1882–1948*. A leading figure was Weitz, who wrote in his diary in 1940, 'It must be clear that there is no room for both peoples in this country . . . After the Arabs are transferred, the country will be wide open for us' (Masalha, p. 131). Eight years later, as the powerful leader of a 'Transfer Committee' and the head of the lands department for the Jewish National Fund, Weitz would advocate for additional 'transfers.' (See examples in the Galilee and Negev cited by Morris, p. 146.) Others in the government, however, argued against this, and many of the remaining Arabs were allowed to stay.

The takeover of Arab lands is described in Morris's *1948 and After* (see, for example, p. 143) and in Segev on pp. 77–78. On pp. 80–82, Segev mentions the concept of 'present absentees.'

The three letters from Arab landowners come from the Central Zionist Archives.

The details on rationing and the role of the Ministry of Supply and Rationing come from the *Israel Government Year Book* for 1950, pp. 198–203, and was corroborated by the Eshkenazis' experience. The *Year Book* (p. 199) describes 'a severance from former sources of supply – the markets of the British Empire . . .'

The Egyptian restrictions in the Suez are mentioned on p. 220

of J. C. Hurewitz's *The Historical Context for Suez 1956: The Crisis and Its Consequences.*

Dalia's memory of her early education about Arabs is corroborated by a review of Israeli school curriculum in *The Arab-Israeli Conflict in Israeli History Textbooks, 1948-2000,* by Elie Podeh, pp. 102-10.

Nasser's appeal as third world leader and a leader of the Arab Nation is discussed in Sayigh's *Armed Struggle and the Search for State,* pp. 27-33. The Suez conflict is described in Erskin Childers's *The Road to Suez,* especially pp. 125-280; Heikal's *Secret Channels,* pp. 100-14; and Shlaim's *The Iron Wall,* pp. 169-78, which analyzed the secret agreement between Israel, France, and Britain to attack Egypt and eliminate Nasser as a perceived threat to their various interests.

The geopolitical background for the conflict, with its involvement in superpower politics and the fading imperial powers in Europe, is worth exploring in some detail:

In 1955, Nasser had sought U.S. backing for his country's massive modernization project, the Aswan High Dam (Sayigh, p. 26). In the meantime, both Israel and Egypt had begun a race to arm themselves: Israel with weapons from France; Egypt from the Soviet Union's client state Czechoslovakia, after its request to the Americans was turned down (Sayigh, p. 19; Morris, *Border Wars,* p. 282). After Egypt formally recognized the People's Republic of China, the United States, led by the cold war secretary of state John Foster Dulles, withdrew its support for the Aswan Dam (Sayigh, p. 26; Heikal, pp. 108-13). Nasser had responded swiftly by nationalizing the British-built Suez Canal, the vital link carved between Africa and Asia, and declaring that revenues from the passage of ships would from now on be used to finance the dam (Heikal, *Secret Channels,* p. 110). Nasser also closed the Straits of Tiran, which represented Israel's only sea link to the Red Sea and Africa.

The Israeli attack in October 1956 was part of a secret plan with leaders of Britain and France, which came to light many years later, to destabilize Nasser and destroy his pan-Arab ambitions; reassert colonial authority by seizing the canal and opening the Straits of Tiran; and, according to some analysts, expand Israel's territory across the Sinai all the way to the Gulf of Suez – in other words, to recarve the physical and political map of the Middle East (Shlaim, pp. 172-84; Sayigh, p. 26; Heikal, p. 112; Herzog, *The Arab-Israeli Wars*, pp. 117-24).

The arrival of more 'Oriental Jews' in 1956 was largely the result of political tensions and violence within Arab nations. An Arab representative, Heykal Pasha, warned the UN General Assembly in 1947 that the creation of a Jewish state 'might endanger a million Jews living in the Moslem countries,' and in fact such violence came to pass, resulting in subsequent flight to Israel. In some cases, however, the exodus was aided by Zionist operations in the Arab countries. For example, a series of bombings in Alexandria, Egypt, in 1954 involving an Israeli espionage operation and later dubbed the 'Lavon affair' stirred outrage and in some cases mob attacks against Egyptian Jews. (See David Hirst, *The Gun and the Olive Branch*, pp. 290-96; Heikal, pp. 106-07; and 'The Lavon Affair,' by Doron Geller, www.jewishvirtuallibrary.org/jsource/History/lavon.html.) Especially after Suez, many Israelis preferred to see the flight of Jews from Arab lands, coupled with the flight of Palestinians in 1948, as an 'exchange of populations' (Israel Gefen interview, June 2004). Some evidence suggests that Zionists staged events to encourage their flight. On January 14, 1951, a hand grenade exploded outside a Baghdad synagogue; later, U.S. intelligence sources and Iraqi Jews themselves would blame Zionists. See, for example, the article by Iraqi Jew Naeim Giladi ('The Jews of Iraq') in *The Link* 31, no. 2, 1998. Another source is former CIA officer Wilber Crane Eveland's *Ropes of Sand*, pp. 48-49.

The 1958 demonstration was recalled by Avraham Shmil, the retired director of the Ramla office of the Histadrut labor federation. Shmil also described the living conditions for many *mizrahi* Jews, their frustrations in finding jobs, the tensions with Ashkenazi Jews, and the pressure he applied on Israel's labor secretary. The virtual taboo on *mizrahis'* listening to classical Arabic music was discussed by Israeli musicologist Yoav Kutner in an interview.

The 'BOULDER-STREWN' quote from the JNF comes from an advertisement in the *Israel Year Book* of 1950, p. 463.

The destruction of the Arab villages is documented from multiple sources. As this may be less familiar to Western readers, documentation here is especially rigorous, starting with Meron Benvenisti's extensive section in *Sacred Landscapes*, pp. 165–67. Another key source is Aharon Shai of the Hebrew University of Jerusalem, whose research in the archives of the Israel Archeological Survey Society documents an extensive program conducted in conjunction with the Israel Lands Administration to demolish abandoned Arab villages. Shai's article 'The Fate of Abandoned Arab Villages in Israel on the Eve of the Six-Day War and Its Immediate Aftermath,' appeared in *Katedra*, no. 105, September 2002, published by Yad Ben Zvi, an Israeli think tank named after the country's second president. Shai's article describes how the Archeological Society 'was for all practical purposes employed by the ILA in its efforts to clear the country of deserted villages. Its officials surveyed the villages intended for destruction . . . Most of the abandoned Arab villages inhabited until 1948 and abandoned in the course of the War of Independence . . . disappear[ed] . . . as a result of a clear and well-designed plan originating with the ILA.' (An English-language abstract of the article is available at http://www.ybz.org.il/?ArticleID=372.)

Other sources include Sharif Kanaana, 'The Eradication of the

Arab Character of Palestine and the Process of Judaization That Accompanied It,' as cited by Benvenisti, (*Sacred Landscapes*, p. 263). Also see Morris (*1948 and After*, p. 122), who quotes Yosef Weitz ordering two settlement officials 'to determine in which villages we will be able to settle our people, and which should be destroyed.' One of those officials, Asher Bobritzky, would later report (Morris, p. 125) 'orders' to accelerate the destruction of the villages. Segev quotes Aharon Cizling, a cabinet minister, describing 'an order to destroy forty villages.' On 'bombing' of villages, see Benvenisti, p. 162; for 'tractors,' see Morris, *1948 and After*, p. 123; reference to 'bulldozers' and army demolition crews comes from my telephone interview with Shlomo Shaked of Kibbutz Gezer based on his eyewitness account. See also *Ha'aretz*, April 4, 1967, which quotes Moshe Dayan as saying, 'There is not a single Jewish village in the country that has not been built on the site of an Arab village.'

The Sabra discussion comes largely from Oz Almog's *Sabra: The Creation of the New Jew* and from interviews with Moshe Melamed and former Knesset member Victor Shemtov. The definition of *tzabar* and the 'elect son' quote are Almog, p. 104. See also Amos Elon's *The Israelis*, pp. 227–28. The serialized novel by Moshe Shamir was recalled by Shemtov, at the time an editor of a Bulgarian-language newspaper in Israel that was tied to the leftist Zionist Mapam Party. Shemtov's 'wash off that old Jew' quote comes from an interview, in his Jerusalem home in June 2004. The Sabra 'uniform' was recalled in numerous interviews, including with Melamed, and is mentioned in *Sabra*, p. 212; additional details can be seen in the permanent exhibit of the Museum of Ramla.

The shame of the Holocaust vis-à-vis Sabra identity is also discussed by Shemtov and in Yablonka's *Survivors of the Holocaust*. The 'difficult human matter' quote is in Yablonka, p. 65; Ben-Gurion's 'human dust' remark comes from Almog,

p. 87; the 'pathetic and helpless people' quote is in Yablonka, pp. 30–31. The attitudes of some Ashkenazi leaders toward some *mizrahi* is well documented by Segev in *1949*, especially pp. 155–94.

The immigrant labels (*'yeke'* and so on) were recalled by several longtime Ramla residents, including Esther Pardo, Yona Sirius, Labib Qulana, and Ya'acov Haran, in interviews, and by Moshe Melamed in correspondence with me.

The disappearance of the tent camps by the mid-1960s was confirmed in the interview with Shmil; Ramla's gritty reputation of the day was recalled by Ramla-born Israeli actor Moni Moshonov and Israeli musicologist Yoav Kutner.

The campaign of the Israeli Lands Administration and the quote from Eshkol are from Benvenisti, *Sacred Landscapes*, pp. 167–68. The position of Nasser in the mid-1960s is described by Heikal (*Secret Channels*, pp. 122–26) and Sayigh (*Armed Struggle and the Search for State*, pp. 132–42), who also describes (pp. 132–37) the role of the PLO and the ANM.

The seeming inevitability of war was recalled by Dalia and during various interviews with the Khairi family.

Chapter 8

This chapter is based on personal and historical accounts of the 1967 war between Israel and the Arab states, known in the West mainly as the Six Day War. Family recollections were gathered in multiple interviews with Dalia and with Bashir, Nuha, and Ghiath Khairi. Historical accounts from 1967, and the years leading up to the war, come from a wide range of perspectives: from the Israeli military point of view, Chaim Herzog's *The Arab-Israeli Wars*; from an analysis of Israeli politics, based on minutes of cabinet meetings and other original documents, Avi Shlaim's *The Iron Wall: Israel and the Arab World*; from an Egyptian perspective, *Secret Channels: The Inside Story of the Arab-*

Israeli Peace Negotiations, by Mohamed Heikal, who was a key aide to Gamal Abdel Nasser; from a Jordanian military and political perspective, Samir Mutawi's *Jordan in the 1967 War*, which is based largely on interviews with key players in Jordan, including King Hussein; from a broad political analysis of the war and how it affected the Palestinian liberation movement, Yezid Sayigh's *Armed Struggle and the Search for State*.

Key portions of the narrative describing the buildup to war rely on declassified U.S. documents from November 1966 to June 1967. These documents, which include minutes of cabinet meetings, CIA intelligence advisories, and telegrams between Israeli, Jordanian, and Egyptian leaders and American officials, are housed at the LBJ Library at the University of Texas at Austin. Many of the documents have been assembled in volumes XVIII and XIX of the *Foreign Relations of the United States 1964-1968*, which are housed at the library and also available online at http://www.state.gov/r/pa/ho/frus/johnsonlb/xix/ and http://www.state.gov/www/about_state/history/vol_xviii/index.html (hereinafter FRUS Vol. XVIII or XIX). For an additional analysis of these events, which draws on many of the same documents, see Stephen Green's *Taking Sides*, pp. 195-211.

The departure of Ramallah Christians, which followed an earlier wave of immigration to the United States that began well before the 1948 war, is confirmed by Palestinian scholar Naseer Aruri. The Ramallah diaspora is now so vast that the list of Ramallah families in the United States alone is contained in a published directory of 237 pages. The description of the political position of the 'host' governments, UNRWA, and the refugees is based on years of interviews with refugees and other Palestinian and Israeli analysts. Bashir's political views in 1967 were in line with those of many Palestinians (see Sayigh, pp. 95-154, for his analysis of the development of Palestinian factions prior to the war).

For more on Nasser as a hero of the Arab masses, see Heikal, pp. 100-38, and Bassam Abu-Sharif, in *Best of Enemies*. Reference to the nonaligned movement is in Heikal, pp. 108-10, and its relationship to the Palestinians is in Sayigh, p. 312, p. 332, and p. 690.

The Palestinian urgency to confront Israel is documented in Sayigh, p. 122 and p. 124. Indeed, at its secret plant in the Negev desert at Dimona, Israel was developing such weapons, though this would not become an 'official secret' for years. See Oren, in *Six Days of War*, pp. 75-76, and Stephen Green, *Taking Sides*, p. 152, for more on Israel's nuclear development and Arab reaction to it. Oren, on p. 120, writes of an Egyptian overflight of the secret nuclear project at Dimona, and on pp. 75-76, he cites Nasser's 1964 remark that if Israel began developing nuclear weapons capabilities, it 'would be a cause for war, no matter how suicidal.' Nasser did not repeat this threat, nor did he ever cite Dimona 'as a motive for his decisions in May,' but Oren argues that Israeli fear of an Egyptian attack on Dimona was a major catalyst for war. Morris, in *Righteous Victims*, p. 307, concurs: 'The Egyptian command on May 24-25 briefly considered and planned a preemptive air offensive against Israeli targets – including the Dimona nuclear plant . . . Nasser countermanded the order on May 26 . . .'

Discussion of Habash, the ANM, and Nasser is in Sayigh, pp. 71-80. Habash's experience in Lydda in 1948 comes from 'Taking Stock: An Interview with George Habash,' *Journal of Palestine Studies* 28, 1 (Autumn 1998): 86-101, and Sayigh, p. 71.

Nasser's stance on Palestine is documented by Sayigh, p. 78 and p. 131, and by Hirst in *The Gun and the Olive Branch*, p. 401, who quotes from Nasser's speech to the Palestine National Council in June 1965: 'If we are today not ready for defense, how can we talk about an offensive?'

The 'special forces' training came from an interview with Bassam Abu-Sharif, former member of Habash's Popular Front for the Liberation of Palestine and coauthor of *Best of Enemies*. Additional details were provided in an interview with another former PFLP member no longer living in the Middle East.

The emergence of Fatah and of Arafat and Abu Jihad is discussed in Sayigh, pp. 80–87 and pp. 119–23. The New Year's 1965 operation is described in Michael Oren's *Six Days of War* as a 'fiasco' (p. 1); and by Sayigh (p. 107) as a 'lacklustre start'; nevertheless, Sayigh writes, 'New Year's Day 1965 was subsequently to be celebrated by all Palestinian organizations as the launch of the armed struggle.'

Tensions over water as part of the buildup to war and Arab discussions around diversion are described by Heikal (p. 121), Oren (p. 23), Herzog (p. 147), Shlaim, p. 232), and my own series, *Troubled Waters*, for NPR in 1997. For a more detailed analysis of the issue, see this case study prepared by American University's Inventory of Conflict & Environment: www.american.edu/projects/mandala/TED/ice/JORDAN.HTM.

Fatah's attacks are described by Sayigh on pp. 119–22, which indicates that most Fatah targets were military and industrial, and that Israeli casualties during this period were low. This is corroborated by a timeline from Israel's Ministry of Foreign Affairs (http://www.mfa.gov.il/MFA/Facts+About+Israel/Israel+in+Maps/1948-1967-+Major+Terror+Attacks.htm). Several of the Israeli casualties were due to explosions when Israeli vehicles drove over land mines planted by Palestinian guerrillas. The Samu raid of November 13, 1966, is described by Oren (pp. 34–35), Sayigh (p. 138), and Shlaim (p. 233), who writes, 'Inside Jordan the effects of the raid were highly destabilizing.' The death toll of twenty-one soldiers comes from Sayigh; Oren mentions fifteen and Shlaim 'dozens.'

Verification of the U.S. condemnation of the Samu raid is

contained in a November 13, 1966 State Department telegram to the American Embassy in Tel Aviv (*Foreign Relations of the United States 1964-1968, Volume XVIII Arab-Israeli Dispute, 1964-67*, ([hereinafter FRUS Vol. XVIII, document number 332, online at http://www.state.gov/www/ about_state/ history/vol_xviii/index.html]). The Rostow 'out of proportion' memo to LBJ is at the same location, document 333. LBJ's November 23 telegram to King Hussein in the LBJ Library archives, 'National Security File, Mideast Crisis, NSC History,' Vol. 1, Tab 10. The CIA 'Special Memorandum' is in FRUS Vol. XVIII, document 338.

The political fallout from Samu is described by Sayigh on pp. 140-42; Heikal (p. 125) reports that 'many Palestinians called for immediate war against Israel.' The crackdown in Jordan is described by Mutawi (*Jordan in the 1967 War*) on p. 80 and by Sayigh on p. 139; Sayigh refers to 'hundreds' of Fatah members in Jordanian prisons in the early part of 1967. The unrest in Jordan and U.S. military aid are mentioned by Herzog on p. 147. Mutawi quotes the 'imperialist agent' and 'ally of Zionism' remarks on p. 83.

April 1967 tensions in the Golan Heights are described in Herzog (pp. 147-48) and Oren (p. 46), and the dogfight is described by Shlaim (pp. 234-36) and Mutawi (p. 85). Shlaim, the Israeli history professor at Oxford, argues that contrary to popular belief in Israel, 'many of the firefights' in the DMZ 'were deliberately provoked by Israel.' Moshe Dayan, in an interview published posthumously in *Ma'ariv*, described how many of the clashes were provoked by Israel (see Shlaim, pp. 235-36).

Nasser's embarrassment over the Israeli victorious dogfight over Syria is indicated by Herzog, p. 148, and Mutawi, p. 85. The response by King Hussein and the Jordan Radio comments are in Mutawi, pp. 85-86. Rabin's threats to topple the Syrian regime came on May 11 or 12 (Shlaim, p. 236; Hirst, p. 342).

This was a significant incident in ratcheting up Arab fears. According to Charles W. Yost, former U.S. ambassador to Syria, 'Israeli public statement between May 11 and 13 . . . may well have been the spark that ignited the long accumulating tinder' (*Foreign Affairs*, January 1968, p. 310). That the closure of the Straits of Tiran would be considered an act of war is made clear by Herzog (p. 147), who fought in the war on the Israeli side. The closure represented more of a political threat and a matter of sovereignty, than an economic peril for Israel: The vast majority of Israel's sea trade was conducted through its Mediterranean ports, not from Eilat in the south.

Whether or not Nasser wanted war in 1967 remains a con-tentious dispute among historians. Nasser's public statements sent a bellicose message to Israel and the world, much like his decision to close the Straits of Tiran (Mutawi, p. 95), but as Shlaim writes in *The Iron Wall*, p. 237, 'There is general agree-ment among commentators that Nasser neither wanted nor planned to go to war with Israel. What he did was to embark on an exercise in brinkmanship that was to carry him over the brink.' Yost, in his 1968 *Foreign Affairs* article, wrote that 'there is no evidence – quite the contrary – that either Nasser or the Israeli Government . . . wanted and sought a war at this juncture.' In a May 12, 1967 background briefing, according to Hirst (p. 343), Aharon Yariv, director of Israeli military intelligence, told reporters, 'I would say that as long as there is not an Israeli invasion into Syria extended in area and time, I think the Egyptians will not come in seriously . . . they will do so only if there is no other alternative. And to my eyes no alter-native means that we are creating such a situation that it is impossible for the Egyptians not to act because the strain on their prestige will be unbearable.'

The specific numbers of troops massing near the common border at the edge of the Sinai Peninsula is also contentious.

Herzog (*The Arab-Israeli Wars*, p. 149 and p. 154) and Oren (p. 63, citing IDF intelligence) suggest close to one hundred thousand Egyptian troops were in Sinai. Israeli general Matitiahu Peled later indicated that the troop concentrations were lower than the figures Herzog and Oren used (Hirst, p. 337).

U.S. officials were also highly skeptical of the one hundred thousand figure. Perhaps most compelling on this point, and generally regarding U.S. diplomatic activity in May and June 1967, and military capabilities of Middle Eastern nations, are the exchange found in documents in the LBJ Library, many of which are housed in FRUS Vol. XIX (available online at http://www.state.gov/www/about_state/history/vol_xviii/index.html). The May 26 CIA memo is in that collection, document 79. Battle's 'slightly insane quote' comes from a summary of a May 24 National Security Council meeting, FRUS Vol. XIX, document 54. The U.S. estimates of fifty thousand Egyptian troops, repeated in at least two separate CIA memoranda: May 25, FRUS Vol. XIX, document 61; and May 26, 'Military Capabilities of Israel and the Arab States,' from 'National Security File–Country File, Middle East Crisis, CIA Intelligence Memoranda,' Folder 3, from which the analysis of Israel's 'political gambit' also comes. Rostow's characterization of Israel's estimates of one hundred thousand Egyptian troops as 'highly disturbing' come from his May 25 'memorandum for the President,' from 'National Security File, Mideast Crisis NSC History,' Vol. 1, Tab 42, document 32. The CIA assessment of Israel's abilities to fight and/or defend various fronts comes from a May 23 memorandum (FRUS Vol. XIX, document 44). Yet another CIA memorandum, on May 26, assessed the 'lack of cohesiveness on the Arab side' and the depletion of Nasser's forces by thirty-five thousand troops ('Military Capabilities of Israel and the Arab States,' 'National Security File–Country File,

Middle East Crisis, CIA Intelligence Memoranda,' Folder 3). The conversation between Abba Eban, McNamara, and LBJ, including McNamara's telling Eban of the conclusions of 'three separate intelligence groups' that the Egyptian Sinai deployments were defensive, and LBJ's 'whip the hell out of them' quote, is summarized in the May 26 'Memorandum of Conversation' (FRUS Vol. XIX, document 77). The Katzenbach 'mop up the Arabs' quote comes from his oral history interview for the LBJ Library (interview number 3, December 11, 1968). For additional background on Eban's trip to Washington, see Heikal (p. 127), Green (pp. 198-204), and Shlaim (pp. 239-240).

King Hussein's concerns about 'USG' favoring Israel were delivered as an 'oral message' to the U.S. ambassador in Amman and cabled to the 'highest USG authorities' in Washington ('National Security File, Mideast Crisis, NSC History,' Vol. 1, Tab 36). The same file, Tab 38, contains Secretary of State Dean Rusk's May 26 'Memorandum for the President,' which notes Israel's conclusion that Egyptian and Syrian attacks were imminent, and Rusk's observation that 'our intelligence does not confirm this Israeli estimate.' LBJ's urgent May 27 telegram to Eshkol is in FRUS Vol. XIX, document 86.

Nasser's 'we are ready!' remark is quoted in Mutawi, p. 94. These statements had special meaning for the Israeli public, for whom 'the memory of the Holocaust was a powerful psychological force that deepened the feeling of isolation and accentuated the perception of threat' (Shlaim, p. 238).

Michail Fanous, an Arab of Ramla, confirmed Dalia's recollection of preparations. Additional detail, including the ten thousand graves, comes from Oren, pp. 135-36. The 'push the Jews into the sea' remark is recalled by Dalia and cited to me in many interviews by both Arabs and Israelis. For perceptions of the strength of the Israeli army, see Shlaim, pp. 239-40.

Numerous Arab sources express skepticism that the 'push them into the sea' comments were ever uttered. Heikel (p. 141) suggests this was 'a remarkably successful piece of disinformation.' He recalls that following Indian president Nehru's concerns about the quoted threat, 'a committee consisting of senior officials from Yugoslavia, India and Egypt was set up to sift through all public remarks by Nasser and Egyptian ministers,' and that they found 'no trace of the alleged comment.' Hirst (p. 417) cites British parliamentarian Christopher Mayhew's offer of five thousand British pounds for anyone who could 'produce any statement by an Arab leader which could be described as "genocidal" in intent,' and that 'no statement was produced.' Still, as mentioned above, the 'push into the sea' remarks are specifically recalled by Arabs and Jews I interviewed, and even if the statement was never uttered in those precise words, the threats of Nasser and other Arab leaders toward Israel, and their effects on the Israeli public, are clear enough.

Heikal, p. 128, cites the visit to Nasser by the Soviet ambassador. Mutawi discusses King Hussein's position on pp. 85-121.

The rupture in Eshkol's cabinet is described by Shlaim, pp. 238-41, where he recounts Rabin's twenty-four-hour attack of 'acute anxiety' and his dressing-down by Ben-Gurion, who told Rabin: 'I very much doubt whether Nasser wanted to go to war, and now we are in serious trouble.'

McNamara's conversation with Meir Amit is summarized in the June 'Memorandum for the Record' (FRUS Vol. XIX, document 124). The 'I, Meir Amit' and 'seven days' quotes appear as a footnote in the memorandum, quoting Amit's recollection of the meeting with McNamara at a 1992 conference on the Six Day War. These and other details are also contained in Richard B. Parker's *The Six-Day War: A Retrospective*, (Gainesville,

Florida: University Press of Florida, 1996, p. 139). Nasser's remark to Mayhew is cited in Mutawi on p. 94. His conversation with Robert Anderson, and the upcoming visit of Mohieddin is summarized in two telegrams to LBJ and Rusk that Anderson sent on June 1 and 2 from the U.S. Embassy in Lisbon, Portugal (FRUS Vol. XIX, documents 123 and 129). Walt Rostow, in a note to LBJ four hours after Anderson's June 2 cable arrived, wrote, 'In the light of this picture of Nasser's mind, we must work out most carefully the scenario for talks with Mohieddin . . . It is urgent that we decide whether we should inform the Israelis of this visit. My guess is their intelligence will pick it up. We would be wise to have Sec. Rusk tell [Israeli Ambassador Avraham] Harman,' (FRUS Vol. XIX, document 129, footnote 1).

Nasser's June 2 telegram to President Johnson is in the LBJ Library, 'National Security File, NSC History, Middle East Crisis, May 12-June 19, 1967,' Tab 101. The June 3 CIA memorandum, 'The Current Focus of the Near East Crisis,' is located in 'National Security File, Country File, Middle East Crisis, CIA Intelligence memoranda,' Folder 3).

The Israeli intelligence analysis is quoted by Schleifer in *The Fall of Jerusalem*, pp. 102 and 113.

See Mutawi, pp. 94-96, for more on Nasser's motivation and intentions. He quotes King Hussein and other prominent Jordanians as saying they did not believe Nasser wanted war. Rabin's 'I do not believe Nasser wanted war' quote comes from Hirst, *The Gun and the Olive Branch*, p. 337, and was published in a *Le Monde* article of February 29, 1968. Rabin added: 'The two divisions he sent into Sinai on May 14 would not have been enough to unleash an offensive against Israel. He knew it and we knew it.' Matitiahu Peled, an Israeli general at the time, and later a prominent member of the Israeli peace movement, told *Ma'ariv* in 1972, 'It is notorious that our

General Staff never told the government that the Egyptian military threat represented any danger to Israel or that we were unable to crush Nasser's army, which, with unheard-of foolishness, had exposed itself to the devastating might of our army.' Oren (pp. 92-97, 119-121), unlike most writers on the 1967 war, makes much of 'Operation Dawn,' an alleged plan by Egyptian war minister Amer to strike first against Israel, though he acknowledges that Nasser may not have even known about 'Dawn' until days before it was to be implemented, raising questions as to whether this was a genuine plan. In any case, Oren writes, Nasser scuttled the alleged plan in late May, and it was never implemented.

The 'strong warning' quote comes from Heikal, at the time a Nasser aide, on p. 126.

The start of the war is described by Herzog on pp. 151-53. Herzog mentions 1:45 as the moment the war began; Oren (p. 170) mentions 7:10. Eshkol's message to King Hussein is quoted by Shlaim on p. 244. The scene on the streets of Ramallah was described in various interviews, including with Nicola Akkel, and is corroborated in descriptions in *Homeland*, a collection of Palestinian oral history interviews, p. 62.

The Voice of the Arabs broadcasts emanating from Cairo are described by Mutawi on p. 133 and Oren on p. 178. Bashir recalls hearing such broadcasts on June 5 and his elation that the Arabs were winning. His cousin Ghiath told me the Umm Kolthum story in an interview.

The destruction of the Egyptian air force and the timing of the Israeli attack are described by Herzog on pp. 151-52. The coded message sent from Egypt to Jordan, containing 'completely false information,' is quoted by Mutawi on p. 123.

King Hussein's mistrust of Eshkol and the Israeli promises not to attack are outlined by Mutawi on p. 130. The 'Brother Arabs' quote comes from archival tape provided me by radio archivist Andy Lanset of WNYC in New York. I used this tape in a December 2001 broadcast on the Arab view of the West for the public radio documentary program *American Radio Works*. Ahmad Said's 'Zionist barracks' declaration is quoted in Morris (*Righteous Victims*, p. 310). The attacks and the destruction of Arab air forces are described in multiple sources, including Herzog (p. 171), Oren (pp. 186-95), and Mutawi (p. 129). The explosions in Ramallah on June 5 and 6 are described by numerous sources, including Bashir; Husam Rafeedie in the oral history *Homeland*, p. 63; and Raja Shehadeh's memoir, *Strangers in the House*, pp. 37-47. Herzog (p. 175) mentions the radio transmitter in Ramallah being 'put out of action' and on p. 176 describes the obliteration of the Jordanian infantry troops coming from Jericho. The reports of the Old City being surrounded is in Herzog, p. 176, and Mutawi, p. 134.

The 'rapidly deteriorating' quote from Riad, the Arabs' choices, and the cables and telegrams between Amman and Cairo are described by Mutawi, pp. 138-39, quoting directly from original documents in Arabic.

The fall of Ramallah is described by Bashir and Akkel and in *Strangers in the House* by Shehadeh, who recalls his father's words, whispered as he was 'totally enveloped in a troubled silence':

It's a repeat of 1948 . . . Just like 1948, so much talk and no action, just bravado: We will show the enemy, the Arabs declare, but when the fighting starts they disappear.

The near defenselessness of the Jordanian army and its retreat late on June 6 are depicted by Mutawi on pp. 138-40; however, he also cites an interview with Habes Majali, commander in chief of the Jordanian armed forces, as saying that the reports of Jordanian losses in the West Bank were exaggerated by field commanders. Clearly, though, without air cover the Jordanian army had become essentially unable to defend itself or the residents of the West Bank against the power of the Israel Defense Forces.

The image of white flags in the form of T-shirts and hand-kerchiefs comes from an interview with Nicola Akkel in Ramallah.

The destruction of Imwas, Beit Nuba, and Yalo is described by numerous historians, including Oren on p. 307. Today there is almost no trace of the villages; in their place is 'Canada Park.' A plaque reads:

> The Valley of Springs in Canada Park has been developed through the generosity of Joseph & Feye Tanenbaum, Toronto, Ontario, Canada. Jewish National Fund.

The flight of at least 200,000 Palestinian refugees during and after the 1967 war is one of the lesser-known effects of those six days. Oren makes no mention of it in *Six Days of War*. He writes that the 'Palestinian community' was 'for the most part retained in [its] prewar positions . . .'

Segev, author of a recent book in Hebrew on the 1967 war, wrote me that the figure of displaced Arabs in 1967 was about 250,000, which included Syrian civilians who fled the Golan Heights. Andrew I. Kilgore, former U.S. ambassador to Qatar and publisher of the *Washington Report on Middle East Affairs*, used a figure in March 1990 (www.washingtonreport.org/backissues/0390/9003017.htm) of 200,000 Palestinians displaced. The Israeli government's Ministry of Foreign Affairs (www.mfa.gov.il/MFA/MFAArchive/2000_2009/2000/2/Displaced+Persons+-+1967.htm) acknowledges 'displaced persons' from the 1967 war but does not use a number.

The Permanent Observer Mission of Palestine to the United

Nations, in a 1998 statement, used a figure of 325,000, part of what it called a 'systematic policy of deportation and forced migration.' Sayigh, on p. 174, describes 'the exodus of another 300,000 refugees' after the 1967 war. John Quigley, professor of international law at Ohio State University, cites a figure of 350,000 in *Palestine and Israel: A Challenge to Justice*, a number 'that represented 25 percent of the population' of the West Bank and Gaza Strip.

A September 1967 UN Special Representative's field investigation report estimated that 200,000 left for the East Bank and more were displaced within the West Bank area. The report also documented specific incidents, including home demolitions and intimidation, which led to the flight of the Palestinian population during and after the war. The UN report states that in the West Bank town of Qalqilya, 'three weeks after they left their city, the population was allowed to go back . . . Upon their return they found that out of a total of some 2,000 dwellings approximately 850 had been demolished' (United Nations General Assembly, 'Report of the Secretary-General under General Assembly Resolution 2252 [ES-V] and Security Council Resolution 237 [1967],' September 15, 1967). Oren, on p. 307, states that 'nearly half the houses in Qalqilya were reportedly damaged, though later repaired by Israel.'

The lawyers' strike was recalled by Bashir in a December 2003 interview and corroborated in my correspondence with George Bisharat, author of *Palestinian Lawyers and Israeli Rule: Law and Disorder in the West Bank*, who reviewed relevant sections of this and later chapters for accuracy. Bashir, characteristically modest, would not say that he was a leader of the strike, but Ghiath Khairi insisted that his cousin was indeed '*the* leader.' Bashir's comments to the Israeli colonel are recalled from his memory, as are the figures of eighty lawyers. Bisharat believes the number was closer to fifty. The establishment of military courts is mentioned in the United Nations 'Report of the Special Committee to Investigate Israeli Practices Affecting the Human Rights of the Population of the Occupied Territories,' October 1, 1976.

The quote of 'no reconciliation' comes from Sayigh, *Armed Struggle and the Search for State*, p. 143. Bashir confirmed the sense of clarity and freedom that settled over many Palestinians immediately following the occupation.

The definition of *fedayi* (plural fedayeen) is from Bassam Abu-Sharif in *Best of Enemies*. Abu-Sharif's account of Habash, of joining the PFLP, and of his own father's dismay is on pp. 52-63. His 'eternal foreigner' and 'rather be dead' quotes are on p. 53.

The stories of Palestinians returning to their old homes are too numerous to count; I have heard dozens over the years, and most involve a spontaneous journey across the 'Green Line,' though some travelers indicated they applied for and received permits. In each case, however, it is important to stress that the border was much less defined: not only less defined than it is now, with the construction of the separation wall and fence, but less even than in the 1980s and 1990s, when tensions led to far more checkpoints and patrols between Israel and the occupied territories.

Chapter 9

The notes for this chapter are comparatively short. The chapter relies largely on recollections from Bashir and Dalia as told to me in more than a dozen interviews in 1998, 2003, 2004, and 2005 and as recounted in Bashir's memoir in Arabic (see notes for chapter 1). Ghiath Khairi, Bashir's cousin who also traveled to Ramla that day, provided additional details in interviews in January 2005.

The conversations between Bashir and Dalia, of course, were

not recorded; the quotes come almost entirely from Bashir's memory and Dalia's. There were cases where Dalia did not recall saying something Bashir attributed to her in his memoir or was sure she did not say; in such cases, I either did not include the quote or noted the discrepancy. Such discrepancies are minor, however: Essentially, Bashir and Dalia agree on what happened in the house in Ramla that day and in their subsequent meetings.

Both Bashir and Dalia have reviewed this and other chapters for accuracy. My hope is that I have reflected the spirit of the exchange as accurately and fairly as possible.

Bashir's talk with his family on his return to Ramallah was conveyed in his memoir and in the interviews with me. That conversations like the Khairis' were taking place across old Palestine in 1967 has been conveyed to me in dozens of stories and interviews over my last twelve years traveling through Israel, the West Bank, Gaza, Jordan, and Lebanon. Bashir's return trip with Kamel is conveyed in Bashir's memoir. That the dream of return was as ferocious as ever is evidenced by the political developments in the Palestinian movement after June 1967, which are conveyed in Sayigh's *Armed Struggle in the Search for State*, especially on p. 147, where he describes the 'heyday of the guerillas.'

The description of Arafat comes from multiple sources, including Bassam Abu-Sharif's account in *Best of Enemies*, from which the 'Palestinian spirit' quote comes (p. 58). The analysis of the limitations of cross-border attacks is also discussed by Abu-Sharif on p. 58. Arafat's relaunching of armed struggle is described by Abu-Sharif on pp. 58–59; by Sayigh on pp. 161–64; and by Said K. Aburish, author of *Arafat: From Defender to Dictator*, on pp. 71–77. These accounts, as well as the Web site of Israel's Ministry of Foreign Affairs, indicate that these particular attacks, during this period, rarely resulted in civilian casualties. The legend of 'Abu Amar' is laid out by Abu-Sharif (p. 59, coffee on fire story) and by David Pryce-Jones, a British journalist and author of *The Face of Defeat* (p. 41). Aburish (pp. 82-83) recalls Arafat's slogans and describes how the Fatah leader shaped his keffiyeh in the shape of historic Palestine. 'The exercise took nearly an hour every morning,' Aburish writes:

He donned the American-style sunglasses, which gave him an air of mystery and which he still wore indoors . . . In many photos he carried a stick, an improvised field marshal's baton; not only did it distinguish him from people around him, it was also something which he could use constantly as a symbol of his power and to point out the locations of heroic acts or Israeli atrocities.

For the lawyers' strike and the impact of the occupation on Palestinian attorneys such as Bashir, see George Bisharat's *Palestinian Lawyers and Israeli Rule*, especially pp. 145-61. For the attitudes of Palestinians toward the Israeli annexation of East Jerusalem, see Aburish, pp. 71-72, and Shehadeh, p. 46 and pp. 55-57. Early Israeli settlements in the West Bank are described by Morris in *Righteous Victims*, pp. 331-34. Military Order 145 is mentioned on p. 147; it was implemented in April 1968, according to the Web site of the Israel Law Resource Center.

Bashir recalled his arrest and incarceration of September 1967 in interviews. The wider context of the Israeli counterinsurgency is discussed by Sayigh on p. 180. The 'no reconciliation' quote comes from Sayigh, p. 143. Portions of the text of United Nations Security Council Resolution 242 of November 22, 1967, are taken from the UN Web site (daccess-ods.un.org/TMP/7167138.html).

For Nasser and King Hussein's attitude toward 242, see Sayigh, p. 143. For the attitudes of many Palestinians, including supporters of the popular factions like the PFLP, see Abu-Sharif, pp. 56-63, and Sayigh, p. 229 and p. 252. Sayigh, on p. 167 and p. 170, discusses Israeli arrests of Palestinian guerrillas and supporters; the figure of '1,000-1,250' activists in prison is on p. 172; this figure would rise to 1,750 (p. 203) by the end of 1968.

The emergence of the PFLP with the airport attack, and its tactical failure, is in Sayigh, p. 167; the date is also mentioned by Abu-Sharif (p. 51) as marking the founding of the PFLP, with a 'manifesto' that 'had only one item: the liberation of Palestine from Israeli occupation by means of armed struggle.'

For Palestinian attitudes toward Habash, see Abu-Sharif, pp. 50-51.

Bashir recalled his arrest on September 17, 1967, and a stay of 'one hundred days'; this would have meant his release in late December.

Oz and his colleagues produced *The Seventh Day: Soldiers' Talk About the Six-Day War*, a book aimed at 'recording in permanent form the effect of the Six-Day War on their generation.' The soldiers' stories and quotes are taken from it. Oz's early stance against the occupation is documented by David Remnick in his *New Yorker* article 'The Spirit Level,' November 8, 2004.

The remainder of the chapter – Dalia and Richard's arrival in Ramallah, their reception by the Khairi family, and the encounter between Dalia and Bashir – is recounted according to their memories, as described at the beginning of the notes for this chapter.

Chapter 10

This chapter is based on a combination of eyewitness interviews, memoirs, secondary sources describing the historical and political context of the day, and interviews with various actors among the Palestinian political factions from 1969 to the mid-1980s. Primary interviews were with Dalia, various members of the Khairi family, Israeli veteran Israel Gefen, former members of the PFLP, and Palestinian men who spent time in Israeli prisons in the 1970s and 1980s. The larger political context is understood through Yezid Sayigh's rigorously researched *Armed Struggle and the Search for State*; the feel of the times is vividly conveyed in the interviews with Dalia and in Abu-Sharif's accounts in *Best of Enemies*.

The events at the Supersol were recalled in a series of interviews I did with Israel Gefen in 2004. Gefen, then eighty-two years old, had a memory full of tiny, compelling details including, strikingly, his mission at the Supersol that day: to buy a container of frozen lemon juice. The Supersol itself, as well as an Israeli-built park, parking lot, and nearby West Jerusalem buildings, were built on a burial site and *waqf* land used by Muslims until 1948, according to the Palestinian Authority's Ministry of Information(http://www.minfo.gov.ps/permenant/ English/ Jerusalem/m_%20j_history.htm).

Details from the Supersol bombing are corroborated by clips from the *Jerusalem Post* in its Sunday, February 23, article, '2 Die, 8 Wounded in J'lem Terror Outrage at Supersol.' (A third victim died later.) The explosion occurred at 10:40 A.M.; a second explosion was averted when an army sapper disarmed a biscuit tin full of explosives.

Bashir does not recall the precise day of his arrest, but it appears to have been at the end of February 1969 or perhaps on March 1. A March 2 article in the *Jerusalem Post* announced, 'Supersol Blast Suspects Held in Round-up of 40'; a follow-up article two days later stated, 'It is understood that a Ramallah lawyer, Bashir Khayri, is also among those arrested.' Habash's 'reassurance and security' quote is from Sayigh, p. 216. Bashir, meanwhile, was named (*Post* article March 6, 'Major Terror Gang Seized') as a 'leader of terrorist activities.'

Early PFLP operations are described by Abu-Sharif on pp. 59–63 by Sayigh on pp. 230–32, and by Morris in *Righteous Victims*, pp. 376–80.

Bashir's incarceration was described in separate interviews with Bashir and Nuha Khairi, and additional confirmation of his presence in Israeli prisons comes from Felicia Langer, at the time an Israeli human rights lawyer. While there are no eyewitnesses beyond Bashir himself (and at one point his sister Nuha) to corroborate his torture, what he describes is consistent with the descriptions summarized in Langer's *With My Own Eyes* and with the numerous interviews I did in the summer of 2004 with Palestinian former prisoners. Josef Odeh's description of his daughter's torture, strikingly similar to the Khairis' description of Bashir's torture, was in the *Times* of London investigation of June 19, 1977. His house demolition is documented in a March 11, 1969 article in the *Jerusalem Post*, 'Houses of 9 West Bank Terrorists Demolished.'

More information on the history of torture in Israel, including the findings of the Landau Commission and the subsequent judicial restrictions on torture, can be found on the Web site of B'tselem, the respected Israeli human rights organization (www.btselem.org/english/Torture/ Torture_by_GSS.asp).

The PFLP tactics are described extensively by Sayigh, including on pp. 232–37; Abu-Sharif (pp. 59–60) describes the 'electrifying vision' of the PFLP operations 'master' Wadi Haddad, who was the author of the 'spectaculars.' Abu-Sharif also describes the entrée that fedayeen enjoyed throughout the Arab world. Aburish (pp. 101–07) describes the tensions between Jordan, Israel, and the Palestinian factions in 1969 and 1970; Sayigh does the same on pp. 243–51. The battle of Karama is detailed by Sayigh on pp. 174–79; by Morris

(*Righteous Victims*, pp. 368-370); by Hirst (*The Gun and the Olive Branch*, pp. 411-14); and by Aburish in *Arafat: Defender to Dictator* on pp. 81-83. The idea of transforming a military defeat at Karama into a political victory is explored by Rashid Khalidi in *Palestinian Identity*, p. 197.

Khalidi (p. 197), Aburish (p. 84), and Abu-Sharif (pp. 65-66) all describe the role of Karama in inspiring new recruits and support from the Left. A March 5, 1969, article in the *Jerusalem Post* quoted Habash saying: 'A Vietnamese-type of revolution is the only way . . . by the *kadaheen* (poor toilers) who are ready to fight because they have nothing to lose but those miserable tents they live in.' Habash's slogan, and the 'inferno' quote, appear in Hirst (*The Gun and the Olive Branch*, p. 419 and p. 410, respectively).

The attitude that Israelis were 'soldiers in civilian clothing' came from an interview with Palestinian scholar Naseer Aruri. Habash's 'when we hijack' quote appeared in *Der Stern* in 1970 and is excerpted in numerous U.S. military Web sites. The Israeli crackdown was recalled by Abu Laila in an interview. He also described the growing tensions within the PFLP and with Jordan. Corroboration comes from Sayigh, pp. 243-55, and Aburish, p. 94 and p. 98. The multiple hijacking to 'Revolution Airport' is described by Sayigh on p. 257 and by Abu-Sharif on pp. 80-90. Abu-Sharif recalls consoling a passenger with, 'Don't worry, it's only a hijack. Nobody will be hurt,' as another PFLP operative began attaching plastic explosives to the seats. 'You expect me to be relaxed?' the astonished man shouted at Abu-Sharif. 'Look at that guy! What the hell is he doing?'

The Jordanian military superiority over the Palestinian factions, and the 'state within a state' in Jordan, is detailed by Sayigh on pp. 263-64. The 'Arab Hanoi' reference is in Hirst, p. 436. The king's request for assistance from Israel, considered a betrayal by many an Arab, was documented in a January 2001 report on BBC television, *UK Confidential*, and is based on British cabinet documents released on January 1, 2001. See news.bbc.co.uk/1/hi/world/middle_east/1095221.stm.

Sayigh estimates the Palestinian death toll during Black September at between three thousand and five thousand (p. 267). The agreement between Arafat and King Hussein is also on p. 267; scenes of Nasser's death come from Sayigh on p. 145 and Heikal on p. 159.

Bashir and his family do not recall the exact day of his conviction, only that it was in 1972. The wording of the sura of Yassin was confirmed by Dr. Hatem Bazian, lecturer in Near Eastern Studies at UC-Berkeley.

Dalia recalled the proximity of the school and the prison; she believes they actually shared a common wall.

The murder of Israeli athletes in Munich is recounted by Sayigh on p. 309; by Hirst on pp. 439-45; and by Morris in *Righteous Victims*, pp. 380-82. The quote from Arafat appears in Sayigh. Sayigh says the attack was under the name of Black September but that the attackers were not part of the original Black September group. The Israeli general was Aharon Yariv, who directed Operation Wrath of God, and his quote comes from Reeve, pp. 160-61. The Habash 'inhuman' quote is in Sayigh, p. 71.

The Israeli assassinations, including the car bomb that killed Ghassan Kanafani and his niece and the letter bomb that maimed Bassam Abu-Sharif, are mentioned in Sayigh, p. 310; by Abu-Sharif, p. 97; and by Morris (*Righteous Victims*, p. 380), who gives the age of Kanafani's niece as seventeen, not twenty-one. Abu-Sharif describes his maiming in graphic detail in *Best of Enemies*, pp. 96-99.

The picture of prison life is drawn from multiple interviews with Bashir and with other Palestinian men who spent time in

Israeli prisons in the 1970s and 1980s. These include Jabril Rajoub, the former Fatah activist and later head of West Bank security under Arafat; Abu Mohammad of Tulkarm in the West Bank; and several current and former members of the DFLP and PFLP who wish to remain anonymous. Most of them, as it happens, spent time in one prison or another with Bashir.

Statistics on incarcerated Palestinian men are listed in Sayigh, p. 608.

Some of Bashir's artwork, including the rendering of the Palestinian peasant and the replica of the Al-Aqsa Mosque, is at his house in Ramallah.

Sadat's visit to Jerusalem and the subsequent Camp David accords are documented by Shlaim in *The Iron Wall* on pp. 355–83. Rabin's 'wall of hate' quote comes from Abu-Sharif, p. 165. Palestinian objections to the accords were reflected in numerous interviews I did, including with Bashir and Abu Laila, and are described by Shlaim on p. 378 and by Edward Said in *The Politics of Dispossession*, pp. 66–67. Shlaim (p. 326), Morris (*Righteous Victims*, pp. 330–336), and Hirst (p. 500–502) describe the rise of Gush Emunim (The Bloc of the Faithful) and the National Religious Party in the governing Likud coalition; Hirst, in particular, describes Sharon's connection to these politics, and the subsequent support of the World Zionist Organization through its 'Master Plan for the Development of Settlement in Judea and Samaria.'

Said, in an essay on Sadat's death, wrote that the Egyptian leader 'worked outside Arab history, society, and actuality . . . in his last years he abused the Arabs mercilessly . . . He seems to have lost touch with his people.'

Bashir's release from prison was recalled by Nuha and Khanom. Khanom believes Bashir's body was scarred with cigarette burns, but Bashir did not comment on this.

Dalia's husband, Yehezkel Landau, recounted his and Dalia's contact with the Anglican priest Audeh Rantisi.

Yehezkel translated the prayer from the Hebrew.

Chapter 11

This chapter is based largely on correspondence between Dalia and Bashir and on interviews with Dalia, Bashir, other Khairi family members, Yehezkel Landau, and Bashir's fellow prisoners, including Jabril Rajoub. Historical context comes from numerous primary and secondary sources, as indicated in the text that follows.

Bashir's time in prison was corroborated in separate interviews with Jabril and by mid-January 1988 articles in the *Times* of London and the *Jerusalem Post*. Both Bashir and Jabril reviewed relevant portions of this chapter for accuracy; their nearly identical recollections (recounted separately) of the same events corroborate the overall story of the prison at Jneid.

Context for the occupation that led to the intifada and the details of the intifada itself come from Meron Benvenisti's chapter 'The Uprising' in his *Intimate Enemies: Jews and Arabs in a Shared Land*, pp. 72–111; from Abu-Sharif in *Best of Enemies*, pp. 224–28; Aburish's *Arafat: From Defender to Dictator*, pp. 199–229; Sayigh's *Armed Struggle and the Search for State*, pp. 607–65; and Shlaim's *Iron Wall: Israel and the Arab World*, pp. 450–60.

The story of the spark that lit the intifada varies in its particulars. Shlaim (p. 451) refers to a 'truck driver' who 'killed four residents' of the Jabalya camp; Sayigh (p. 607) mentions 'an agricultural vehicle' that 'drove into two cars carrying workers from Gaza'; Abu-Sharif (p. 225) writes that 'a truck carrying Palestinian workers was ambushed by Israeli soldiers'; Gerner, in *One Land, Two Peoples* (p. 97), says, 'An Israeli tank transporter collided with a line of cars filled with Palestinian workers.' All accounts agree that four Palestinians were killed and that rumors, false or otherwise, gripped occupied Gaza.

Dilip Hiro, in *Sharing the Promised Land*, p. 185, provides the 'brother doctors' quotes.

Shlaim (p. 454) discusses the reversal of the Palestinian image internationally; on p. 453, he describes how Rabin 'greatly underestimated the gravity of the situation,' and on p. 451 he makes mention of the 'Palestinian war of independence.' Benvenisti refers to the 'war of liberation' on p. 73.

The reference to Yassin's home village is from Walid Khalidi's *All That Remains: The Palestinian Villages Occupied and Depopulated by Israel in 1948*, pp. 116–17. The roots of Hamas and its philosophy are discussed by Sayigh on p. 631. Israel's initial encouragement of Hamas, 'in the hope of weakening the secular nationalism of the PLO,' is mentioned by Shlaim on p. 459.

Details of how the intifada was organized, including the tax revolt, come from an interview with Elias Rishmawi, a pharmacist in the West Bank town of Beit Sahour, near Bethlehem, in *Homeland: Oral Histories of Palestine and Palestians*. Additional details, including the 'victory gardens' and chickens hatching in old fridges, come from an interview with Palestinian scholar Naseer Aruri.

The Hebrew prayer is known as 'Rebbe Nachman's Prayer for Peace' and is attributed to Rabbi Nachman ben Feiga of Breslov, 1773–1810 (www.pinenet.com/rooster/peace.html).

Rabin's policy of 'force, might and beatings' was widely publicized at the time and is mentioned by Shlaim (p. 453), Hiro (p. 186), and Sayigh (p. 619); Sayigh also indicates figures on arrests, administrative detentions, and the closure of schools. The bone-breaking policy is alluded to by Shlaim (p. 453), Gerner (p. 98), and Hiro (p. 186); Hiro refers to a CBS television report showing 'Israeli soldiers beating bound

Palestinians in order to break their bones.' Morris (*Righteous Victims*, pp. 589–90) also describes the bone-breaking policy.

Dalia's husband, Yehezkel, confirmed some of the details of Dalia's hospital stay from his own memory.

Bashir and Jabril Rajoub confirm the scene at the Jneid prison as they were escorted out. That they had abandoned their appeal of the deportations is confirmed in articles in the *Times* of London, January 13–15, 1988. The 'game was fixed' and 'among the leaders' quotes come from a January 14 article in the *Jerusalem Post*. The articles refer to UN and U.S. objections to Israel's deportations policy. United Nations Security Council Resolution 607 of January 5, 1988, 'calls upon Israel to refrain from deporting any Palestinian citizens from the occupied territories.'

Jabril Rajoub recalled his own comments to the military judge. Bashir described Rabin's visit to the prison in an interview. Jabril and Bashir recalled the trip in blindfolds in the van and then into the helicopters; each stressed, in separate interviews, that they had no idea where they were going.

The Israeli presence in Lebanon is discussed by Benvenisti in *Intimate Enemies*, p. 79, as a means to 'destroy the independent power base of Palestinian nationalism in Lebanon'; additional context is provided by Shlaim, pp. 384–423, and Sayigh, pp. 495–521. See also *Israel's Lebanon War* by Ze'ev Schiff, Israel's leading military correspondent, and Ehud Ya'ari; and *Pity the Nation* by Robert Fisk. The 'Israel's Vietnam' reference was made as early as 1983, as evidenced from this article from Israel's Ministry of Foreign Affairs: www.mfa.gov.il/MFA/Foreign+Relations/Israels+Foreign+Relations+since+1947/1982–1984/111+Interview+with+Defense+Minister+Arens+on+Israe.htm.

Bashir and Jabril each recalled their arrival in southern Lebanon, as did Salah Salah, their PFLP escort, in interviews.

The State Department's 'deep regret' and Netanyahu's 'totally legal' comments are from the *Times* of London and *Jerusalem Post* articles. The death of Yonatan (also known as Jonathan) Netanyahu in the raid on Entebbe is described in an online article, 'Entebbe Diary,' published by the official Web site of the Israel Defense Forces. Netanyahu was killed while leading a raid to free hostages from a plane that had been hijacked by the PFLP to Idi Amin's Uganda. He was the only casualty. That his younger brother, 'Bibi,' formed or at least hardened some of his personal and political convictions following the death of Yonatan was underscored to me several times by Dalia.

Rabin's 'courage that deserves respect' quote comes from Heikal's *Secret Channels*, p. 384; there, Heikal describes the beginning of Rabin's 'shift toward moderation'; Shlaim also explores this shift (on p. 467), which would be expressed only later; the continuing 'iron fist' policies are discussed on pp. 453-55.

Dalia's 'Letter to a Deportee' appeared in the editorial pages of the *Jerusalem Post* on January 14, 1988, and is printed in full at www.friendsofopenhouse.org/article3.cfm.

The general political context of the Palestinian presence in Lebanon is described in Fisk and specifically in Sayigh, pp. 282-317 and especially on p. 291. Hezbollah's founding purpose is described by Fisk in *Pity the Nation*; Shlaim (p. 559) states that the 'main aim of its militancy was to expel Israel from its toehold in southern Lebanon.' Friedman, in *From Beirut to Jerusalem*, mentions a secondary goal of establishing an Islamic state in Lebanon. The funneling of Israeli funds to the Lebanese militias is documented in Schiff and Ya'ari's *Israel's Lebanon War*, p. 18.

The historical context for the 'Lebanese Quagmire,' as Shlaim called it, including the various factions fighting one another, is beyond the scope of this book, but a few things are worth noting. Tensions after 1970 were heightened both by the presence of the Palestinian factions and by the Israelis. These tensions played out largely along religious lines, with Muslims by and large supporting the Palestinians and many Maronite Christians, with their Phalangist militias, supported by Israel and periodically demanding their own separate Christian state. In addition, the Muslim population was growing faster than the Christian, even though many of the Muslims were Palestinians living in squalid refugee camps and denied citizenship or the right to live elsewhere or work in most occupations. As the tensions grew, a fragile, religious-based political balance, established by the colonial French when carving up the Middle East with Britain in 1916, would shatter entirely. Civil war broke out in Lebanon in 1975 when Christian militiamen near Beirut opened fire on a busload of Palestinian civilians. Within days, reprisals and counterreprisals would escalate into full-blown civil war, as Beirut was effectively divided between the Christian east and the Muslim west. Car bombings, kidnappings, and executions would become the norm for years.

The Israeli invasion of Lebanon, including numbers of weapons and casualties, the siege of Beirut, and the PLO resistance, is described in detail by Sayigh on pp. 522–43.

Sharon's 'razed to the ground' quote is from Schiff and Ya'ari, p. 211. The motives of the Israeli invasion are described by Shlaim on pp. 405–06. The departure of the Palestinian *cadres* is in Sayigh, p. 537. Arafat's boarding of the Greek ship is in Shlaim, p. 413. The 'fifteen days' promises to Palestinian refugees in 1948, and their unrelenting desire, fifty-six years later, to return to their old homes, were conveyed to me many times during interviews in the camps in Lebanon.

The Sabra and Shatilla massacres are detailed in Sayigh on p. 539 and in Loren Jenkins's account in the *Washington Post*, September 23, 1982.

The 'having disregarded' quote comes directly from the official findings of Israel's Kahan commission of inquiry of February 8, 1983. The Kahan report, which details the use of Israel Defense Forces flares to light up the Sabra and Shatilla camps, and describes the proximity of IDF officers to the camps, can be read in its entirety at http://www.jewishvirtuallibrary.org/jsource/History/kahan.html. The report also makes it clear that defense minister Ariel Sharon explicitly approved the entry of the Phalangist militia into the camps on September 16, 1982.

Bashir's 'only solution is return' and 'we demand' comments were quoted in news accounts in January 1988, including in the *Jerusalem Post*. Jabril Rajoub's candid 'Salah paid' comments were made to me in an interview, after I had read him this section of the chapter. I half expected him to explode in anger or denial. Instead, he replied unflinchingly; perhaps he was relieved to acknowledge publicly, and indirectly to his old friend Salah, what had happened and why. After acknowledging Salah paid for his speech, Jabril looked at me and added: 'I am embarrassed by that. I was a young man.'

The *Al-Awda* story was told to me in interviews with Bashir and with Hilda Silverman, a Boston peace activist who was in Athens and planning to board the ship back to Haifa. Additional details come from an October 1988 article by Alfred Lilienthal in the *Washington Report on Middle East Affairs* and by the Belgian journalist Mon Vanderostyne, who was in Athens to cover the story. The 'criminals' quote comes from Vanderostyne's report.

The assassination of Abu Jihad is described in Sayigh on pp. 618-19 and by Hiro on pp. 216-17. Ehud Barak's role in the assassination has been reported in various newspapers, including in Israel, and is documented on the Web site of the Jewish Agency for Israel (www.safi.org.il/education/jafi75/

timeline7i.html). News accounts of that week, including an AP dispatch on April 16, indicate a surge in the intifada following Abu Jihad's assassination. The visit by Ghiath and Nuha Khairi to Dalia's hospital room on May 8, 1988, was recorded in Dalia's journal entry of May 9, and all description and dialogue from this section comes from that entry. The birth of Raphael was described in interviews with Dalia and Yehezkel.

The increasing political divisions in the Palestinian movement are described by Hiro on pp. 187–90 and Sayigh on pp. 643–50; on pp. 650–53, he discusses the role of Hamas. Shlaim analyzes the same period from the Israeli political perspective on pp. 463–66. Abu-Sharif describes his political shift, from Habash to Arafat, on pp. 224–46. His 'Dr. George' remark was recalled in an interview, as were memories of the fading cold war. Arafat's trip to Geneva is in Abu-Sharif's personal account on pp. 257–62.

The continuing split in the Palestinian movement was described in interviews with Bashir, Abu Laila in Ramallah, and a former PFLP member no longer living in the Middle East.

Bashir and Salah each recalled their Tunis exile in separate 2004 interviews.

Dalia recalled her journey from Jerusalem to Ramla to meet with Michail Fanous. I interviewed both of them about that first meeting, and their memories corroborate each other's stories. Both Dalia and Michail recall their shared vision for the place they would call Open House; Dalia, indeed, recalled Michail looking at her and saying, 'We can dream together.'

Chapter 12

This chapter is based on interviews with Dalia and Yehezkel Landau and Bashir, Nuha, Ghiath, and Khanom Khairi; on original documents from the Oslo agreements; on firsthand accounts, investigations, and newspaper clippings describing the Oslo process and the 'second intifada,' which began in September 2000; and on my own reporting in the region, which began in 1994.

The Oslo 'accords' refer to a series of agreements, beginning with the 'Declaration of Principles' (DOP), that grew out of secret discussions between Israeli and PLO negotiators in the Norwegian capital beginning in 1992. Rabin's and Arafat's exchange of letters was part of the DOP, cited in *Documents on Palestine: Vol. II*, published by the Palestinian Academic Society for the Study of International Affairs (PASSIA), p. 142. The text of the DOP is on pp. 145–50. Polls showing the early popularity of Oslo among Palestinians, and the early measures of sovereignty, including Palestinian stamps, are part of the PASSIA timeline in *Documents on Palestine*, pp. 371–98. The description of separate wings and jurisdictions and the 'remains responsible' quote come from the 'Gaza-Jericho Autonomy Agreement of May 4, 1994,' Annex I, Article X.

The planned new Israeli housing units and bypass roads come from my own observation in the region in 1994 and after and are listed in the PASSIA timeline, pp. 371–88.

Baruch Goldstein's massacre of Palestinians is mentioned by Benny Morris on p. 624 of *Righteous Victims: A History of the Zionist Arab Conflict, 1881–2001*. The link between Goldstein's attack and subsequent civilian attacks by Hamas was made in two analysis pieces by Danny Rubinstein in *Ha'aretz*, September 28 and October 23, 1998. The suicide attacks are documented in the PASSIA timeline and in 'Major Palestinian Terror Attacks Since Oslo' at www.jewishvirtuallibrary.org/jsource/Terrorism/TerrorAttacks.html. Hamas's claims that these attacks were in response to Israeli attacks on Palestinian civilians is documented by Amira Hass in a March 22, 1999, article in *Ha'aretz*.

House demolitions are documented by the United Nations

Commission on Human Rights in periodic reports; see, for example, its note of February 19, 1996. Human Rights Watch's documentation of sleep deprivation and other practices was made periodically, including in a written statement to the commission on March 15, 1996.

The roundups of Palestinians by Palestinian police are mentioned in numerous news articles during the period and are cited in the August 1995 B'tselem report 'Neither Law Nor Justice: Extra-Judicial Punishment, Abduction, Unlawful Arrest, and Torture of Palestinian Residents of the West Bank by the Palestinian Preventive Security Service.' For more on the Palestinian Authority's censorship tactics, see 'Critique of the Palestinian Press Law of 1995' by the Palestinian Center for Human Rights (www.pchrgaza.org/files/S&r/English/study 1/Section2.htm). Said's 'Vichy' remark comes from his scathing essay 'The Middle East "Peace Process,"' published in his *Peace and Its Discontents: Essays on Palestine and the Middle East Peace Process*, p. 159.

The anger at Arafat and contrasting images of rich and poor were documented in large part from my trips to Gaza beginning in 1994; additional details in this paragraph, including the 'profiteers' quote, is from David Hirst's article 'Shameless in Gaza,' which appeared in the *Guardian Weekly* on April 27, 1997. (I was in Gaza at the time, and the article caused a stir – officials were infuriated and many others elated; there was also a sense among some Palestinians that it was 'too early' to be airing the Palestinians' dirty laundry to the world 'while we are still under occupation.')

The October 1995 poll, showing plummeting approval for Oslo among Palestinians, was conducted by the respected Jerusalem Media and Communication Center and is cited on p. 387 of *Documents on Palestine*; only 23.7 percent 'strongly' supported the agreement.

Yehezkel Landau discussed the atmosphere of Israel during the Oslo period and recalled Rabin's remarks about 'Bagatz and B'tselem.'

The Netanyahu quote is cited in dozens of articles, including the June 2004 piece 'Israel's Wayward Prime Ministers' by Daniel Pipes, posted at the online magazine *American Daily*: www.americandaily.com/article/2547.

The doctored posters depicting Rabin in a Nazi uniform and the attacks on Rabin by the religious and political Right were recalled vividly by Dalia and Yehezkel, who also recalled the use of the word *rodef*. More details are mentioned in *Righteous Victims*, pp. 634-35. Dalia recalled her feelings of outrage at the depictions of Rabin during interviews in the summer of 2005. She and Yehezkel recalled the challenges of 'the whole coexistence approach' during this period.

The particulars of the rally during which Rabin was killed come from Yehezkel and are corroborated by Morris on p. 635. Additional details of the assassination are in Shlaim's *The Iron Wall*, pp. 548-50. Dalia's recollection of Rabin saying, 'Enough of the struggle for war,' may have its origins in a speech Rabin gave to the Knesset on October 5, 1995, in which he said, 'We can continue to fight. We can continue to kill – and continue to be killed. But we can also try to put a stop to this never-ending cycle of blood. We can also give peace a chance.'

Yigal Amir's 'I acted alone' remark has been widely quoted. Shlaim, on p. 549, adds this from Amir: 'When I shot Rabin, I felt as if I was shooting a terrorist.'

The account of Camp David is pieced together from numerous sources. A large part of it comes from an exchange of Camp David 'versions' published in the *New York Review of Books*, from Barak through Benny Morris (June 13, 2002) and from Robert Malley and Hussain Agha (June 27, 2002). Also important in my telling here is Charles Enderlin's *Shattered*

Dreams, which reconstructed the summit 'through accounts, filmed during the weeks following the meeting, as well as the notes that several participants, Israeli and Palestinian, took in real time.' Another valuable account is Clayton E. Swisher's *The Truth About Camp David: The Untold Story About the Collapse of the Middle East Peace Process*, which is based on extensive interviews with parties from all sides. Other sources include Dennis Ross's *The Missing Peace: The Inside Story of the Fight for Middle East Peace*; Madeleine Albright's *Madam Secretary*; the diaries of Saeb Erekat, one of the principal Palestinian negotiators; and 'The Camp David Papers' by Akram Hanieh, another member of the Palestinian team and editor-in-chief of the Palestinian daily *Al-Ayyam*, and the diaries of Saeb Erekat, one of the principal Palestinian negotiators, as given in a speech in Bethlehem which was translated and posted at http://homepages.stmartin.edu/ Fac_Staff/rlangill/PLS%20300/ Camp%20David%20Diaries.hitm. Erekat, in personal correspondence with me, confirmed the authenticity of the diaries.

The accounts vary in tone and ascribing of blame for Camp David's failure, depending on the perspective of the narrator. Small details also vary, with one narrator recalling a yellow portion of a map where another remembers it being brown. The quotes are taken verbatim from the sources cited, but they are not likely exact, as the participants recalled the conversations after the fact. Occasionally there is slight disagreement on the dates certain conversations took place, though it is also possible similar conversations were repeated ad nauseam over the fourteen days of Camp David. I have used quotes only when there is more than one source for a conversation.

Ross's 'same old bullshit' comment comes from his memoir, p. 669. Clinton's outburst at Abu Ala is quoted by Enderlin (p. 202); slightly different versions appear in Ross, p. 668, and Albright, *Madam Secretary*, p. 488, where the 'got drenched' quote also appears. Clinton's banging his fist on the table comes from Barak's account to Morris in the *New York Review of Books* article. Arafat's response comes from the Erekat diaries. Clinton's appeal to Arafat on the eve of his departure for the G-8 summit is documented by Enderlin on p. 239, by Albright on p. 490, by Ross on p. 696E, and by Swisher on p. 299, where Clinton's 'price you have to pay' quote also appears, attributed to the recollection of Sandy Berger. Arafat's pointed response to Clinton after his return from Okinawa, including the 'small island' and 'I will not sell Jerusalem' quotes, are from Hanieh's *Camp David Papers*. Arafat's famous invitation to attend his own funeral is quoted in various forms in nearly every account. His 'revolution is easier than peace-making' comes from the Erekat diaries.

The exact percentage of the West Bank and Gaza discussed at Camp David as the basis of a solution remains in dispute, in part because few if any written offers were made and because sections of East Jerusalem and other areas were not considered in the calculation. According to Malley and Agha, 'The ideas put forward at Camp David were never stated in writing, but orally conveyed.' Some estimates of what was actually on the table are as low as 80 percent. See Naseer Aruri's *Dishonest Broker: The U.S. Role in Israel and Palestine*. Others insist the figure was as high as 95 percent.

The 'most contested' status for Haram al-Sharif/Temple Mount is one of the few undisputed things about it. The importance of the site to Muslims, not only in the Middle East, was brought home to me on a visit to a Muslim slum on the island of Mindanao in the Philippines, where families had tacked pictures of the Al-Aqsa Mosque on their walls and where, upon hearing of my reporting in the Middle East, they launched into discussions of the importance of Jerusalem to Muslims.

The figure of 1,500 police comes from the Israeli Ministry of

Foreign Affairs (mfa.gov.il). The events of September 29 are described in the final report of the impartial Sharm El-Sheikh Fact-Finding Committee, better known as the Mitchell Commission after its chair, former U.S. senator George Mitchell. The report indicates the Palestinian demonstrators did not fire weapons on September 29, citing U.S. State Department findings. More details can be found in Amnesty International's October 19, 2000, report.

The 'grand plan' quote comes from Barak in the interview with Benny Morris in the *New York Review of Books*, and the sentiment is corroborated by Israel's statements to the Mitchell Commission. The commission was among the fact-finding teams which determined that most of the early demonstrations did not involve 'deploying children to stand in front of' armed men. The commission did, however, criticize the statement in June 2000, four months before the Al-Aqsa intifada began, by Abu Ali Mustafa, a PLO and PFLP leader: 'The issues of Jerusalem, the refugees and sovereignty will be decided on the ground and not in negotiations. On this point it is important to prepare the Palestinian public for the next step, because without doubt we shall find ourselves in conflict with Israel in order to create new facts on the ground.' Mustafa added that any future conflict 'will be more violent' than the first intifada. Fifteen months later, he was assassinated by Israeli security forces.

The crisis, Israel concluded, was 'an armed conflict short of war,' a claim the Palestinians said was only an excuse 'to justify its assassination policy, its collective punishment policy, and its use of lethal force.'

Statistics on early casualties come from investigations by human rights groups, including the Israeli group B'tselem, which found in a December 2, 2000, report that 264 Palestinians had been killed in the occupied territories since September 29, 204 of them civilians 'killed by IDF forces, of them 73 minors aged 17 and under.' During the same period, twenty-nine Israelis were killed, sixteen of them members of the security forces. The figure of ten thousand injured comes from the same B'tselem investigation, which concluded: 'Israel did not develop non-lethal methods to disperse demonstrations or train its soldiers to confront such demonstrations.' B'tselem reported that 'according to IDF figures, 73 percent of the incidents [from September 29 to December 2, 2000] did not include Palestinian gunfire.'

The death of thirteen Israeli Arabs is documented in the U.S. State Department's 'Country Reports on Human Rights Practices' of February 23, 2001. According to one respected Israeli pollster, by 2002, 46 percent of Israelis supported 'transfer' (expulsion) of Palestinians from the occupied territories, and 31 percent supported 'transfer' of Israeli Arabs. See 'Israeli Public Opinion on National Security 2002' by Asher Arian, director of the National Security Policy and Public Opinion Project at Tel Aviv University. Rehavam Zeevi's 'transfer' position was widely known. See, for example, 'Israel Mints Ultranationalist Hero,' *Christian Science Monitor*, October 10, 2002. The U.S. State Department 'Country Report' of February 28, 2005, referred to Israel's investigation and findings into the deaths of the Israeli Arabs: 'The Orr Commission of Inquiry (COI) was established to investigate those killings. It recommended a number of measures, including criminal prosecutions. The Cabinet adopted those recommendations in June.'

The Israeli anger over the death of the two soldiers in Ramallah, perhaps more than anything, contributed to a shift to the right in Israel after 2000. According to the Mitchell report, 'For Israelis, the lynching of two military reservists, First Sgt. Vadim Novesche and First Cpl. Yosef Avrahami, in Ramallah on October 12, reflected a deep-seated Palestinian hatred of Israel and Jews.'

The New Year's Day bombing in Netanya was mentioned in a Reuters article of January 2, 2001: 'Barak Doubts Clinton Can Forge Mideast Peace Deal.' Barak's 'deep doubts' comment comes from this article.

Progress in the talks at Taba was considered genuine by analysts on both sides and by independent observers. One European diplomat sought me out in 2001 to underscore this. He cited the findings of Miguel Moratinos, the EU envoy who was a party to the talks at Taba. In February 2002, *Ha'aretz* published the Moratinos Document, which can be viewed online at www.arts.mcgill.ca/MEPP/PRRN/papers/moratinos.html. Seen through Moratinos's eyes, Taba represented substantial movement toward a comprehensive settlement, with progress on Palestinian sovereignty over East Jerusalem, including some religious sites in the Old City and, for the first time, limited Israeli acknowledgment of UN Resolution 194 and the Palestinian right of return, which had now been on the table for more than fifty years. Barak's remark, made to Morris in the *New York Review of Books* article of June 13, 2002, after his defeat to Sharon, is unyielding on right of return, yet the Moratinos Document clearly states that the Israeli delegation at Taba, ostensibly led by Barak, declared otherwise. It is not clear whether this discrepancy says more about the negotiations at Taba, the accuracy of Moratinos's document, or Barak's own personal and political considerations at the time he made the remark.

The assassination of Abu Ali Mustafa is chronicled in Graham Usher's 'As the Dominoes Fall' in *Al-Ahram Weekly* of Cairo, August 30, 2001. The assassination of Zeevi is described in wire service accounts, including an AP article, 'Israel's Tourism Minister Killed,' from October 17, 2001.

Sharon's words are from a speech in Jerusalem recorded by CNN.

Casualties from the suicide bombings are documented at the Jewish Virtual Library(www.jewishvirtuallibrary.org/jsource/ Terrorism/ TerrorAttacks.htm). The Apache helicopter attacks are cited by *Al-Ahram Weekly*'s correspondent Khaled Amayreh in an article on December 6. Israel's attack on Arafat's compound and the Israeli cabinet's declaration that Arafat was 'irrelevant' come from a December 13 article, 'Israel Launches Attacks After Declaring Arafat "No Longer Relevant,"' israelinsider.com/channels/security/articles/sec_0158.htm. The shelling of the Voice of Palestine is documented in a CNN online article at archives.cnn.com/2002/ WORLD/meast/ 01/18/mideast.violence.

Arafat's article 'The Palestinian Vision of Peace' was published on the op-ed page of the *New York Times* on February 3, 2002. The later attacks on the *muqata*, as Arafat's headquarters in Ramallah was known, as well as the 'steadfast resistance' quote, are mentioned in the February 2002 'Chronological Review of Events Relating to the Question of Palestine, Monthly Media Monitoring Review,' by UNISPAL, the UN Information System on the Question of Palestine, at domino.un.org/UNISPAL. The image of a tattered flag was captured by photographer George Azar.

The incident at the Arab Care hospital is described in an April 2001 article in the British *Guardian*. The attack on Jenin is chronicled in the 'Report of the Secretary-General Prepared Pursuant to General Assembly Resolution ES-10/10' and is online at un.org/peace/jenin. The joke comparing Ramallah to Jenin was told to me by the Palestinian folklorist Dr. Sharif Kanaana.

Statistics on house demolitions are at the Web site of the Israel Committee Against House Demolitions (www.icahd.org/ eng/faq.asp?menu=9&submenu=1), which states, 'Since 1967, 12,000 houses [sic] Palestinian homes have been demolished in the Occupied Territories.' This figure includes East Jerusalem, which Israel annexed after the 1967 war. See also B'tselem's November 2004 report, 'Through No Fault of Their Own: Israel's Punitive House Demolitions in the al-Aqsa Intifada,' which found that 'on average, 12 innocent people lost their home for every person suspected of participation in attacks against Israelis.'

Rosen-Zvi's 'refusenik' stance was documented in *Ha'aretz*, 'Reservist Jailed for Refusal to Serve in Territories,' on June 15, 2001.

Details of the suicide attack on Dalia, Yehezkel, and Raphael's neighborhood of Kiryat Menachem come from interviews with Dalia and Yehezkel, augmented by press accounts, including a November 21, 2001, article in the British *Guardian*, 'Jerusalem Suicide Bombing Kills 11.' Abu-Hilail's father's comment and the reoccupation of Bethlehem were reported at the CBS News online Web site in a November 22 article, 'Israel Retaliates for Bus Bomb.' Arafat's 'blind terrorism' comment comes from a James Bennet article in the *New York Times* of November 22.

Dalia and Yehezkel recalled the shrine at the bus station and the content of the handmade signs. Additional details come from Yehezkel's article 'Religious Responses to Atrocity,' in *Tikkun* 18, no. 5 (September–October 2003). The stabbing of the Arab resident was reported by Agence France-Presse on November 24 and recalled by Dalia and Yehezkel; they also described the attack on the Palestinian baker.

Yehezkel's decision to address what he called a 'global spiritual crisis' led him, more and more, to Hartford, Connecticut, while Dalia stayed in Jerusalem.

Chapter 13

Notes for this chapter are comparatively short, as the chapter is based largely on interviews with Dalia and Bashir and on my own observations as I spent time with them in Jerusalem, Ramallah, and Bulgaria.

Additional details of the monastery come from www. visitbulgaria.net/places/bachkovomonastery/index.shtml. The information about Yad Vashem and the Bulgarian bishops can be found at www1.yadvashem.org.

The story of Bashir's release from Israeli detention in Ramallah comes from an old friend of Bashir's who did not want his name used. Bashir, characteristically, would not elaborate on the story.

The death of Iman al-Hams on October 5, 2004, was widely reported at the time, including in the *Philadelphia Inquirer* on October 6. The 'horrific statistics' quote and details come from Gideon Levy's column in *Ha'aretz*, 'Killing Children Is No Longer a Big Deal', from October 17, 2004. Lengthy waits at checkpoints are familiar to all travelers to and from the West Bank. The story of the violinist was also widely reported and is mentioned in an AP story from December 29, 2004, 'Palestinian Fiddler Gets Earful of Israeli Hospitality', which describes Tayem's trip to an Israeli kibbutz. Tayem was invited by kibbutzniks who, according to a fellow violinist, 'wanted to show him that Israel is not just about terror and violence, that you can also find warmth and good people.'

The description of Dalia's trip to Ramallah comes from my own notebooks. I was driving the rental car and waved my blue American passport. For some reason, the Israeli soldiers did not ask for Dalia's identification, which likely would have aborted our journey; we headed north, amazed, with the wall to our left. The 'duty-free' is a wry slogan of Palestinians, including Nidal.

Description of the 'security fence' (which is partly a twenty-five-foot-high wall) and its construction comes from the Israeli government Web site, www.securityfence.mod.gov.il/Pages ENG/execution.htm. The 'sole purpose' quote comes from a statement by Israel on July 23, 2001. Palestinian objections to the barrier, including the Palestinian Authority's characterization of it as an 'apartheid wall,' are documented at www.mofa.gov.ps/positions/2004/19_1_04.asp. See also the Reuters article of July 10, 2004, which details Palestinian objections to the barrier's route and describes the ruling by the International Court of Justice. White House spokesman Scott McClellan's 'political issue' quote is from that article; John Kerry's 'legitimate act' and 'not a matter' quotes come from his presidential campaign and can be found at www.jewishvirtual-library.org/jsource/US-Israel/kerryisrael.html.

In the encounter between Dalia and Bashir, they spoke a few words to each other in English, but most of it was translated by Nidal, who wrote furiously so as to capture every phrase and faithfully repeat Dalia's words to Bashir and vice versa.

Chapter 14

I learned of the death of the lemon tree on my first trip to Open House in the early part of 1998, when I was working on my radio documentary for the NPR program *Fresh Air*. I remember looking down at one of the hard-shelled lemons and wondering if I should take it for a souvenir while I worked on my story. But I left it on the ground.

INDEX